Scientific Papers of Tjalling C. Koopmans

Volume II

Papers of Tjalling C. Koopmans

Scientific Papers of Tjalling C. Koopmans. New York: Springer, 1970.
Scientific Papers of Tjalling C. Koopmans, volume II. Cambridge, Mass.: MIT Press, 1985.

mo

Scientific Papers of Tjalling C. Koopmans

Volume II

with a foreword by Herbert E. Scarf

The MIT Press
Cambridge, Massachusetts
London, England

This book was reproduced from the original documents and printed and bound in the United States of America.

Library of Congress Cataloging in Publication Data
(Revised for volume 2)

Koopmans, Tjalling Charles, 1910–1985
Scientific papers of Tjalling C. Koopmans.

Vol. 2 published: Cambridge, Mass.: MIT Press.
"Publications of Tjalling Charles Koopmans":
v. 1, p. [595]–600; v. 2, p.
Includes bibliographical references.
1. Econometrics—Addresses, essays, lectures.
2. Economics, Mathematical—Addresses, essays, lectures. I. Title.
HB139.K636 1970 330′.028 76-95566
ISBN 0-262-11106-3 (v. 2)

Contents

Foreword xi

1
T. C. Koopmans
Note on a Social System Composed of Hierarchies with Overlapping Personnel 1
Orbis Economicus 13, no. 3/4 (1969) (special issue in honor of P. de Wolff), pp. 61–71

2
R. Beals and T. C. Koopmans
Maximizing Stationary Utility in a Constant Technology 13
SIAM Journal of Applied Mathematics 17, no. 5 (1969), pp. 1001–1015

3
T. C. Koopmans and J. M. Montias
On the Description and Comparison of Economic Systems 29
Comparison of Economic Systems: Theoretical and Methodological Approaches, ed. A. Eckstein (Berkeley: University of California Press, 1971), pp. 27–78

4
T. C. Koopmans
Representation of Preference Orderings with Independent Components of Consumption 81
Decision and Organization: A Volume in Honor of Jacob Marschak, ed. C. B. McGuire and R. Radner (Amsterdam: North-Holland, 1972), pp. 57–78

5
T. C. Koopmans
Representation of Preference Orderings over Time 103
Decision and Organization: A Volume in Honor of Jacob Marschak, ed. C. B. McGuire and R. Radner (Amsterdam: North-Holland, 1972), pp. 79–100

6
T. Hansen and T. C. Koopmans
On the Definition and Computation of a Capital Stock Invariant under Optimization 125
Journal of Economic Theory 5, no. 3 (1972), pp. 487–523

7
T. C. Koopmans
Some Observations on 'Optimal' Economic Growth and Exhaustible Resources 163
Economic Structure and Development: Essays in Honour of Jan Tinbergen, ed. H. C. Bos, H. Linnemann, and P. de Wolff (Amsterdam: North-Holland, 1973), pp. 239–255

8
T. C. Koopmans
Is the Theory of Competitive Equilibrium With It? 181
American Economic Review 64, no. 2 (1974), pp. 325–329

9
T. C. Koopmans
Proof for a Case where Discounting Advances the Doomsday 187
Review of Economic Studies, Symposium on the Economics of Exhaustible Resources, 1974, pp. 117–120

10
T. C. Koopmans
Concepts of Optimality and Their Uses 191
Les Prix Nobel en 1975 (Stockholm: Nobel Foundation, 1976)

11
T. C. Koopmans
Examples of Production Relations Based on Microdata 209
The Microeconomic Foundations of Macroeconomics: Proceedings of a Conference held by the International Economic Association at S'Agaro, Spain, ed. G. C. Harcourt (London: Macmillan, 1977), pp. 144–178

12
T. C. Koopmans
Economics Among the Sciences 237
American Economic Review 69, no. 1 (1979), pp. 1–13

13
T. C. Koopmans
Alternative Futures With or Without Constraints on the Energy Technology Mix 251
Directions in Energy Policy: A Comprehensive Approach to Energy Resource Decision-Making, ed. B. Kurşunoğlu and A. Perlmutter (Cambridge, Mass.: Ballinger, 1979), pp. 103–113

14
T. C. Koopmans
The Transition from Exhaustible to Renewable or Inexhaustible Resources 263
Economic Growth and Resources, volume 3: Natural Resources (Proceedings of the Fifth World Congress of the International Economic Association held in Tokyo, Japan), ed. C. Bliss and M. Boserup (London: Macmillan, 1980), pp. 3–11

15
G. Debreu and T. C. Koopmans
Additively Decomposed Quasiconvex Functions 273
Mathematical Programming 24, no. 1 (1982), pp. 1–38

Publications of Tjalling C. Koopmans, 1969–1985 311

Index 313

Scientific Papers of Tjalling C. Koopmans

Volume II

Foreword

During the last half-century, economic theory and econometrics have undergone a vital transformation. Formal mathematical models have become the major vehicle for the presentation of economic ideas—ideas which can then be examined with the logical precision and special methods of argument made available by the language of mathematics. Tjalling C. Koopmans was, and is, one of the leaders of this intellectual revolution.

I have been privileged to know Tjalling Koopmans as a close personal friend and professional colleague since 1957. Despite my great familiarity with his work, a rereading of these articles is still capable of eliciting feelings of awe, admiration, and aesthetic delight. Few economists of his stature have consistently displayed such intellectual freshness, conceptual originality, and stylistic clarity over such an extended period of time. Koopmans has had many laurels bestowed on him and has frequently beckoned the profession of economics into new and fruitful areas of inquiry; nevertheless, his work continues to have the directness and simplicity customarily associated with a young researcher in the early stages of his professional journey.

Although his work so frequently displays powerful and sophisticated mathematical arguments, Koopmans is not a detached and abstract mathematical economist. Throughout his career he has continued to insist that a line of inquiry in economics, if it is to be valuable, must ultimately be useful. His early work on linear programming and on the role of prices in the optimal allocation of resources was stimulated by the transportation problem, a specific practical problem that arose at the Combined Shipping Adjustment Boards in 1942. His work on econometric methodology in the late 1940s established the framework—and provided the primary theoretical stimulus—for the development of large macroeconomic models of the economy. Koopmans's first papers on economic growth theory do present theorems and mathematical models, but his preoccupation with the usefulness of formal arguments resulted in the articles in this volume on energy scarcity and on the more general problem of exhaustible resources. This same motivation prompted him, in 1975, to accept the chairmanship of the Modeling Resources Group of the Committee on Nuclear and Alternative Energy Systems (CONEAS) of the National Academy of Sciences. Under Koopmans's guidance, that group compared the results of a number of long-range energy models of the economy. His 1978 presidential address to the American Economic Association will give the reader a clear indication of the importance with which Koopmans views the study of specific policy choices based on detailed economic and engineering data. The topics cited in the references to this address are illuminating: underground power transmission, alternative energy growth patterns, helium conservation, energy modeling for an uncertain future, and the costs and benefits of automobile emission controls.

As many of the articles in this volume indicate, Tjalling Koopmans has a remarkable ability to attract a variety of collaborators to his professional ventures. He is gregarious, bold, inquisitive, and capable of initiating and maintaining fruitful relationships with economists, mathematicians, engineers, and scientists from all parts of the world. His qualities of leadership and intellectual involvement have been displayed during his long association with the Cowles Commission and the Cowles Foundation for Research in Economics. For many years, younger scholars have been guided by him in the choice of research topics and the methods of written and spoken exposition, and visitors have been reminded that the requirements of clarity and logical coherence were never to be discarded when entering the seminar room.

Leaders of a scientific revolution combine judgment, intellectual penetration, and personal force. The articles in this volume testify to the presence of these qualities in one of the most distinguished economists of our time.

Herbert E. Scarf
January 1985

1

Note on a Social System Composed of Hierarchies with Overlapping Personnel*

Tjalling C. Koopmans**

Orbis Economicus 13, no. 3/4 (1969) (special issue in honor of P. de Wolff), pp. 61–71

Introductory remarks

Casual observation shows that many people are subject to supervision by different superiors for different activities (economic, political, scientific, recreational, social, educational, religious, ...) in which they engage. At the same time, one can view many societies as being composed of organizations that have an essentially hierarchical internal structure. The purpose of this note is to show that these two observations are logically entirely compatible. They are reconciled if we regard the supervision relation that generates hierarchical structure as being not total, but limited to one or a few specific activities in each instance. Since this is a matter of a formal, logical or mathematical, character we can deal with it without facing the more difficult sociological questions as to what "supervision" really consists of and on what terms it is accepted by the supervisee. [1]) Neither need we spell out in the present context what the activities in question are or might be, thus maintaining flexibility of interpretation.

---

*) The ideas developed in this note originated from a joint investigation with J. Michael Montias, the results of which will be published as a paper, "On the Description and Comparison of Economic Systems," in a volume edited by Alexander Eckstein, reporting on a Conference on Comparison of Economic Systems held at the University of Michigan, Nov. 1968. I am indebted to Truus W. Koopmans, Gerald Kramer and J. M. Montias for valuable comments.

**) Center for Advanced Study in the Behavioral Sciences, Stanford, Cal., and Cowles Foundation for Research in Economics at Yale University. The research for this paper was carried out under a grant from the National Science Foundation to the CASBS.

[1]) For discussions of these questions, see, for instance, H. A. Simon, "A Formal Theory of the Employment Relation," Econometrica, Vol. 19, July, 1951, pp. 293-305, reprinted in H. A. Simon, Models of Man, Wiley, 1957. Also P .M. Blau and W. R. Scott, "Formal Organizations," Chandler, 1962.

Let **A** denote a finite set of *activities*, a, a^{I} ..., in which people engage, **B** a finite set of *persons*, b, b^{I}, ..., each of whom pursues one or more of these activities. (One may think of persons as individuals, but also as committees, boards, governing bodies with specific decision-making procedures). Denote by $c = (a, b)$ an *engagement*, that is, a pair composed of an activity a and a person b engaged in it.

Denote by **C** the set of all engagements $c = (a, b)$ assumed or observed to be in operation in a given state of society. Then **C** is a given subset

P1 $$\mathbf{C} \subset \mathbf{A} \times \mathbf{B}$$

of the set of all imaginable engagements (a, b) in any activity a of **A** by any person b of **B**, technically known as the "Cartesian product"

$$\mathbf{A} \times \mathbf{B} = \{ (a, b) \mid a \varepsilon \mathbf{A}, \ b \varepsilon \mathbf{B} \}$$

of **A** and **B**.

For each activity a of **A** we define the set

D1 $$\mathbf{B}_a = \{ b \mid (a, b) \ \varepsilon \mathbf{C} \}$$

of all persons engaged in that activity. On that set we define a supervision relation, denoted by

$$b^{\mathrm{I}} \overset{1}{>}_a b ,$$

and interpreted as " b^{I} supervises b in activity a ." We postulate that

P2 $$b^{\mathrm{I}} \overset{1}{>}_a b , \quad b^{\mathrm{II}} \overset{1}{>}_a b \ \text{ imply } \ b^{\mathrm{I}} = b^{\mathrm{II}} ,$$

a roundabout way of saying that each person b engaged in an activity a has at most one supervisor in that activity.

By iterated application of the supervision relation $\overset{1}{>}_a$ we define an n-th superior b^n of b in activity a by:

D2 $b^n \overset{n}{>}_a b$ if there exists a sequence of n—1 persons $b^1, \ldots , b^{n-1}$, where $n \geqq 2$, such that

$$b^n \overset{1}{>}_a b^{n-1} \overset{1}{>}_a \cdots \overset{1}{>}_a b \overset{1}{>}_a b .$$

It follows from P2 that for each n there exists at most one n-th superior. If one exists for given n, the sequence $b^1, b^2, \ldots, b^{n-1}$ consists of the unique 1st, 2nd, $(n-1)$th superiors, provided we define the first superior as the supervisor of b. If we add the postulate

P3 for no a, b, n does $b \overset{n}{>}_a b$ hold,

then no one is superior to himself in any activity (a good organisational rule!), the persons $b^1, \ldots, b^n$ in D2 are all distinct, and the number n is also unique, given b^n. Finally we define the general superiority relation for the activity a by

D3 $b^{\mathrm{I}} >_a b$ means $b^{\mathrm{I}} \overset{n}{>}_a b$ for some $n \geqq 1$.

In order to explore the organizational structure implicit in these definitions and postulates, we define, for any $a \varepsilon \mathbf{A}$ and $b \varepsilon \mathbf{B}_a$,

D4 *the hierarchy* $H_a(b)$ *for the activity* a, *headed by* b, is the set of all persons to whom b is superior for a, with b himself added in.

As a special case, $H_a(b)$ may consist of the single member b. If more than one member exist, one readily verifies that, for any two distinct members b^{I}, b^{II} of $H_a(b)$, one of the following mutually exclusive statements holds,

(i) $b^{\mathrm{I}} >_a b^{\mathrm{II}}$,
(ii) $b^{\mathrm{II}} >_a b^{\mathrm{I}}$,
(iii) neither (i) nor (ii) hold, and there exists a unique b^{III} with the properties
 (α) $b^{\mathrm{III}} >_a b^{\mathrm{I}}$ *and* $b^{\mathrm{III}} >_a b^{\mathrm{II}}$,
 (β) there exists no b^{IV} *for which* $b^{\mathrm{III}} >_a b^{\mathrm{IV}} >_a b^{\mathrm{I}}$ *and* $b^{\mathrm{IV}} >_a b^{\mathrm{II}}$.

The member b^{III} may be called the *lowest common superior* of b^{I} and b^{II}. The situation is clarified if one represents $H_a(b)$ as in Figure 1 by a directed linear graph or *digraph* [2]) $D_a(b)$, in which the members of

[2]) See, for instance, F. Harary, R. Z. Norman and D. Cartwright, Structural Models: An Introduction to the Theory of Directed Graphs, Wiley, 1965.

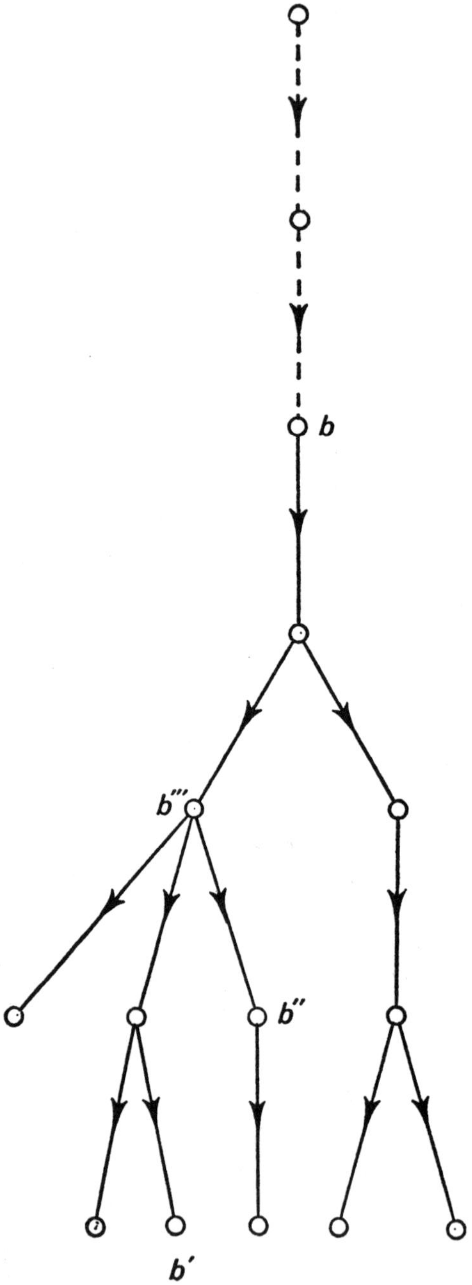

Figure 1

$H_a(b)$ are shown as *nodes,* all instances of supervision within $H_a(b)$ as *directed arcs.* For any given member b^{I}, there is a unique directed chain (sequence of nodes with successive directed connecting arcs) leading from b to b^{I} (a single node only if $b^{\mathrm{I}} = b$). Cases (i) and (ii) arise if one of the chains leading to b^{I} and b^{II}, respectively, is contained in the other. Case (iii) arises if each chain has at least one node with connecting arc outside the other chain. The member b^{III} corresponds to the node from which the two chains bifurcate.

A digraph with the properties required so to represent a hierarchy for a single activity is known as a *directed tree from* b *:* every node is connected with b, and no cycle can be formed from any set of arcs.

Figure 1 also shows, by dotted arcs drawn from nodes outside $D_a(b)$, the possible existence of superiors of b for a. We now define:

D5 *a complete hierarchy* $H_a(b^*)$ *for an activity* a is a hierarchy for a whose head b^* has no supervisor for a,

and prove the following theorem:

T1 Each person b engaged in an activity a belongs to one and only one complete hierarchy $H_a(b^*)$ for a.

To construct one such hierarchy from any given such b, take $b^* = b$ if b has no supervisor for a. If b has a supervisor b^1 construct the unique sequence $b^1, b^2, \ldots, b^n$ of successive supervisors (as in D2) until a superior b^n is met who has no supervisor. Take $b^* = b^n$. To show there is only one such hierarchy, assume that $b \varepsilon H_a(b^*)$, $b \varepsilon H_a(b^{**})$ with $b^* \neq b^{**}$. Then, in graph language, the supervision chains leading from b^* and b^{**}, respectively, to b would meet (see Figure 2) at a member b^{I} (which could be b) having two supervisors for a, a violation of P2.

As a corollary of T1 we have

CT1 The set $\mathbf{B}_a$ of persons engaged in an activity a can be partitioned into (regarded as the union of non-overlapping) complete hierarchies for that activity.

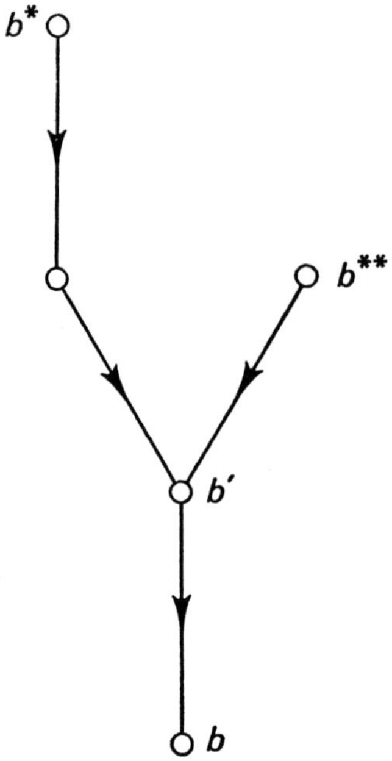

Figure 2

A graph consisting of a union of directed trees no two of which have a common node is called a *directed forest.*

Hierarchies for a Set of Activities

Everything said so far would apply equally if only a single activity were pursued in the society considered. If more than one activity is present, connections between hierarchies for different activities also need to be explored. A useful image [3] is to think of a sheet of paper (an underlay, say) on which one node has been drawn in for each person of **B**. For each activity a of **A**, one then imagines a transparent overlay on which, in a color specific to a, nodes for all persons engaged in a have been dotted, and arcs for all instances of supervision in a have been drawn in. A picture of the entire hierarchical structure of society is obtained if all overlays are placed in proper position over the underlay.

The discussion of hierarchies for a set of activities is helped by a change in terminology and notation. We now define a supervision relation $>^1$ on the set **C** of all engagements as follows:

D6 $(a^I, b^I) >^1 (a, b)$ implies $a^I = a$,

$(a, b^I) >^1 (a, b)$ if and only if $b^I \overset{1}{>}_a b$.

The first condition in D6 limits supervision, as before, to persons engaged in the same activity. The second changes notation in such a way that $>^1$ now combines the information previously contained separately in all the $\overset{1}{>}_a$, $a \varepsilon$**A**. It is represented by the graph obtained when all overlays are in position, provided each node b originally on the underlay is regarded as generating a different new node (a, b) in every instance in which it is found dotted in a specific color.

As before, we can define a superiority relation $>$ on **C** by iterating $>^1$. It satisfies conditions obtained from D6 by omitting all superscripts 1 to the relation symbols.

We further change both the meaning of, and the notation for, the term "hierarchy for a single activity" by applying

---

[3]) Suggested to me by Lloyd Shapley.

it now to a set of engagements rather than to a set of persons. The new definition is

D7 $$\mathbf{H}_a(b) = \{ (a, b^{\mathrm{I}}) \mid b^{\mathrm{I}} \varepsilon H_a(b) \},$$

in which every person b^{I} originally in the hierarchy is replaced by his "engagement" (a, b^{I}) in the activity a in question. The set of persons involved is now renamed the *personnel* of the hierarchy, and continues to be denoted by $H_a(b)$. We now define

D8 a *hierarchy* $\mathbf{H}_A(b)$ *for a set* A *of activities* is the union $\mathbf{H}_A(b) = \bigcup_{a \varepsilon A} \mathbf{H}_a(b)$ of a set of hierarchies $\mathbf{H}_a(b)$, one for each $a \varepsilon A$, all having the same head b;

D9 *a complete hierarchy* $\mathbf{H}_A(b^*)$ *for a set* A *of activities* is a hierarchy for that set of which each component hierarchy $\mathbf{H}_a(b^*)$ is complete.

As an example of a hierarchy for a set A of activities let A consist of all the activities pursued in the blast furnace department of an integrated iron and steel plant, and let b be the head of that department. Then $\mathbf{H}_A(b)$ consists of all engagements (a, b^{I}), $a \varepsilon A$ to which (a, b) is superior, that is, all engagements (a, b^{I}) in blast furnace operation activities by persons b^{I} linked to b by a chain of successive supervisors in one and the same activity $a \varepsilon A$. As one goes up a step in any such chain of supervisors, the set of all activities engaged in by the supervisor remains the same or expands. The head b is engaged in all activities of A. Figure 3 gives a simplified example with A consisting of just three activities, a, a^{I}, a^{II}.

In this example $\mathbf{H}_A(b)$ is not complete if b has one or more superiors in at least one activity of A, such as the head of the integrated plant, and possibly a board of directors above him. In that case, however, $\mathbf{H}_A(b)$ can be supplemented to form a complete hierarchy $\mathbf{H}_A(b^*)$ for the *same* set A of activities *only* if any superior b^{I} of b in any activity of A is a superior of b in all activities of A. If so, then the highest superior b^* to b in any $a \varepsilon A$ is also

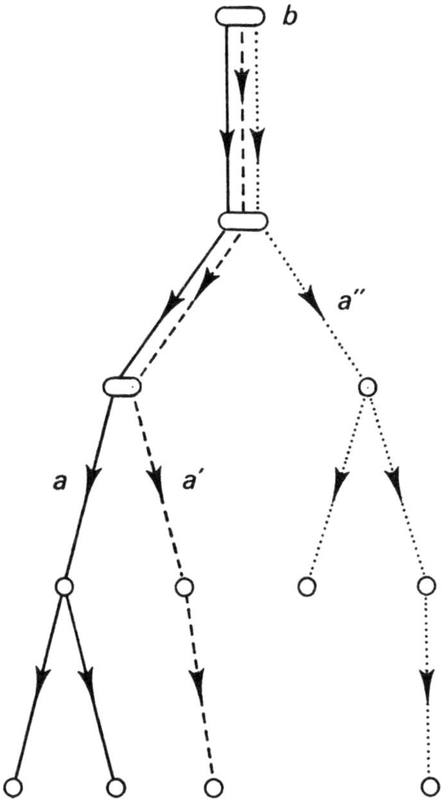

Figure 3

highest superior to b in all $a \varepsilon A$, and $\mathbf{H}_A(b^*)$ is a complete hierarchy for A.
Note that the personnel of $\mathbf{H}_A(b^*)$ may contain additional persons, other than b, who are neither superior to nor supervised by b in any $a \varepsilon A$.

Complete Hierarchies

It is natural to ask whether the set of activities A for which $\mathbf{H}_A(b^*)$ is a complete hierarchy can be further expanded. In the example just given, $\mathbf{C}$ may be such that A can be expanded, hence also the personnel $H_A(b^*)$ of $\mathbf{H}_A(b^*)$ enlarged, by adding in all engagements of the steelmaking and possibly other departments, supervised by the same head b^*. The following definition expresses this idea.

D10 A complete hierarchy $\mathbf{H}(b^*)$ is the union of all complete hierarchies $\mathbf{H}_a(b^*)$ for single activities a, of which b^* is the head.

This definition leads directly to our second theorem:

T2 each engagement $(a, b) \varepsilon \mathbf{C}$ belongs to one and only one complete hierarchy $\mathbf{H}(b^*)$.

To construct this hierarchy uniquely from any given $(a, b) \varepsilon \mathbf{C}$, first find the complete hierarchy $\mathbf{H}_a(b^*)$ for a containing (a, b), which by T1 is unique. Next find the set A of all activities pursued by the head b^* of $\mathbf{H}_a(b^*)$ in which he has no supervisor. Then the unique complete hierarchy containing (a, b) is $\mathbf{H}(b^*) = \mathbf{H}_A(b^*)$.

It will be seen from this construction that the complete hierarchy containing any arbitrary engagement in a blast furnace operation by an employee of the integrated iron and steel plant considered excludes the private practice that the medical director of the company may pursue on the side — provided that medical care for private patients is interpreted as an activity different from those he engages in as a medical director. It includes those activities by members of the family of the head of the integrated plant that he supervises — unless he is in turn supervised by a board of directors in the running of the integrated plant, but *not* in the engagements of his family.

Putting T2 in a different way,

CT2 The set **C** of all engagements partitions into complete hierarchies.

Concluding Remarks

Whether the definitions and postulates here proposed lead to a meaningful concept of complete hierarchies depends on a trait of real-life hierarchic organizations not recognized in these postulates. Often, and for good reasons, the set of activities engaged in by the personnel of a hierarchy, for which ultimate responsibility is placed in the same individual or supervisory body, is determined on the basis of interdependence [4]) of the activities concerned. By introducing one or more relations of interdependence on the set of activities, one may be able to refine the definition of a complete hierarchy in such a way as to avoid the inconsistency that the family activities supervised by, or the boy scout group led by, a member of the firm is included with a complete hierarchy containing that firm if the member is its head but not if he is second in command.

Some activities of governments, especially in countries with central planning and direction of the economy, can be naturally fitted into the concepts introduced. A fuller coverage can be obtained if besides a relation of supervision of engagements one introduces a relation of suppression of engagements. In that way the law-making activities of governments can be looked upon as defining, and the law enforcement activities as aimed at suppressing, illegal engagements.

---

[4]) For further discussion of the concept of interdependent activities, see Koopmans and Montias [paper 3 in present volume].

2

Maximizing Stationary Utility in a Constant Technology*

Richard Beals† and Tjalling C. Koopmans‡

SIAM Journal of Applied Mathematics 17, no. 5 (1969), pp. 1001–1015

1. Introduction. This paper is concerned with a problem in the optimal control of a nonstochastic process over time. It can also be looked on as a problem in convex programming in a space of infinite sequences of real numbers. Because the problem arose in the theory of optimal economic growth, we shall use some economic terminology in describing it.

Consider the problem of maximizing a utility function $U(x_1, x_2, \cdots)$ subject to production feasibility constraints $x_t = z_{t-1} + g(z_{t-1}) - z_t \geqq 0$, $z_t \geqq 0$, where x_t is consumption per worker in time period t, z_t is capital stock per worker at end of time period t, an initial capital stock $z_0 = z$ is given, and we have assumed that a single commodity serves both as consumption good and as capital. Then the consumption program $(x_1, x_2, \cdots)$ is a single-valued function of the capital program $(z_0, z_1, \cdots)$. Equivalently, we want to choose a feasible capital program with $z_0 = z$ so as to maximize an objective function $W(z_0, z_1, \cdots)$ implicit in U, g.

For a fairly general class of problems with a *stationary utility function* (see below) we show the following: (a) for each initial stock $z = z_0$ there is a unique optimal capital program $(\hat{z}_0, \hat{z}_1, \cdots)$; (b) in this optimal program $\hat{z}_t$ either increases, decreases, or is constant with respect to time t; (c) the direction of change with respect to time and the limit $\hat{z}_\infty = \lim \hat{z}_t$ as $t \to \infty$ can be determined explicitly from the initial stock z. We also obtain the "marginal" conditions for optimality in terms of the first derivatives of U and g, and show that in contrast to the usual situation, e.g., of finite time horizon, these necessary conditions are not sufficient. Finally, we consider some iterative procedures for constructing optimal programs. Our primary concern is with (b) and (c) above, and with the construction methods. Existence and uniqueness follow immediately from our assumptions and, in fact, from much less restrictive ones.

Several papers on optimal economic growth (see [8], [1], [4], [6], [7] and other papers cited there) consider a utility function of the form

$$U(x_1, x_2, \cdots) = \sum_{t=1}^{\infty} \alpha^{t-1} u(x_t), \qquad 0 < \alpha < 1, \tag{1}$$

where $u(x)$ is a strictly concave, increasing *single-period utility function*. Then α is called a *discount factor* and $\rho = (1 - \alpha)/\alpha$ is called a *discount rate*. A generalization of (1) has been proposed under the name *stationary utility*. This class of functions has been derived from postulates of continuity, sensitivity, limited independence

* Received by the editors March 14, 1968, and in revised form October 10, 1969. This work was supported in part by the Office of Naval Research.

† Department of Mathematics, University of Chicago, Chicago, Illinois 60637.

‡ Cowles Foundation of Research in Economics at Yale University, New Haven, Connecticut 06520. The work of this author was completed under a grant from the National Science Foundation.

between consumption in successive time periods, stationarity, and the existence of a best and worst program [2], [5], [3]. A function in this class satisfies a recursive relation

(2) $$U(x_1, x_2, x_3, \cdots) = V(x_1, U(x_2, x_3, \cdots)).$$

One obtains (1) from (2) by the particular choice $V(x, U) = u(x) + \alpha U$. The natural generalizations of α and ρ to general stationary utility are given by

(3) $$\alpha(x) = \frac{1}{1 + \rho(x)} = \left(\frac{\partial V(x, U)}{\partial U}\right)_{U = U(x,x,x,\ldots)}$$

The solution of (c) above is given in terms of the discount rate ρ associated with that constant consumption program which maintains the initial capital stock z.

Precise assumptions on U, V, and the production function g, used in the present study, are given in the next section. Results (a) and (b) are obtained in § 3, and the marginal conditions and result (c) are obtained in § 4. Constructive methods are investigated in § 5, and in that connection it is shown that the marginal conditions are not sufficient for optimality.

2. Definitions, notations and assumptions. We assume discrete time t, and a single commodity serving as capital (amount per worker z_t at end of period t) and also as consumption good (consumption flow per worker x_t during period t). Technology is constant and is represented by a net per worker production function $g(z)$. If the labor force is assumed constant, $g(z_t)$ is proportional to output in period $t + 1$, net of depreciation of capital. If the labor force grows exponentially at a given rate $v > 0$, $g(z)$ represents (gross) output per worker less $\lambda z = (\mu + v)z$, where μz allows for proportional depreciation of capital in one time period, and vz is the additional net investment needed to keep z_t constant, that is, to keep the absolute capital stock growing in proportion to the labor force. We require $\lambda \geqq 0$

A *capital path* is a sequence ${}_0z = (z_0, z_1, \cdots)$, $0 \leqq z_t \leqq \bar{z}$, $z_t < \infty$, where $0 < \bar{z} \leqq +\infty$. We denote by ${}_tz$ the tail $(z_t, z_{t+1}, \cdots)$ and by ${}_sz_t$ the finite segment $(z_s, z_{s+1}, \cdots, z_t)$.

A *consumption path* is a sequence, ${}_1x = (x_1, x_2, \cdots)$, $x_t \geqq 0$. We define the tail ${}_tx$ and the segment ${}_sx_t$ as above.

For any constant a, we denote by ${}_{\text{con}}a$ the constant (capital or consumption) path $(a, a, a, \cdots)$.

The capital path ${}_0z$ is said to be *feasible* for the initial capital stock z if $z_0 = z$ and

(4) $$z_{t+1} \leqq z_t + g(z_t), \qquad t = 0, 1, \cdots.$$

If ${}_0z$ is feasible for z, the *associated consumption path* ${}_1x$ with

(5) $$x_{t+1} = z_t + g(z_t) - z_{t+1} \geqq 0, \qquad t = 0, 1, \cdots,$$

is also said to be feasible for z. Let $\mathscr{Z}_z$ and $\mathscr{X}_z$ be the collections of capital paths and consumption paths, respectively, which are feasible for z.

Let the closed interval $\mathscr{I}$ be defined by

$$\mathscr{I} = \begin{cases} [0, \bar{z}] & \text{if } \bar{z} < \infty, \\ [0, \bar{z}) & \text{if } \bar{z} = \infty. \end{cases}$$

We assume the following:

(I) The production function $g(z)$ is continuous and continuously differentiable on $\mathscr{I}$. Moreover $g(0) = 0$, $0 < g'(0)$, g is concave, and the function $h(z) = z + g(z)$ is an increasing function mapping $\mathscr{I}$ onto itself. Hence

$$h(\bar{z}) = \lim_{z \to \bar{z}} h(z) = \bar{z}, \tag{6}$$

and, if $\bar{z} < \infty$, then $g(\bar{z}) = 0$, $g'(\bar{z}) < 0$. If $\bar{z} = \infty$, we assume $\lim_{z \to \infty} g'(z) = 0$.

To interpret these assumptions, let $F(Z, L)$ represent total (gross) output before depreciation, Z the total capital stock, L the labor force. The standard assumptions $F(0, L) = F(Z, 0) = 0$, F continuously differentiable and homogeneous of degree 1, $F_Z > 0$, $F_{ZZ} < 0$ for all $Z \geqq 0$, $L > 0$, then imply, through $F(Z, L) = Lf(Z/L) = Lf(z)$, $g(z) = f(z) - \lambda z$, the assumptions made about g. Since $F(Z, 0) = 0$ implies $\lim_{z \to \infty} f'(z) = 0$, we have $\bar{z} = \infty$ only if $\lambda \leqq 0$, hence $\lambda = 0$, which requires a rate $-v$ of contraction of the population equal to the rate μ of depreciation of capital. In particular, $\bar{z} = \infty$ if $\mu = v = 0$, an important special case discussed by Koopmans [4] in relation to the utility function (1).

If $\bar{z} < \infty$ and $g(z)$ is defined and concave on $[0, \bar{\bar{z}}]$, $\bar{\bar{z}} > \bar{z}$, then, for $\bar{z} < z_0 < \bar{\bar{z}}$, feasibility requires $z_t < \bar{z} + \varepsilon$ for any $\varepsilon > 0$ and large enough t (see Fig. 1). From assumptions on U made below we shall see that optimality requires $z_t < \bar{z}$ eventually. On the other hand, for $0 \leqq z_0 < \bar{z}$, feasibility precludes $z_t \geqq \bar{z}$, whereas $z_0 = \bar{z}$ requires $z_t \leqq \bar{z}$. For these reasons we consider only values $z_0 \in \mathscr{I}$. We note for future use that if $0 < z'_0 < \bar{z}$, feasibility permits $\lim_{t \to \infty} z'_t = \bar{z}$; see Fig. 1.

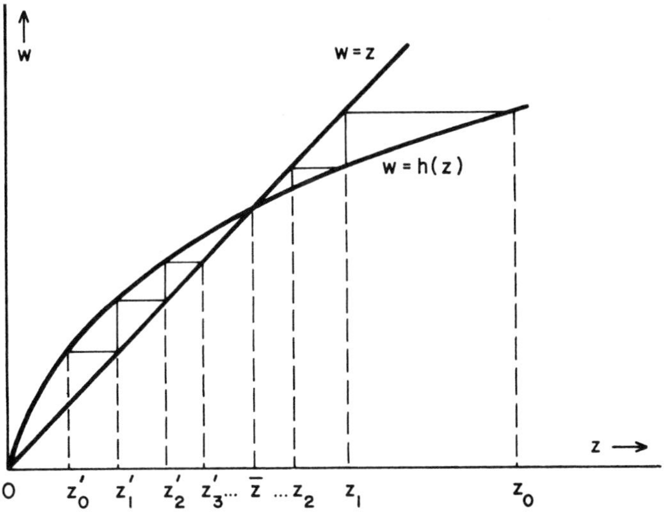

FIG. 1. *Two capital paths with zero consumption*

(II) $U({}_1x)$ is defined on the union $\mathscr{X} = \bigcup_{z\in\mathscr{I}}\mathscr{X}_z$ of all feasible sets, satisfies the recursive relation (2), and is continuous on each $\mathscr{X}_z$ with respect to the product topology.[1]

An example where $U({}_1x)$ is continuous on each $\mathscr{X}_z$ but not on $\mathscr{X}$ is given below.

(III) $U({}_1x)$ is strictly quasi-concave on $\mathscr{X}$.

That is, ${}_1x(\lambda) = \lambda({}_1x) + (1 - \lambda)({}_1x'), 0 < \lambda < 1$, and ${}_1x \neq {}_1x'$ imply

(7) $$U({}_1x(\lambda)) > \min\{U({}_1x), U({}_1x')\},$$

a standard assumption in utility theory. In general, it expresses a decreasing desire for one commodity or commodity bundle relative to another as the other is traded for the one at a constant barter ratio.

(IV) $V(x, U)$ has positive continuous derivatives $\partial V/\partial x, \partial V/\partial U$, on $(\mathscr{I} - \{0\}) \times \mathscr{U}$, where $\mathscr{U}$ is the range of $U({}_1x)$. Moreover $V(x, U)$ is continuous at $x = 0$ for all U, and $\lim_{x\to 0}\partial V(x, U)/\partial x = \infty$ for all U.

It follows from (II) and (IV) that $U({}_1x)$ strictly increases with each x_t.

The condition on $\partial V/\partial x$ as $x \to 0$ ensures that $z_0 > 0$ implies $\hat{x}_t > 0$ for all t, where ${}_1\hat{x}$ denotes the optimal consumption path; see Lemma 2 below. This simplifies some of the statements and proofs, but is not actually necessary for most of the results.

From the identity $U({}_{\text{con}}x) = V(x, U({}_{\text{con}}x))$ implied in (2) one finds by differentiation that (IV) implies

(8) $$0 < \alpha(x) < 1,$$

hence $0 < \rho(x)$, for all $x > 0$ with ${}_{\text{con}}x \in \mathscr{X}$.

(V)

$$D(x, U) = -\left(\frac{dU}{dx}\right)_{V(x,U)=\text{const.}} = \frac{\partial V(x, U)/\partial x}{\partial V(x, U)/\partial U}$$

is strictly decreasing in x on $\mathscr{I} - \{0\}$ for given U.

To interpret this condition, let

$$V_2(x, y; U) = V(x, V(y, U)),$$

(9) $$D(x, y; U) = -\left(\frac{dy}{dx}\right)_{V_2(x,y;U)=\text{const.}} = \frac{\partial V_2(x, y; U)/\partial x}{\partial V_2(x, y; U)/\partial y},$$

and note that assumption (IV) implies that $D(x, y; U) \to \infty$ as $x \to 0$, $y \neq 0$, while $D(x, y; U) \to 0$ as $y \to 0$, $x \neq 0$.

Now, given (IV), condition (V) is equivalent to the following condition.

(V′) For given $y(\neq 0)$, U, $D(x, y; U)$ is strictly decreasing in x on $\mathscr{I} - \{0\}$. Together with an assumption we will not need, viz., that $D(x, y; U)$ strictly increases with y, (V′) is implied in the following plausible assumption, illustrated in Fig. 2:

[1] For a definition of the product topology see [9], or use the distance function defined by $D({}_1x, {}_1x') = \sum_{t=1}^{\infty} \delta^t|x_t - x_t'|/(1 + |x_t - x_t'|)$, where δ is any number with $0 < \delta < 1$.

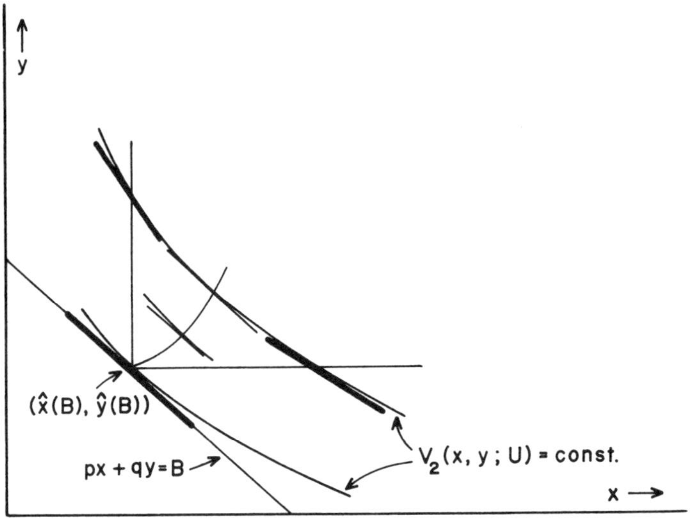

FIG. 2. *Noninferiority of consumption in periods* 1 *and* 2

The first- and second-period consumptions $\hat{x}(B)$, $\hat{y}(B)$ that maximize $V_2(x, y; U)$ for given U, if bought at given positive prices p, q within a budget $px + qy \leqq B$, are strictly increasing with B. Economically, consumption in neither period is inferior to that in the other period, in the way potatoes are inferior to steak.

Two questions arise: whether the assumptions on $U({}_1x)$ in (I), (II), and those on $V(x, U)$ in (III), (IV), (V) are compatible, given (2), and whether a set of conditions on either $U({}_1x)$ or $V(x, U)$ alone could have served instead. In § 6 we answer the first question by exhibiting a large class of examples, and we summarize available results and other considerations bearing on the second question.

3. Optimal capital paths. Given a feasible capital path ${}_0z$, let ${}_1x$ be the associated consumption path given by (5). Define $W({}_0z)$ by $W({}_0z) = U({}_1x)$. If ${}_0z$ and ${}_0z'$ are in $\mathscr{Z}_{z_0}$, then the concavity of the production function $g(z)$ implies that any convex combination ${}_0z'' = \lambda({}_0z) + (1 - \lambda)({}_0z')$, $0 < \lambda < 1$, is also in $\mathscr{Z}_{z_0}$, and that the associated consumption path ${}_1x''$ has $x_t'' \geqq \lambda x_t + (1 - \lambda)x_t'$ for all t. This, the monotonicity and the strict quasi-concavity of U imply that W is also strictly quasi-concave.

A capital path ${}_0\hat{z}$ is *optimal for* z if ${}_0\hat{z} \in \mathscr{Z}_z$, and $W({}_0\hat{z}) \geqq W({}_0z)$ for all ${}_0z \in \mathscr{Z}_z$.

A capital path ${}_0z$ is *strictly monotone in time* if one of the following conditions holds:

(i) $z_t < z_{t+1}, t = 0, 1, 2, \cdots$;
(ii) $z_t = z_{t+1}, t = 0, 1, 2, \cdots$;
(iii) $z_t > z_{t+1}, t = 0, 1, 2, \cdots$.

The assumptions (I)–(V) in § 2 imply the following theorem.

THEOREM 1. *For any initial capital stock $z \in \mathscr{I}$ there is a unique optimal capital path ${}_0\hat{z}$. This path varies continuously with z and is strictly monotone in time. Each $\hat{z}_t$ increases strictly with z.*

Given $z \in \mathscr{I}$, let ${}_0z^* \in \mathscr{Z}_z$ be the path with no consumption, hence $z_0^* = z$, and

$$z_{t+1}^* = h(z_t^*), \qquad t = 0, 1, \cdots . \tag{10}$$

If we define $h^{(n)}(z)$ recursively by

$$h^{(n)}(z) = h(h^{(n-1)}(z)), \qquad h^{(0)}(z) = z, \tag{11}$$

then by (10) the set $\mathscr{Z}_z$ is contained in the product $\mathscr{Z}_z^*$ of the closed intervals $[0, h^{(n)}(z)]$, $n = 0, 1, 2, \cdots$. The latter set is compact with respect to the product topology, by the theorem of Tychonov, and $\mathscr{Z}_z$ is easily seen to be a closed subset, hence likewise compact. Continuity of U on $\mathscr{X}_z$ implies continuity of W on $\mathscr{Z}_z$. Then the continuous, strictly quasi-concave function W assumes a maximum at a unique element ${}_0\hat{z}$ of the compact convex set $\mathscr{Z}_z$. The remainder of this section is devoted to showing continuity and strict monotonicity of this unique optimal capital path ${}_0\hat{z}$.

Given $z \in \mathscr{I}$, let ${}_0\hat{z}$ be the optimal capital path for z and set $\hat{W}(z) = W({}_0\hat{z})$.

LEMMA 1. *$\hat{W}(z)$ is strictly increasing and continuous from the left.*

Proof. If $0 \leqq z < z' \leqq \bar{z}$, and if ${}_0\hat{z}$ is optimal in $\mathscr{Z}_z$, let ${}_0z' \in \mathscr{Z}_{z'}$ be given by $z'_0 = z'$, ${}_1z' = {}_1\hat{z}$. Then, for the associated consumption paths ${}_1x'$, ${}_1\hat{x}$, we have $x'_1 > \hat{x}_1$ and ${}_2x' = {}_2\hat{x}$, so $\hat{W}(z') \geqq W({}_0z') > W({}_0\hat{z}) = \hat{W}(z)$. Therefore $\hat{W}$ is increasing.

If $0 < z \leqq \bar{z}$, then along the optimal consumption path ${}_1\hat{x}$ associated with ${}_0\hat{z}$, some $\hat{x}_t$ is the first to be positive. Then $\hat{z}_{t'} > 0$ for $0 \leqq t' \leqq t - 1$, and for a sufficiently small $\varepsilon > 0$ there is a $\delta > 0$ such that the path $({}_1\hat{x}_{t-1}, \hat{x}_t - \varepsilon, {}_{t+1}\hat{x}) = {}_1x$ is feasible for $z - \delta$. Then $U({}_1x) \leqq \hat{W}(z - \delta) < \hat{W}(z)$. As $\varepsilon \to 0$ one has $\delta \to 0$, $U({}_1x) \to U({}_1\hat{x}) = \hat{W}(z)$, proving continuity from the left.

We can now show that ${}_0\hat{z}$ depends continuously on z. Suppose $z^{(n)} \to z \in \mathscr{I}$. For some $z' \in \mathscr{I}$, $z^{(n)} \leqq z'$ for all n. Then $\mathscr{Z}_{z^{(n)}} \subseteq \mathscr{Z}_{z'}^*$ for all n. Since the latter set is compact, the corresponding sequence of optimal paths, ${}_0\hat{z}^{(n)}$, has at least one convergent subsequence, and it suffices to show that any convergent subsequence must converge to ${}_0\hat{z}$, the optimal path for z. Dropping terms and renumbering, we may assume ${}_0\hat{z}^{(n)}$ itself converges to some ${}_0z \in \mathscr{Z}_z$. By the continuity of W, Lemma 1, and the optimality of ${}_0\hat{z}$ in $\mathscr{Z}_z$, respectively, $W({}_0z) = \lim W({}_0\hat{z}^{(n)}) = \lim \hat{W}(z^{(n)}) \geqq \hat{W}(z) = W({}_0\hat{z})$. Therefore $W({}_0z) = W({}_0\hat{z})$, so ${}_0z = {}_0\hat{z}$ by the uniqueness of ${}_0\hat{z}$, thus proving continuity of ${}_0\hat{z}$.

To show that $\hat{z}_t$ increases with z, we note that $z = 0$ forces $\hat{z}_t = 0$, $\hat{x}_t = 0$ for all t as the unique feasible, hence optimal, path, and prove two lemmas.

LEMMA 2. *Suppose ${}_0\hat{z}$ is optimal for $z > 0$, and let ${}_1\hat{x}$ be the associated consumption path. Then $\hat{x}_t > 0$, $\hat{z}_t > 0$, for $t = 1, 2, \cdots$.*

Proof. Suppose one of the pair $(\hat{x}_t, \hat{x}_{t+1})$ is positive. Then feasibility requires $\hat{z}_{t-1} > 0$. Let $(\hat{x}, \hat{y}) = (\hat{x}_t, \hat{x}_{t+1})$ and $U = U({}_{t+2}\hat{x})$. Then $(\hat{x}, \hat{y})$ maximizes $V_2(x, y, U)$ subject to the constraint, derived from (5),

$$h(h(\hat{z}_{t-1}) - x) - y = \hat{z}_{t+1},$$

where $0 \leqq \hat{z}_{t+1} < h(h(\hat{z}_{t-1}))$. It is clear from the properties of h and of the slope $D(x, y, U)$ noted after assumption (V) that both $\hat{x}$ and $\hat{y}$ must be positive. Clearly $\hat{x}_t$ is positive for some t; working backwards and forwards in time we see that $\hat{x}_t > 0, t = 1, 2, \cdots$, hence $\hat{z}_t > 0, t = 1, 2, \cdots$.

LEMMA 3. *Suppose $z, z' \in \mathcal{I}$, $z < z'$, and let ${}_0\hat{z}$ and ${}_0\hat{z}'$ be the corresponding optimal paths. Then $\hat{z}_1 < \hat{z}'_1$.*

Proof. If $z = 0$, then $\hat{z}_1 = 0 < \hat{z}'_1$ by Lemma 2. Now assume $0 < z$. The stationarity of U (see (2)) implies that for each t, ${}_t\hat{z}$ is optimal for $\hat{z}_t$. Therefore if $\hat{z}_1 = \hat{z}'_1 \neq 0$, then ${}_1\hat{z} = {}_1\hat{z}'$. Suppose this is so, and let ${}_1\hat{x}$ and ${}_1\hat{x}'$ be the associated consumption paths. Then $0 < \hat{x}_1 < \hat{x}'_1$ and $0 < \hat{x}_2 = \hat{x}'_2$, ${}_3\hat{x} = {}_3\hat{x}'$. Write $U_3 = U({}_3\hat{x}) = U({}_3\hat{x}')$. Then $(\hat{x}_1, \hat{x}_2)$ maximizes $V_2(x, y; U_3)$ subject to $h(h(z) - x) - y = \hat{z}_2$, and similarly for $\hat{x}'_1, \hat{x}'_2$, with z' replacing z. But this is seen to contradict assumption (V), since $\hat{x}_1 < \hat{x}'_1$, $\hat{x}_2 = \hat{x}'_2$ and $h(z) - \hat{x}_1 = \hat{z}_1 = \hat{z}'_1 = h(z') - \hat{x}'_1$, and in view of the concavity of h, the strict quasi-concavity of U, hence of V_2 (see Fig. 3).

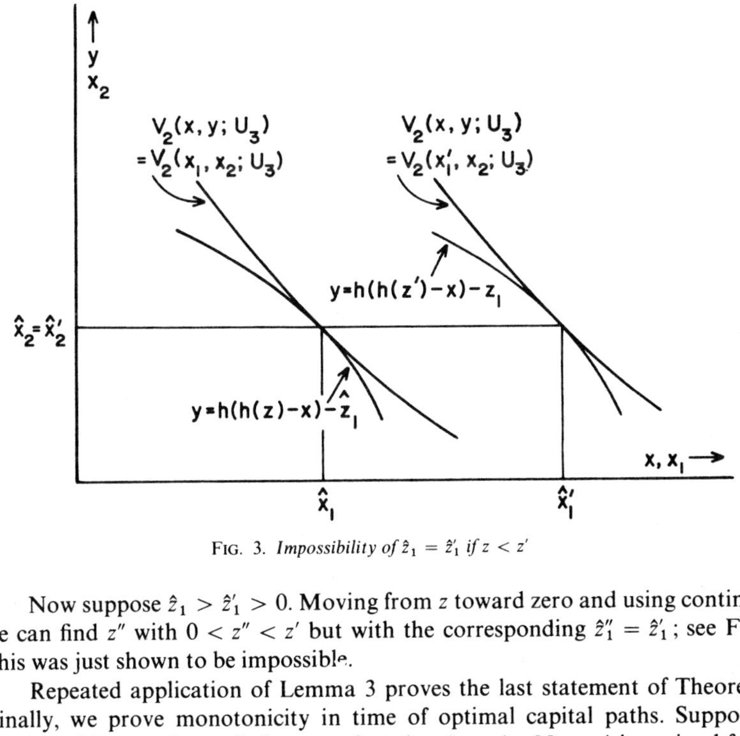

FIG. 3. *Impossibility of $\hat{z}_1 = \hat{z}'_1$ if $z < z'$*

Now suppose $\hat{z}_1 > \hat{z}'_1 > 0$. Moving from z toward zero and using continuity, we can find z'' with $0 < z'' < z'$ but with the corresponding $\hat{z}''_1 = \hat{z}'_1$; see Fig. 4. This was just shown to be impossible.

Repeated application of Lemma 3 proves the last statement of Theorem 1. Finally, we prove monotonicity in time of optimal capital paths. Suppose ${}_0\hat{z}$ is optimal for $z \in \mathcal{I}$, $z > 0$. Suppose first that $\hat{z}_0 < \hat{z}_1$. Now ${}_1\hat{z}$ is optimal for $\hat{z}_1$, so Lemma 3 implies $\hat{z}_1 < \hat{z}_2$. Inducing, we get $\hat{z}_t < \hat{z}_{t+1}$ for all t. The cases $\hat{z}_0 = \hat{z}_1$ and $\hat{z}_0 > \hat{z}_1$ are handled similarly.

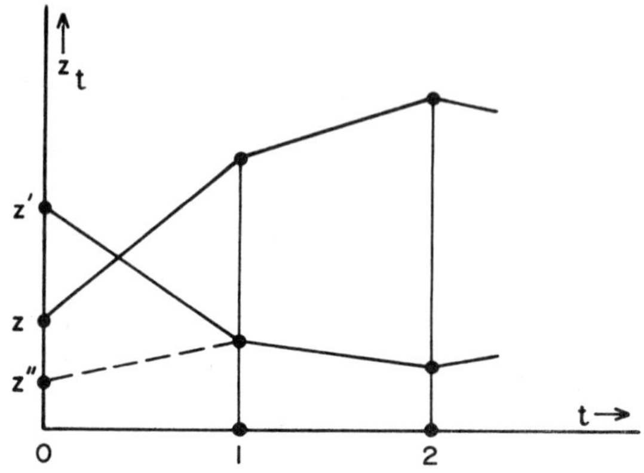

FIG. 4. *Impossibility of* $\hat{z}_1 > \hat{z}'_1$ *if* $z < z'$

4. Asymptotic behavior of optimal paths. Monotonicity in time of the optimal path ${}_0\hat{z}$ implies that the (possibly infinite) limit $\hat{z}_\infty = \lim_{t\to\infty} \hat{z}_t$ exists. We want to determine, for each initial capital stock z, whether $\hat{z}_t$ increases, is constant, or decreases over time, and what its limit is.

Suppose the pair $(\hat{x}, \hat{y})$ maximizes $V_2(x, y; U) = V(x, V(y, U))$ subject to the constraint $h(h(z_0) - x) - y = z_2$, where U, z_0, and z_2 are given, with $z_0 > 0$ and $z_2 < h(h(z_0))$. Let $\hat{z}_1 = h(z_0) - \hat{x}$ and $\hat{U}_2 = V(\hat{y}, U)$. It follows from the proof of Lemma 2 that $\hat{x} > 0$, $\hat{y} > 0$, and, in particular,

$$\frac{\partial}{\partial x} V(\hat{x}, \hat{U}_2) = \frac{\partial}{\partial U} V(\hat{x}, \hat{U}_2) \cdot \frac{\partial}{\partial y} V(\hat{y}, U) \cdot h'(\hat{z}_1). \tag{12}$$

Conversely, (12) implies that $(\hat{x}, \hat{y})$ is optimal for the given problem.

Similarly ${}_1\hat{x}_n$ with each $\hat{x}_t > 0$ maximizes $V_n({}_1x_n, U) = V(x_1, V(x_2, \cdots, V(x_n, U) \cdots))$ subject to ${}_1x_n$ being obtained by (5) from ${}_0z_n$ with z_0, z_n, U prescribed, if and only if

$$\frac{\partial}{\partial x} V(\hat{x}_t, \hat{U}_{t+1}) = \frac{\partial}{\partial U} V(\hat{x}_t, \hat{U}_{t+1}) \cdot \frac{\partial}{\partial x} V(\hat{x}_{t+1}, \hat{U}_{t+2}) \cdot h'(\hat{z}_t), \tag{13}$$

$t = 1, 2, \cdots, n-1$, where $\hat{U}_t = V_{n-t+1}({}_t\hat{x}_n, U)$, $\hat{U}_{n+1} = U$, and $\hat{z}_0 = z_0$, $\hat{z}_t = h(\hat{z}_{t-1}) - \hat{x}_t$.

A path ${}_0z$ with associated consumption path ${}_0x$, where $x_t > 0$ for all t, cannot be improved by changing finitely many of the z_t, $t \geqq 1$, if and only if the corresponding equations (13) hold for all t. Thus ${}_0z$ cannot be improved by finitely many changes if and only if it cannot be improved by a single change. It is shown in § 5 below that the equations (13) are not sufficient for optimality.

Given $z \in \mathscr{I}$, $z > 0$, the consumption path associated with ${}_{\text{con}}z$ is ${}_{\text{con}}x$, where $x = g(z)$. Since $g(\bar{z}) = 0$, ${}_{\text{con}}\bar{z}$ is not optimal for $\bar{z}$ by Lemma 2. Let $z < \bar{z}$ and

$U = U({}_{\text{con}}x)$. If ${}_{\text{con}}z$ were optimal we could divide (12) by $\partial V(x, U)/\partial x$ to get, using (3),

$$\alpha(g(z))h'(z) = 1, \tag{14}$$

equivalent to $g'(z) = \rho(g(z))$. In economic terms, a necessary condition for the optimality of a constant capital path at a level $z > 0$ is the equality of the marginal net per-worker productivity $g'(z)$ of per-worker capital z to the "associated" discount rate $\rho(g(z))$. (We shall see later that this condition is also sufficient.)

Proceeding from this observation, we partition $\mathscr{I}$ into the following disjoint sets:

$$\begin{aligned} \mathscr{I}^{=} &= \{z \mid \text{either } z = 0 \text{ or } 0 < z < \bar{z} \text{ and } g'(z) = \rho(g(z))\}, \\ \mathscr{I}^{>} &= \{z \mid 0 < z < \bar{z} \text{ and } g'(z) > \rho(g(z))\}, \\ \mathscr{I}^{<} &= \{z \mid 0 < z \leqq \bar{z}, \quad z < \infty \text{ and } g'(z) < \rho(g(z)) \text{ if } z < \bar{z}\}. \end{aligned} \tag{15}$$

Then $\mathscr{I}^{=}$ is closed, $\mathscr{I}^{>}$ and $\mathscr{I}^{<} - \{\bar{z}\}$ are open. (If $\bar{z} < \infty$, then by (6), (8), for some $\varepsilon > 0$, $g'(z) < 0 < \rho(g(z))$, hence $z \in \mathscr{I}^{<}$, when $\bar{z} - \varepsilon \leqq z < \bar{z}$.)

THEOREM 2. *Let* ${}_0\hat{z}$ *be optimal for* $z \in \mathscr{I}$. *Then*

(a) *if* $z \in \mathscr{I}^{=}$, ${}_0\hat{z}$ *is the constant path* ${}_{\text{con}}z$;

(b) *if* $z \in \mathscr{I}^{>}$, *then* $\hat{z}_t$ *increases with t and* $\hat{z}_\infty$ *is the smallest number in* $\mathscr{I}^{=}$ *which is larger than z; if no such number exists,* $\hat{z}_\infty = \infty$;

(c) *if* $z \in \mathscr{I}^{<}$, *then* $\hat{z}_t$ *decreases and* $\hat{z}_\infty$ *is the largest number in* $\mathscr{I}^{=}$ *which is smaller than z.*

A path ${}_0\hat{z}$ optimal for z is called *stable* if, for every path ${}_0\hat{z}'$ optimal for z' which has z' sufficiently near z, $\hat{z}'_\infty = \hat{z}_\infty$. We have the following consequence of Theorem 2 (see Fig. 5).

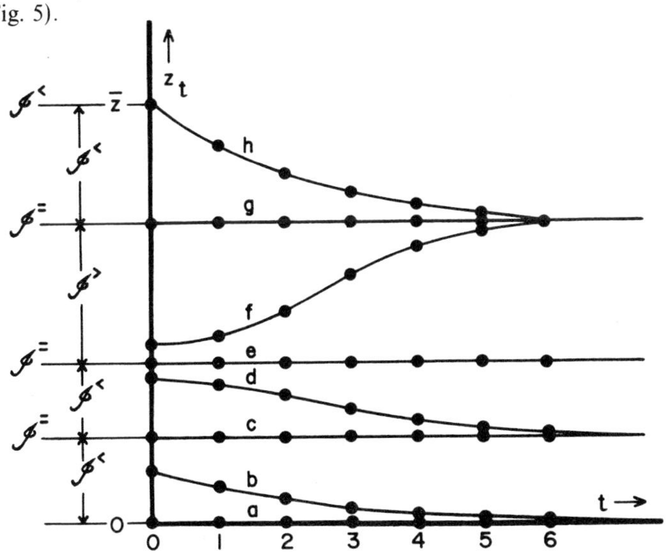

FIG. 5. *Optimal paths for* $\bar{z} < \infty$. *All except c, e are stable*

COROLLARY. *Let ${}_0\hat{z}$ be optimal for z. Then ${}_0\hat{z}$ is stable unless $z \in \mathscr{I}^=$ and is also in the closure of $\{z'|z' \in \mathscr{I}^>, z' > z\}$ or of $\{z'|z' \in \mathscr{I}^<, z' < z\}$.*

If $z = 0$, only ${}_{\text{con}}z$ is feasible and statement (a) of Theorem 2 follows.

If $z \in \mathscr{I}^=$, $0 < z$, then (14) shows that the equations (13) are satisfied by the path ${}_0z = {}_{\text{con}}z$. Therefore ${}_0z$ cannot be improved by changing only finitely many of the z_t, $t \geqq 1$. Statement (a) of Theorem 2 is thus implied by the following lemma.

LEMMA 4. *Let ${}_0z$ be a feasible capital path with $0 < z_t \leqq z^* < \bar{z}$ for all t. Suppose $W({}_0z) \geqq W({}_0z')$ for all ${}_0z'$ with $z'_0 = z_0$ and ${}_mz' = {}_m\hat{z}$ for some m. Then ${}_0z$ is optimal.*

Proof. Suppose ${}_0z'' \in \mathscr{Z}_{z_0}$ with $z''_t > 0$ for all t. For any n there is a path ${}_0z^{(n)} \in \mathscr{Z}_{z_0}$ with ${}_0z^{(n)}_n = {}_0z''_n$ and ${}_mz^{(n)} = {}_mz$ for sufficiently large m (depending on n, z''_n and ${}_0z$); this follows from the last remark in the discussion of assumption (I) above. Then $W({}_0z) \geqq W({}_0z^{(n)})$, and ${}_0z^{(n)} \to {}_0z''$, so $W({}_0z) \geqq W({}_0z'')$.

It is clear from the proof of Lemma 4 that the assumption that z_t is bounded away from $\bar{z}$ is stronger than necessary. What is needed is that ${}_tz$ can always be caught up with, even from a late and bad start.

Next we consider the effect of finitely many downward changes in ${}_{\text{con}}z$ when $z \in \mathscr{I}^>$.

LEMMA 5. *Suppose $z \in \mathscr{I}^>$. If ${}_0z \in \mathscr{Z}_z$ and $z_t \leqq z$ for $t < n$, while ${}_nz = {}_{\text{con}}z$, then $W({}_0z) \leqq W({}_{\text{con}}z)$. Moreover, equality holds only if ${}_0z = {}_{\text{con}}z$.*

Proof. We use induction on n. By assumption $z_0 = z$, so for $n = 1$ there is nothing to prove. Suppose the statement is true for $n = m \geqq 1$ and suppose $z_t \leqq z$ for $t \leqq m$ while ${}_{m+1}z = {}_{\text{con}}z$. If $z_m = z$ then ${}_mz = {}_{\text{con}}z$ and the statement holds, by assumption. Suppose $z_m < z$. Choose a path ${}_0z' \in \mathscr{Z}_z$ with $z'_t = z$, $t \neq m$ and $z'_m = z + \delta$, $\delta > 0$ (see Fig. 6). The corresponding value of W satisfies

$$W({}_0z') - W({}_{\text{con}}z) = (\alpha(x))^{m-1}\frac{\partial V}{\partial x}(x, U)[\alpha(x)h'(z) - 1]\cdot\delta + \varepsilon(\delta)\cdot\delta,$$

where $x = g(z)$, $U = W({}_{\text{con}}z)$, and $\varepsilon(\delta) \to 0$ as $\delta \to 0$. Since $z \in \mathscr{I}^>$, the factor in square brackets is positive. Therefore, for small positive δ,

$$W({}_0z') > W({}_{\text{con}}z). \tag{16}$$

Now $z_m < z < z'_m$, so there is a convex combination ${}_0z'' = \lambda({}_0z) + (1 - \lambda)({}_0z')$, $0 < \lambda < 1$, with $z''_m = z$. Clearly $z''_t \leqq z$ for $t < m$ and ${}_mz'' = {}_{\text{con}}z$. The induction assumption implies that $W({}_0z'') \leqq W({}_{\text{con}}z)$. Strict quasi-concavity of W implies that $W({}_0z'') > \min\{W({}_0z), W({}_0z')\}$. But $W({}_0z') > W({}_{\text{con}}z) \geqq W({}_0z'')$, so $W({}_0z'') > W({}_0z)$. Therefore $W({}_{\text{con}}z) > W({}_0z)$, completing the proof.

A similar argument shows that if $z \in \mathscr{I}^<$, any change in ${}_{\text{con}}z$ moving finitely many z_t upward is a change for the worse.

We can now prove (b) of Theorem 2. Suppose $z \in \mathscr{I}^>$ and let ${}_0\hat{z}$ be the optimal path for z. We know from (14) that ${}_0\hat{z}$ is not constant, so by Theorem 1 it either increases or decreases. Suppose it decreased. By Lemma 2, $\hat{z}_t > 0$ for all t. Hence, as in the proof of Lemma 4, there would be a sequence of paths ${}_0z^{(n)} \in \mathscr{Z}_z$ such that ${}_0z^{(n)} \to {}_0\hat{z}$, $z^{(n)}_t \leqq z$ for all t, and ${}_mz^{(n)} = {}_{\text{con}}z$ for large m. By Lemma 5, $W({}_0z^{(n)})$

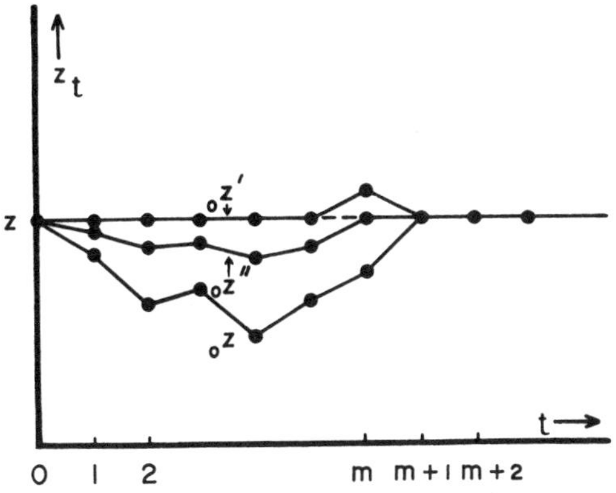

FIG. 6. *Proof of Lemma* 5

$\leqq W({}_{\text{con}}z)$ for all n. Therefore $W({}_0\hat{z}) \leqq W({}_{\text{con}}z)$, contradicting the nonoptimality of ${}_{\text{con}}z$. Thus ${}_0\hat{z}$ increases.

Let z' denote the smallest number in $\mathscr{I}^=$ larger than z, if there is one, and let $z' = \infty$ otherwise. If $z' < \infty$, then ${}_{\text{con}}z'$ is optimal for z', and the last statement of Theorem 1 shows that $\hat{z}_t < z'$ for all t. Hence $\hat{z}_\infty \leqq z'$, which remains true if $z' = \infty$. Now suppose $\hat{z}_\infty = z'' < z'$. Then ${}_T\hat{z}$ satisfies equations (13) for all T and all n, if we write $\hat{U}_{n+1} = W({}_{T+n-1}\hat{z})$. But ${}_t\hat{z} \to {}_{\text{con}}z''$ as $t \to \infty$. By continuity ${}_{\text{con}}z''$ will also satisfy equations (13) with $\hat{U}_{n+1} = W({}_{\text{con}}z'')$, so $z'' \in \mathscr{I}^=$, contradicting $z'' < z'$, since $z = \hat{z}_0 < \hat{z}_t < \hat{z}_\infty = z''$. Hence $z'' = z'$. This completes the proof of (b). The proof of (c) is parallel, with 0 taking the place of ∞.

If ${}_0\hat{z}$ is an optimal capital path and ${}_1\hat{x}$ is the associated consumption path, then ${}_1\hat{x}$ obviously has the following properties:

$$\hat{x}_{t+1} < g(\hat{z}_t) \quad \text{if } \hat{z}_t \text{ increases;}$$

$$\hat{x}_{t+1} > g(\hat{z}_t) \quad \text{if } \hat{z}_t \text{ decreases;}$$

$$\hat{x}_\infty = \lim_{t\to\infty} \hat{x}_{t+1} = \lim_{t\to\infty} g(\hat{z}_t).$$

It is not clear whether our assumptions guarantee that $\hat{x}_t$ is also monotone with respect to time. That it is monotone when U has the special form (1) was shown by Koopmans [4] for a continuous time variable, and is implied in equation (13) for discrete time.

5. Construction of optimal paths. We give two procedures for constructing the optimal capital path as a limit of a sequence of paths each obtained by solving the optimization problem for finite time. Each procedure has certain disadvantages, theoretical or practical.

Given a path ${}_0z \in \mathscr{Z}_z$ and an integer $n \geqq 1$, let $T_n({}_0z)$ be the path ${}_0z' \in \mathscr{Z}_z$ which maximizes $W({}_0z')$ with constraints (4) and ${}_0z'_{n-1} = {}_0z_{n-1}$, ${}_{n+1}z' = {}_{n+1}z$.

Thus $T_n({}_0z)$ is obtained from ${}_0z$ by making the best feasible adjustment in z_n alone. Then T_n is an operator from $\mathscr{Z}_z$ to $\mathscr{Z}_z$. Note that $W(T_n({}_0z)) \geqq W({}_0z)$, with equality only when $T_n({}_0z) = {}_0z$.

Let S_n be the iterated operator $S_n = T_n T_{n-1} \cdots T_1$, and suppose $z \in \mathscr{I}, z > 0$. Start with some path ${}_0z^{(0)}$ in $\mathscr{Z}_z$ and define a sequence of paths inductively by

$$ {}_0z^{(n+1)} = S_{n+1}({}_0z^{(n)}). $$

Thus ${}_0z^{(n+1)}$ is obtained by improving ${}_0z^{(n)}$ in the first $n + 1$ places, in order. We cannot be sure that ${}_0z^{(n)}$ will converge to the optimal path; in fact a poor initial choice ${}_0z^{(0)}$ will ensure that it does not. To see this, note that the optimal path ${}_0\hat{z}$ gives positive consumption in each time period, so $\hat{x}_1 > 0$, $\hat{z}_1 < h(z)$. Choose z_1^* with $\hat{z}_1 < z_1^* < h(z)$, and let $z_{t+1}^* = h(z_t^*)$, $t = 1, 2, \cdots$. Any feasible path ${}_0z$ with $z_1 \leqq z_1^*$ must have $z_t \leqq z_t^*$, all $t \geqq 1$. Now there are paths ${}_0z^{(0)} \in \mathscr{Z}_z$ with $z_t^{(0)} > z_t^*$, all $t \geqq 1$; we can even choose ${}_0z^{(0)}$ so that there is positive consumption in each time period. From the preceding remarks we see that any ${}_0z \in \mathscr{Z}_z$ differing from ${}_0z^{(0)}$ in only finitely many time periods has $z_1 > z_1^* > \hat{z}_1$. Therefore ${}_0\hat{z}$ cannot be the limit of any subsequence of the sequence ${}_0z^{(n)}$ obtained from such a ${}_0z^{(0)}$.

Since as noted above $\mathscr{Z}_z$ is compact, starting from any ${}_0z^{(0)} \in \mathscr{Z}_z$, some subsequence ${}_0z^{(n_j)}$ of ${}_0z^{(n)}$ will converge to a path ${}_0z \in \mathscr{Z}_z$. Since

$$ W({}_0z^{(m)}) \leqq W(T_1({}_0z^{(m)})) \leqq W(S_{m+1}({}_0z^{(m)})) = W({}_0z^{(m+1)}), $$

we have $W(T_1({}_0z)) = W({}_0z)$. Hence, by strict quasi-concavity of W, the adjustment of z_1 in the definition of $T_1({}_0z)$ leaves z_1 unchanged, and $T_1({}_0z) = {}_0z$. Inductively, suppose $T_j({}_0z) = {}_0z$ for $j \leqq n - 1$. Then $T_n({}_0z) = S_n({}_0z)$, and the same argument shows $W(S_n({}_0z)) = W({}_0z)$, so $S_n({}_0z) = {}_0z$. If $z_t \leqq z^* < \bar{z}$ for all t, then, by Lemma 4, ${}_0z$ is optimal. Moreover, *if* ${}_0z$ *is optimal*, then any other convergent subsequence of ${}_0z^{(n)}$ will converge to a ${}_0z'$ with $W({}_0z') = W({}_0z)$. Hence the whole sequence ${}_0z^{(n)}$ will converge to ${}_0z$.

As noted above, the limit need *not* be optimal, however. On the other hand, if ${}_0z^{(0)}$ allows $x_t^{(0)} > 0$ for some t then

$$ U({}_{\text{con}}0) < U({}_1x^{(0)}) = W({}_0z^{(0)}) \leqq W({}_0z) = U({}_1x), $$

hence $x_t > 0$ for some t, and, by the proof of Lemma 2, for all t. Therefore, the equations (13) for a path with positive consumption in all periods are not sufficient for optimality. Some such paths cannot be improved by any finite number of changes, but can be improved by an infinite number of changes.

We conjecture that if ${}_0z^{(0)}$ is chosen to show a monotonic approach from z to the $\hat{z}_\infty$ of Theorem 2, and if $\hat{z}_\infty < \infty$, then ${}_0z$ is optimal, and such a choice of ${}_0z^{(0)}$ gives relatively faster convergence. We have not succeeded in proving these statements.

An optimum can be guaranteed by the following method. Given $z \in \mathscr{I}, z > 0$, choose some $z' \in \mathscr{I} - \{\bar{z}\}$. (A computationally helpful choice of z' is again $\hat{z}_\infty$, provided $\hat{z}_\infty < \infty$.) For some N there is a path ${}_0z' \in \mathscr{Z}_z$ with ${}_Nz' = {}_{\text{con}}z'$. For any

$n \geqq N$ there is a unique ${}_0z^{(n)} \in \mathscr{Z}_z$ maximizing $W({}_0z)$ subject to ${}_nz = {}_{\text{con}}z'$. Let ${}_0\hat{z}$ be optimal for z. As in the proof of Lemma 4 there is a sequence of paths ${}_0\tilde{z}^{(n)} \to {}_0\hat{z}$ such that, for each n, the tail ${}_m\tilde{z}^{(n)}$ is eventually ${}_{\text{con}}z'$. Then $W({}_0\tilde{z}^{(n)}) \leqq W({}_0z^{(m)})$, so $\lim W({}_0z^{(m)}) = W({}_0\hat{z})$. It follows that ${}_0z^{(m)} \to {}_0\hat{z}$.

The practical difficulty with this method is that it involves solving optimization problems for more and more time periods, rather than for one period at each step as in the first method. Let us note that each such problem can be solved by iterating the one-period solution. Suppose ${}_0z^{(0)} \in \mathscr{Z}_z$ and $n \geqq 1$. A modification of the argument above shows that ${}_0z^{(m)} = (S_n)^m({}_0z^{(0)})$ converges to the path ${}_0z \in \mathscr{Z}_z$ which maximizes $W({}_0z')$ subject to ${}_{n+1}z' = {}_{n+1}z^{(0)}$.

6. Comments on the assumptions made. We establish compatibility of the assumptions (I) through (V) by constructing a general class of examples, as follows. Let $g(z)$ be concave and continuously differentiable on $\mathscr{I} = [0, \infty)$, with $g(0) = 0$, $g'(0) > 0$, and $\lim_{z\to\infty} g'(z) = 0$, so $\lim_{z\to\infty} g(z)/z = 0$. Define $\mathscr{Z}_z$ and $\mathscr{X}_z$ accordingly. Given $z \in \mathscr{I}$, let ${}_0z^* \in \mathscr{Z}_z$ be the path with no consumption, ${}_0z \in \mathscr{Z}_z$ any feasible path, and ${}_1x$ the associated consumption path. Then (5) implies $z_t \leqq z_t^*$ for all t. Therefore (10) implies that, for any $\varepsilon > 0$, there exists $T = T(\varepsilon)$ such that

$$x_{t+1} \leqq h(z_t) \leqq h(z_t^*) \leqq (1 + \varepsilon)z_t^* \leqq \cdots \leqq (1 + \varepsilon)^{t-T+1} z_T^* \qquad \text{for all } t \geqq T.$$

This shows that for any $z \in \mathscr{I}$ and any $\varepsilon > 0$ there is a constant c such that

$$x_t \leqq c(1 + \varepsilon)^t \quad \text{for all } {}_1x \in \mathscr{X}_z \quad \text{and} \quad t = 1, 2, \cdots. \tag{17}$$

Now let $V(x, U)$ be a function defined on $\mathscr{I} \times \mathscr{I}$, satisfying assumptions (IV) and (V) on $(\mathscr{I} - \{0\}) \times \mathscr{I}$. Suppose also that V is nonnegative and strictly concave and that there are constants $c_0 > 0$ and $0 < \alpha < 1$ such that

$$V(x, 0) \leqq c_0(1 + x), \qquad \frac{\partial V}{\partial U}(x, U) \leqq \alpha, \qquad \text{for all } x, U. \tag{18}$$

Set $V_1(x, U) = V(x, U)$ and $V_{t+1}({}_1x_{t+1}, U) = V_t({}_1x_t, V(x_{t+1}, U))$, $t = 1, 2, \cdots$. It is easily seen that

$$0 \leqq \frac{\partial V_t}{\partial U}({}_1x_t, U) \leqq \alpha^t \qquad \text{for all } {}_1x_t, U.$$

Suppose ${}_1x \in \mathscr{X}_z$ and c is chosen so that (17) holds. Then

$$\begin{aligned} 0 \leqq V_{t+1}({}_1x_{t+1}, 0) - V_t({}_1x_t, 0) &= V_t({}_1x_t, V(x_{t+1}, 0)) - V_t({}_1x_t, 0) \\ &\leqq c[1 + (1 + \varepsilon)^t]\alpha^t, \qquad \text{for all } t. \end{aligned}$$

If ε has been chosen so that $\alpha(1 + \varepsilon) < 1$, we see from this that

$$U({}_1x) = \lim_{t\to\infty} V_t({}_1x_t, 0) \tag{19}$$

exists and is continuous on $\mathscr{X}_z$ in the product topology. Clearly $U({}_1x)$ satisfies (2). Concavity of $V(x, U)$ implies concavity of each V_t, by induction, so $U({}_1x)$ is concave. Finally, concavity of $U({}_1x)$, equation (2), and the fact that $V(x, U)$ is strictly concave and strictly increasing in x and U are easily seen to imply strict concavity of $U({}_1x)$. Thus assumptions (I)–(V) are satisfied.

In particular, take $g(z)$ as above and take $V(x, U) = x^\gamma + \alpha U$ with $0 < \alpha$, $\gamma < 1$. Then the $U({}_1x)$ given by (19) is the same as that given by (1), with $u(t) = x^\gamma$, and all assumptions are satisfied. Note that in this example $U({}_1x)$ is not defined on all of $\mathscr{I} \times \mathscr{I} \times \cdots$, and is not continuous on all of $\mathscr{X}$: since $h(z) \geqq z$ for all $z \in \mathscr{I}$, the path ${}_1x^{(n)}$ with $x_t^{(n)} = 0$ for $t \neq n + 1$ and $x_{n+1}^{(n)} = \alpha^{-n/\gamma}$ is feasible for the initial capital $z^{(n)} = \alpha^{-n/\gamma}$. As $n \to \infty$, the sequence of paths ${}_1x^{(n)}$ converges to ${}_{\text{con}}0$ in the product topology; but $U({}_1x^{(n)}) = 1$ for all n, while $U({}_{\text{con}}0) = 0$.

The assumptions (I)–(V) have been adapted to the present concern with existence and characteristics of an optimal path. Results of axiomatic studies cited in § 1, based on slightly different and in part more restrictive assumptions about $U({}_1x)$, may help clarify the connections between $U({}_1x)$ and $V(x, U)$. For $\bar{z} < \infty$, assumptions about $U({}_1x)$ made in these studies imply the recursive relation (2) with $V(x, U)$ continuous and increasing in x, U. If $\phi(x)$ is a continuous, increasing function from the range of $U({}_1x)$ to the real line, then

$$(20) \qquad U^*({}_1x) = \phi(U({}_1x)), \qquad V^*(x, U^*) = \phi(V(x, \phi^{-1}(U^*)))$$

preserves (2), and the substitution of $U^*({}_1x)$ for $U({}_1x)$ does not affect the optimality of any path. However in the second study cited it is found that ϕ can be chosen so as to have

$$(21) \qquad U^* > U^{*\prime} \quad \text{implies } V^*(x, U^*) - V^*(x, U^{*\prime}) \leq U^* - U^{*\prime}$$

for all x; moreover there is strict inequality for a "large majority" of the $(x, U^*, U^{*\prime})$, with equality as an often (perhaps always) avoidable special case. This suggests the degree of generality of the second part of (18) above. If, analogously to (18), we restrict the class of $U({}_1x)$ somewhat further by requiring that for some ϕ and some α, $0 < \alpha < 1$, we have in (21)

$$V^*(x, U^*) - V^*(x, U^{*\prime}) \leqq \alpha(U^* - U^{*\prime});$$

then $U({}_1x)$, assumed continuous in the sup topology in the references cited, is continuous in the product topology as well (as assumed here), and can be determined from a given $V(x, U)$ as in (19).

Neither differentiability nor concavity assumptions are involved in the above considerations. The present introduction of differentiability assumptions can be reconciled with (20) by stipulating that $\phi(U)$ shall possess a positive derivative for all U. Note that quasi-concavity of $U({}_1x)$ is preserved by (20). However, conditions on $V(x, U)$ equivalent to quasi-concavity of $U({}_1x)$ and invariant for (20) have not been found, and could not take the simple form of (noninvariant) concavity or quasi-concavity conditions on $V(x, U)$. The authors therefore both acknowledge and bypass this gap in present knowledge by attaching a quasi-concavity condition to $U({}_1x)$, although the other conditions are more naturally attached to $V(x, U)$.

Acknowledgment. The authors are indebted to David Cass and to the referees for valuable comments.

REFERENCES

[1] D. Cass, *Optimum growth in an aggregative model of capital accumulation*, Rev. Econ. Stud., 32 (1965), pp. 233–240.

[2] T. C. Koopmans, *Stationary ordinal utility and impatience*, Econometrica, 28 (1960), pp. 287–309.

[3] T. C. Koopmans, P. A. Diamond and R. E. Williamson, *Stationary utility and time perspective*, Econometrica, 32 (1964), pp. 82–100.

[4] T. C. Koopmans, *On the concept of optimal economic growth*, The Econometric Approach to Development Planning, North-Holland, Amsterdam, and Rand McNally, Chicago, 1965, pp. 225–287.

[5] ———, *Structure of preference over time*, Cowles Foundation Discussion Paper 206, 1968, 71 pp.

[6] ———, *Objectives, constraints and outcomes in optimal growth models*, Econometrica, 35 (1967), pp. 1–15.

[7] E. Malinvaud, *Croissances optimales dans un modèle macro-économique*, The Econometric Approach to Development Planning, North-Holland, Amsterdam, and Rand McNally, Chicago, 1965, pp. 301–384.

[8] F. P. Ramsey, *A mathematical theory of saving*, Economic J., 38 (1928), pp. 543–559.

[9] J. L. Kelley, *General Topology*, Van Nostrand, Princeton, 1955.

3

On the Description and Comparison of Economic Systems

Tjalling C. Koopmans and John Michael Montias

Comparison of Economic Systems: Theoretical and Methodological Approaches, ed. A. Eckstein (Berkeley: University of California Press, 1971), pp. 27–78

1. Introduction

The traditional comparison of economic systems starts from the trichotomy of capitalism, socialism, and communism. It goes from there to recognize a certain diversity of patterns within each of these three prototypes.

The last twenty years have seen a great deal of relatively independent experimentation with organizational techniques and institutional forms within each of the prototypes, and some borrowing of devices and forms between prototypes. In addition, the rather different institutional problems of less developed economies have received greatly increased attention. As a result, a rich and, indeed, somewhat bewildering variety of organizational forms and systems is now spread before us, which defies simple classification according to a few prototypes.

To the researcher the new situation offers a double advantage. Not only is the number of possible comparisons substantially increased, but, at the same time the greater variety of systems provides opportunities for comparison between economies that are alike in most respects and differ notably only in one or two of their critical traits or dimensions—a type of comparison that may permit the tracing of effects of specific traits on outcomes with greater chance of success. For instance, it may be more easily possible to compare the role of market prices and government controls in Belgium and the Netherlands, or of investment policies of Poland and Rumania—in both cases pairs of countries with many common traits—before proceeding to the more complex comparisons of the total systems of countries that are more widely disparate in their institutions, size, and resources.

In general, we believe the new circumstances invite approaches to the comparison of economic systems that altogether avoid prior classification according to the grand "isms" and instead start from comparisons of organizational arrangements for specific economic functions. Among these we should wish to consider the coordination of production activities by distinct organizations, the accumulation and utilization of means of production of new or existing types, the research and development for new methods and means of production, the distribution of currently produced goods and services among the participants and beneficiaries of the system, the maintenance of aggregate stability, and the protection of individuals from harmful effects of the economic actions of others.

Our decision to shun the "isms" as a basis for classification of observed economic systems does not preclude comparing models of admittedly hypothetical pure systems, representing one variant or another of one of the "isms" or of any other system proposed or contemplated. However, our decision leaves us without suitable terms for referring to categories of observed economies professing allegiance to the respective "isms." Reaching into geography for substitute labels, we shall occasionally and metaphorically use "East" for the diverse group of countries in which a communist party is the leading political organ; "West" for the developed "capitalist" and mixed "capitalist-socialist" countries; and "South" for the less developed noncommunist countries, regardless of their individual locations. It will then be understood that Cuba is in "East," while Australia and Finland are in "West." Yugoslavia, which does not seem to fit with either "East" or "West" in its economic institutions, will be mentioned separately when the need arises.

Although the conference to which this paper is a contribution is attended almost exclusively by economists, the importance of political and (non-economic) social factors, both in the realities of the systems to be compared and in the criteria (or "norms") entering into the comparisons, is apparent to all. Your authors herewith disclaim professional expertise in the socio-political sciences, but they have preferred the risk of making uninformed observations to that of not recognizing the crucial political and sociological aspects of the topic under discussion. Even so, our professional preoccupations may well have led us to follow some economic twigs while stopping short on some political limbs.

The main aim of the present paper is to suggest, without particular claim to novelty, one possible framework for the description and comparison of economic systems. For an objective comparison the descriptions of the systems being compared should be couched as much as possible in system-free terms. It is in the nature of this undertaking that definitions and terminology take up an inordinate part of the paper. The ideal is that the *primitive* (undefined) terms entering into these definitions be few in number and universal in applicability and prior meaning. Preferably they should be drawn from fields such as engineering, psychology, physiology, that have a relatively system-free status. Terms such as "individuals," "preferences," "commodities," "production," "perception," "communication," "constraints on behavior," come close to meeting this requirement. Terms such as "price," "supervision," "organization," "decentralization," "planning," whose meanings may be system-bound or otherwise ambiguous, should then be defined for the purposes of the comparison, using the primitive terms.

We have not attained this ideal. Within the available time and space we have used more than a minimum of primitive terms in an exploratory attempt to block out what seem to us important aspects of both the conceptual and the statistical problems of system description and system comparison. We may well have neglected or dealt too cursorily with other aspects of comparable importance.

As a test of relevance, we do provide illustrative examples to convey contexts for the definitions and suggest possible uses for the concepts introduced. Finally, we rather liberally insert conjectures of regularities that more systematic empirical investigation might confirm or refute, again to suggest rather than demonstrate possible uses of the concepts.

2. A Conceptual Framework

2.1. Environment and System

Following Grossman[1] and others, we shall think of comparisons of economies or of their systems as being made via models of these economies or systems. That is, instead of comparing economies A and B directly, models M_A and M_B are abstracted from our knowledge of A and B, respectively, and are compared with each other as well as with the realities whose salient features they seek to embody. Of course, the choice of the models again depends on the particular purpose of the comparison to be made.

In the models here suggested for demonstration purposes, we distinguish (representations of) the *environment*, the (economic) *system*, *actions*, *outcomes*, and *norms* with respect to which the outcomes are evaluated and the systems compared. All of these are defined with reference to a particular time period to which the description or the comparison applies. Briefly, the *environment of the economy* includes *resources*, *initial technology*, *external factors* (including technology available from other economies), and the impact of *random events* on each of these. It also includes *initial preferences*, and *incomplete interactions* (as of the initial date of the period of comparison).

Resources, in turn, include *natural resources* proper (including climatic conditions), the *initial capital stock* (available means of production and goods in inventory or in process at the beginning of the period), and the *initial population*, its age distribution, health, skills, and education levels. Resources evolve over time by prospecting, investment, conservation or neglect of physical and biological surroundings of man, and also by

[1] G. Grossman, *Economic Systems*, Englewood Cliffs, N.J., 1967.

human reproduction, medical services, education, learning from experience, aging and death.

Technology (at any time) is thought of as a long list of commodity specifications, together with a long list of descriptions of possible activities. An *activity* is defined by its inputs (kinds and quantities), by its effects, and, if greater specificity is required, by the kind of repeatable *action* or sequence or combination of actions that, by the state of the arts at the time, is known to produce the effects whenever the inputs are available. The effects will be outputs (kind and quantity) in the case of production activities of goods and some services, maintenance of states of health or of satisfaction levels in the case of consumption activities, increases in the knowledge or skills of individuals in the case of instructional activities, and so forth. The inputs are efforts, the use of facilities or equipment, and in most cases other goods, services or resources. Technology evolves by the addition of new commodities and activities through research and development or through their introduction from other economies, and by the demise of old ones as a result of disappearance of demand or of requisite skills.

External factors are all traits of the rest of the world, other than of the economy in question, pertinent to economic processes in the economy. This includes the geographical position, resource endowment and purchasing power of important actual or potential trading partners, the existence and proximity of political or military rivals, protectors, or clients, and the systems in operation in each of these.

Random events give rise to uncertainty about the availability of resources, about the outputs (or even about the input or action requirements) of given activities, about the external factors, and may require definition in terms of subjective or objective probability distributions. Other kinds of uncertainty, arising from unpredictable aspects of behavior of economic agents within the economy, are characteristic of the system rather than of the environment.

The initial population has been included with the resources because of its productive potentialities. Its *initial preferences* must be recorded separately as a baseline from which subsequent preferences evolve. The standard description of preferences (at any time) associates with each individual a *preference ordering* (possibly represented by a *utility function*) of all alternative current and future consumption paths of that individual and possibly of his family ("private preferences"). The ordering can be thought extended to express also his "social preferences" concerning the consumption paths of others (living and as yet unborn) as well as more general system traits. The "social preferences" of central planners, for example, may be thought to guide their allocation decisions, which affect the welfare of the future as well as the present population.

However, the concept of preference ordering, whether it applies to individuals, to planners, or to other participants making allocation decisions on behalf of groups of system participants, does not require that the ordering of possible states be complete. How far into the future a decision maker attempts to discriminate among possible states or paths to these states and the efforts he may exert to specify and detail his preferences among these states or paths may also differ from system to system.

The term "utility function" is less appropriate for goals imputed to or proposed for organizations, including the economy as a whole. In those instances, we shall therefore use less specific terms, such as *goal function* and *norm*, to be introduced more fully below.

The representation of preferences by a goal function is normally associated with a model of consumers', citizens', organizational, or national choice that maximizes goal attainment among available alternatives. Progress in utilizing generalizations of that model to include realistic elements of habituation, of "satisficing,"[2] of random behavior,[3] of coping with uncertainty,[4] and of learning from experience[5] has been incomplete and uneven. Whichever model one adopts, the important implication it has for system description is the *decision rule* describing how consumer's choice or organizational or civic action depend on available opportunities and prospects. In particular, for statistical inter-system comparisons of consumers' behavior, studies of demand functions representative of entire populations or large subsets thereof will usually have to be substituted for a conceptually fuller description of choice. For these reasons, the skeptical reader may want to think in terms of "decision rules" wherever in the sequel we use the term "preferences," or "utility function," or "goal function."

Incomplete interactions include all orders not yet fulfilled (contracts to deliver goods or services, quotas in production plans) and commitments (repayment of loans, payment of pensions) required by, or compatible with, the system, which are outstanding at the beginning of the period to which the comparison applies.

The *system* is hardest to define because of the widely inclusive nature of the concept and because of the difficulty of separating economy from polity. In greatest generality, the *total system* includes all political, social

[2] H. A. Simon, *Models of Man*, New York, 1957, Ch. 14.

[3] D. Davidson and J. Marschak, "Experimental Tests of a Stochastic Decision Theory," in Churchman and Ratoosh, eds., *Measurement Definitions and Theories*, New York, 1959, Ch. 13.

[4] L. J. Savage, *The Foundations of Statistics*, New York, 1954.

[5] T. C. Koopmans, "On Flexibility of Future Preferences," in Shelly and Brian, eds., *Human Judgments and Optimality*, New York, 1964, Ch. 13, pp. 243–254.

and economic institutions, organizational structure, laws and rules (and the extent of their enforcement and voluntary observance), and all traditions, religious and secular beliefs, attitudes, values, taboos, and the resulting systematic or stochastic behavior patterns. The total system includes all these phenomena both as initially present and as evolving over the period of comparison through organizational change, new legislation or rulings, or new trends in attitudes and behavior. The provisions for creating or dissolving organizations, modifying relations between organizations, amending the rules, and influencing attitudes and behavior are themselves considered part of the system.

Depending on the comparison to be made, the comparor may feel that he can designate as *economic system* only that part of the total system, which directly or indirectly affects economic behavior and outcomes in at least one of the systems being compared.[6] So as not to prejudge this issue in general, we shall from here on use the term *system* in an open-ended way to refer to all or to the economically relevant part of the total system, leaving the burden of proof of nonrelevance with the comparor.

One may wish to extend the concept of the system to include perception of the environment, of the system, and of the interaction of its participants—as distinct from that environment, system, interaction taken by itself or as perceived by the comparor. This view recognizes the system participants' perception of the economy's environment and of their respective individual environments (defined below) as itself a system characteristic. Examples abound: A presumption of racial superiority may prevent an employer from perceiving the skills of a racial minority. A strong attachment to central planning may lead a planner to underrate the impact of random events in such industries as agriculture or fisheries. An entire literature on less developed economies deals with the obstacles that traditions, attitudes, and vested interests place in the way of the perception of technological opportunities.

In these examples the term "perception" is used in a sense somewhat broader than its primarily cognitive connotation in psychological parlance. Especially if we speak of the *perceived system*, we may think of an image of the system formed in the minds of its participants, which the comparor may infer or extract from expressions of views or opinions by these participants and from modes in which the participants address each other for purposes of persuasion. If we include in this discussion perceptions of one system by the members of another, it will be clear that such images, sometimes even caricatures, are formed under the influence of the observer

[6] Applying this notion symmetrically to the political comparor who designates as "*political system*" that part of the total system directly or indirectly affecting political behavior and outcomes, we must expect a very substantial overlap between the political and the economic system.

or critic's own institutional system and of information emanating from other observed systems. Where information about a system is manipulated by some of its participants for the purpose of influencing fellow-participants or participants in other systems, it is termed *propaganda*. Another closely related influence on an individual's perception of his or of other total systems is his *ideology*, a more or less stable pattern of frequently untestable ideas, symbols, and symbol clusters, usually expressed in widely disseminated printed, broadcast, or televised material, which supply him with a more or less coherent view or explanation of, and a definite attitude to, a broad range of the world's phenomena.

Actions differ from activities in that they are thought of as taken by a specific participant at a specific time, whereas activities are types of possible actions not dated or connected with a participant (though their possibility may be limited by time of inclusion in the technology or by skill requirements). Generally, an *action* changes the environment of the economy or of the participants or both in some minor or major way.

Taking actions as the elementary building blocks of economically relevant behavior, we may use the term *decisions* for commitments to several simultaneous or successive related actions and *policies* as classes of decisions adopted in order to economize on decision time and effort and, in many cases, made known in order to create stable expectations about future decisions.

The boundary between system and policies is not a sharp one and may depend on the length of the period for which a comparison is made. For instance, a market economy in which the central government follows a fiscal policy of a balanced annual government budget may be considered as a system somewhat different from that of the same economy in which a fiscal and monetary full-employment policy is pursued. If within a longer period the former system is succeeded by the latter, one may alternatively speak of a market system in which a policy change occurred at some point of time.

The policies, decisions, and actions of all participants other than a specific one, together with the outcomes of these policies, decisions, and actions, must be included with the environment of the economy to define the *environment of that specific individual*. The latter, in particular, includes both the technology available from outside the system and that generated by other participants within the system. That part of a participant's environment that he actually perceives is called his *information set*.[7]

Outcomes are all aspects or consequences of the system, and of the policies, decisions, or actions of all participants to which positive or

[7] Note that a participant may know about the existence of a technology, yet the technology itself may not be part of his information set, since it may be protected by patents or restricted by high communication or learning costs.

negative value is attached in at least one of the norms entering into a comparison. This may include any valuable or deleterious man-made changes in the environment during the period involved in the comparison and any "evolutionary" changes in the system that are made or come about in a manner compatible with it. It is also bound to include levels of consumption activities or of satisfactions and changes over time thereof, as well as aggregates, distributions, and possibly other functions of these levels or changes in levels. In Section 3 we give examples of important outcomes (there called "desiderata"), of which some are common to most systems, others are specific to one or more systems. In Section 4 we give examples of important categories of activities, ranging from some that are common to all systems to some others whose character or even existence is specific to the systems in which they occur.

Finally we come to the concept of a *norm* (criterion).[8] We believe that no meaningful comparison of economies or of their systems is possible without at least the implicit application of some norm. Even a seemingly entirely descriptive comparison must select from a vast multitude of traits that smaller number deemed sufficiently interesting (a value concept!) to be entered into the comparison. A norm may be implicit rather than explicit; it may be limited by the perception of the comparor; or its presence and nature may escape the perception of some or most of his readers. But the conscious and unconscious motivations of the investigator and the natural selection by which individual studies enter into the cumulative record of social science results tend to introduce, and make apparent over time, the underlying norms.

Norms become more visible when observed inter-system differences in various system traits are brought together and weighed against each other. We define an *explicit norm* (hereafter often briefly a *norm*) formally as an evaluation function (utility function, goal attainment function) of all outcomes which represents the preferences of some individual or group pertinent to the comparison.

The scientific character of a comparison is enhanced if any underlying norm is made explicit to the extent possible. Furthermore, it is instructive to make the same comparisons in the light of a number of alternative pertinent norms. These may include:

A. A norm perceived as a *prevailing norm* in any of the two or more economies being compared. This may be a norm explicitly adopted and imposed by a majority or minority enabled by the system to

[8] We choose the word "norm" without the connotation of disapproval of dissenters which sometimes adheres to it. While the term "criterion" is more value-free, it does not contain any hint that the interesting criteria are those to which at least some people attach a normative value.

make it the prevailing norm. If no such group exists, it may be a norm that embraces, or is explicit in, the outcome of the processes of adjustment of diverse interests inherent in the system.

B. A norm attributed by the comparor to groups of the population (minorities or majorities) whose preferences are given little weight in, or overruled by, the prevailing norm, in short, an *unavailing norm*.

C. Norms adduced by the comparor for purposes of discussion. This category may explicitly include (if he wishes) a norm he himself deems pertinent or even advocates. In regard to economies where a prevailing norm is imposed by a minority, or also where it is accepted by an inattentive and unreflecting majority, the category may further include a comparor's tentative but explicit estimate of a better balance of interests, possibly arrived at with the help of attitudinal surveys, legal documents, and more general past and current social thought. Finally, it may contain norms he explicitly attributes to groups of his readers, or to the intended beneficiaries of his knowledge and insights—regardless of the standing of these norms in the economies being compared.

2.2. Comparison of Economies and Comparison of Economic Systems

Differences in observed outcomes in different economies will in general reflect such differences as are present in all of the components of environment, system and policy we have distinguished. Symbolically, if e denotes *e*nvironment, s *s*ystem, p_s *p*olicies pursued by the participants under the system s, and o *o*utcomes, then we may write

$$o = f(e, s, p_s)$$

for the grand relationships we would all like to know and understand. Even though our actual knowledge is pitifully small compared with the complexity of the relationships in question, writing them out in this explicit way may help in their discussion. The implied assumption is that the laws of physics, chemistry, technology, agronomy, human and animal physiology and psychology—the same fields from which the primitive terms are drawn—circumscribe what can be achieved by any given economic organization, in a manner subject in principle to objective inquiry and explicit description.

A system may be more suited to one environment than to another, in the sense that more desirable combinations of consumption, growth, and national security may be attained by that system in one environment than in another. (It may be argued that some systems may not even be viable unless certain environmental conditions are met.) The interdependence between the environment of the economy and the system is cited by

Wittfogel, who suggests that in certain environments special forms of hierarchic organization, run by bureaucracies with virtually unlimited powers over the participants in their system, may have arisen in response to the need for coping with drought (through irrigation), with floods (through flood control), and with other negative factors in their environment.[9] Another example, much discussed in the literature, is the strong influence of the mere size of an economy on the optimal degree of enterprise specialization.[10] A third example, perhaps more conjectural, is the tendency of a low level of skills in an economy to favor a more centralized system.[11]

But even if differences in environment were not to favor corresponding differences in system, a statistical comparison of systems under some given norm would still require that one allow for the inevitable effect of environmental variables on system performance under the norm. The initial capital-labor ratio, mineral wealth, climate and soil, the geographical location of other nations important for trade, national security or influence, are all examples of environmental variables that codetermine, say, the consumption-growth-security locus attainable with the "best" of systems. The use of observations on economies with markedly different environments for the empirical comparison of systems therefore requires the econometric estimation of the vector function f, or at least of the first and possibly second derivatives of important outcomes in f with respect to those environmental variables for which the data present important differences.

A similar problem arises with respect to the policy variables p_s. The very nature (as distinct from the numerical values) of these variables will in general depend on the system. This is particularly true for the policies of ruling organizations. It may well be true also for those of other participants. One may wish to compare systems under the policies actually or typically in use in each system during the period(s) of the comparison. In that case, separating the effects of policies from those of the system raises no new econometric problem. However, the principal reason for the distinction between system and policies is the greater ease of changing policies than systems. One may therefore also wish to compare systems on

[9] K. Wittfogel, *Oriental Despotism: A Comparative Study of Total Power*, New Haven: 1957.

[10] See, for instance, G. J. Stigler, "The Division of Labor is Limited by the Extent of the Market," *Journal of Political Economy*, LIX:3 (1951) 185–193.

[11] For pertinent comment, see A. Eckstein, "Individualism and the Role of the State in Economic Growth," *Economic Development and Cultural Change*, VI:2 (1958) 81–87; A. O. Hirschman, *The Strategy of Economic Development*, New Haven, 1958, p. 65; R. C. Wallich, "Some Notes Towards a Theory of Derived Development," in Agerwala and Singh, eds, *The Economics of Underdevelopment*, Oxford (1958) pp. 189–204.

the assumption that in each system, at least on the level of ruling organizations, the policies applied are the best available within the institutional and normative constraints of the system. In addition to estimation of the values $f(e_0, s_i, p_{s_i})$ of the outcome vectors f for some standardized environment e_0 and for the (s_i, p_{s_i}) combinations observed in the economies labeled $i = 1, 2, \ldots, k$, this would require the further estimation of first and second derivatives of important outcomes in f with regard to important components of p_{s_i} in those countries where policy is deemed clearly nonoptimal.

As in other relatively simpler problems in econometrics, the very limited opportunities for experimentation, the limited number of periods and of economies for which observations are available, and economic history's inherent selectivity in regard to the range of vector variables presented to view in any given economy and period do not permit such estimation without resort to *a priori* assumptions about the properties of the functions f and about their deduction from underlying, more autonomous, relationships. For instance, the activity–analysis model of production may be used in a first approximation as a source of mathematical constraints on the way in which important environmental variables enter into f. Likewise, ideas from organization theory may be drawn upon to spot crucial system and policy variables and to circumscribe the manner in which they enter into f. In Section 5 we seek to explore some possibilities in that direction with regard to system variables. As a third example that anticipates the "utility version" of the efficiency norm,

$$n(o) = n(f(e, s, p_s)),$$

a function of the outcome vector o to be introduced in Section 3.2, we need to draw on the theory of consumers' choice when faced with given market prices.

Whether these particular approaches are helpful or should be discarded for better ones is not the issue here. The main point is that the principles regarding the use of *a priori* postulates for the identification of economic relationships and for the tracing of causal chains, developed in connection with other fields of application of econometric methods,[12] also bear, *mutatis mutandis*, on the comparison of economic systems. In fact, in such comparisons, the dependence on *a priori* assumptions is the greater, the more numerous the differences between the economies to be compared.

[12] See W. C. Hood and T. C. Koopmans, eds., *Studies in Econometric Method*, New York (1953) especially Chs. I (J. Marschak), II (T. C. Koopmans), III (H. A. Simon); also Simon, *Models of Man*, *Op. Cit.* (n. 2) Chapters 1 and 3; and T. C. Koopmans and A. F. Bausch, "Selected Topics in Economics Involving Mathematical Reasoning," *SIAM Review*, I:2 (1959) 79–148, topic 11.

An ability to trace the effects of differences or changes in environment, system, or policies is crucial to the ultimate purpose of the comparison of economic systems: to find ways of improving the performance of any given economy or system in the light of some adopted norm. The use of models of the economies compared is therefore bound up in the normative character of the comparisons.

2.3. Organizational Structures and System Descriptions

We propose to describe a system for comparative purposes with the aid of the following terms and concepts in addition to those already introduced. We wish to stress that our ultimate purpose of facilitating the comparison of systems lies at the basis of our classification of institutions and of other system characteristics in the taxonomic material in this and in the following sections. We are mindful, for example, that the organizations, activities, actions and messages in a system may be subdivided into much smaller and more homogeneous categories than we suggest in this paper. Alternative classifications of approximately the same degree of "coarseness" also come readily to mind.

To demarcate a system, we specify a set of *participants* whom we identify as all individuals, and possibly groups of individuals acting with a specific group decision procedure (boards, committees, parliaments), that take economically relevant actions.

Participants' actions, including messages, may become part of the environment of other participants, who may respond to them if they so desire or if they are obligated to do so. This response is also an action.

We call *interaction* a set of actions, simultaneous, sequential, or of both kinds such that each participant in the interacting subset of participants directly affects the environment or information set or both of every participant in that subset. The relation is thus symmetrical: If person i interacts with person j, i's actions impinge on j and vice versa.

Orders are dated messages calling for a specific response (to act or desist) from the participant(s) to whom they are addressed; *rules* are messages stipulating or constraining the actions of a set of participants for an indefinite period and under specified conditions. The set of participants is explicitly defined in the message but not necessarily by listing them individually.

We conceive of participants as associating in organizations. An *organization* is defined with reference to a specific set of activities. It consists of a set of persons called *members* of the organization (which must include at least one participant of the system considered), who regularly interact with each other, by communication and possibly in other ways, in the process of carrying on one or more activities of the set. To be precise, for any two members i, q, of the organization, we require that there be a *chain* of interactions connecting them, that is, a sequence i, k, l, . . . , p, q, of different members such that (i, k), (k, l), . . . , (p, q) are interacting pairs[13] (not necessarily for the same activity or activities in the set). In particular, as we shall see below in Section 5.4.1, all participants form an organization in this sense for the set of all activities engaged in by at least one of them.

It will be convenient to use the word *entity* for either an individual or an organization.

To differentiate *associations*, *hierarchies*, and *quasi-hierarchies*, the three basic types of organizations we shall deal with in Section 5, we require the concepts of *supervision* and *superordination*.

A member of an organization *supervises* another member if he has the power to issue orders to, and exert significant influence on the actions of, that member with reference to one or more of the activities in which the organization is engaged or could engage.[14] If member i supervises member j who in turn supervises member k, and so forth, then i is said to be *superordinate* (or *superior*) to j, k, . . . , and j, k, . . . , *subordinate* to i, whether or not i actually also supervises k, ... Note that a member may be superior to another for one activity and subordinate or neither-superior-nor-subordinate for another activity.

An *association* for an activity or a set of activities is an organization, none of whose individual members is superior to another member in carrying out any of these activities.

A *hierarchy* for an activity is an organization with the following properties:

1. For each pair of members of the organization *either* one member is subordinate (for that activity) to the other *or* both are subordinate to the same third member of the organization.
2. If one member is subordinate to another in the organization, there is a unique chain of successive supervisors (for that activity) connecting the two.

From this definition it may be inferred that a hierarchy has a unique head and that every other member in a hierarchy is directly supervised by precisely one member. These properties differentiate hierarchies as we have defined them from *quasi-hierarchies*, the third, residual, category of organizations, in which a supervision relation occurs between at least one pair of members, but where members need not be related to each other by a single chain of supervision, and more than one member may head the

[13] For an alternative, broader definition of an organization where the necessity for regular interaction *within* each pair of members (i, k), (k, l) . . . , (p, q) in a chain is relaxed, see section 5.4.1.

[14] On the supervision relation, see also below, section 5.3.

organization. (Among modern nuclear families consisting of father, mother, and children such quasi-hierarchies are frequently encountered.) A hierarchy or quasi-hierarchy may itself be a member of an association, or vice versa, if all the members of the member-organization act according to or abide by the decision procedures of that organization.

This classification of organizations will be used in Section 5, where we put forward two conjectures on the efficiency of alternative organizations, including markets (which we conceive of as associations of a special type).

We call *ruling organizations* for a system certain organizations (usually structured as hierarchies) that have the power to issue *rules* or *orders* to some designated set of system participants to which they are addressed; these may include both members and non-members of these organizations. We shall call these rules laws. The *legal framework of the economy* is the set of all laws pertinent to the economic processes in the system.

We describe a system in terms of the patterns of interaction among its participants and in terms of the rules governing these interactions imposed by ruling organizations. A complete system description presupposes that an information set (see Section 2.1) and either a preference ordering (say, a utility function) or a decision rule can be attributed to each of the participants. If a utility function is attributed, the participant's *motivation* is then defined as a function that associates with each course of action open to him the utility of that outcome which, on the basis of his information set, he expects to result from that course of action.[15] If his information takes the form of a (subjective or objective) probability distribution of the outcomes of at least some courses of action, the term "expected utility" may be substituted for "utility" in this definition, or another model for choice under uncertainty may be employed.

The motivation for a participant's decision to comply or not to comply with an order from a supervisor in the organization of which he is a member depends, among other things, on his assessment of the loss or inconvenience he would suffer if he were forced to leave the organization—a possible outcome of failure to comply, once or repeatedly. Although the goals and policies of an organization are likely to constrain the actions of all of its members (with the possible exception of the head of a hierarchy if the goals and policies he is able to impose accurately reflect his personal preferences), we allow for the possibility of actions by members in conflict with the goals and policies of the organization as

[15] The behavior model suggested in this paragraph is in the tradition of the economist's theory of maximizing behavior already referred to in Section 2.1. A psychologist would note that changes in information would receive more attention than unchanged information. An organization theorist would note that the utilities of alternatives quite different from the one presently pursued would receive more attention when the participant's fortunes are strongly threatened.

interpreted by their superiors, as well as actions by members adversely affecting fellow members in terms of the latters' goals.

We shall find that the notions of price and of ownership, which will be defined when they are introduced in Section 5, can be fitted without strain into the conceptual framework we have set forth.

3. Norms (Criteria)

3.1. Outcomes, Desiderata, Indicators

We have defined outcomes as *all aspects or consequences of system, policy, decisions, or actions to which positive or negative value is attached in at least one of the norms entering into a comparison.* In turn, a norm was defined as *an evaluation function of all outcomes that represents the preferences held by some individual or group pertinent to the comparison.* The mathematical definition of a function then permits a norm to depend in fact on only a subset of all outcomes, indicating that the individual or group in question is interested only in some of the outcomes. We shall call *desiderata* for any given norm those outcomes on which the norm in fact depends positively. (Any *odiosa* can be transformed into desiderata by a change of sign.)

Before listing examples of important desiderata occurring in pertinent norms, we make a few more general observations.

The insertion of the word "aspect" in the above definition of an outcome entails that any trait of a system or policy can itself be a desideratum in some norm if value is attached to it in that norm, possibly because of presumed noneconomic effects. For instance, decentralization of economic decisions may be valued in itself because it is looked upon as strengthening the self-reliance of individuals. In contrast, in another system centralization may be valued in itself, because it is thought to help maintain central control over political and cultural decisions desired in the prevailing norm. In comparisons the fact that these system traits appear as outcomes valued in opposite ways in different norms must be taken into account.

The inclusion in a norm of, or the giving of extra weight to, a desideratum merely because of its presumed relation to some unnamed, perhaps noneconomic, desideratum introduces into the norm an assumption about causal relationships that may be mistaken. This element of speculation is present, to a smaller or larger degree, in almost all adoption and weighting of desiderata. It is enhanced by the fact that the more ulterior desiderata are often harder to quantify, and therefore proximate desiderata which are more easily measurable must represent the ulterior ends in question.[16]

[16] Cf. E. Kirschen and L. Morrissens, "The Objectives and Instruments of Economic Policy," in B. Hickman, ed., *Quantitative Planning of Economic Policy*, Washington D.C., 1964.

The use of statistical *indicators* as proxies for desiderata or odiosa raises problems of representativeness and comparability. Two countries may have a desideratum in common but may pursue different proximate goals to attain it. Most societies, for example, wish to minimize economic strife (for reasons related to desideratum y_5 to be defined in Section 3.2) and to preserve a reasonable degree of stability in the distribution of power and rewards. In some economies where labor is autonomously organized, man-days lost by strikes may be used as an indicator of strife and tension. But no such measure is available for economies in which strikes are illegal.

Another example concerns the volume of unfinished construction, an indicator likely to be relevant for comparing the intertemporal efficiency of alternative systems. Comprehensive data on this variable can only be obtained for the Soviet Union and for the East European economies. In market economies these data, if they are collected at all at the level of the construction enterprise, are generally not aggregated, presumably because neither the decision makers in the governmental hierarchy nor those in any nongovernmental organization have felt or articulated a need for them in reaching their decisions.

3.2. Common or Similar Desiderata in Various Norms

We begin our listing with some *common desiderata* that we believe to be present in the prevailing norms of most systems in the modern world. It is not implied that the relative weights given to the various desiderata are the same in the several norms in which they are held in common. Neither is a desideratum recognized as common necessarily expressible in the same form in regard to different systems. Nevertheless, a list of common desiderata is a first step toward a methodology of comparison of economic systems that may gain acceptance by economists living under different systems.

y_1 a high level of *per capita consumption* of goods and services desired by or for consumers.[17]

Although some individuals have sought a life of austerity and self-denial, as far as majorities of participants go this desideratum has a long history. It is practically universal in the modern world without any signs of an approach to saturation even in the wealthiest economies.

Currently almost as universal is the desire for

y_2 *growth* in the per capita consumption of goods and services through technical advances and through accumulation of physical and human capital.

[17] The words "by or for" allude to a system difference to be discussed further in connection with desideratum y*.

This is in part a matter of intertemporal distribution of consumption and of dissatisfaction with present consumption levels, especially in the less developed countries. It is also derived from another desideratum

y_6 to maintain or extend one's influence and power in the world,

which we mention here somewhat out of sequence while postponing further comment. Finally, especially in the more affluent countries with private property and enterprise, a given growth of population produces an at least corresponding growth in capital almost painlessly through the desire for continuity of income into the retirement period.[18] Additional sources of technical advance are the desire of the young to acquire skills and knowledge that have market value besides their personal value, the competition between business firms, nation-states, and systems in the technological race, and the pressure from scientists for funds to pursue their intellectual interests. One feels that in these circumstances, given the rate of population growth, a comparable all-over growth rate would have resulted in the most advanced countries of West even if growth had not enjoyed public and official acclaim as a national goal in itself—provided a full-employment policy was successfully pursued.

The three desiderata listed so far introduce the three major contenders for the aggregate use of resources in modern systems. The next three desiderata deal more with the apportioning of consumption by types of goods and by recipients. It is therefore appropriate here to make the point that simultaneous pursuit of the first three desiderata, whatever their (positive) weights in the pertinent norm, implies a derived desideratum of

y_* *efficiency* in the use of resources.

Perfect efficiency of an entire economy, an unattainable ideal, is defined, in the "commodity version" common to East, West, and South, as a choice of the kinds and levels of production activities in use such that within the bounds of the given resource availabilities it is not technologically possible to produce (or secure) more of any good or service (including leisure) desired by some participant except at the opportunity cost of producing less of some good or service desired by some participant. In another more inclusive "utility version," called Pareto optimality, or consumers' sovereignty, and rating higher in West than elsewhere, the definition says instead "... that ... it is not possible to increase the utility

[18] J. Tobin has calculated that the United States capital stock corresponds in size to what would be implied in a life-cycle theory of saving that extends the suggestions made in F. Modigliani and R. Brumberg, "Utility Analysis and the Consumption Function: An Interpretation of Cross-Section Data," in Kurihara, ed., *Post-Keynesian Economics*, New Brunswick, N.J., 1954, pp. 388–436. See J. Tobin, "Life Cycle Saving and Balanced Growth," in W. Fellner et al., *Ten Economic Studies in the Tradition of Irving Fisher*, New York, 1967, pp. 231–256.

of any one individual without decreasing that of another." The former efficiency concept applies just to allocation of resources in production, the latter to distribution to consumers as well. The latter concept expresses the phrase "desired *by* consumers" in the definition of y_1. The former concept is implied in the latter (assuming nonsaturation), but standing by itself needs to be supplemented by a specification of the ratios[19] in which goods are "desired *for* consumers."

Neither the definition of efficiency nor the desiderata implying it go into the difficult organizational problems that are the main topic in the comparison of economic systems: How does one achieve or approach efficiency? Is its attainment harder and less complete if the growth rate is higher? What is its cost in terms of other desiderata yet to be mentioned? It is, therefore, desirable to have a measure of attainment of efficiency. Debreu has proposed such a measure for the utility version, which is not affected by ordinality of the participants' utility functions.[20] His "coefficient of resource utilization" is defined as the smallest identical fraction of all actual primary inputs that would still permit attaining the same utility level for each individual by a more efficient allocation and distribution. Even though hard to evaluate numerically, this measure may be a good starting point for the search for more easily determined measures.

Single-period efficiency (in either version) is obtained if all the inputs and outputs (or utilities) in the definition refer to one single time period.[21] In that interpretation, one must specify in the definition of efficiency that, in comparisons with other allocations (and distributions), the amounts of all goods to be held over for use in later periods be kept constant. *Intertemporal efficiency* is obtained if the same good available in different periods is interpreted as so many different goods, the while holding the initial and (for a finite horizon) terminal capital stocks constant. This concept implies single-period efficiency in all periods in question, but the converse is not true. Hence intertemporal efficiency is the stricter and indeed more meaningful desideratum of the two. For a sufficiently long horizon, it also reflects efficiency in choosing the size and composition of investment. However, it suffers from an implication of perfect foresight as regards technology, preferences, and actual allocation and distribution for $n \leqq \infty$ periods ahead. A suggestion for a more flexible concept is made below.

[19] See, for instance, L. V. Kantorovich, *Ekonomicheskii raschet nailuchshego ispol'zovania resursov* (The Best Use of Economic Resources), Academy of Sciences of the USSR, 1959 (English translation, Cambridge, Mass., 1965).

[20] G. Debreu, "The Coefficient of Resource Utilization," *Econometrica*, July XIX:3 (1951) 273–292.

[21] This concept is also somewhat inaccurately named "static efficiency," a term better reserved for efficiency attained in a hypothetical stationary state with all variables constant over time.

While single-period efficiency in some sense implies maximal consumption y_1 in that period compatible with the stipulations in its definition, intertemporal efficiency is of course compatible with high or low growth, stationarity, decline, or fluctuation of per capita consumption. The growth desideratum y_2 adds to this a specific preference as regards *aggregate* intertemporal distribution of consumption.

A concern with distribution among individuals is expressed by

y_3 *equity* in the distribution of the conditions of living, or at least of opportunity in that regard, among contemporaries,

which is more strongly held in East and West than in South. The "conditions of living" include consumption levels (current as well as lifetime prospects), health care, opportunity for gainful employment, protection from adverse working conditions, absence of non-functional discrimination, and dignity in human interactions. We prefer the hard-to-define ethical term "equity" to the more definite term "equality," which ignores differences in need arising, for instance, from different states of health or from different numbers of dependents or providers. It also ignores the socially desirable incentive effect of income responding positively to productive effort. So what we mean is something like "fairness and efficiency modifying a desideratum of equality."

Particularly in West and South, social services and public goods are largely provided by mechanisms different from those by which other consumption goods are supplied. For this reason, we shall recognize a separate desideratum, which is a further stipulation within the consumption desideratum y_1.

y_4 provision of *social services and public goods.*

This desideratum rates higher, by and large, in East than in South and West, in relation to resources. However, the modern emphasis on increasing levels of widespread education, mentioned already in connection with the growth desideratum y_2, is almost universal. Likewise, the protection of the physical and biological surroundings of man from the adverse effects of economic activities, which we include under the desideratum y_4, is currently gaining strength in both East and West.

The following intertemporal aspect of the conditions of living deserves separate mention:

y_5 *stability* of employment and incomes.

In West policy makers use monetary and fiscal policy toward this goal. With respect to South, efforts are made to protect the value of exports against price fluctuations and overproduction by arrangements modifying the operation of markets in important raw materials. In East direct controls over investments and restrictions on short-term credits are used to maintain macroeconomic stability.

There remains the crucial desideratum y_6 already mentioned. We extend its definition here.

y_6 (*national strength*) to ensure the continuation of national existence and of national or ideological independence; where possible to extend national or ideological influence, prestige and power.

As between different countries or systems this desideratum is *similar* rather than common. It has the same definition, except that in each case a different name of country or system is written in.

The economic significance of this largely political desideratum is very great. It competes with all the foregoing desiderata by the absorption of resources in military preparedness and, if the case arises, in armed international conflict. A lesser but noticeable complementarity between y_6 and earlier desiderata arises from the benefits to production for civilian consumption thrown off by military research. A definite positive value for some of the other desiderata arises from some primarily nonmilitary activities motivated by y_6. This includes the emphasis on rapid industrialization in South and East and ventures in oceanographic or space research in the most highly developed countries.

Another important desideratum, similar in intent but possibly quite different in form of application as between different systems, is

y_7 *provision for orderly change in a system* to permit adjustment to changing circumstances without endangering its essential continuity.

System changes themselves were mentioned among possible outcomes in Section 2.1. Normally, system change desiderata differ considerably within one and the same economy as between prevailing and other contending norms. The prevailing norm tends to favor little or no change, while the contending norms favor a variety of not necessarily compatible changes. We return to these relationships in Section 3.5.

3.3. Desiderata Specific to Various Norms

As alluded to above, West favors and practices

y_8 *widely dispersed economic decisions* through inheritable private property, through individual and corporate enterprise, and through a legal framework enforcing contracts while permitting limited liability of corporations.

To different degrees in different countries of West and possibly South the concern for business enterprise is carried to the point of

y_9 *commercialism*, a tolerant attitude toward uninformative competitive advertising, sales pressure, and the influencing of essentially educational and cultural activities by business interests,

in some comparors' norms the tolerance of an odiosum rather than a positively valued desideratum.

The traditional desideratum of East,

y_{10} *centralized*[22] *decisions and control* over the composition of output and consumption,

has been abandoned in Yugoslavia and to a significant degree in Hungary, and is currently under hesitant and partial reconsideration in a few other countries because of its conflict with y_*.

3.4. Some Possible Comparors' Desiderata

The comparor may wish to improve the formulation of desiderata already recognized or to propose as pertinent some desiderata not previously formulated. An example of the former is

y_1' *a flexible intertemporal efficiency* concept capable of recognizing uncertainty about technology at any future date, which will diminish as the date is approached, as well as similar uncertainty about future consumers' or planners' preferences.

The analytical difficulties in the way of such a conceptual refinement are considerable. An exploratory discussion of flexible preferences has already been referred to.[23]

An example of a newly proposed desideratum might concern the coexistence characteristics of various mixtures of economic systems. The comparor might wish to propose the study of unilaterally initiated or mutually agreed self-reforms of coexistent systems to

y_{11} *reduce both the cost of the balance of deterrence and the probability or destructiveness of armed conflict* between countries having similar or different systems.

The crucial importance of this (proximate rather than ultimate) desideratum for the future of mankind contrasts sharply with the difficulties of obtaining clarity and, if needed, agreement on policies promoting this desideratum. It is not even clear what bearing economic policies may have on its attainment, except for a general presumption that the increasing

[22] Again, "centralization" as understood in East.
[23] Koopmans, "On Flexibility" *op. cit.* (n. 5).

interdependence of economies in the modern world is likely to increase the importance of various system characteristics to coexistence problems.

Obviously, our list of desiderata could be extended indefinitely, and other authors might have regarded some other desiderata more important than some of those we have listed. Many proximate goals not specifically mentioned so far can be derived from our desiderata. For example, the defense of the balance of payments may be motivated by a desire for stability of employment and incomes, for growth in per capita consumption, for national strength, for equity in distribution, or for a combination of any of these desiderata.

3.5. Interaction between Prevailing Norms, Other Norms, and Systems

The very concept of what is a prevailing norm differs between systems. In a highly centralized system, the prevailing norm is essentially the norm of those who exercise power in the system. In a pluralistic society, where interest groups are clearly visible and in explicit competition through political processes, through collective bargaining, strikes, and threats of strikes, market strategy, persuasion through various media, demonstrations and other means, what we might call the prevailing norm can only be inferred from actual policies and decisions, rather than being read in declarations or programs. In such a society, the rules of the struggle for influence, power and wealth are an important part of the system. Knowledge of these rules, and of the contending groups and their specific norms, is essential for an understanding of the prevailing norms and their change over time. Undoubtedly similar processes take place in the more centralized systems in a submerged manner escaping any but conjectural and inferential contemporary analysis.

Systems and norms influence each other in many ways. The most important example concerns *system change*, which is itself included among the outcomes. System change tends to be resisted by those participants on whom the system bestows wealth, influence or power, a resistance aided by traditional values and the advantages of stability. The ideology of the dominant group, which may be spread among the participants through propaganda, advertising, proselytization, or other vehicles of persuasion, reinforces these conservative tendencies. It follows from this bias that comparison between two systems with similar environments on the basis of the prevailing norm of either will favor the system whose prevailing norm instructs the comparison. Even if the list of desiderata were to be the same in the two prevailing norms, any difference in the weights given to the desiderata in the respective prevailing norms will make either system bend the outcomes to its own norm, other things being equal. Total system change nevertheless occurs either when those in situations of power are dissatisfied with the performance of the system and are desirous of bringing about its reform or overhaul, or when a group of individuals who are not among the top power holders and feel disadvantaged or otherwise dissatisfied with the system can force a modification to give greater effect to their own norms. The pressure for change on the part of persons in and out of power depends on the information generated by the system about its performance, itself a system characteristic. It has been conjectured, for instance, that the amount and quality of information percolating to power holders will vary inversely with the political coercion and restrictions they impose upon society.[24] The change effected in the system is *evolutionary* if it takes place clearly within the framework and procedures recognized by the system. This requires that the prevailing norm give weight to y_7, provision for change in the system. A *revolutionary* change takes place if a group has ways to force a system change according to its norm which supersedes the previous total system outright. These are extremes of a scale, and intermediate forms of system change are frequent. In revolutionary change, the part of the system that changes most is the institutions, organizations, laws and rules. The regular patterns of behavior are not generally capable of abrupt change.[25]

As another, final example of an effect of system on norms, we refer to the observation by March and Simon in a discussion of ideas on organizational learning by Robert Merton: that system traits may over time become infused with value through a more or less unconscious process, called "goal displacement."[26] The authors cited state that the repeated choice of specific acceptable means to a valued end causes a gradual transfer of the preference from the end to the means adopted. The means itself may be a proximate goal, or an institutional device for reaching such a goal.

Finally, we note that the presence of one desideratum in the prevailing norm of a system may affect the meaning of another desideratum. In any system in which consumers' choice influences the incomes of managers in individual enterprises and in which advertising is a part of business operation, the very consumers' preferences that enter into the efficiency desideratum (utility version) are affected and at times distorted by advertising. To the extent that this happens, the tolerance of commercialism qualifies, and detracts from the merit of, the desideratum of efficiency in the utility version. Thus, the prevailing norm of that system (West) that attaches the greatest weight to consumers' sovereignty at the same time impairs its significance. Corresponding effects occur in the sphere of

[24] D. Apter, *The Politics of Modernization*, Chicago, 1965 p. 40.

[25] There is an analogy here with technological change. Important new knowledge can become available overnight. Its incorporation in new capital stock and a (re–) trained labor force takes much longer.

[26] J. G. March and H. A. Simon, *Organizations*, New York, 1958.

public goods and services. Observers, such as Eisenhower and Galbraith, have pointed to the influence that producers of military goods exercise on government expenditures.[27] The latter has also referred to the relative neglect of expenditures on those other public goods and services for which pressure from private producers is less pronounced or absent.[28]

4. Activities, Interactivities, Custody

4.1. Technological Activities

It will help in the discussion of organization in Section 5 if we insert here three brief, illustrative, and nonexhaustive lists of important categories of activities. The first list leans to the more purely technological activities, which at the same time are the more universal activities across systems. The sequence of categories within any one list is somewhat arbitrary.

A. *Categories of "technological" activities.*
- Recognizing and locating natural resources (such as water, minerals, soils, forests, game, fish)
- Specifying and/or designing commodities to be produced. We distinguish:
  - commodities not for final consumption, to be embodied or used up in production of other commodities, and means of production of some durability (including consumers' durable goods)
  - commodities for final consumption (including the services rendered by consumers' durable goods)
- Producing all commodities of both types, choosing inputs and methods of production from among those available
- Research and development of new methods of production
- Transportation and delivery of output from producer to user or consumer
- Maintaining inventories of storable goods
- Labor force participation
- Human reproduction, care of the young, education and training in the technological activities
- The *rendering* of health services

With some flexibility of interpretation the activities in these categories can be fitted into the definition of activity given in Section 2.1. In all

[27] President Dwight D. Eisenhower, "Farewell Address to the American People," Jan. 7, 1961, *Public Papers of the Presidents of the U.S.*, 1960–61, Paper 421; J. K. Galbraith, *The New Industrial State*, Boston (1967), especially Ch. 27.

[28] J. K. Galbraith, *The Affluent Society*, Boston (1957).

economic systems there is some degree of functional specialization among participants in performing the technological activities, which is the more detailed the larger the scale of the economy. This specialization is due to the indivisibility of the human carrier of skill and expertise and to the greater productivity of a finer subdivision of specializations whenever scale permits full use of at least one individual of each specialized skill.[29] The resulting specializations are so similar in different modern economies or systems that, where languages differ, makers of dictionaries have had little difficulty in finding equivalent functional or occupational designations (often derived from the same root).

4.2. Interdependence of Activities

The second list contains activities arising from the technological interdependence of those on the first list. Two or more activities are called *interdependent* if efficient allocation of resources requires at least one of the following:

i. the activities make use of the same indivisible input(s) (example: different tasks to be carried out on one lathe in the same day)
ii. they contribute to the same indivisible output(s) (building a house)
iii. they must be carried out jointly (one man holds the horse, the other shoes it) or simultaneously (individuals whose travel converges on a common meeting place)
iv. they must be carried out in a certain sequence because an output of one activity becomes an input to another (transferring liquid iron from a blast furnace to a foundry)
v. their levels must stand in a certain proportion, because two of their respective inputs originate from, or two of their respective outputs are required for, a single activity characterized by constant proportions of outputs or inputs.

The interdependencies i., ii., iii. are often absolutes. Interdependencies iv. and v. become a matter of degree if alternative sources of input or uses of output exist at moderate cost differentials. On the other hand, chains made up of pairs of activities whose interdependence is of type iv. or v. create secondary, tertiary, . . . interdependencies of similar types that attenuate further as the number of links in the chain increases.

The coordination problems of production, transportation, distribution, consumption take their form in large part from the nature of the interdependencies between the activities involved. We believe that the literature

[29] See, for instance, G. J. Stigler, *op. cit.* (n. 10). By an indivisible factor of production we mean a factor that is not available for productive use in any quantity smaller than a positive smallest unit.

on activity analysis[30] can contribute elements to a formalization of these coordination problems that provides a background against which the solutions offered by different systems can be compared. Sections 4.3 and 4.4 contain further observations toward such a marriage of activity analysis and organization theory.

4.3. Custody and Transfers of Custody

We conjecture that in most modern systems almost any resource,[31] means of production, or good in process is at any time in the *custody* of some entity (operator, foreman, plant department, sales department, owner, manager, trader). In the case of a means of production or resource, the *custodial entity* controls its use in time and as between claimants. In the case of a material, good in process, or finished good, the custodial entity determines the next disposition of the good, such as leaving or placing it in inventory, continuing its processing, entering it into the next stage of processing, or making it available for consumption, in some of these cases while transferring its custody to another entity.

Transfers of custody tend to occur, for good and rather obvious efficiency reasons, in those states of each good between processing stages, to be called *transfer states*, in which one or more of the following applies:

a. the good is capable of being handled (automobiles) and/or stored (steel billets) and/or delivered (electric power) without serious loss of quality,
b. the specifications describing the transfer state are standardized, and
c. the transferrer or the transferee or both can expect to have a choice between more than one transferee or transferrer, respectively, who may belong to different entities engaged in the same production activities, or who may differ in the processing activity that preceded transfer,[32] or that is to take place after transfer (coal).

If a custodial entity is an organization, efficiency often requires that it be clear to all concerned to which member of the organization the custody

[30] See, for instance, T. C. Koopmans, ed., *Activity Analysis of Production and Allocation*, New York, 1951, and A. M. Manne and H. Markowitz, eds., *Studies in Process Analysis*, New York, 1963.

[31] There is one important category of resources not subject to specific custody. This category consists of generally accessible resources, with regard to which the use, the extraction and possible degradation are not easily controlled: air, the ocean and its mineral and biological content, inland water, in earlier periods land, increasingly in modern periods streets and highways. We return below (Sec. 5.4.4.) to the adverse effects on efficiency that may be connected with such absence or insufficient effectiveness of custody arrangements.

[32] For a description of an integrated steel plant simultaneously using steel obtained from different processes see T. Fabian, "Process Analysis of the U.S. Iron and Steel Industry," in Manne and Markowitz, *op. cit.*, Ch. 9.

of which good is delegated, even if subject to reversal by a supervisor for the custodial activity in the case of a (quasi-) hierarchy. For goods not in continual use (television set in the family) delegation may extend to all members of an organization on a first-come-first-served basis, again subject to reversal.

In any system in which one or more of the above types of goods or resources are privately owned, custody normally goes with ownership or is delegated by the owner.[33] For this and other reasons, forms of ownership of resources and of man-made means of production are usually regarded as a major system characteristic.

Transfers of custody or of delegated custody may take place between entities embedded in the same hierarchy or between entities not belonging to the same hierarchy for the activity or set of activities in question. Whether the transfer of a given type of good of similar specification in two systems falls in one or the other of these two cases will in general depend on the system. The relative frequency of transfers within, as against between, hierarchies is indeed an important system characteristic. However, we conjecture that there is a very substantial similarity and overlap between systems in the specifications, not only of finished goods and services, but also of the unfinished transfer states in the production of these commodities. We surmise further that the particular bundle of production activities taking place between two successive transfer states that two systems have in common depends less on system characteristics than on the scale of the economy or of the enterprise and, given a modicum of efficiency, on the environment. Among pertinent environmental factors, the relative scarcities of aggregate basic inputs, such as labor, resources, and capital, to the economy as a whole are particularly important.

We adduce three reasons for these conjectures. First, technology does not stop or change much in character at the boundaries between systems. Acceptability of technology is usually unrelated to the system of origin, and information on advanced technology circulates widely and is given constant attention. The second reason follows from the first. The economies inherent in the characteristics a., b., c. of transfer states listed above are rather apparent, and their perception is not much affected by system characteristics. Finally (the third reason), both scale and factor proportions are likely to enter into the bundle of production activities occurring between successive transfer states, scale because of the indivisibilities of human operators and pieces of equipment, factor proportions because even moderate efficiency demands reasonably full use of available factors.

Although the above reasoning has been given largely in terms of production of goods, similar reasoning applies, *mutatis mutandis*, to most

[33] Further remarks on the relation of custody and ownership are given in section 5.

industrial services as well, if performance of a service is substituted for transfer of custody of a good. This includes transportation, in which case only transport-relevant characteristics of the goods shipped need be taken into account.

4.4. Interactivities

We now list categories of activities, the need for which arises from the interdependence of activities in list A (Sec. 4.1). All the actions of which these activities consist are part of interactions and it is therefore natural to speak of *interactivities*.

B. *Categories of interactivities for the assignment and scheduling of technological activities*

Assigning, directing, or coordinating tasks for technological activities requiring simultaneous or successive actions by two or more individuals

Arranging the transfer of custody of a specific batch, quantity, or item of a specific good to the next using, processing, or consuming entity, which has a demand for it

Arranging for the use of a given resource or fraction thereof by a specific producer or household, during a given time

(Within the household) determining which quantity of which consumption good available to it is consumed by which member of the household at which time.

4.5. System-bound Activities and Actions

Although the activities of list B need to be performed under any system, their character depends on the organizational structure and operating procedures of the system more than do those in list A. However, in most systems the activities in list B are only a part of the organizational activities required by the system. One could, it is true, imagine a command system capable of perfect coordination, in which all the activities exemplified by lists A and B were implemented by commanded actions of individuals belonging to one large hierarchy. In that case, the commanded transfers of custody would themselves define the demands they meet and the supplies from which they are made. In all systems of record, many other activities intervene to determine these demands and supplies and to serve various other desiderata. The nature of these activities depends strongly on the system in which they occur. For that reason we are forced, in listing a few of these by way of examples, to use some terms which while perfectly familiar to the reader have not yet found a place in the framework of concepts developed so far, because they anticipate essentially organizational concepts to be introduced in Section 5.

C. *Examples of system-bound activities*
Activities determining capabilities to acquire custody of additional means of production through credit from financial institutions that absorb savings by individuals and organizations or from governmental credit institutions that may obtain their funds from tax revenues.
Activities that spread risk by pooling
Protection of individuals from ill effects of adverse conditions of labor (for instance, as provided by labor unions in interaction with employers)
Education and training for managerial and other system-bound activities
The *provision* of health services.

Additional more specific system-bound activities of an organizational character are discussed in Section 5, largely in terms of the kinds of actions and interactions they consist of. There is a good reason for this shift in terminology. We have defined activities as kinds of repeatable action, and the term "activity" is most serviceable where the action in question is in fact repeated in a rather routine manner. Organizations, however, the most system-bound aspect of an economy, are primarily concerned with coping with change, with the new and unexpected.[34] An organizational model for a stationary state, if at all conceivable, helps little in understanding the nature of organizational problems in any real-life system. For that reason, the expectation of repetition of an organizational action of precisely the same kind or form is generally much weaker, and the terminology of "actions" and "interactions" is more appropriate in an organizational context.

5. The Organizational Structure of Systems

5.1. Participants and Ruling Organizations

To be precise enough for both conceptual and statistical purposes, the description of each system entering a comparison should specify the set of its participants. For some purposes it may be useful to include in this set all the individuals located within certain geographical boundaries

[34] This applies particularly to economic organizations. Some other organizations, such as schools, churches, political organizations serve in addition to spread knowledge, faith or power, or to preserve any of these from attrition due to the predictable change arising from human aging and death.

during the period of comparison; another possible definition would include all individuals of a given nationality irrespective of their location; still another would include all individuals associated with organizations incorporated (or having their headquarters) in a certain nation or region. The definition of the set of participants in each system will determine the scope of the interactions that are considered to be "across systems," to be discussed in Section 6. In comparisons involving nation-states with dual economies, one may wish to treat each "economy" as a separate subsystem and consider the interactions between the subsystems as one would consider the external economic relations of any economy considered to be sufficiently homogeneous to qualify as having a single system.

As we saw in Section 2.2, ruling organizations set bounds to the actions of individuals and organizations. They also facilitate certain interactions, such as transfers of custody in exchange for a compensation, by sanctioning one or more means of payment (legal tender) for discharging all debts and obligations, and by supervising weights and measures used in defining the quantity of certain goods.

In most nations today, the diverse organizations known in their aggregate as the *government* are the only ruling organizations empowered to issue rules at least nominally binding on all participants in the system.[35] However, the power of these organizations to issue laws may be circumscribed by certain prior rules endowed with a higher status or by certain principles or values which may or may not be codified. Prior rules include compacts, constitutions, treaties, and collective agreements; principles and values include taboos, religious documents, ideological pronouncements and so forth that happen to be accepted as binding or restraining by the dominant group in the total system.

Within ruling organizations modern systems have developed specialized suborganizations for issuing laws, for inducing most participants to conform to these laws, for adjudicating disputes arising from conflicting interpretations of the laws, and for identifying entities that have violated laws and deciding on sanctions.

Whether or not all component organizations under a ruling organization are bound by the laws issued by competent organizations within this ruling organization may be a critical trait differentiating one total system from another. With regard to the economic system, a gain in efficiency is

[35] In the United States, Federal, state and local governments, together with the agencies whose powers emanate from them, are the only legally sanctioned ruling units. In the Soviet Union the Party is in practice a ruling unit alongside, and in some respects above, the government. In early modern times, the Catholic Church in Europe was a ruling unit emitting both rules (e.g., prohibition on interest–taking) and general orders (the tithe). Illegal ruling units include racketeering organizations such as the Mafia. In the process of modernization in West, the state gradually suppressed all competing legitimate ruling units.

likely to accrue from the settlement of disputes arising from conflicts of interests according to a regular, well-defined procedure, with the final adjudication conforming to certain durable principles, precedents, or both: Such a procedure will help define the limits within which decision makers may operate without fear of restraint or retribution and will foster expectations of regular behavior on the part of other participants in the system and thus reduce the risks of decision-making.

5.2. Actions and Interactions

To distinguish *informational* from *effective actions*, we require the concept of *message*, information conveyed by one or more participants to one or more other participants. An informational action changes only the environment of some other participants except for interactions associated with the process of communication itself. We call all other actions effective.

Informational actions comprise: 1. offers and acceptances, including, in particular, those concerning the transfer of custody of goods in transfer states, with or without payment in return; 2. rules and orders and responses thereto; 3. *communications*, messages containing information about activities, processes and preferences; 4. threats, appeals, and other messages aiming to exert influence.

Among the principal types of effective actions may be cited the actual transfer of custody of goods and the performance of services, financial transactions, the hiring or conscription of individuals for specific activities, strikes, sabotage, and production actions resulting in pollution (insofar as it affects other entities). An effective action may also carry a message. A gift may be bestowed or a service performed with the aim of creating an obligation on the part of the recipient to reciprocate the favor at some future time. Initiatives of this type are important in promoting commodity exchanges in pre-modern societies and in wielding influence in many modern ones. Similarly the information conveyed to invidious neighbors by the conspicuous display of clothing, furnishings, or cars may prompt them to purchase similar goods for the sake of keeping up.

In general, effective actions, once they have been registered in the information set of the participants they affect, have either a direct or an indirect impact on their utility function. Informational actions, in contrast, affect a participant's welfare only insofar as they influence his expectations of subsequent effective actions.

Effective actions may further be classified according to the presence or absence of mutuality in the interaction of which they are a part. *Complete mutuality* prevails in actions that require the consent of all parties affected (e.g., a sale prepared by an exchange of messages or by a jointly issued message known as a contract). *Partial mutuality* prevails in an interaction when an individual undertaking an effective action incurs some, possibly temporary, disutility in order (a) to forestall an action by one or more participants which would inflict on him an even greater loss in utility, or (b) to accumulate credits for future benefits, or in recognition of the legitimacy of certain claims. In all such cases, the interacting participants are involved in an ongoing relation, which they consider to be acceptable if not actually desirable (e.g., employees interacting with their employers, taxpayers with government officials). In all remaining instances of interactions, there is *no mutuality* among the interacting participants.

The same initiating action may belong simultaneously to one interaction, characterized by complete mutuality for some participants, and to another interaction characterized by partial or no mutuality for others. Thus the owners of a landsite near a highway, an advertising agency, and an outdoor display company may all agree to put up a billboard, whose sight may offend motorists traveling along that highway.

A two-way classification of interactions may be made according to the type of actions that initiated them and according to the degree of mutuality that characterized them. A number of instances of interactions are classified according to this principle in Table 1.

The exchange of messages may enable two or more participants to discover the mutually advantageous effective actions they might undertake without exposing them to the risk of the losses that a series of inferior effective actions might give rise to. Bargaining to reach a mutually acceptable price or a wage settlement is an example of such exploratory behavior in a market system. Planning procedures also usually call for exploratory interactions between members of the organization issuing the plan.[36] These preliminary explorations may involve contacts between members of different organizations, especially where the planning organization, as in France, for instance, is only empowered to issue an *indicative* plan (one which is not even nominally binding on the organizations concerned). Where the plan consists of a set of orders, as in the Soviet Union, the entities to which the plan is addressed normally belong to the same *complete hierarchy* as the ruling organization issuing the plan.[37]

Evidence about the degree of mutuality characterizing an interaction cannot be used mechanically to infer the presence or absence of Pareto optimality.[38] Although the sale of a good to a customer by a monopolist for example, may be accomplished with the freely given consent of both buyer and seller, the transaction does not lead to Pareto optimality for

[36] These remarks were inspired by Dr. Pavel Pelikán's comments on an earlier draft of this paper.

[37] See below, Section 5.4.3.

[38] For a definition of Pareto optimality, see section 3.2.

Table 1
Mutuality Basis of Some Interactions Touched Off By Various Initiating Actions

Initiating action(s) \ *Degree of mutuality characterizing interaction*	*Mutual agreement*	*Pratial mutuality based on legitimacy of claim or punitive sanction*	*No mutuality*
Offer	Sale of a good	—	—
Rule or order calling for effective action	Payment of check by bank	Subordinate's compliance with an order in a hierarchy	Conscription of individual for military service
Communication	Sale of a patent	Repurchase of good by seller upon disclosure of misrepresentation	Unauthorized adoption of a process described in patent
Threat or other message aimed at exerting influence	—	Wage settlement on threat of strike	Performing forced labor for another individual on threat of life
Implicit message conveyed via effective action	—	Giving of present or favor in expectation or reciprocity	Sabotage, purchase and use of drumset in retaliation against neighbors' piano playing
Unilateral action unheralded by message	—	Traveling in a crowded subway	River pollution, theft

both participants, because there is some income transfer from buyer to seller, accompanied by a reduction in price and an adjustment in the monopolist's output and supply which would make both better off.

An action taken by one or more participants without the explicit consent of the other participants affected is likely to produce a situation deviating from Pareto optimality, whether or not the affected participants are made better or worse off by this action. "Transaction costs" and institutional obstacles may prevent the realization of the potential gains from mutually beneficial exchanges starting from such a nonoptimal situation.[39]

The relative importance of the differing degrees of mutuality and conflict underlying effective actions varies widely from system to system with putative, but not always ascertainable, consequences for the relative efficiency and equity of the systems compared. We have only one remark to make on this score: The effective actions based on orders involving partial or no mutuality as well as those based on complete mutuality all entail costs. No mutuality inflicts losses in efficiency due to the lower productivity of services rendered under compulsion (such as slave labor). In general, incomplete mutuality entails costs due to the necessity of assigning scarce labor to data-collecting, inspection, and control to ensure a close correspondence between orders and complying actions (and the morale effects of such control). In the case of complete mutuality, costs are incurred in making personal contacts, in information exchange and negotiations, in the persuasion necessary to achieve mutuality, in the verification of performance, and in actions to challenge nonperformance.

It may be noted that most effective actions based on mutual agreement involve participations in joint actions that are pairs, triples, or *n*-tuples of simultaneous and complementary single actions. Examples include transfers of custody within or between hierarchies, with or without simultaneous payment, and all loans and contracts for future delivery or performance. Certain rules issued by ruling organizations are designed to induce contracting parties to adhere to these agreements, even in the face of most random events but not of certain improbable events which, when they do occur, tend to be highly correlated and are therefore uninsurable. (These events are known in West as "acts of God.")

In modern systems, either transfer prices or exchange prices are an integral part of virtually all contracts. The *exchange price* offer for a good or service may be defined as an option for transferring to a different entity custody, other property rights, or both of one unit of a good or service against payment of a certain number of units of legal tender at a certain time. A *transfer* price differs from an exchange price only insofar as the option refers to a transfer between component entities of the same hierarchy or quasi-hierarchy rather than between separate entities, and in that actual payment may not be called for (e.g., bookkeeping transactions).

A message containing a price offer expressed in monetary units for a particular good will not generally call forth an acceptance by another

[39] On the relation between degree of mutuality and "externalities" see H. Demsetz, "Toward a Theory of Property Rights," *American Economic Review*, LVII:2 (1967) 347–359 and "The Cost of Transacting," Quarterly Journal of Economics, LXXXII:1 (1968), 33–53.

entity, unless the characteristics of the good have become part of the potential buyer's information set either through direct inspection or because its standardization has led him to expect predictable characteristics. The standardization of commodities effectively widens the intersection (the common subset) of the information sets of potential sellers and buyers and makes it possible for effective interaction to take place with significantly less prior transfer of information.[40] Standardization thus economizes on information costs and facilitates the transfer of goods, irrespective of other rules and patterns of interaction prevailing in a modern system.

5.3. Motivation

In the preceding section we briefly discussed the impact of messages on decision makers in terms of the mutuality that may or may not be required for the interaction to result in an effective action. Consent is, of course, a necessary but not a sufficient condition to be met if the message is to trigger an effective response, especially one consistent with the intent of the sender.[41] Even though, for instance, the legitimacy of a tax law may be recognized, the actual payment may fall short of and be significantly inferior to the amount actually due because of concealment of sources of income. A ministerial order to an enterprise in a centrally coordinated economy may not be carried out, in spite of possible sanctions. Likewise, a contract between two firms in a market economy may not be respected if its fulfillment eventually runs contrary to the essential interests of at least one of the parties. The precise response of a decision maker to an informational action will be conditioned by his motivation, which we have already defined as a function associating with each course of action the utility of the outcome of the probability mixture of expected outcomes.

Each individual in an organization may be presumed to apply his own utility function to the outcome of his actions, but in a hierarchy or quasi-hierarchy the preferences of superiors will tend to constrain the options left to subordinates. Constraints are more likely to be imposed whenever the preferences of superiors and subordinates diverge seriously and the fuller delegation of authority might lead to undesirable outcomes from the

[40] In the case of nonstandardized goods, price catalogues containing detailed information are normally circulated by potential suppliers. This routine, which presupposes experience leading to stable expectations on the part of potential buyers with respect to the accuracy of the information contained in these complex messages, also economizes on the costs of inspection and contact.

[41] Note, however, that under the hypothesis of perfect competition in a market economy, the entity quoting the price is assumed to be agreeable to any response or lack of response. Hence "intent" may not be strictly relevant in this limiting case.

superiors' point of view. The ability of superiors to impose on an organization such preferences as they hold in common will depend in part on the information they are able to collect about the outcomes of subordinates' decisions, as well as on the effectiveness of the sanctions they may administer to subordinates for deviant behavior. Because of the costs of obtaining complete compliance with orders mentioned in Section 5.2, we are led to suspect that a unique goal function cannot be invoked, let alone constructed, which would satisfactorily account for all the decisions made in an organization. Furthermore, in large complex organizations whose component organizations are engaged in different sets of activities, these divergent sets of preferences are likely to be important enough to engender conflicts between components or members or both. Where the size and complexity of organizations are themselves system coordinates, the presence or absence of these conflicts may be of considerable interest to the comparor.

Nevertheless, we shall occasionally refer to the putative goal function of an organization as if the managers were able to effect decisions on the part of their entire personnel consistent with a utility function acceptable to themselves.

To discuss one broad basis of motivation in organizations we shall need the term *profits*. This term applies when the inputs to an entity's activities are transferred from, and the outputs transferred to, the custody of other entities (for the set of activities under consideration.) The profits of an entity per period are then reckoned as the algebraic sum of the (negative) value of inputs and the (positive) value of outputs, both valued at transfer or exchange prices, whichever apply.

On the basis of rather casual observation or indirect reasoning, economic theorists in West have posited that decision makers—especially managers of "enterprises"—acted in such a way as to maximize the value of some outcome function, such as profits in market economies and the income from bonuses for fulfillment and overfulfillment of plan targets in the centrally coordinated economies.

Other economists have criticized these simple explanations of managerial behavior by pointing to the importance of other motives, which often conflict with profit maximization: Managers may wish to limit the time and effort they put into the job; they may prefer steady growth to higher profits; they may maximize their discounted expected utility accruing over time, a maximand that will not coincide with discounted profits if their utility-of-income function is strictly concave; they may choose outcomes that will be satisfactory without being optimal in any sense (as in the "satisficing behavior" described by Herbert Simon[42]); in a large hierarchy they may

[42] See Simon, *Models of Man*, Ch. 14 and 15, and the introduction to Part IV.

balance their immediate earnings against enhanced chances of advancement in the hierarchy, lowered chances of dismissal or punishment, or both.

To cite only one example, the offer of a license for a new technology is likely to be received differently depending on whether the recipient manager maximizes short-run profits, the enterprise's equity (if the system allows for a capital market), the growth rate of his enterprise, or its share of the market for his products over the next three years.

The rules governing the use and disposition of an economy's means of production—objects of a certain durability, capable of being used in a productive activity—usually place constraints on managers' actions and influence the objectives they pursue. Whether a manager of an enterprise maximizes short-run profits or the discounted sum of future profits may depend, for instance, on whether he owns part of the enterprise's means of production (on his "equity" in the enterprise) or at least on whether his income hinges in some way on their efficient utilization or disposition. Ownership refers to legally sanctioned rights of utilization and disposition by individuals or organizations over resources, goods in process, means of production or consumption goods, or over claims to shares in these rights. These rights may be exclusive, or hemmed in by legal or conventional restrictions, such as laws of entail forbidding the parcelling out of estates or their sale to unauthorized entities; or they may be abrogated under certain conditions in favor of the public at large or of ruling organizations (eminent domain, "fair housing" laws, collection of works of art "owned" by foundations that must make provision for the admission of the public).

Ownership normally implies custody, which may be delegated or separated in the case of organizations or individuals whose legal rights have been curtailed (e.g., due to the mental incapacity of an individual or to an enterprise's condition of receivership). In West the delegation of custody by the stockholders of a corporation to its managers may at times turn out to be irreversible, especially if the latter also own stock in it. In any case, ownership of means of production includes the right of the owner or his custodian to buy and sell them and to draw benefits from their productive use, an aspect with important consequences for equity which we shall not dwell on here.

The efficiency of resource allocation in any system must depend to a crucial extent on both the content of messages (e.g., in a market economy on whether prices reflect relative scarcities, or in a centrally coordinated economy on whether orders correspond to efficient input allotments and output targets) and on the responses of the makers of economic decisions to these messages (maximizing behavior in a market economy, compliance with orders implementing the principal production and allocation decisions in a centralized economy). In a competitive market economy, in particular, efficiency cannot be attained unless all resources and means of production are in the custody of some participant and are managed by these participants in such a way as to maximize the discounted stream of their future rents, corresponding to nondiscriminating rentals based on efficiency prices.[43] Access to resources held in common and not subject to such custody and management—pastures, forests, and even arable land in certain developing economies, crowded highways and city streets in developed economies, fishing grounds especially in international waters—is often not sufficiently restricted for their efficient utilization under a market system without the intervention of ruling organizations. Under unrestricted conditions, pastures tend to be overgrazed, timber overcut, land overworked, roads excessively congested, and species of fish threatened with extinction. In the absence of custodial entities restricting access to these resources or man-made facilities, directly or by an efficient rental charge, potential users are guided by the average costs they must bear—e.g., the average congestion delay on a road—which does not take into account the total additional costs imposed on other users by their decision to share in its common utilization.

5.4. Patterns of Interaction

5.4.1. Organizational graphs. In Section 2.3 we have defined an organization for a set of activities as a set of persons regularly interacting with each other in the process of carrying on one or more activities of that set. The theory of *linear graphs* offers a convenient device for representing the organizational structure of a system. Each participant is represented by a point (a *vertex*), each interaction by an *arc* connecting the vertices of the two interacting participants. For each category of interactions of interest, the corresponding graph contains the vertices of all participants engaged in such an interaction and all arcs representing instances of it. The category may be chosen to be strictly functional, such as making offers, accepting offers, supervising; or strictly substantive, such as interacting in truck gardening; or a combination of both, such as trading in vegetables. Figure 1 illustrates the device.

A graph is called *connected* if every pair of vertices in it can be connected by a chain (as defined in Section 2.3) that runs inside the graph. If the graph of all interactions in the system in a category of interest (such as the internal operations of truck gardening anywhere in the system) is not connected, each of its components (maximal connected subgraphs)

[43] For further discussion of the role of pricing in attaining efficient allocation See T. C. Koopmans, *Three Essays on the State of Economic Science*, New York, 1957, Essay I.

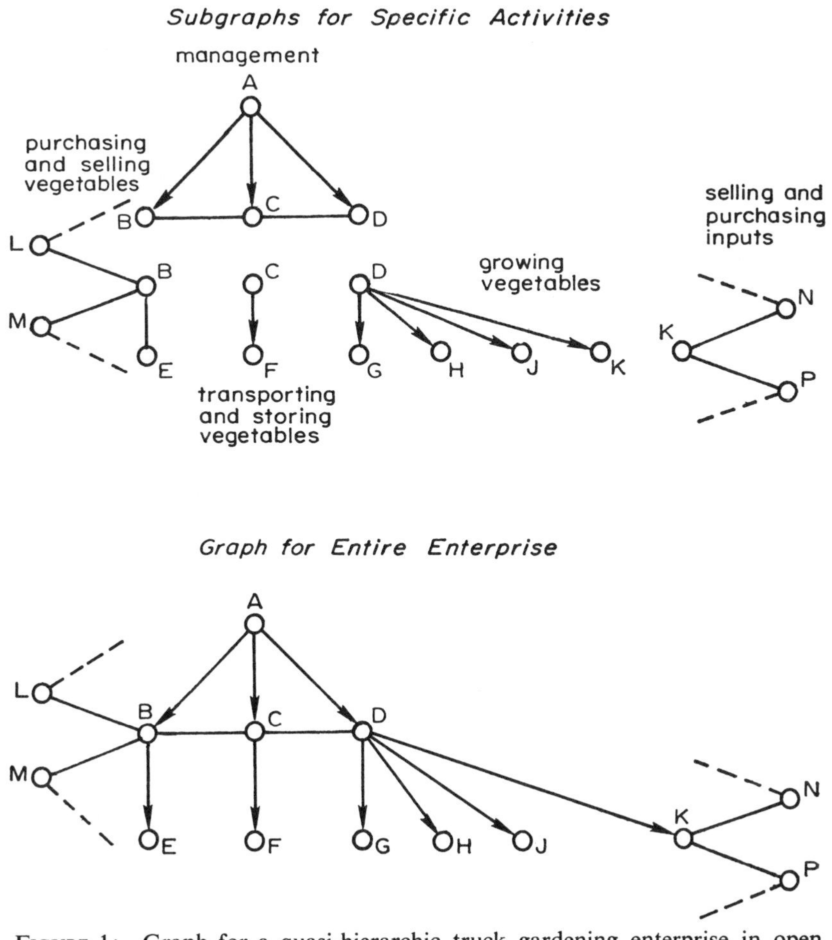

FIGURE 1: Graph for a quasi-hierarchic truck gardening enterprise in open ended association with several markets. Arrows indicate supervision, absence of arrows mutuality

represents a separate organization (a truck gardening enterprise) by the definition given in Section 2.3. If the category of interactions is enlarged (by the inclusion of trading in vegetables, say), a graph previously not connected may become connected.

By a sufficiently inclusive choice of the category of interactions, the entire set of participants in any modern system can be regarded as belonging to one and the same organization as defined. For, every participant is either a member of one of the following groups of interacting persons or belongs to a household that contains a member of one of these groups: 1. employees; 2. members of cooperatives; 3. self-employed or unemployed persons interacting through market relations; 4. institutionalized persons; 5. persons receiving pensions, gifts, or charities. Moreover, it may safely be assumed that there does not exist any subset of persons in the system no member of which interacts in some way with one or more members not in that subset. Thus we can represent and study every modern system through a connected graph generated as the union of the graphs corresponding to a given classification of all pertinent types of interaction.

Some interactions, such as supervision, are asymmetric. In Figure 1, this is represented by adding an arrow pointing from supervisor to supervisee to each such arc. A graph in which all arcs are given a direction is called a *directed graph* (briefly, a *digraph*). In particular, all hierarchies can be represented by digraphs.

The digraph notion may also be used to define an organization somewhat more broadly than we did in Section 2.3. Suppose that, in the pursuit of activities of a set A, person i either interacts with j or regularly sends messages to j without getting messages from him in return. We shall describe this relation by writing that i addresses j. We now draw a digraph showing a directed arc for each "ordered" pair of persons in which the first person in the pair addresses the second in the conduct of a given set of independent activities. If both address each other ("interact"), two arcs of opposite directions join their vertices. (This may, for instance, occur in a hierarchy if a member imparts information to his supervisor or to a higher superordinate, at the latter's request.) Call a *directed chain* a sequence i, k, l, . . . , p, q of members (vertices) such that (i, k), (k, l), . . . , (p, q) indicate directed arcs of the graph. An organization for a set A of activities is then represented by a graph such that each pair of vertices, say (i, q), is connected by a directed chain. (This implies that another chain for the pair (q, i) must also occur in the graph.)

For the study of the internal structure of organizations, especially hierarchies, engaged in several activities a slightly different interpretation of the organizational graph may be preferable, and will be used in Section 5.4.3. In this interpretation a vertex represents not a person, but the pairing of a person with an activity, which we shall call an *assignment*.[44] This device allows the same person to have different supervisors for different activities.

5.4.2. Organizational change. If we choose a period of time short enough to be able to disregard change in the number of participants in the system, we may represent the creation or dissolution of an organization merely as a change in the graph for the entire system. A complete system description, however, may have to keep a record of the organizations to which the members of a new organization formerly belonged, because they will contribute to the new organization information that would otherwise be unavailable to its members. For example, the reorganization of Soviet industry in 1957 involved the creation of new assignments and supervision relations and thereby brought into existence a new set of organizations comprising virtually the same set of participants as belonged to the old system. The chains of supervision that used to follow industrial lines (sets of industrial activities) now followed regional lines, at least for directors of enterprises and their superiors in the complete hierarchy for the Soviet economy. The members of the new organizations contributed their experience of previous activities and interactions in another organizational structure. These antecedents may have helped to smooth the transition to the new system.[45]

Every description of an organizational change in a system may thus be said to involve two sets of coordinates, one set belonging to the system before the change and one to the new state. The first set describes the procedures for modifying the system and identifies the persons belonging to one or more organizations of the old system who have the power to initiate or to carry out such changes or both. The second set describes the interactions between members of the new organizations and between them and persons still belonging to those old organizations from which they were recruited. Significant differences between systems may be detected in data pertinent to these coordinates. In particular, if the head of a new hierarchy remains subordinate to a member of one of the parent hierarchies, we may speak of the *centralized* creation of new organizations, a system trait with implications for attaining pertinent desiderata.

The creation of new and the dissolution of old organizations is also a crucial factor in the intertemporal efficiency of an economy in any system. New organizations usually are not confined to the activities of the organizations from which their personnel has been recruited. They are a vehicle for introducing new technologies and patterns of organization as

[44] The term allows an activity to be self-assigned.

[45] This interesting observation was made by Professor Arthur Wright in an informal talk at the Economic Growth Center of Yale University.

well as new modes of interaction with other entities. The dissolution of old organizations often does away with inefficient routines that cannot be eliminated without restructuring existing patterns of interaction. In East, ruling organizations have the exclusive responsibility for creating and winding up "enterprises on cost accounting," that is, economic organizations calculating their costs, receipts, profits and losses, and paying a part of their profits to, or receiving subsidies from, superior entities in the hierarchy. In part because rates of industrial growth are high in this group of countries and new supervisory personnel is systematically trained in educational institutions, the creation of such new enterprises can usually be effected without dissolving old ones, and rarely encounters effective opposition from vested interests.[46] In West (as well perhaps as in Yugoslavia) new enterprises frequently represent a serious threat to existing ones, especially if they compete for the same markets. To forestall such threats, existing enterprises may, and often do, resort to various devices to prevent newcomers from intruding on their territory, often with adverse effects on equity and on consumers' sovereignty. Access to the industry (the set of activities in which existing firms are engaged) may be restricted by the rules and orders of ruling organizations, or by barring potential newcomers either from their markets or from the resources required for their operations with the cooperation of banks, labor unions, railroads, and other organizations enjoying a protected status in their own industry. Attempts to engross trade to protect interests vested in existing organizations are not confined to privately owned enterprises. We conjecture that they will occur whenever 1) the interests of the managers of enterprises, whether publicly or privately owned, are bound up with the financial results of their enterprise's activities, 2) means to restrict unwanted entry exist, and 3) the heads of the threatened organizations do not perceive competition as being in the interest of the larger hierarchy of which they are a part. In Great Britain, for example, nationalized enterprises fend off competition from other nationalized enterprises, especially within the fuels and transportation sectors. Apparently no ruling organization is sufficiently mindful of the interests of the consumers of the products of these nationalized industries to defend them against the successful efforts of these industries to protect their markets.

5.4.3. Hierarchies and quasi-hierarchies. From here on we shall limit ourselves to a consideration of existing organizations, and resume our

[46] Where growth ceases or slackens, as happened in Czechoslovakia in the 1960s, the restructuring of organizations to promote efficiency presents acute problems, especially where it entails the dissolution of organizations in the less developed parts of the country.

discussion of hierarchies[47] and quasi-hierarchies. We now take the view that the supervision relation applies to assignments rather than to members. We stipulate in addition that supervision of a member in an activity implies that the supervisor is also (at least nominally) engaged in that activity.

To ensure the comparability of hierarchies embedded in dissimilar systems, the supervision relation should be broadly interpreted. An order issued by a supervisor may consist in the delegation of responsibility for certain tasks to a member of the organization or to a committee; a supervisor may also settle conflicts by arbitration, parcel out scarce resources, and so forth. Consultation of experts and mediation of conflicts, however, would not be covered by the supervision relation, because the advice or decisions of consultants and mediators usually have suasive rather than coercive power. In almost all hierarchies, subordinates may, under certain conditions, appeal to members of the organization standing above their supervisor for the activities connected with an order if they consider this order illegal (according to the rules of the organization or of the ruling organization to which it is subject) or if they deem the order extremely deleterious to their interests or to those of the part of the organization for which they hold or share responsibility. Subordinates may also kick upstairs problems that they are unable or unwilling to solve on their own. Although the simple conceptual scheme in Sections 2.3, 5.3, and 5.5 does not make explicit allowance for the right of appeal or for the referral of troublesome questions to higher ups for final decisions, it is flexible enough to encompass these variants of the supervision relation.

It follows from statements in Section 2.3 that the organization graph for the supervisory relation in a hierarchy for a single activity is what is called in graph theory a *tree*. The tree starts with the head of the hierarchy and, in the usual reproduction of an organization table, grows downward, ramifying at every vertex representing a participant supervising more than one other participant in the activity in question. A hierarchy in which all assignments involve one and the same activity is called a *hierarchy for a single activity*. It is called *complete* if 1) every branch of the tree has been traced down to the last participant supervised in the activity in question, and 2) if the head has no supervisor in the activity.

A *hierarchy for a set of activities* is a set of assignments and a supervision relation on that set, which can be thought of as obtained by joining (forming the *union* of) two or more hierarchies for a single activity, all of

[47] For a wide-ranging discussion of hierarchical structures in nature and in society, see H. A. Simon, "The Architecture of Complexity," *Proceedings of the American Philisophical Society*, CVI:6 (1962) 469–482.

which have the same person at the head. This head is then simultaneously engaged as ultimate supervisor in all the activities in which the hierarchy engages. Such a hierarchy is called a *complete hierarchy* if i) every component hierarchy is itself complete and ii) the hierarchy cannot be enlarged by admitting further hierarchies for additional activities. Under certain restrictions it can be shown[48] that, as a logical implication of these definitions, every assignment in the system belongs to precisely one complete hierarchy. (In the case of a self-employed person, this could be a one-man hierarchy.)

Examples for a market economy: The personnel of the blast furnace department in an integrated steel plant make up a hierarchy for activity a where a is the making of pig iron. The entire steel plant under one owner-head is a hierarchy for A, the set of all activities involved in the making of steel. The plant will be a complete hierarchy for A if the head of the steel plant is superior to every employee in the plant, irrespective of that employee's assignment in A (such as, for instance, the head of its medical service, whose assignment is an ancillary activity in A). However, should ownership rest with a body of stockholders supervising the head through a board of directors, then these two collective participants would need to be added before the hierarchy can be called complete for A. Finally, should the *same* body of stockholders also own and effectively supervise one other manufacturing enterprise, then this enterprise would have to be added in before the hierarchy can be called complete.

In a Soviet-type economy, the set of all persons either in the government supervising economic activities or in socialized economic sectors, together with the Communist Party hierarchy, including the Politbureau of the Central Committee, may be said to form a complete hierarchy. Under the above definitions, however, the use of this term is based on the presumption that no person engaged in a given activity is directly supervised *in the exercise of that activity* by both a Party member and by a different member of the government hierarchy. In other words, one-man leadership (*edinonachalie*) is assumed to prevail: Party channels are used to convey orders pertinent to Party activities (including control of the direction of economic activities exercised by members of the government hierarchy) and government channels to convey orders pertinent to the activities of the government hierarchy. To the extent that this principle is regularly violated, we should be dealing with one or more quasi-hierarchies. Yet we suggest that the fit may be close enough to warrant a discussion of the Soviet economy in terms of a complete hierarchy and its component hierarchies.

[48] For further details, see T. C. Koopmans, "Note on a Social System Composed of Hierarchies with Overlapping Personnel" [paper 1 in present volume].

Before the principle of one-man leadership was established and enforced in the Soviet system in the early 1930's, there were parallel lines of command, and many members of the quasi-hierarchy were subject to the orders of several immediate superiors—typically in the government, the Communist Party, and the trade unions—in the exercise of the same function.[49] The elimination of at least some of the overlapping or criss-crossing lines of command, particularly at lower levels, presumably made for greater efficiency in this case. Where objectives and priority among them are clearly defined for all decision makers, and where actions must be taken rapidly in response to orders, we suspect that quasi-hierarchies are less efficient than hierarchies. In other situations, including research and development activities, the case for a unique line of command is much less evident.

5.4.4. Two conjectures. We now define key attributes of hierarchies to be used in the conjectures. The *length* of any chain between two members i and j of the hierarchy is the number of members in the chain, including i and j. The *height* of the hierarchy is defined as the length of the longest chain extending from the head of the hierarchy to a member who is not superior to any other member in the hierarchy in any of its activities. A *tier* is the set of all persons related to the head of the hierarchy by chains of the same length (the head being the first tier).

The information drawn by superiors in a hierarchy from the information sets of subordinates, from their own environment, or from both depends on the activities that have been assigned to them (control, resolution of disputes within the hierarchy, coordination of interdependent activities, and so forth). To be carried out efficiently, the coordination by a superior of a sequence of interdependent activities requires detailed knowledge of each of the procurement, production, transportation, and transfer activities in the sequence as well as of the possibilities of substituting other activities for some of these wherever this may be efficient. To acquire this detailed knowledge himself, a superior might have to extract from his subordinates virtually their entire information sets. There are, however, limits to this information-collecting process: Information is expensive to collect; the capacity of superiors to process, store, and retrieve information is limited; and information that is not immediately communicated becomes obsolete as the participants' environment changes. With improvements in the technology and equipment for information-handling, these constraints have become less stringent. Nevertheless, whether information has been obtained from samples or aggregated from exhaustive reports, in transferring it from each tier to the next, losses and distortions in content and delays have remained unavoidable.

[49] See G. Bienstock, S. Schwartz and A. Yugow, *Management in Russian Industry and Agriculture*, Oxford (1944) 13 and 35.

A superior in a higher tier desiring to avoid such losses of information may send inspectors to the field (e.g., to the lowest tier) or try to see for himself. As we already pointed out in Section 5.3, however, inspection whether carried out by the highly placed member himself or by other members of his hierarchy[50] is expensive in terms of alternative uses of the personnel involved.

The interdependence between activities may hinge on the circumstances of a given moment, so that a particular assignment may be efficient for certain environments but not for others. In the face of this complexity, superordinates may not perceive the best opportunities for scheduling activities in a concrete situation. Thus the efficiency of assignment of activities, as well as their coordination, depends on the information available in the coordinating tier.

Let us now make the extreme assumption, which will later be relaxed, that no two members of a given hierarchy not in the same chain of supervision and responsible for different but interdependent activities can engage in informational interaction with each other. Coordination is thus effected exclusively through common superiors in the hierarchy. Suppose further that we take as given the quality of supervising personnel, the amount and accuracy of the information required by superiors to make effective coordination decisions, and all other variables affecting the efficiency of such decisions.

One would then seek to assign activities in a hierarchy in such a way that the most highly interdependent activities would be assigned to members with a common supervisor. When this assignment exceeded a supervisor's efficient span of control, it would become necessary to assign some still strongly interdependent activities to members whose nearest common superior was two (or more) tiers up the chain of command. Our presumption is that the number and degrees of interdependencies of activities in a modern economy are such, relative to the efficient span of control of supervisors, that even the best feasible assignment of activities from the point of view of efficient coordination through superiors would still leave pairs of activities of substantial interdependence to be coordinated by a nearest common superior many tiers up the chain. (Example: weaving fabrics for the upholstery of automobiles and making automobile bodies.)

Consider two hierarchies H and H', say, two plants initially engaged in disjoint sets of activities A and A' that have substantial interdependence between activities a, a' of the two sets, respectively. We conjecture that the

[50] The high-tier member normally is fully occupied with the information flowing to him through channels; attempts by that member to bypass them in seeking more precise or up-to-date information will usually entail delays in attending to current affairs.

longer the chains (for the interdependent activities) between the two heads of H and H' and their nearest common superior, the more likely it is that each of the two plants will initiate activities already belonging to the set of the other. Each will do so, we reason, because it will wish to ensure better coordination with its own activities of some of the activities initially carried on in the other plant. Furthermore, its incentive for this expansion will be the stronger, the more ineffective the coordination by the common superior in the initial situation. This ineffectiveness, we presume, will be the more serious the longer the chains separating the common superior from the heads of the two plants. How many common activities both plants will ultimately undertake will depend on variables other than the economies of information, such as the availability of equipment and other factors affecting costs of production (to the extent that costs matter).

Suppose that in the initial situation the two plants had been permitted and encouraged to interact directly, that is, to exchange information and to coordinate their own activities within certain limits set by their superiors. The incentive for *organizational autarky*—the phenomenon we have just described—would have been weaker. We conjecture that if complete mutuality were permitted, including the exchanges of goods or services at mutually acceptable prices, specialization between any two hierarchies in the system would be carried further than under a more restrictive arrangement.

We suspect that the phenomenon of autarky among hierarchies that may or may not belong to the same complete hierarchy occurs both in centrally coordinated and in market economies. We suggest that it might be instructive to study whether or not weaknesses in the coordinating functions of markets in these economies show up in the inefficient pursuit of an excessively wide range of activities in existing enterprises.[51] Or, to put the same point in a different way, we wonder whether the existence of small, highly specialized enterprises in certain developed market economies is not rendered possible by the presence of smoothly functioning markets for the inputs and the products of these enterprises' activities. In the case of the centrally coordinated economies of the Soviet Union and of Eastern Europe, evidence has frequently been cited of enterprises engaging in a very wide gamut of ancillary activities—such as maintaining inventories, facilities for producing crucial inputs, personnel engaged in procuring

[51] For example, it has been observed that the privately owned and operated railroads in the United States sometimes found it to mutual advantage to do classification work (assembling or reassembling cars into trains) for each other. However, if the need of railroad A for such work by railroad B lacked a reverse need, no trade took place because the practices of the industry did not include making money payments for such services.

inputs, repair facilities for machinery—the apparent or sometimes explicit aim being that of protecting themselves from the vagaries of an undependable centrally supervised distribution system. A verifiable implication of our conjecture is that plants belonging to different ministries would be more likely to take over each other's activities than those belonging to the same ministry, because their lowest common superior would be further up the hierarchy and there would presumably be less direct interaction between them.

We now set forth a related conjecture involving the conflicting interests of two hierarchies engaged in production activities which possess heads who are in the same tier of their complete hierarchy. We assume that both hierarchies have custody of their means of production and that the remuneration of at least some members with decision-making power in either organization depends on the outcomes of the activities of their respective organizations (such as volume of output, costs, sales proceeds, profits, and so forth).

Suppose now that some members of one of the two hierarchies, in the pursuit of its objectives and without prior agreement with the other, undertake an activity that adversely affects outcomes of the other. Suppose also that the decision makers in the adversely affected hierarchy cannot or may not obtain, through mutual agreement, compensation for the action that is fully equivalent in their preferences to its adverse effect. The action has thus given rise to an "external diseconomy."

If the heads of the two hierarchies involved on both sides of this action are supervised by the same member of a complete hierarchy, the conflict of interests will normally come to his attention. The common superior may or may not order that compensation be made, possibly depending on the effect of such action on the interests of the component hierarchy which he heads (strictly speaking, depending on the superior's interpretation of these interests). He will also have to decide whether a repetition of the action should or should not be prevented by a restraining order. If, however, this nearest common superior is several tiers up, the matter will be more difficult to resolve to the satisfaction of either organization, because the common superior will have less accurate information about the interests affected than a supervisor. We conjecture, therefore, that the likelihood of an efficient resolution of conflicts of this type will be the smaller, the longer the chain separating the parties in the dispute from their nearest common superior.

The conjectures on the efficient coordination of interdependent activities and on the efficient resolution of conflicts involving external diseconomies are clearly two facets of the same general problem of optimizing the interaction between two entities in a complete hierarchy when a mutually satisfactory cooperation is precluded by the rules and orders of superiors, by high transaction costs, or because the interests of the parties cannot be reconciled without such rules and orders (e.g., through mutuality).[52]

Indeed in a market system an entity inflicting damage on another will generally not feel compelled to compensate the latter for its losses or even to abstain from inflicting further damage. However, ruling organizations, through the issuance of rules restraining the behavior of private organizations, through nationalization orders followed by such restraints, or through the compulsory merger[53] of the conflicting entities, may be in a position to salvage some measure of efficiency in these situations. However, the serious pollution of the air over such cities as Chicago, Los Angeles, and Budapest suggests that those problems cannot easily be solved either in market or in centrally coordinated systems.

6. Interaction Between Systems

Since the boundaries between systems more or less coincide with boundaries between nations, interactions between nonruling entities in different systems cannot be discussed without at the same time considering interactions between governments pursuing political as well as economic objectives. One may take the view that the determination of the fraction of output allocated to military preparedness and other policy decisions that may affect the risk or the probable outcome of armed conflict are exogenous to economic systems but have to be taken into account as important environmental factors in studying both the operation and interaction of systems. One may alternatively regard both the political and economic interactions between systems as interdependent parts of a larger complex and consider the chain of causation *from* the economic and political traits of these systems, *through* their political and economic policies and interactions, *to* their presumed effects on pertinent desiderata such as the level of consumption, the risks of limited or large-scale loss of life, goods and resources, and the risk of impairment of national independence.

Whichever view one takes, the economic interactions between ruling

[52] It was argued in Section 5.2 that "externalities" create situations where mutually advantageous transactions are possible provided that all parties affected may freely interact and transaction costs are low. Restrictions on interaction may have complicated the Lake Baikal dispute in the Soviet Union between paper-mills polluting the water and the fisheries. There are also frequent cases where negotiations cannot take place because the perpetrator cannot readily communicate with the entities he adversely affects. How can people who would like to swim in a river, *if* it were not polluted, be compensated?

[53] A suggestion made by L. Hurwicz, "Conditions for Economic Efficiency of Centralized and Decentralized Structures" in G. Grossman, ed., *Value and Plan* Berkeley, 1960, pp. 162–175.

or nonruling entities belonging to two or more economies with similar or different systems reflect system traits, or rather traits of constellations of systems, which are of great interest in the present context.

Over the last century, the economic interactions between entities belonging to different nation-states have become ever closer and more intensive. These interactions may be classified into three groups. They may involve: 1) the transfer across state or system boundaries of goods, services, patents, licenses, franchises, news and weather information, and the movement of tourists consuming goods and services; 2) contacts between members of organizations whose membership or range of activities extends across these boundaries, including all interactions such as direct investments, transfers of know-how, and so forth, taking place within multinational, privately or publicly owned companies and other international organizations; and 3) other informational interactions, such as exchanges of students or scholars in pertinent professions; informal contacts between members of labor unions located in different countries but not belonging to the same international union; exchanges of views between business or government leaders of different states who are not members of the same complete hierarchies, and others.

These more strictly economic interactions across systems may likewise affect every desideratum listed in Section 3. They have special relevance for y_1 and y_2, insofar as international specialization promotes the efficiency of allocation in each economy participating in trade and, withal, the level of living of its nationals and the economy's growth in per capita consumption. Since some of these interactions are often thought to interfere with y_5 (stability of employment and incomes) and y_6 (national strength and prestige), the governments of the nation-states responsible for regulating these interactions frequently evaluate their decisions in this area of policy in terms of a trade-off between the advantages they perceive in interactions across state boundaries through desiderata y_1 and y_2 and their disadvantages due to losses expected through y_5 and y_6.

The second group of interactions is of special interest in view of our emphasis on organizations. These interactions nowadays frequently take place within multi-national organizations, structured as complete hierarchies, embracing activities carried out in more than one nation or employing personnel belonging to several nations, or both. The executives situated at their apex impose more or less uniform rules, procedures, and patterns of organization over component organizations located in countries with widely disparate systems and levels of development. This relatively new phenomenon, together with the accelerated mobility of executives across national borders and the even more pronounced trend toward training executive personnel according to certain common precepts of business efficiency, in West, South, and also in Yugoslavia, has tended to diminish the differences between the patterns of organization prevailing in those groups of countries.

Private multi-national organizations are normally subject to the laws issued by the ruling organizations of the countries in which they have been founded or incorporated. In some instances, these laws govern the permissible actions of the foreign affiliates of the organization as well as of the components of the organization situated in domestic territory. These circumstances may produce jurisdictional disputes in cases where a component organization is nominally subject to the conflicting laws of two or more nations. It may also enable the ruling organization of one country to extend the reach of its strategic policies beyond its boundaries. For example, the United States has been able to impose certain restrictions on trade with Eastern Europe on affiliates of American enterprises incorporated in Western Europe.

In view of these possibilities, the government leaders of nation-states frequently look askance at the growth in their countries of the affiliates of multi-national enterprises. Among other reasons they fear that their foreign economic policies will be subverted by these organizations, which operate within their territories and thereby escape some of the provisions regulating across-system interactions. The protection of indigenous economic organizations, the advancement of nationals in preference to foreigners in the affiliates of multinational organizations situated on home territory, and the broad diffusion of available know-how and innovations are some of the areas where government leaders and representatives of multi-national companies have come into conflict.[54] When nation-states have been weak, as in some parts of South, it has at times been possible for multi-national companies to influence, if not to dominate, their governments, thereby resolving the conflicts in their favor. Colonialism and the dominant relation referred to in East, South, and some parts of West as neocolonialism are extreme versions of this same phenomenon.

Multi-national enterprises may, on the other hand, mitigate incipient conflicts between states because the web of common interests they have woven cannot be undone without palpable harm to all parties concerned. This statement applies especially to multi-national organizations that are under the joint management of several nation-states, such as the European Coal and Steel Community, or under the supervision of an international organization, such as the United Nations.

Governments in West have usually assumed at least partial responsibility for those economic activities of their nationals which transcend their state boundaries. It is usually up to the branches of the government dealing with foreign affairs to avert or to moderate the conflicts which these

[54] See, in particular, R. Vernon, "Economic Sovereignty at Bay," *Foreign Affairs*, XLVII:1 (1968) 114–117.

nationals, operating by themselves or within private or public organizations, may engender in conducting their activities abroad. The comparor can only note that the resentments aroused by certain types of economic interactions may not always be fully realized by all the governments concerned. For this reason, we have formulated a separate desideratum bearing on the co-existence characteristics of systems that would evaluate negatively characteristics that may jeopardize the political relations between states.

The authors are indebted to Gabriel Almond, Abram Bergson, Joseph Berliner, Albert O. Hirschman, Truus W. Koopmans, Janos Kornai, Charles E. Lindblom, Leon Lipson, Richard Loewenthal, Alan S. Manne, Thomas Marschak, Pavel Pelikán, Frank P. Penna, Frederic L. Pryor, Herbert A. Simon, Harvey M. Wagner, Martin Weitzman, and Arthur F. Wright for valuable information and comment.

4

Representation of Preference Orderings with Independent Components of Consumption

Tjalling C. Koopmans

Decision and Organization: A Volume in Honor of Jacob Marschak, ed. C. B. McGuire and R. Radner (Amsterdam: North-Holland, 1972), pp. 57–78

1. Introductory Remarks

A standard model in the theory of consumer's choice assumes that the consumer maximizes a *utility function* under given budgetary constraints. Even in the case of the individual consumer planning for a single period's consumption, however, the time-honored concept of a utility function is not an entirely satisfactory primary concept. One may wish to look on it as a numerical representation of an underlying *preference ordering*, a more basic concept to be more fully defined below. Once this step is made, one will also want to know which class of preference orderings permits such a representation. Moreover, one will not want to exclude *a priori* the consideration of preference orderings that do not permit such a representation.

The present Chapter 3 presents a basic proposition stating sufficient conditions under which a given preference ordering is representable by a continuous function. It goes on to state, and supply proof for, a second proposition concerning the implications, for such a representation, of independence of different components of consumption in the given preference ordering. These propositions are presented for their own interest as well as for their application in Chapter 4. In the latter chapter, both propositions are applied in discussing the choice of a criterion for the evaluation of growth paths, starting from postulates about a preference ordering

---

This chapter reports on research carried out under a grant from the National Science Foundation. It is a revision of Sections 1–4 of Koopmans (1966). I am indebted to Kenneth Arrow and Gerard Debreu for extremely valuable comments.

Note: "Chapter 3" and "Chapter 4" correspond to papers 4 and 5 in the present volume.

of such paths. The labeling of results and propositions is consecutive over the two chapters.

In both chapters, we aim for the simplest proposition of each type, capable of proof by relatively elementary mathematical methods, rather than for propositions and proofs of greatest generality.

In some sections technical parts of the reasoning are set off in starred subsections bearing the same number. These can be passed up by readers interested in results rather than proofs. Equality by definition will be denoted by $\equiv$. References to the literature for both chapters are listed at the end of Chapter 4.

2. Preference Orderings and Representations Thereoof

We shall now define and describe the mathematical concept of a *preference ordering* on a *prospect space*.

The prospect space $\mathscr{X}$ is the set of all alternative *prospects* between which choice may conceivably arise. The term "space" is a geometric metaphor, and the prospects will sometimes be called "points." In the static model of consumer's choice, the prospects are usually interpreted as bundles of consumption goods imagined used or used up in consumption in a stated period. (A bundle specifies the amount of each good on the list.) Instead of attaching preference to the use of goods, some authors have suggested attaching it to characteristics of goods (LANCASTER (1966a, b)), or to the levels of consuming activities each involving either the use or the disappearance of one or more goods (GALE (1967, 1968, pp. 209, 217, 218)). Everything that follows is compatible with any of these interpretations of the coordinates of the points x of the prospect space. Accordingly, we shall use the term *vector* to refer either to a bundle of commodities, or to their characteristics, or to a statement of the levels of specified activities.

A complete preference ordering is a relation (to be denoted $\gtrsim$) between the prospects $x, y, \ldots$ in $\mathscr{X}$, compared pairwise, such that

(*transitivity*) if $x \gtrsim y$ and $y \gtrsim z$ then $x \gtrsim z$,

(*completeness*) for any pair of prospects x, y of $\mathscr{X}$

either $x \gtrsim y$ or $y \gtrsim x$ or both.

The relation $x \gtrsim y$ is interpreted as "x is at least as good as y," or synonymously "x is *preferred or equivalent* to y." *Preference* ($\succ$) and *equivalence* ($\sim$) are again transitive relations, derived from $\gtrsim$ by saying that "$x \succ y$"

means "$x \gtrsim y$ but not $y \gtrsim x$," and is also denoted "$y \prec x$," and that "$x \sim y$" means "$x \gtrsim y$ and also $y \gtrsim x$."

A *partial* preference ordering is obtained if we substitute for the completeness requirement above

(*reflexivity*) for all x of $\mathscr{X}$, $x \gtrsim x$.

Completeness implies reflexivity (take $x = y$), but the converse is, of course, not true. Hence, in a partially ordered space there may be pairs of prospects that are not comparable.[2]

By a numerical representation of a complete[3] preference ordering $\gtrsim$ we mean a function f, defined in all points x of the prospect space $\mathscr{X}$, and whose values $f(x)$ are real numbers, such that

(2.1) $$f(x) \geqq f(y) \text{ if and only if } x \gtrsim y.$$

Using the above definitions of preference and of equivalence, one sees readily that this is logically equivalent to (2.2a), which in turn implies (2.2b):

(2.2a) $$f(x) > f(y) \text{ if and only if } x \succ y,$$

(2.2b) $$f(x) = f(y) \text{ if and only if } x \sim y.$$

The usefulness of a representation by a continuous function, if one exists, lies primarily in the availability of stronger mathematical techniques in that case. There is a temptation to look on the values, and the differences between values, assumed by a representing "utility function" as numerical measures of satisfaction levels, and of differences thereof, associated with the prospects in question. Such interpretations may have heuristic usefulness because of the brevity of phrasing they make possible. However, their observational basis is not really clear. An observed choice between two prospects reveals at best the fact and the direction of preference, not its strength. A descriptive theory of choice thus stays somewhat closer to what is verifiable by observation if it is built on postulates about the underlying preference ordering.

---

[2] What is called a "preference ordering" here is called a "preordering" by DEBREU (1959, p. 7). ARROW (1963, pp. 13, 35) uses "weak ordering" for our "complete preference ordering," and "quasi-ordering" for our "partial preference ordering." In mathematical literature, the term "weak order," or "weak ordering," is used whenever (as here) equivalence ($x \sim y$) does *not* necessarily imply equality ($x = y$).

[3] If the preference ordering is not complete, a numerical representation is a function f such that $f(x) > f(y)$ if $x \succ y$, and $f(x) = f(y)$ if $x \sim y$, together with a specification of the set of pairs (x, y) of prospects x, y in $\mathfrak{X}$ which are indeed comparable. Such representations have been considered by AUMANN (1964b).

A similar remark applies to normative theory. One can better inspect and appraise a recommendation couched in terms of actual choices in various situations, than one derived from measures of "satisfaction" whose operational significance is unclear.

We shall now describe the results of two postulational studies in the literature, as illustrations of the points just made, and for use in what follows. In Chapter 3 and 4 (except for Section 6 of Chapter 4), we shall discuss only complete preference orderings, without always repeating the adjective.

3. Representation of a Continuous Preference Ordering

Intuitively, one would call a preference ordering continuous if a small change in any prospect cannot drastically change the position of that prospect in the ranking of all other prospects. Starting from a sharp definition of this concept, Debreu (1959, Section 4.6) has shown conditions under which a *continuous preference ordering* can be represented by a continuous utility function.[4] In Subsection 3* we show that the definition used by Debreu is logically equivalent to the following one.

The notion of a "small" change in a prospect can be made precise by assuming a given *distance function* in the prospect space.[5] This is a function $d(x, y)$, defined for all pairs (x, y) of points in $\mathscr{X}$, with the following properties usually associated with a distance:

$$
(3.1)\qquad \begin{cases} d(x, y) = d(y, x) \geqq 0 \text{ for all } x, y, \\ d(x, y) = 0 \text{ if and only if } x = y, \\ d(x, z) \leqq d(x, y) + d(y, z) \text{ for all } x, y, z. \end{cases}
$$

We shall call the preference ordering $\succsim$ continuous on $\mathscr{X}$ if (see Fig. 1)

$$
(3.2)\qquad \begin{cases} \text{for any } x, y \text{ of } \mathscr{X} \text{ such that } x \succ y, \text{ there exists a number } \delta > 0 \text{ such that} \\ (a)\ z \succ y \text{ for all } z \text{ in } \mathscr{X} \text{ such that } d(z, x) \leqq \delta, \text{ and} \\ (b)\ x \succ w \text{ for all } w \text{ in } \mathscr{X} \text{ such that } d(y, w) \leqq \delta. \end{cases}
$$

(Note that this is vacuously the case if all prospects in $\mathscr{X}$ are equivalent.) The same continuity concept is obtained from many, but not from all, different choices of the distance function.[6] We now have

---

[4] See also Wold (1943).

[5] The prospect space thereby becomes a *metric space*.

[6] These include, for instance, the Euclidean distance $d(x, y) = [\Sigma_i (x_i - y_i)^2]^{\frac{1}{2}}$.

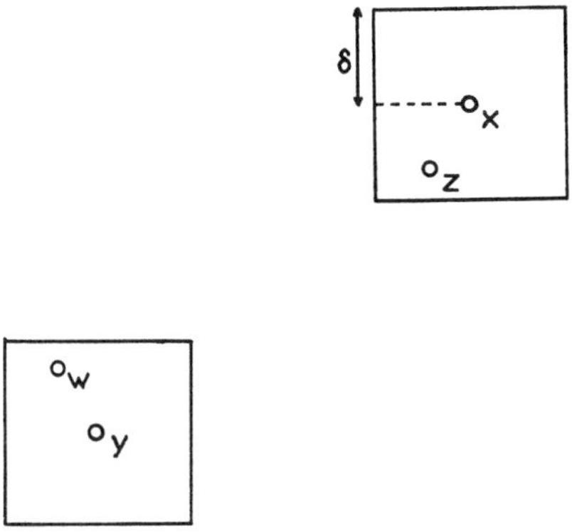

Fig. 1

PROPOSITION 1 (DEBREU (1959)). *A continuous*[7] *complete preference ordering* $\succsim$ *defined on a connected subset* $\mathscr{X}$ *of n-dimensional Euclidean space*[8] $\mathscr{E}^n$ *(n finite) can be represented by a utility function* $u(x)$ *defined and continuous in* $\mathscr{X}$.

Not every conceivable preference ordering is continuous. If any increase, however small, in this year's food supply, is deemed preferable to any increase, however large, in next year's food supply, we have an example of the discontinuous *lexicographic ordering.*

If $u(x)$ is a continuous representation of $\succsim$, and if φ is any continuous and strictly increasing function defined for all values assumed by $u(x)$ on $\mathscr{X}$, then

$$u^*(x) \equiv \varphi(u(x)) \tag{3.3}$$

[7] Continuity of $\succsim$ and of $u(x)$ is defined using the *same* distance function. Fig. 1 uses $d(x, y) = \max|x_i - y_i|$, if x_i, $i = 1, \ldots, n$, are the coordinates of x. While this distance function depends on the units of measurement of the amounts x_i, $i = 1, \ldots, n$, the continuity concept defined by it is again independent of these units.

[8] Depending on the interpretation, the prospect space $\mathscr{X}$ may be the set of all points x with all coordinates $x_i \geqq 0$, or any other representation of the range of alternative prospects suitable in a given problem. $\mathscr{X}$ is called (arcwise) *connected* if any two points of $\mathscr{X}$ can be connected by a continuous curve contained in $\mathscr{X}$. Debreu credits a paper by EILENBERG (1941) as containing the mathematical essence of Proposition 1. For a stronger theorem establishing existence of a continuous representation without assuming connectedness or finite dimensionality see DEBREU (1954, 1964) and RADER (1963).

[9] The proof of this statement is implied in the last paragraph of Subsection 4* below: take $x = x_P$ and replace the pair $(U(x), u(x))$ of (4.4) by the pair $(u^*(x), u(x))$ of (3.3).

is likewise a continuous representation of $\succsim$. Conversely, if $u(x)$ and $u^*(x)$ are two continuous representations of $\succsim$, then such a function φ exists for which (3.3) holds.[9] Therefore, a remark already made in Section 2 about representations in general applies equally to continuous representations: Only the notion of "higher" or "lower" among the levels of $u(x)$ has significance, not the numerical values $u(x)$ themselves or the differences thereof. In particular, even if $\succsim$ should possess a differentiable representation $u(x)$, there is no intrinsic meaning in the "marginal utility" $\partial u/dx_i$ of any single commodity. This is often expressed by the statement that $u(x)$ is an *ordinal*, not a *cardinal*, utility. However, even if $u(x)$ is only ordinal, for given units of commodities i, j, the ratio

$$\frac{\partial u^*(x)}{\partial x_i} \Bigg/ \frac{du^*(x')}{\partial x'_j} \tag{3.4}$$

of two "marginal utilities" at the same point ($x = x'$), or at two equivalent points ($x \sim x'$), is invariant. That is, the ratio (3.4) is independent of the choice of a differentiable φ in (3.3), hence is a quantity meaningful in terms of the given ordering $\succsim$.

Whenever $\mathscr{X}$ contains two nonequivalent points, one can by suitable choice of φ in (3.3) make the range $\mathscr{U}^* = u^*(\mathscr{X})$ of $u^*(x)$ coincide with any interval of positive, finite or infinite, length, that includes the left and/or right endpoint depending on whether $\mathscr{X}$ contains a worst and/or best element of $\succsim$. Existence of a worst and/or best element does not preclude $\mathscr{U}^*$ being unbounded from below and/or above if the values $-\infty$ and/or $+\infty$ are adjoined to the range of u^*.

3. Equivalence of two definitions of continuity of an ordering.* The definitions to be compared are

D If $\lim_{n\to\infty} y_n = y$ then "$x \succsim y_n$ for all n" implies "$x \succsim y$," and "$y_n \succsim z$ for all n" implies "$y \succsim z$."

D' If $y \succ x$ there exists $\delta > 0$ such that (a) $d(y, w) \leqq \delta$ implies $w \succ x$, and (b) $d(w, x) \leqq \delta$ implies $y \succ w$.

Assume "*D'* and not *D*." Then there exist either x, y_n with $x \succsim y_n$ for all n but $\lim_{n\to\infty} y_n = y \succ x$, or z, y_n with $y_n \succsim z$ for all n but $z \succ y = \lim_{n\to\infty} y_n$. Taking the case $y \succ x$, we choose δ in *D'* such that $d(y, y') \leqq \delta$ implies $y' \succ x$, and N in the definition of limit such that $d(y, y_N) \leqq \delta$. Then $y_N \succ x \succsim y_N$, a contradiction. The case $z \succ y$ is similar.

Assume next "D and not D'," and take $\delta_n = 1/2^n$. Then, for some x, y such that $y \succ x$, there exists either a sequence y_n such that $d(y, y_n) \leqq \delta_n$ but $x \succsim y_n$, or a sequence x_n such that $d(x_n, x) \leqq \delta_n$ but $x_n \succsim y$. By D, both cases imply $x \succsim y$, contradicting $y \succ x$.

Two statements such that the negation of either contradicts the other are equivalent.

4. Separable Representation in the Presence of Two Independent Components of Consumption

The problem of deriving special forms for a utility function from assumptions about independence among components of consumption has been studied by several authors, including LEONTIEF (1947a, b) and SAMUELSON (1947, Ch. 7). We shall follow DEBREU (1960) because he avoids assumptions of differentiability of the utility function that seem unrelated to the essence of the problem.

To illustrate the independence concept in terms of the traditional commodity space, one may wish to assume that preferences between food bundles are independent of the amounts of various articles of clothing and of other commodities consumed, and similarly for preferences between clothing bundles, etc.; furthermore that preferences between food-and-clothing bundles are independent of the amount of other commodities consumed, and so on.

In this section we shall derive a preliminary result for the case of two independent components of consumption. Let $\succsim$ denote a preference ordering on the space

$$\mathscr{X} = \mathscr{X}_P \times \mathscr{X}_Q \tag{4.1}$$

of all vectors $x = (x_P, x_Q)$ such that x_P is in a given space $\mathscr{X}_P$, x_Q in $\mathscr{X}_Q$. In mathematical terminology, $\mathscr{X}$ is called the (Cartesian) *product* of the spaces $\mathscr{X}_P$, $\mathscr{X}_Q$, the latter *factor spaces* of $\mathscr{X}$.

To express the required independence assumption we use an arbitrary but fixed *reference vector* in $\mathscr{X}$,

$$z = (z_P, z_Q), \tag{4.2}$$

to define two orderings, $\succsim_P^z$ on $\mathscr{X}_P$ and $\succsim_Q^z$ on $\mathscr{X}_Q$, induced by $\succsim$, as follows,

$$\begin{aligned} x_P \succsim_P^z y_P &\text{ means } (x_P, z_Q) \succsim (y_P, z_Q), \\ x_Q \succsim_Q^z y_Q &\text{ means } (z_P, x_Q) \succsim (z_P, y_Q). \end{aligned} \tag{4.3}$$

In general, the induced orderings depend on the reference vector, in the sense that $\succsim_P^z$ depends on z_Q, and $\succsim_Q^z$ on z_P. The independence assumption will say that this dependence-in-principle is not a dependence-in-fact. In Subsection 4* we show, following DEBREU (1960),

RESULT A. *Let a preference ordering* $\succsim$ *on a product space* $\mathscr{X} = \mathscr{X}_P \times \mathscr{X}_Q$ *be representable by a utility function* $U(x)$, *and let the ordering* $\succsim_P^z$, $\succsim_Q^z$ *induced by* $\succsim$ (as defined above) *be independent of the reference vector* z. *Then* $U(x)$ *has the form*

$$U(x) = F(u(x_P), v(x_Q)), \tag{4.4}$$

where F *is an increasing function of both* u *and* v. *Moreover, if* $\mathscr{X}$ *is connected,* $U(x)$ *continuous, then* $u(x_P)$, $v(x_Q)$ *and* $F(u, v)$ *are continuous, and the ranges of* $u(x_P)$, $v(x_Q)$ *are intervals.*

A function of this form has been called a *utility tree* by STROTZ (1956, 1959), and a *separable utility function* by GORMAN (1959a, b). In the case of two independent components of consumption, therefore, instead of one function U of $n_P + n_Q$ variables (there are a great many such functions!) we have a triple of functions, one (F) of two variables, one (u) of n_P, and one (v) of n_Q variables. In some sense the "number" of such triples forms a much smaller infinity. The utility $U(x)$ of x depends only on the utility levels $u(x_P)$, $v(x_Q)$ associated with x_P, x_Q in their respective spaces, rather than on these vectors in their full detail.

4*. *Proof of Result A.* We define, for some fixed reference vector z^0,

$$u(x_P) \equiv U(x_P, z_Q^0), \qquad v(x_Q) \equiv U(z_P^0, x_Q), \tag{4.5}$$

and consider two vectors x, y in $\mathscr{X}$ such that

$$u(x_P) = u(y_P), \qquad v(x_Q) = v(y_Q).$$

Since U represents $\succsim$, we then have

$$(x_P, z_Q^0) \sim (y_P, z_Q^0), \qquad (z_P^0, x_Q) \sim (z_P^0, y_Q),$$

Since $\succsim_P$ and $\succsim_Q$ are independent of the choice of z^0, we have further

$$x = (x_P, x_Q) \sim (y_P, x_Q) \sim (y_P, y_Q) = y$$

(choose the alternative reference vector $z = (y_P, x_Q)$). Hence $x \sim y$, and $U(x) = U(y)$. This means that the value of $U(x)$ for any vector x in $\mathscr{X}$ depends only on the values of $u(x_P)$, $v(x_Q)$ assumed for the subvectors x_P, x_Q of x, respectively, confirming (4.4).

Moreover, from the independence of $\succsim_P^z$ from z, using the definition of $\succ$ in terms of $\succsim$ we have, for all z_Q, that

$$x_P \succ_P^z y_P \text{ if and only if } (x_P, z_Q) \succ (y_P, z_Q).$$

It follows that F increases with u, and similarly with v.

Finally, by (4.5), continuity of $U(x)$ implies that of $u(x_P)$, $v(x_Q)$, connectedness of $\mathscr{X}$ that of $\mathscr{X}_P$, $\mathscr{X}_Q$. Hence, for any fixed z in $\mathscr{X}$, the ranges of the functions $U(x)$, $u(x_P)$, $v(x_Q)$, $U(x_P, z_Q)$, $U(z_P, x_Q)$ for all x_P in $\mathscr{X}_P$, x_Q in $\mathscr{X}_Q$ are intervals, nondegenerate unless $u(x_P)$ and/or $v(x_Q)$ is constant. But then $F(u, v(z_Q))$ and $F(u(z_P), v)$ are, for any fixed z in $\mathscr{X}$, increasing functions of u and v, respectively, defined on one interval and taking on all the values in another. This is possible only if $F(u, v)$ is continuous in u for each v, and in v for each u. Since $F(u, v)$ increases in both u, v, it follows that $F(u, v)$ is continuous in u and v jointly.

5. Additively Separable Representation in the Case of Three Independent Components of Consumption

Three independent components of consumption suffice to show the essential traits of the case with n such components, where $n \geqq 3$. We shall therefore in this section consider a preference ordering $\succsim$ on a product

$$\mathscr{X} = \mathscr{X}_P \times \mathscr{X}_Q \times \mathscr{X}_R \tag{5.1}$$

of three spaces. To make sure that this is really three for the purpose of our reasoning, we shall need a concept of sensitivity of $\succsim$ in a factor space. We shall say that $\succsim$ is *sensitive* in $\mathscr{X}_P$ if there exist x_P, y_P, z_Q, z_R such that

$$(x_P, z_Q, z_R) \succ (y_P, z_Q, z_R). \tag{5.2}$$

This will ensure that the induced ordering $\succsim_P^z$ will not declare all vectors x_P equivalent.

Given a reference vector $z = (z_P, z_Q, z_R)$, $\succsim$ now induces six orderings, $\succsim_P^z$, $\succsim_Q^z$, $\succsim_R^z$, $\succsim_{P,Q}^z$, $\succsim_{Q,R}^z$, $\succsim_{P,R}^z$ on various factor spaces, defined along the following lines:

$$\begin{cases} x_P \succsim_P^z y_P \text{ means } (x_P, z_Q, z_R) \succsim (y_P, z_Q, z_R) \\ (x_P, x_Q) \succsim_{P,Q}^z (y_P, y_Q) \text{ means } (x_P, x_Q, z_R) \succsim (y_P, y_Q, z_R), \text{ etc.} \end{cases} \tag{5.3}$$

PROPOSITION 2 (DEBREU (1960), 3 components only, modified). *Let* $\succsim$ *be a continuous preference ordering of all consumption vectors* $x=(x_P, x_Q, x_R)$ *such that* x_P, x_Q, x_R *belong to spaces* $\mathscr{X}_P, \mathscr{X}_Q, \mathscr{X}_R$, *which are connected subsets of Euclidean spaces of* n_P, n_Q, n_R *dimensions, respectively. Let* $\succsim$ *be sensitive in each of P, Q, R, and let* $\succsim^z_P, \succsim^z_Q, \succsim^z_R, \succsim^z_{P,Q}, \succsim^z_{Q,R}$ (as defined above) *be independent of z. Then there exist functions* $u^*(x_P)$, $v^*(x_Q)$, $w^*(x_R)$, *defined and continuous on* $\mathscr{X}_P, \mathscr{X}_Q, \mathscr{X}_R$, *respectively, such that* $\mathscr{X}$ *is represented by*

$$U^*(x) = u^*(x_P)+v^*(x_Q)+w^*(x_R). \tag{5.4}$$

This representation is unique up to a linear transformation

$$u'(x_P) = \beta_P+\gamma u^*(x_P), \qquad v'(x_Q) = \beta_Q+\gamma v^*(x_Q), \tag{5.5}$$

$$w'(x_R) = \beta_R+\gamma w^*(x_R), \qquad \gamma>0.$$

In principle, the representation (5.4) is still ordinal. That is, any function $U'(x)$ obtained from $U^*(x)$ by (3.3) is likewise a continuous representation of $\succsim$. However, unless φ happens to be linear as in (5.5), the representation $U'(x)$ cannot be written simply as a sum of functions each depending on one of the vectors x_P, x_Q, x_R only, as $U^*(x)$ is written in (5.4). It is only in this limited sense that the representation by $U^*(x)$ can be called cardinal.

In the proof of Proposition 2 given in Subsection 5* we shall follow the general ideas of Debreu's beautiful geometrical proof, and of the work of BLASCHKE and BOL (1938) on which it builds forth. We modify his reasoning in one respect in order to avoid making the assumption that the sixth induced ordering, $\succsim^z_{P,R}$, is also independent[10] of z.

5*. *Proof of Proposition 2.* Since the Cartesian product

$$\mathscr{X} \equiv \mathscr{X}_P \times \mathscr{X}_Q \times \mathscr{X}_R$$

is a connected subset of a Euclidean space of $n=n_P+n_Q+n_R$ dimensions,

[10] The redundancy of that assumption, as well as the importance of that redundancy for the analysis of utility over time, were perceived and demonstrated by GORMAN (1965, 1968a) for the case of differentiable utility functions. In a recent paper, GORMAN (1968b) has given a complete discussion of the structure of representations with regard to separability and additive separability, without differentiability assumptions. His results imply that, in Proposition 2, the premises that $\succsim^z_P, \succsim^z_Q, \succsim^z_R$ are independent of z are also implied in those made about $\succsim^z_{P,Q}$ and $\succsim^z_{Q,R}$. This further strengthening, important in itself, turns out to be less crucial to the particular application of Proposition 2 made in Chapter 4 than the dropping of the assumption that $\succsim^z_{P,R}$ does not depend on z.

the premises of Proposition 1 are satisfied. Hence $\succsim$ is represented by a continuous function

$$U(x) \equiv U(x_P, x_Q, x_R) \tag{5.6}$$

defined on $\mathscr{X}$. Since an additive constant does not affect the representation, we shall anchor $U(x)$ by requiring that, for some specific reference vector z,

$$U(z) = 0. \tag{5.7}$$

The five induced orderings $\succsim_P, \succsim_Q, \succsim_R, \succsim_{P,Q}, \succsim_{Q,R}$ (superscripts z have been dropped because these are now independent of z) are therefore represented by the continuous functions

$$\begin{cases} u(x_P) \equiv U(x_P, z_Q, z_R), \quad v(x_Q) \equiv U(z_P, x_Q, z_R), \\ \qquad\qquad\qquad\qquad\qquad\qquad w(x_R) \equiv U(z_P, z_Q, x_R), \\ W(x_P, x_Q) \equiv U(x_P, x_Q, z_R), \quad \bar{U}(x_Q, x_R) \equiv U(z_P, x_Q, x_R), \end{cases} \tag{5.8}$$

respectively. Since the domains of all these functions are connected, the range of each is an interval. For three of the ranges we introduce the notations

$$\mathscr{U} = u(\mathscr{X}_P), \quad \mathscr{V} = v(\mathscr{X}_Q), \quad \mathscr{W} = w(\mathscr{X}_R). \tag{5.9}$$

Since $\succsim$ is sensitive in each of P, Q, R, none of the five intervals collapses to a point, and, by suitable choice of z, one can ensure that the point

$$u(z_P) = v(z_Q) = w(z_R) = W(z_P, z_R) = \bar{U}(z_Q, z_R) = 0 \tag{5.10}$$

is interior to all five ranges.

We now apply Result A twice to $U(x)$, once with the partitioning $x = (x_P, (x_Q, x_R))$, and once with $x = ((x_P, x_Q), x_R)$. With reference to the proof of Result A, this gives us the existence of increasing functions $F(W, w)$ and $G(u, \bar{U})$, such that, for all x in $\mathscr{X}$,

$$U(x) = F(W(x_P, x_Q), w(x_R)) = G(u(x_P), \bar{U}(x_Q, x_R)). \tag{5.11}$$

The domains of the arguments W, w of F and u, $\bar{U}$ of G are intervals over which the functions denoted by the same symbols range, respectively. Since these functions as well as $U(x)$ are continuous, F and G are continuous. To avoid repetition of similar reasoning, we announce in advance that the functions F^{-1}, g, f, H, h yet to be introduced are likewise continuous and increasing on the nondegenerate intervals, or products thereof, over which their arguments range.

By inserting $x_R = z_R$ in (5.11), using (5.10) and (5.8), one has

$$F(W(x_P, x_Q), 0) = G(u(x_P), v(x_Q)),$$

and, if F^{-1} is the inverse of $F(W, 0)$,

$$W(x_P, x_Q) = F^{-1}(G(u(x_P), v(x_Q)) \equiv g(u(x_P), v(x_Q)), \tag{5.12}$$

say, and symmetrically

$$\bar{U}(x_Q, x_R) = f(v(x_Q), w(x_R)). \tag{5.13}$$

We can now shed the variables x_P, x_Q, x_R. From (5.11), (5.12), and (5.13) we have

$$F(g(u, v), w) = G(u, f(v, w)) \equiv H(u, v, w) = H(t), \text{ say,} \tag{5.14}$$

where $t \equiv (u, v, w)$. Here $H(t)$ is defined on the three-dimensional cell $\mathscr{I} \equiv \mathscr{U} \times \mathscr{V} \times \mathscr{W}$, of which the origin $o = (0, 0, 0)$ is an interior point. The ordering $\succsim$ on $\mathscr{X}_P \times \mathscr{X}_Q \times \mathscr{X}_R$ represented by $U(x)$ induces an ordering on $\mathscr{I}$, which we likewise denote by $\succsim$, and which is represented by $H(t)$.

We shall study the level curves of $H(u, v, 0)$ and of $H(0, v, w)$. In the plane $w = 0$ we arbitrarily select (see Fig. 2) an indifference curve κ not passing

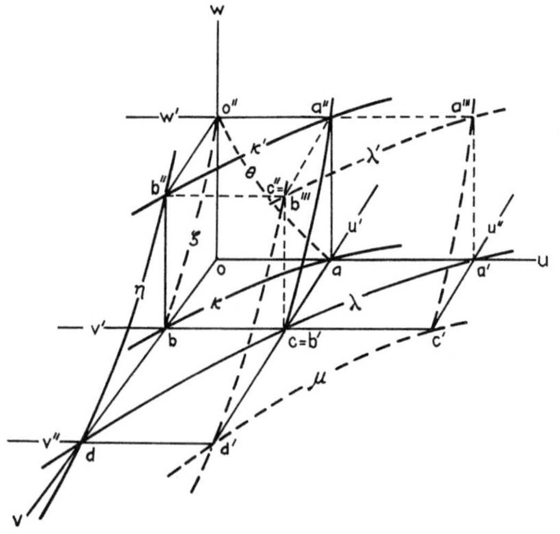

Fig. 2

through o, but close enough to o for all the intersection points sought in the following construction to exist. If κ intersects the u- and v-axes in $a = (u', 0, 0)$ and $b = (0, v', 0)$, respectively, we have

$$a \sim b, \text{ implying } g(u', 0) = g(0, v') \tag{5.15}$$

by taking $w = 0$ in the first member of (5.14). At most one intersection point exists in each case because $g(u, v)$ is increasing in each variable. Precisely one will exist if κ passes close enough to o, because of the continuity of $g(u, v)$.

It will save words to refer to two points s, t of $\mathscr{I}$ as *u-congruent* if they differ only in their u-coordinate,

$$s = (u^{(1)}, v, w), \quad t = (u^{(2)}, v, w) \quad u^{(1)} \neq u^{(2)}.$$

Similarly we shall speak of v- and w-congruence.

We find $c \equiv (u', v', 0)$, v-congruent to a, u-congruent to b, and draw through c an indifference curve λ in the plane $w = 0$, which intersects the u-axis in $a' \equiv (u'', 0, 0)$, the v-axis in $d \equiv (0, v'', 0)$. In particular,

$$c \sim a', \text{ implying } g(u', v') = g(u'', 0)\,. \tag{5.16}$$

Finally we find $c' \equiv (u'', v', 0)$, v-congruent to a', u-congruent to b, and $d' \equiv (u', v'', 0)$, u-congruent to d, v-congruent to a.

We now wish to prove that $d' \sim c'$. In Section 7 we shall show that Proposition 2 does not hold for a partitioning of x into only two components.[11] Therefore, we shall need to go into the third dimension to prove that $d' \sim c'$.

On the indifference curve η through d in the plane $u = 0$, we find $b'' \equiv (0, v', w')$, w-congruent to b. Then

$$d \sim b'', \text{ implying } f(v'', 0) = f(v', w') \tag{5.17}$$

by the second member of (5.14). Finally we find $o'' \equiv (0, 0, w')$ on the w-axis, v-congruent to b'', and $a'' \equiv (u', 0, w')$, u-congruent to o'', w-congruent to a. Then, by taking $w = w'$ in the first member of (5.14), we see that (5.15) in its turn implies $a'' \sim b''$. (In fact the indifference curves κ and κ' are point-by-point w-congruent.) Hence $c \sim d \sim b'' \sim a''$, and therefore

$$c \sim a'', \text{ implying } f(v', 0) = f(0, w')\,. \tag{5.18}$$

The second round of the construction is similar to the first. It employs the points $a''' \equiv (u'', 0, w')$, u- and w-congruent to o'' and a', respectively, and

[11] See Section 7 below.

$c'' \equiv b''' \equiv (u', v', w')$, u-, v-, and w-congruent to b'', a'', and $c = b'$, respectively. We have

$$\left.\begin{array}{l}(5.17) \text{ implies } d' \sim b''' \\ (5.16) \text{ implies } c'' \sim a''' \\ (5.18) \text{ implies } a''' \sim c'\end{array}\right\} \text{ so } d' \sim c'.$$

Hence d' and c' are on the same indifference curve μ in the plane $w = 0$.

The rectangle $acc'a'$ has the following characteristics relative to the indifference curves κ, λ, μ:

incidence:					congruence type of				
	a	c	c'	a'		a,a'	c,c'	a,c	a',c'
is on	κ	λ	μ	λ	is	u	u	v	v

We shall call such a rectangle *inscribed in the curves* κ, λ, μ. Since the origin could have been chosen anywhere in $\mathscr{I}$, we have found the following result, illustrated in Fig. 3.

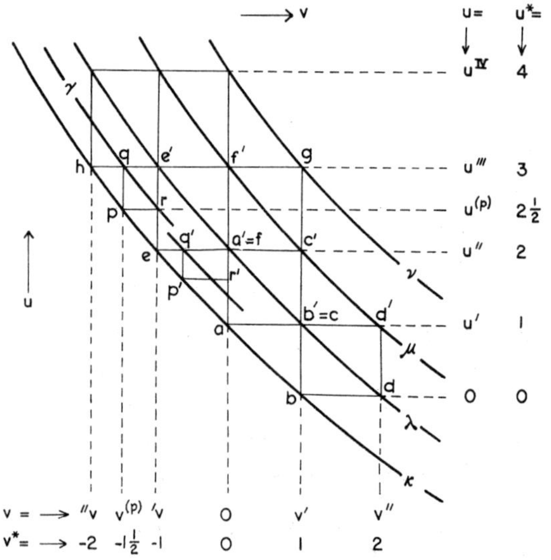

Fig. 3

RESULT B. *If three indifference curves* κ, λ, μ *possess an inscribed rectangle* $acc'a'$ *then* κ, λ, μ *possess adjoining inscribed rectangles* $bdd'b'$, $b' = c$, *and*

$eff'e'$, $f=a'$, provided only that the intersection points required by their construction exist.

The remainder of the proof is based on the "geometry of webs" of BLASCHKE and BOL (1938). On any three indifference curves κ, λ, μ one can construct a sequence of such rectangles as indicated in Fig. 3, going as far in both directions as the intervals $\mathscr{U}$ and $\mathscr{V}$ permit. If there should be an infinite sequence of such rectangles inscribed in κ, λ, μ, such a sequence cannot have a finite point of accumulation t' in $\mathscr{I}$, because by the continuity of $\mathrm{H}(t)$ such a point would belong to each of κ, λ, μ, which is a contradiction. Hence if $\mathscr{U}$ and $\mathscr{V}$ are bounded, an infinite sequence of inscribed rectangles can only have an accumulation point on the boundary of $\mathscr{I}$, and not belonging to $\mathscr{I}$.

A second sequence of rectangles can be inscribed in λ, μ, ν if ν contains, for instance, the point g, u-congruent to c' and v-congruent to f'. In this way the intersection of $\mathscr{I}$ with the plane $w=0$ is covered by rectangles inscribed in a sequence of indifference curves ..., κ, λ, μ, ν, ..., except possibly for uncovered margins near the endpoints (if finite) of $\mathscr{U}$, $\mathscr{V}$.

Furthermore, one can interpolate an indifference curve γ "between" κ and λ, say, by choosing p on eh (Fig. 3) so that $q \sim r$, and drawing γ through q and r. This construction can be extended over the full length of κ and λ, repeated between λ and μ, etc. and possibly into any uncovered margins, and repeated again between κ and γ, etc.

Let $\mathscr{U}'$ be the set of all u-coordinates $(0, u', u'', \ldots)$ of vertices of inscribed rectangles occurring in this construction repeated indefinitely, $\mathscr{V}'$ that of all v-coordinates. Then $\mathscr{U}'$ is dense in $\mathscr{U}$, $\mathscr{V}'$ in $\mathscr{V}$. We assign new coordinates (u^*, v^*) to all points of $\mathscr{U}' \times \mathscr{V}'$ in the manner indicated in the margins of Fig. 3. Then

$$u^* = \pi(u), \qquad v^* = \varphi(v), \tag{5.19}$$

are continuous and increasing functions on $\mathscr{U}'$ and $\mathscr{V}'$, respectively, for which

$$\pi(0) = \varphi(0) = 0. \tag{5.20}$$

These functions are extended to $\mathscr{U}$, $\mathscr{V}$, while retaining these properties by

$$\pi(u) \equiv \sup_{\substack{u' \leqq u \\ u' \in \mathscr{U}'}} \pi(u'), \qquad \varphi(v) \equiv \sup_{\substack{v' \leqq v \\ v' \in \mathscr{V}'}} \varphi(v').$$

It follows from the construction that for any two equivalent points (u, v),

(u', v') of $\mathscr{U}' \times \mathscr{V}'$ one has

$$u^* + v^* = \pi(u) + \varphi(v) = \pi(u') + \varphi(v') = u'^* + v'^* .$$

By continuity of $H(u, v, 0)$ this property extends to $\mathscr{U} \times \mathscr{V}$. Therefore, if we now define functions

$$u^*(x_P) = \pi(u(x_P)), \qquad v^*(x_Q) = \varphi(v(x_Q)),$$

the ordering $\succsim$, restricted to points of $\mathscr{X}$ for which $w(x_R) = 0$, is represented by the continuous function

$$u^*(x_P) + v^*(x_Q). \tag{5.21}$$

By the independence of $\succsim_{P,Q}$, the same representation applies to any set of points of $\mathscr{X}$ on which $w(x_R)$ takes another constant value.

To extend this representation to all of $\mathscr{X}$, we return to Fig. 2 to note that (5.18) also implies $b \sim o''$. It follows that, had we carried out the preceding construction in the plane $u = 0$ instead of in $w = 0$, starting from ζ instead of from κ, we would have arrived at the same demarcation point d by intersecting the v-axis with the indifference curve through b'' as we obtained by intersection with λ through b'. Moving the origin successively to b, d, ..., we obtain that the same sequence of demarcation points o, b, d, ... on the v-axis would have been obtained starting from ζ instead of from κ. But then the same must hold for the sequence of demarcation points o, $'b$, b, $'d$, d, ... (not shown in the figures) obtained from o, b, d, ... by interpolation, because the interpolated sequence could as well have been obtained without interpolation by starting with an indifference curve $'\kappa$ (not shown) defined by

$$w = 0, \qquad \pi(u) + \varphi(v) = \tfrac{1}{2} .$$

Since this reasoning extends to any number of interpolations, the construction starting from ζ would have led to the same function $v^*(x_Q)$, along with a similar function $w^*(x_R)$. It follows that $\succsim$ is continuously represented, on any set of points of $\mathscr{X}$ for which $u^*(x_P)$ takes a constant value, by

$$v^*(x_Q) + w^*(x_R). \tag{5.22}$$

We shall finally show that $\succsim$ is represented on $\mathscr{X}$ by the continuous function[12]

$$U^*(x) = u^*(x_P) + v^*(x_Q) + w^*(x_R). \tag{5.23}$$

---

[12] There is an affinity between the following reasoning and a study by Arrow (1952).

Consider two vectors $x=(x_P, x_Q, x_R)$, $x'=(x'_P, x'_Q, x'_R)$. By (5.11), (5.12), (5.13), (5.19) their order depends only on the corresponding utility vectors

$$(5.24) \qquad (u^*, v^*, w^*), \qquad (u'^*, v'^*, w'^*),$$

where $u^* = u^*(x_P)$, etc. Extending the usual notation $[m, m']$ for the interval $m \leqq u \leqq m'$ to

$$|[m, m']| \equiv \begin{cases} [m, m'] \text{ if } m \leqq m' \\ [m', m] \text{ if } m' < m, \end{cases}$$

we consider the set

$$\mathscr{S} \equiv |[u^*, u'^*]| \times |[v^*, v'^*]| \times |[w^*, w'^*]| .$$

This is a *block* (rectangular parallelepiped) of which each vertex has each coordinate in common with one or the other of the points (5.24), as shown in Fig. 4. On the points of each edge of $\mathscr{S}$ the ordering $\gtrsim$ is (strictly) monotonic as indicated by arrows, because of the monotonicity of H in (5.14), and each such *edge ordering* is represented by the corresponding term in (5.23).

We must show that, for all possible dimensions of the block, the ordering $\gtrsim$ of each of the pairs (a, h), (b, e), (c, f), (d, g) is represented by (5.23). For (a, h) this is already implied in the edge orderings $a \succ b \succ f \succ h$.

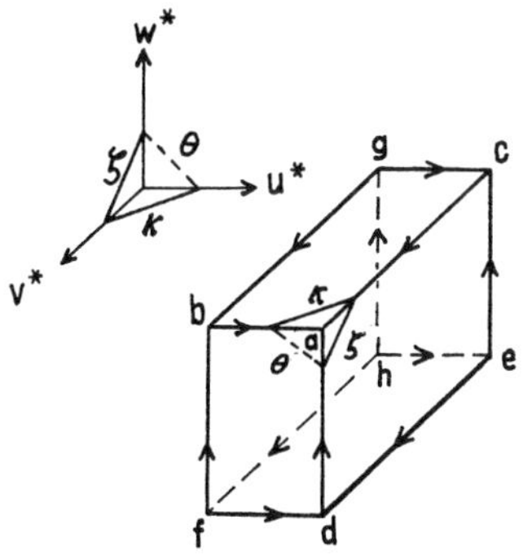

Fig. 4

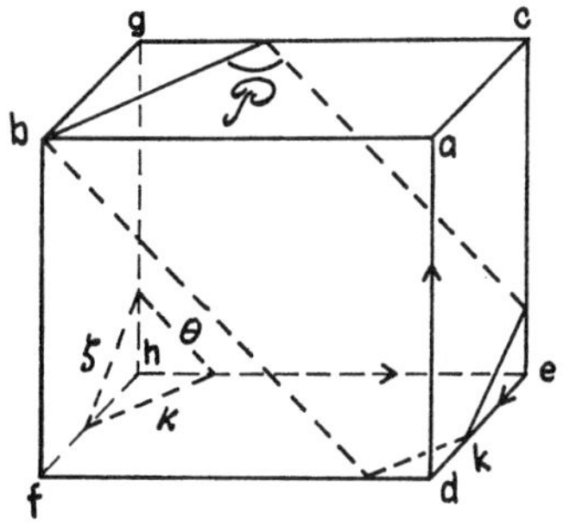

Fig. 5

Assume first that $v^* \neq v'^*$. Then if either $u^* = u'^*$ or $w^* = w'^*$, the remaining comparisons are settled by (5.22) or (5.21), respectively. Assume therefore that the block $\mathscr{S}$ is three-dimensional. We shall make use of the equivalences

$$(u^*, v^*, w^*) \sim (u^*+p, v^*-p, w^*) \sim (u^*+p, v^*-p+q, w^*-q) \sim \ldots,$$

implied in (5.21), (5.22) as long as we make sure that all points so compared are in $\mathscr{S}$. This means that all points of any line segment in $\mathscr{S}$ parallel to either κ or ζ are equivalent, and these equivalences are represented by (5.23).

As an example, Fig. 5 shows the comparison of b and e. We intersect $\mathscr{S}$ with a plane $\mathscr{P}$ through b parallel to both κ and ζ. Since a, h are on opposite sides of $\mathscr{P}$, the intersection is a two-dimensional convex polygon $\mathscr{Q}$ with edges parallel to κ, ζ or θ. Now $\mathscr{P}$ and hence $\mathscr{Q}$ must intersect the broken line $h\ e\ d\ a$ in precisely one point k. Fig. 6, drawn in $\mathscr{P}$, shows how a broken line in $\mathscr{Q}$ with a finite number of segments parallel to κ and ζ can be drawn to connect b and k. This establishes the equivalence of b and k, and its representation by (5.23). The comparison of k and e then is made through the edge orderings on $h\ e\ d\ a$, again represented by (5.23). In Fig. 5 $b \sim k \succ e$.

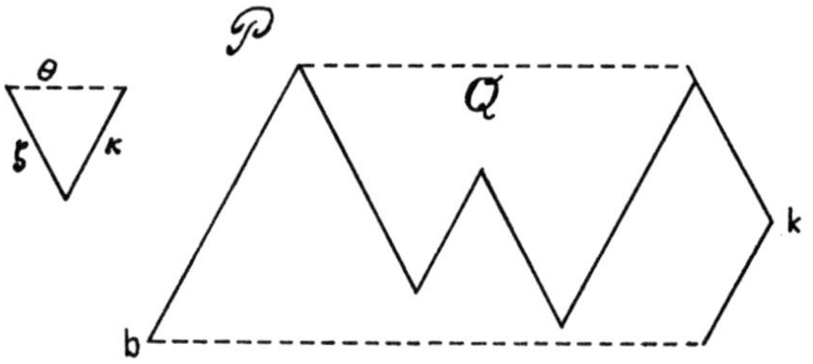

Fig. 6

It is clear from the two-dimensionality of $\mathscr{Q}$, from the condition on the slopes of its sides, and from the Archimedean property of real numbers, that the above reasoning can be carried through regardless of the dimensions of $\mathscr{S}$, and of the pair of opposite vertices compared (see Fig. 5).

On the other hand, if $v^* = v'^*$, we first use (5.25) with either $p \neq 0$ or $q \neq 0$ to obtain

$$(u''^*, v''^*, w''^*) \sim (u^*, v^*, w^*), \text{ say, with } v''^* \neq v^*,$$

and continue from there with the above reasoning. This procedure is unavailable with regard to *both* (u^*, v^*, w^*) and (u'^*, v'^*, w'^*) only if each is either $(\underline{u}, \underline{v}, \underline{w})$ or $(\bar{u}, \bar{v}, \bar{w})$, where $\underline{u}$, $\underline{v}$, $\underline{w}$, are finite lower endpoints of $\mathscr{U}^* \equiv u^*(x_P)$, $\mathscr{V}^*$, $\mathscr{W}^*$, included in $\mathscr{U}^*$, $\mathscr{V}^*$, $\mathscr{W}^*$, respectively, and $\bar{u}$, $\bar{v}$, $\bar{w}$ are similar upper endpoints. But then $v^* = v'^*$, $\bar{v} > \underline{v}$ forces $(u^*, v^*, w^*) = (u'^*, v'^*, w'^*)$, equality implying equivalence, represented by (5.23).

Finally, to discuss the uniqueness of (5.23), we note first from (5.10), (5.19), (5.20) that

$$u^*(z_P) = v^*(z_Q) = w^*(z_R) = 0 .$$

Now assume that $\succsim$ is also represented by the continuous function

$$U'(x) = u'(x_P) + v'(x_Q) + w'(x_R) .$$

We define

$$\beta_P \equiv u'(z_P), \text{ etc., } u''(x_P) \equiv u'(x_P) - \beta_P , \text{ etc.}$$

Then there exists $h(U^*)$ such that, for all x in $\mathscr{X}$,

$$u''(x_P) + v''(x_Q) + w''(x_R) = h(u^*(x_P) + v^*(x_Q) + w^*(x_R)) .$$

Inserting $x_R = z_R$, and thereafter $x_Q = z_Q$, or $x_P = z_P$, or both, we have, for all values of the omitted arguments x_P, x_Q, x_R,

$$u'' + v'' = h(u^* + v^*), \quad u'' = h(u^*), \quad v'' = h(v^*), \quad 0 = h(0) ,$$

hence

$$h(u^* + v^*) = h(u^*) + h(v^*), \quad h(0) = 0 ,$$

for all (u^*, v^*) in $\mathscr{U}^* \times \mathscr{V}^*$.

This in turn implies

$$h(nu^*) = n h(u^*)$$

for all integer n and all u^* such that u^* and $n\, u^*$ are in the interval $\mathscr{U}^*$. Among continuous functions $h(u^*)$, this property is possessed only by the linear functions

$$h(u^*) = \gamma u^* ,$$

where $\gamma > 0$ because h is increasing. This establishes the transformation (5.5). The proof of Proposition 2 is now complete.

6. Extensions to the Case of More than Three Independent Components of Consumption

Debreu has extended Proposition 2 to the case of $k > 3$ independent components of consumption. If we write

$$\mathscr{X} = \mathscr{X}_1 \times \mathscr{X}_2 \times \ldots \times \mathscr{X}_k \tag{6.1}$$

for the factorization of the prospect space by independent components (with respect to each of which $\succsim$ is sensitive), he has assumed that the orderings induced by $\succsim$ on every product.

$$\mathscr{X}_{i_1} \times \mathscr{X}_{i_2} \times \ldots \times \mathscr{X}_{i_j}, \quad 1 \leqq j \leqq k-1, \tag{6.2}$$

of j out of the k spaces are independent of the reference vector.

We have already seen that for $k=3$ independent components only five out of the six such assumptions are needed. As mentioned in Footnote 10 above, GORMAN (1968b) has cut this down further to only two. In the same paper he has given minimal assumptions for the generalization of Proposition 2 to k independent components. To avoid duplication, we mention here only one straightforward extension of Proposition 2 that helps prepare for Chapter 4.

RESULT C *Let the following orderings, induced on factor sets by a continuous ordering $\succsim$ on the product* (6.1) *of connected subsets of finite-dimensional Euclidean spaces be independent of the reference vector z,*

$$\begin{cases} \succsim_i \text{ on } \mathscr{X}_i, & i = 1, 2, \ldots, k, \quad k \geqq 3, \\ \succsim_{i,i+1} \text{ on } \mathscr{X}_i \times \mathscr{X}_{i+1}, & i = 1, 2, \ldots, k-1. \end{cases} \tag{6.2}$$

Let $\succsim$ be sensitive in each $\mathscr{X}_i$. Then $\succsim$ is represented on $\mathscr{X}$ by a continuous function of the form

$$U(x) = u_1(x_1) + u_2(x_2) + \ldots + u_k(x_k), \tag{6.3}$$

unique up to an increasing linear transformation.

6.* *Proof of Result C.* By Proposition 2, the statement is true for $k=3$. Suppose it is true if k is replaced by $j-1$, where $4 \leqq j \leqq k$, and consider the ordering $\succsim^z_{1,\ldots,j}$ induced by $\succsim$ on the space

$$\mathscr{X}^{(j)} = \mathscr{X}_1 \times \mathscr{X}_2 \times \cdots \times \mathscr{X}_j,$$

using a reference vector z. Then Proposition 2 can be applied to the factorization

$$\mathscr{X}^{(j)} = \mathscr{X}^{(j-2)} \times \mathscr{X}_{j-1} \times \mathscr{X}_j$$

to give the existence of a continuous representation of the form

$$u^{(j-2)}(x_1, \ldots, x_{j-2}) + u^*_{j-1}(x_{j-1}) + u^*_j(x_j).$$

We compare the representation of $\succsim^z_{1,\ldots,j-1}$, obtained by holding x_j

constant in this expression, with

$$u_1(x_1)+ \dots +u_{j-1}(x_{j-1}),$$

given by the inductive hypothesis made. The reasoning used at the end of Section 5* to establish the essential uniqueness of additively separable representation then gives, with $\gamma>0$,

$$u_1(x_1)+ \dots +u_{j-2}(x_{j-2}) = \gamma u^{(j-2)}(x_1, \dots, x_{j-2})+\delta$$

$$u_{j-1}(x_{j-1}) = \gamma u^*_{j-1}(x_{j-1})+\delta^*,$$

from which, by introducing $u_j(x_j)=\gamma u_j^*(x_j)$, one validates the inductive hypothesis for $\succsim^z_{1,\dots,j}$. By continued induction one obtains (6.3), unique up to an increasing linear transformation.

7. Reconsideration of the Case of Two Independent Components of Consumption

To show that the case of $k \geqq 3$ independent components of consumption leads to a more special class of representations than the case $k=2$, we must show that not every function of the separable form (4.4) can be transformed into the additively separable form

(7.1) $$U^*(x) = u^*(x_P)+v^*(x_Q).$$

One readily verifies that any ordering representable by (7.1) must satisfy the condition that

(7.2) $$\left.\begin{array}{l}(x_P, x'_Q) \sim (x'_P, x_Q) \\ (x_P, x''_Q) \sim (x''_P, x_Q)\end{array}\right\} \text{ implies } (x'_P, x''_Q) \sim (x''_P, x'_Q).$$

Given any continuous representation of the separable form (4.4) of an ordering $\succsim$ on $\mathscr{X} = \mathscr{X}_P \times \mathscr{X}_Q$, the test (7.2) can be expressed in terms of the values

$$(u, u', u'') = (u(x_P), u(x'_P), u(x''_P)), \quad (v, v', v'') = (v(x_Q), v(x'_Q), v(x''_Q)),$$

assumed by the functions $u(x_P)$, $v(x_Q)$ in the points x, x', x''. The configuration of points and indifference curves expressing the test is shown in Fig. 7. It is more general than that of the corresponding points a, b, d, d', c', a' in Fig. 3, but includes the latter as a special case. Since the latter configuration was already found, in the proof of Proposition 2, to be sufficient for the existence of the representation (7.1), either condition, (7.1) or (7.2), is both necessary and sufficient for such representability.

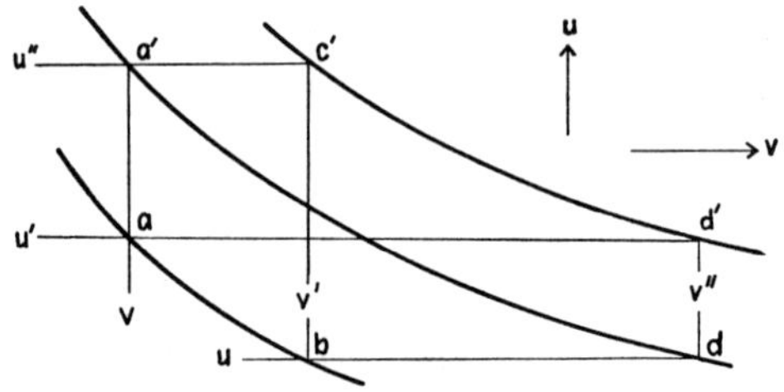

Fig. 7

The separable function

$$U(x) = (1+u)(1+u+v), \quad u = u(x_P) \geqq 0, \quad v = v(x_Q) \geqq 0,$$

fails to meet this test for a choice of points x, x', x'' and functions u, v such that

$$(u, u', u'') = (0, 1, 2), \qquad (v, v', v'') = (0, 3, 8).$$

Hence it cannot be transformed to the form (7.1).

Note: The references for [paper 4] are included with those of [paper 5].

5

Representation of Preference Orderings over Time

Tjalling C. Koopmans

Decision and Organization: A Volume in Honor of Jacob Marschak, ed. C. B. McGuire and R. Radner (Amsterdam: North-Holland, 1972), pp. 79–100

1. Preference over Time

In Section 1 of Chapter 3 we have argued the desirability of formalizing the idea of consumer's preference in terms of a *preference ordering* on a *prospect space*, before discussing the possibility of representing such an ordering by a *utility function*. The considerations there adduced have still greater force with regard to problems of evaluative comparison of growth paths for an indefinite future. If one interprets this as an infinite future, neither the concept of a utility function depending on infinitely many variables, nor that of a preference ordering on a space of infinitely many dimensions, has an obvious intuitive meaning. To start from the more basic one – the preference ordering – is therefore even more desirable in that case, in that it may help avoid implicit assumptions one is not aware of.

In the present chapter, therefore, the propositions of Chapter 3 are applied to the representation of preference orderings over time. Because of the close connections between the two chapters, the notations are almost identical, and a single list of references to the literature appears at the end of Chapter 4.

Before getting into details, a word is in order on the question whose preference is being studied. This question concerns the interpretation and relevance of the analysis, as distinct from the logical connections between

[1] This chapter reports on research under a grant from the National Science Foundation. It revises and extends Sections 5–9 of Koopmans (1966). I am indebted to Kenneth Arrow and Gerard Debreu for extremely valuable comments.

Note: "Chapter 3" and "Chapter 4" correspond to papers 4 and 5 in the present volume.

the properties of the ordering and the mathematical form of its representation. In regard to preference over time, the simplest interpretation of the orderings that have been studied most thus far is a normative one. One looks at various possible preference orderings that may be adopted, by whatever decision process, for the planning of an economy with a constant population size. New problems arise if population is expected to grow indefinitely or to keep changing in other ways.

Another possible interpretation is that one wishes to study descriptively the preference ordering of an individual with regard to his life-time consumption program, assuming that such an ordering is implicit in his decisions. For this interpretation the finite life span and the bequest motive need to be considered as well. For applications of such a preference ordering, see YAARI (1964).

Finally – the ultimate goal of a theory of preference over time for an economy with private wealth – one may wish to examine whether, or under what conditions, an aggregate preference ordering over time can be imputed, on an "as if" basis, to a society of individual decision-makers each guided by his own preference ordering over time.

In all these interpretations, normative or descriptive, the most intriguing problems arise from the fact that the future has a beginning but no discernible end. In contrast to this central problem, the question whether to use a discrete or a continuous time concept seems in the present state of knowledge primarily a matter of research tactics rather than of substance. So far the indications are that axiomatic analysis is somewhat simpler if one chooses discrete time. On the other hand, the maximization of a utility function of a given form under given technological constraints is often simpler with continuous time. We shall therefore here choose discrete time on the basis of expedience without further excuse or explanation.

2. Postulates Concerning a Preference Ordering over Time

We shall adopt a set of five postulates about a preference ordering $\succsim$ on a space ${}_1\mathscr{X}$ of *programs*, that is, of infinite sequences, denoted

$$ {}_1x \equiv (x_1, x_2, x_3, \ldots), \tag{2.1} $$

of vectors

$$ x_t \equiv (x_{t1}, x_{t2}, \ldots, x_{tn}) \tag{2.2} $$

associated with successive time periods $t = 1, 2, 3, \ldots$. The *program space*

${}_1\mathscr{X}$ is the space of all such sequences, in which each vector x_t is a point of the same (single period) *choice space* $\mathscr{X}$. Thus the components x_{ti} of x_t refer to a list of commodities, characteristics, or activities (as the case may be), which is the same for all t.

The postulates are modeled after those used in two earlier studies by KOOPMANS (1960) and by KOOPMANS, DIAMOND and WILLIAMSON (1964). The main difference is that the former studies presupposed the existence of a continuous representation. In the present study, the postulates refer to a continuous ordering, and the proximate aim of the study is to derive the existence of a continuous representation. Further differences will be noted in connection with the third and fifth postulates.

The problem of logical independence of the postulates is not investigated. The formulation and sequence of postulates is chosen primarily from the point of view of naturalness of interpretation. One case of recognized dependence between postulates is noted in Footnote 4.

It will be useful occasionally to employ short notations for finite or infinite segments of the program sequence, as follows,

$$(2.3) \qquad {}_1x \equiv (x_1, {}_2x) \equiv (x_1, \ldots, x_{t-1}, {}_tx) \equiv ({}_1x_{t-1}, {}_tx).$$

In an infinite-dimensional space such as ${}_1\mathscr{X}$, the choice of the distance function is crucial for the meaning of the continuity concept implied in it. We shall adopt the function[2]

$$(2.4) \qquad D({}_1x, {}_1y) \equiv \sup_t d(x_t, y_t)$$

where $d(x_t, y_t)$ is the distance between the t-th period installments x_t, y_t of the programs ${}_1x$, ${}_1y$, according to the definition

$$(2.5) \qquad d(x_t, y_t) \equiv \max_i |x_{ti} - y_{ti}|.$$

POSTULATE 1 (Continuity). *The program space ${}_1\mathscr{X}$ is the space of all programs ${}_1x$ such that, for all t, x_t is in a choice space $\mathscr{X}$, which is a connected subset of n-dimensional Euclidean space. On the program space there exists a complete preference ordering $\succsim$, which is continuous with regard to the distance function* (2.4).

[2] The symbol $\sup_t d_t$ denotes the largest of the numbers d_t, $t = 1, 2, 3, \ldots$, if there is a largest, or the smallest number not exceeded by any d_t if there is no largest. Such a number exists whenever $\mathscr{X}$ is bounded, that is, when the range of $d(x, y)$ for all x, y in $\mathscr{X}$ is bounded. If $\mathscr{X}$ is unbounded we admit the possibility that $D({}_1x, {}_1y) = \infty$.

Postulate 2 (Sensitivity). *There exists a program* ${}_1x$ *in* ${}_1\mathscr{X}$ *and a vector* y_1 *in* $\mathscr{X}$ *such that*

$$ {}_1x = (x_1, x_2, x_3, \dots) \succ (y_1, x_2, x_3, \dots). $$

The first purpose of P2 is to exclude the trivial case where all programs in ${}_1\mathscr{X}$ are equivalent. However, P2 does more than that. It also excludes orderings in which the standing of any program ${}_1x$ relative to other programs is independent of any vector x_t pertaining to any specific period t, but does depend on the asymptotic behavior of x_t as t tends to infinity.[3]

Next we introduce two independence postulates, P3′ and P3″, both of which will be maintained throughout Sections 2–6. In Section 7 we comment briefly on the case where P3″ is omitted. In these postulates we employ an arbitrary but fixed reference program,

$$ {}_1z = (z_1, {}_2z) = (z_1, z_2, {}_3z), \tag{2.6} $$

to define five orderings, induced by $\succsim$ on factor spaces of ${}_1\mathscr{X}$, and denoted $\underset{1}{\overset{z}{\succsim}}$, $\underset{2}{\overset{z}{\succsim}}$, ${}_1\underset{2}{\overset{z}{\succsim}}$, $\underset{3}{\overset{z}{\succsim}}$, $\underset{2}{\overset{z}{\succsim}}$, as follows:

$$ \left\{ \begin{array}{lll} x_1 \underset{1}{\overset{z}{\succsim}} y_1 & \text{means} & (x_1, {}_2z) \succsim (y_1, {}_2z) \\ {}_2x \; {}_2\overset{z}{\succsim} \; {}_2y & \text{means} & (z_1, {}_2x) \succsim (z_1, {}_2y) \\ (x_1, x_2) \; {}_1\underset{2}{\overset{z}{\succsim}} (y_1, y_2) & \text{means} & (x_1, x_2, {}_3z) \succsim (y_1, y_2, {}_3z) \\ {}_3x \; {}_3\overset{z}{\succsim} \; {}_3y & \text{means} & (z_1, z_2, {}_3x) \succsim (z_1, z_2, {}_3y) \\ x_2 \underset{2}{\overset{z}{\succsim}} y_2 & \text{means} & (z_1, x_2, {}_3z) \succsim (z_1, y_2, {}_3z) \end{array} \right. \tag{2.7} $$

Postulate 3′ (Limited Independence). *The two orderings* $\underset{1}{\overset{z}{\succsim}}$, $\underset{2}{\overset{z}{\succsim}}$ *are independent of the reference program* ${}_1z$.

Postulate 3″ (Extended Independence). *The ordering* ${}_1\underset{2}{\overset{z}{\succsim}}$ *is independent of* ${}_1z$.

For convenient reference, we also introduce

Postulate 3 (Complete Independence). *Both* P3′ *and* P3″ *hold.*[4]

---

[3] A simple example of such an ordering $\succsim$ satisfying all postulates except P2 is that in which $\mathscr{X}$ is one-dimensional and $\succsim$ is represented by $\lim_{T\to\infty} \sup_{t \geq T} x_t$. This ordering looks only at the highest consumption level that is, ultimately, and again and again thereafter, at least temporarily reached or arbitrarily closely approached. (Note the contrast between succinct mathematical notation and involved equivalent verbal statement$_1$.)

[4] By Gorman (1968b) (see Footnote 10 of Chapter 3), the independence of ${}_1\underset{2}{\overset{z}{\succsim}}$ and ${}_2\overset{z}{\succsim}$ implies that of $\underset{1}{\overset{z}{\succsim}}$.

Whenever one or both of P3′, P3″ are assumed in what follows, the corresponding orderings will be denoted $\succsim_1, \succsim_2, {}_1\succsim_2$. Note that ${}_1\succsim_2$ would have been denoted $\succsim_{1,2}$ in Chapter 3.

In the earlier studies referred to above, the implications of P3′ were pursued at length, those of P3 only briefly mentioned. In this study, the emphasis is reversed.

Neither P3′ nor P3″ can be regarded as realistic. Taken together, they will be found to preclude all complementarity between the consumption of different periods. P3′ by itself will be seen to permit a limited complementarity among the utility levels to be associated with consumption in successive periods, but still no complementarity between individual commodities or activities in different periods. P3 or P3′ should therefore be looked upon as first approximations, made to facilitate exploration of the implications of the fourth postulate, the real objective of this study:

Postulate 4 (Stationarity). *There exists a first period vector x_1^* in $\mathscr{X}$ with the property that the programs*

$$ {}_1x = (x_1^*, {}_2x) = (x_1^*, x_2, x_3, \ldots) $$

$$ {}_1y = (x_1^*, {}_2y) = (x_1^*, y_2, y_3, \ldots) $$

are such that ${}_1x \succsim_1 {}_1y$ if and only if the programs[5]

$$ {}_1v = (v_1, v_2, v_3, \ldots) = (x_2, x_3, x_4, \ldots) = {}_2x, $$

$$ {}_1w = (w_1, w_2, w_3, \ldots) = (y_2, y_3, y_4, \ldots) = {}_2y, $$

defined by $v_t \equiv x_{t+1}$, $w_t \equiv y_{t+1}$, $t = 1, 2, \ldots$, are such that ${}_1v \succsim_1 {}_1w$.

Before interpreting this postulate in less formal language, we note that, if one particular $x_1 = x_1^*$ in $\mathscr{X}$ has this property, then by P3′ every x_1 in $\mathscr{X}$ has this property. Using this, P4 says that if two programs ${}_1x$, ${}_1y$ have a common first-period vector $x_1 = y_1$, then the programs ${}_1v$, ${}_1w$ obtained by deleting x_1 from ${}_1x$ and from ${}_1y$, respectively, and advancing the timing of all subsequent vectors by one period, are ordered in the same way as ${}_1x$, ${}_1y$.

It is worth emphasizing that in this statement nothing is said or implied about the ordering of "then future" programs ${}_2x$, ${}_2y$ that may be applied

[5] In the notations ${}_2x$, ${}_2y$ as used here, there is no longer a necessary connection between the presubscript of ${}_2x$ and the timing of the first installment x_2 of that program. That is, x_2 simply means the vector that happened to represent second period consumption in the program ${}_1x$. In the program ${}_2x = {}_1v$, that same consumption occurs in the first period. With this point established, the notations ${}_1v$, ${}_1w$ will no longer be needed in what follows.

after the first period has elapsed. That is, no question of consistency or inconsistency of orderings adopted at different points in time is raised.[6] Only the ordering $\succsim$ applying "now" is under discussion. Applied repeatedly, P4 implies that the present ordering of two programs $(x_1, \ldots, x_{t-1}, {}_tx) \equiv ({}_1x_{t-1}, {}_tx)$ and $({}_1x_{t-1}, {}_ty)$ that start to differ in a designated way only from some point t in time onward is independent both of what that point in time is, and of what the common values ${}_1x_{t-1}$ up to that point are.

The fifth and last postulate asserts, roughly, that the end result of an infinite sequence of improvements starting from some given program is itself an improvement over that program. If only a finite number of future periods is affected by all but a finite number of the improvements, such an assertion is already implied in P1, P3′, P4. For simplicity we will refer only to a sequence of improvements made to successive vectors in the program, taken one at a time. A similar postulate has been used by DIAMOND (1965). An alternative postulate in terms of improvements affecting several periods at a time is briefly considered in Subsection 6* below.

POSTULATE 5 (Monotonicity). *If* ${}_1x$, ${}_1y$ *are programs such that, for all* $t = 1, 2, \ldots, (x_1, x_2, \ldots, x_{t-1}, y_t, y_{t+1}, y_{t+2}, \ldots) \precsim (x_1, x_2, \ldots, x_{t-1}, x_t, y_{t+1}, y_{t+2}, \ldots)$ *then* ${}_1y \precsim {}_1x$.

It can be shown that, given all other postulates, P5 is implied in the following stronger postulate, used in a previous study (KOOPMANS (1960)).

POSTULATE 5′ (Extreme Programs). *There exist in* ${}_1\mathscr{X}$ *a best and a worst program.*

There is some interest in avoiding that stronger statement wherever possible, with a view to problems of optimal growth under continuing technical change.

On the basis of the postulates set out, we seek to construct a representation of $\succsim$ on the entire program space ${}_1\mathscr{X}$, or on as large a subspace of it as we can. Our strategy will be first to find such representations on suitably chosen subspaces of ${}_1\mathscr{X}$.

3. Representation of $\succsim$ on Any Subspace of Ultimately Identical Programs

Since the space ${}_1\mathscr{X}$ is infinite-dimensional, Proposition 1 cannot be directly applied to the ordering $\succsim$ given on it.[7] For this reason, we shall

[6] For a discussion of that question, see STROTZ (1957).

[7] While it is true that Proposition 1 can be extended to infinite-dimensional spaces having the topological property of "separability" (see DEBREU (1954, 1964)), the distance function (2.4) does not endow ${}_1\mathscr{X}$ with that property.

in the present section study $\gtrsim$ on the subspace ${}_1\mathscr{X}_T^z$ of all programs of the form

$$(3.1) \qquad {}_1x = ({}_1x_T\,,\, {}_{T+1}z),$$

where ${}_1z$ is again an arbitrary but fixed reference program. Since programs in this subspace differ only in the segments ${}_1\mathscr{X}_T$, the ordering $\gtrsim$ on ${}_1\mathscr{X}$ restricted to the subspace ${}_1\mathscr{X}_T^z$ induces an ordering of sequences ${}_1x_T$ of length T on the space ${}_1\mathscr{X}_T$. We shall denote this ordering by ${}_1\gtrsim_T$. In Subsection 3* we shall prove

RESULT D. *For all T, the ordering* ${}_1\gtrsim_T$ *is independent of* ${}_1z$, *and is represented by a function of the form*

$$(3.2) \qquad U_T({}_1x_T) = u(x_1) + \alpha u(x_2) + \cdots + \alpha^{T-1} u(x_T), \quad 0<\alpha<1.$$

Here $u(x)$ *is a continuous function defined on* $\mathscr{X}$, *and both* α *and* $u(x)$ *are independent of* T.

The proof proceeds through a succession of statements which we label (*Da*), (*Db*), ..., recording in each case the postulates and/or previous results used in the proof. The notations for induced orderings extend those of (2.7).

(*Da*; P3′, P4) The induced ordering ${}_t\gtrsim^z$ of sequences ${}_tx$, defined by restricting $\gtrsim$ to the set of programs $({}_1z_{t-1}\,,\, {}_tx)$ is independent of ${}_1z$ and of t.

(*Db*; P3′, P4) The induced ordering $\gtrsim_t^z$ of vectors x_t is independent of ${}_1z$ and of t.

(*Dc*; P3, P4) The induced ordering ${}_{t-1}\gtrsim_t^z$ of vectors $(x_{t-1}\,,\, x_t)$ is independent of ${}_1z$ and of t.

(*Dd*; *C*, *Db*, *Dc*) The induced ordering ${}_1\gtrsim_T^z$ of sequences ${}_1x_T$ is independent of ${}_1z$, and is represented by a continuous function of the form

$$(3.3) \qquad U_T({}_1x_T) = u_1(x_1) + u_2(x_2) + \cdots + u_T(x_T),$$

unique up to a linear transformation similar to (5.5) in Chapter 3.

(*De*; *Dd*, P4) One can choose the $u_i(x_i)$ in (3.3) in such a way that (3.2) holds with $\alpha>0$, where α is unique, and where $u(x)$ is unique up to a linear transformation

$$(3.4) \qquad u^*(x) = \beta + \gamma u(x), \qquad \gamma>0.$$

(*Df*; *De*, P5) $\alpha<1$.

3*. *Proof of Result D.* Clearly the continuity of $\gtrsim$ entails the continuity of all restricted orderings induced by it.

(*Da*). P3′ allows us to write

$$\precsim_1^z = \precsim_1, \qquad {}_2\precsim^z = {}_2\precsim. \tag{3.5}$$

Using the symbol ⇔ to denote logical equivalence, these statements are made explicit by

$$\text{for all } {}_2x^*, x_1, y_1, \quad (x_1, {}_2z) \precsim (y_1, {}_2z) \Leftrightarrow (x_1, {}_2x^*) \precsim (y_1, {}_2x^*), \tag{3.6}$$

$$\text{for all } x_1^*, {}_2x, {}_2y, \quad (z_1, {}_2x) \precsim (z_1, {}_2y) \Leftrightarrow (x_1^*, {}_2x) \precsim (x_1^*, {}_2y). \tag{3.7}$$

In particular, choosing for x_1^* in (3.7) the x_1^* occurring in P4, we have from P4

$$\text{for all } {}_2x, {}_2y, \quad (z_1, {}_2x) \precsim (z_1, {}_2y) \Leftrightarrow {}_2x \precsim {}_2y, \tag{3.8}$$

an implication which can be applied once more to give

$$(z_1, z_2, {}_3x) \precsim (z_1, z_2, {}_3y) \Leftrightarrow (z_2, {}_3x) \precsim (z_2, {}_3y) \Leftrightarrow {}_3x \precsim {}_3y, \text{ etc.}$$

These results are summarized in

$$_t\precsim^z = {}_t\precsim = \cdots = {}_2\precsim = \precsim \qquad t = 2, 3, \ldots, \tag{3.9}$$

keeping in mind the notational practice explained in Footnote 5.

(*Db*). From (3.8) and (3.6), we have, for all ${}_1x^*$,

$$(z_1, x_2, {}_3z) \precsim (z_1, y_2, {}_3z) \Leftrightarrow (x_2, {}_3z) \precsim (y_2, {}_3z) \Leftrightarrow$$

$$\Leftrightarrow (x_2, {}_3x^*) \precsim (y_2, {}_3x^*) \Leftrightarrow (x_1^*, x_2, {}_3x^*) \precsim (x_1^*, y_2, {}_3x^*).$$

This reasoning and its repetition yield

$$\precsim_t^z = \precsim_t = \cdots = \precsim_2 = \precsim_1, \quad t = 1, 2, 3, \ldots. \tag{3.10}$$

(*Dc*). We now bring in P3″, written as ${}_1\precsim_2^z = {}_1\precsim_2$. Together with (3.8) this implies that, for all ${}_1x^*$,

$$(z_1, x_2, x_3, {}_4z) \precsim (z_1, y_2, y_3, {}_4z) \Leftrightarrow (x_2, x_3, {}_4z) \precsim (y_2, y_3, {}_4z) \Leftrightarrow$$

$$\Leftrightarrow (x_2, x_3, {}_4x^*) \precsim (y_2, y_3, {}_4x^*) \Leftrightarrow (x_1^*, x_2, x_3, {}_4x^*) \precsim (x_1^*, y_2, y_3, {}_4x^*).$$

Since this can again be repeated, we have

$$_{t-1}\precsim_t^z = {}_{t-1}\precsim_t = \cdots = {}_2\precsim_3 = {}_1\precsim_2, \quad t = 2, 3, \ldots. \tag{3.11}$$

(*Dd*). We consider ${}_1\precsim_T^z$, and note that $\precsim_t^z$, $t = 1, \ldots, T$ and ${}_{t-1}\precsim_t^z$, $t = 2, \ldots, T$, are all independent of ${}_1z$. By P2, $\precsim_1$ permits $x_1 \succ_1 y_1$, and by (3.10) a similar statement holds for $\precsim_t$, $t = 2, 3, \ldots$. The premises of Result C of Section 6 in Chapter 3 are therefore satisfied, and the representation

(3.3) follows. Hence ${}_1\succsim_T^z$ is independent of z, and we write ${}_1\succsim_T$ from here on.

(*De*). By (3.8) and (3.3), ${}_2\succsim_T$ is represented on ${}_2\mathscr{X}_T$ by either of the functions

$$u_2(x_2)+u_3(x_3)+\cdots+u_T(x_T),$$

$$u_1(x_2)+u_2(x_3)+\cdots+u_{T-1}(x_T).$$

It follows, along the lines of the uniqueness proof of Proposition 2, that, for all x in $\mathscr{X}$ and all $T \geqq 3$,

$$u_{t+1}(x) = \beta_t + \alpha u_t(x), \quad t = 1, \ldots, T-1, \quad \alpha > 0.$$

Since we are free to choose each $u_t(x)$, $t=2, \ldots, T-1$, so as to have $\beta_t = 0$ for all t, (3.2) results, with $u(x) = u_1(x) \equiv u^{(T)}(x)$, say, which might still depend on T. However, by comparing the representation (3.2) of ${}_1\succsim_T$ in terms of $u^{(T)}(x)$ with that in terms of $u^{(T+1)}(x)$ obtained from (3.2) with $T+1$ sustituted for T, one finds, again using the uniqueness argument, that the same $u^{(T)}(x) = u(x)$ can be used for all $T \geqq 3$, and hence, by holding ${}_3x$ constant, also for $T = 1, 2$.

(*Df*). The proof of *Df* will be given in Section 4.

4. Representation of $\succsim$ on the Space of Ultimately Constant Programs

In this section we choose a favorable ground on which to face the infinite horizon by first restricting ourselves to the space ${}_{\text{con}}\mathscr{X}$ of *constant programs*

(4.1) $${}_{\text{con}}x \equiv (x, x, x, \ldots),$$

that is, of programs ${}_1x$ for which $x_t = x$ for all t.

The points of ${}_{\text{con}}\mathscr{X}$ are in a one-to-one correspondence

(4.2) $${}_{\text{con}}x \leftrightarrow x$$

to those of $\mathscr{X}$. Because for all x, x' in $\mathscr{X}$,

(4.3) $$D({}_{\text{con}}x, {}_{\text{con}}x') = d(x, x'),$$

this correspondence preserves the distance function, and therewith the continuity concept. Moreover, if x, y are vectors of $\mathscr{X}$ such that $y \precsim_1 x$, then, by *Db* and P5, if ${}_{\text{con}}x_T$ denotes the sequence $(x, x, \ldots, x)$ of T identical vectors x,

(4.4) $${}_{\text{con}}y \precsim (x, {}_{\text{con}}y) \precsim \cdots \precsim ({}_{\text{con}}x_T, {}_{\text{con}}y) \precsim \cdots \precsim {}_{\text{con}}x.$$

The continuous ordering $\succsim_1$ on $\mathscr{X}$ is therefore transformed by the correspondence (4.2) into the ordering $\succsim$ restricted to ${}_{\text{con}}\mathscr{X}$. In particular,

RESULT E. *Any continuous representation $u(x)$ of $\succsim_1$ on $\mathscr{X}$ is at the same time a continuous representation of $\succsim$ restricted to ${}_{\text{con}}\mathscr{X}$.*

Note that only limited independence (P3′) was used in the proof of Result E.

Next we consider the space $\mathscr{X}_{\text{con}}$ of *ultimately constant programs*, that is, of programs such that, for some $T \geqq 0$,

$$(4.5) \qquad {}_1x = ({}_1x_T, {}_{\text{con}}x) = (x_1, \ldots, x_T, x, x, \ldots)$$

(for $T=0$ the term ${}_1x_T$ is absent). One readily verifies that the reasoning that led to Result *De* also applies in any subspace $\mathscr{X}_{\text{con}}^{(T)}$ of $\mathscr{X}_{\text{con}}$ consisting of programs (4.5) *with a fixed T*. The only difference consists of an added term in (3.2). One now finds for all $T \geqq 2$ a continuous representation of $\succsim$, restricted to $\mathscr{X}_{\text{con}}^{(T)}$, by the function

$$(4.6) \qquad u(x_1) + \alpha u(x_2) + \ldots \alpha^{T-1} u(x_T) + f_T(u(x)), \quad 0 < \alpha,$$

where $f_T(u)$ is continuous and increasing. From this representation we can derive two representations of $\succsim$ restricted to $\mathscr{X}_{\text{con}}^{(T-1)}$, one (4.7a) by setting $x_1 = x_1^*$ and applying P4, the other (4.7b) by setting $x_T = x$, as follows,

$$(4.7a) \qquad U^{(a)}({}_1x) \equiv \alpha u(x_1) + \cdots + \alpha^{T-1} u(x_{T-1}) + f_T(u(x))$$

$$(4.7b) \qquad U^{(b)}({}_1x) \equiv u(x_1) + \cdots + \alpha^{T-2} u(x_{T-1}) + \alpha^{T-1} u(x) + f_T(u(x)).$$

By Result C these representations are, for all $T \geqq 3$, unique up to a linear transformation. Comparison of the first terms shows that

$$U^{(a)}({}_1x) = \alpha U^{(b)}({}_1x) + \beta,$$

which implies that

$$f_T(u) = \alpha^T u + \alpha f_T(u) + \beta.$$

Since $f_T(u)$ is increasing, we must have $\alpha < 1$, that is, *Df* above, thus completing the proof of Result D. Solving for $f_T(u)$ and dropping the constant term, we have

RESULT F. *On the space $\mathscr{X}_{\text{con}}$ of ultimately constant programs $\succsim$ is represented by the continuous function* (*with* $0 < \alpha < 1$)

$$(4.8) \quad U({}_1x) = U({}_1x_T, {}_{\text{con}}x) \equiv u(x_1) + \alpha u(x_2) + \cdots + \alpha^{T-1} u(x_T) + \frac{\alpha^T}{1-\alpha} u(x),$$

unique up to a linear transformation.

Note that in this function T itself depends on the given ultimately constant program ${}_1x$. For definiteness one can specify that $T+1$ is the earliest time from which onward ${}_1x$ is constant. However, the same value of $U({}_1x)$ is obtained if one allows $T+1$ to be any time, earliest or not, beyond which ${}_1x$ is constant. It is for that reason that the function (4.8) represents $\succsim$ on the space $\mathscr{X}_{\text{con}}$ for *all* ultimately constant programs, regardless of the values of their "minimal" T.

5. Representation of $\succsim$ on the Space of Programs Bounded in Utility

It is now possible to indicate a large subspace of the program space on which the ordering $\succsim$ is represented by

$$U({}_1x) \equiv \sum_{t=1}^{\infty} \alpha^{t-1} u(x_t), \quad 0<\alpha<1. \tag{5.1}$$

We shall call a program ${}_1x$ *bounded in utility* if there exist vectors x, $\bar{x}$ in $\mathscr{X}$ with $\underline{x} \prec_1 \bar{x}$ such that

$$\underline{x} \precsim_1 x_t \precsim_1 \bar{x} \text{ for all } t = 1, 2, \ldots. \tag{5.2}$$

We can then show

PROPOSITION 3. *On the space* ${}_1\mathscr{X}^*$ *of all programs bounded in utility, the ordering* $\succsim$ *is represented by the continuous function* (5.1).

It is to be noted that for ultimately constant programs the function (5.1) is identical with that in (4.8). Hence Proposition 3 includes Result F.

5*. *Proof of Proposition 3.* We first note that if ${}_1x$ is bounded in utility, then,

$$u(\underline{x}) \leqq u(x_t) \leqq u(\bar{x}) \text{ for all } t,$$

and, since $0<\alpha<1$, the series in (5.1) is absolutely convergent, hence its sum exists and is continuous with respect to ${}_1x$.

Now let ${}_1x$ and ${}_1y$ be two programs bounded in utility, and define bounds applicable to both ${}_1x$ and ${}_1y$ by

$$\underline{z} \equiv \begin{cases} \underline{x} \text{ if } \underline{x} \precsim_1 \underline{y} \\ \underline{y} \text{ if } \underline{y} \prec_1 \underline{x} \end{cases}, \qquad \bar{z} \equiv \begin{cases} \bar{x} \text{ if } \bar{x} \succsim_1 \bar{y} \\ \bar{y} \text{ if } \bar{y} \succ_1 \bar{x} \end{cases},$$

$$\underline{u} \equiv u(\underline{z}), \qquad \bar{u} \equiv u(\bar{z}), \qquad \text{so } \underline{u} \leqq \bar{u}.$$

Assume first that $U({}_1x) > U({}_1y)$, and write

$$U({}_1x) - U({}_1y) \equiv 3\Delta > 0.$$

For comparison purposes we consider two programs

$${}_1x^{(T)} = ({}_1x_T, {}_{\text{con}}\underline{z}), \qquad {}_1y^{(T)} = ({}_1y_T, {}_{\text{con}}\bar{z}),$$

where T is chosen large enough to have

$$\left(\sum_{t=T+1}^{\infty} \alpha^{t-1}\right)(\bar{u} - \underline{u}) = \alpha^T \cdot \frac{\bar{u} - \underline{u}}{1 - \alpha} \leqq \Delta.$$

Because of $\underline{u} \leqq u(x_t) \leqq \bar{u}$ and similar inequalities for y_t we then have

$$U({}_1x) - U({}_1x^{(T)}) = \sum_{t=T+1}^{\infty} \alpha^{t-1}(u(x_t) - \underline{u}) \leqq \Delta, \qquad U({}_1y^{(T)}) - U({}_1y) \leqq \Delta,$$

and therefore

$$U({}_1x^{(T)}) - U({}_1y^{(T)}) \geqq \Delta > 0.$$

Since ${}_1x^{(T)}$, ${}_1y^{(T)}$ are ultimately constant, this implies ${}_1x^{(T)} \succ {}_1y^{(T)}$ by Result F. But then, using P5, ${}_1x \succsim {}_1x^{(T)} \succ {}_1y^{(T)} \succsim {}_1y$, which yields

(5.3) $$U({}_1x) > U({}_1y) \text{ implies } {}_1x \succ {}_1y,$$

confirming the representation (5.1) in this case.

Assume next that, for two programs ${}_1x$, ${}_1y$ bounded in utility,

(5.4) $$U({}_1x) = U({}_1y) \text{ but } {}_1x \prec {}_1y.$$

Then there exists t_0 such that

(5.5) $$x_{t_0} \prec_1 y_{t_0}, \text{ so } u(x_{t_0}) < u(y_{t_0}),$$

because "$x_t \succsim_1 y_t$ for all t" would contradict "${}_1x \prec {}_1y$" by P5.

Using the connectedness of $\mathscr{X}$, we draw an arc $\mathscr{A}$ in $\mathscr{X}$ connecting x_{t_0} and y_{t_0} (see Fig. 1). Then, by the continuity of $u(x)$, we can find a point x on $\mathscr{A}$ such that

(5.6) $$u(x) = u(x_{t_0})$$

while, for each $\delta > 0$, there exists x' on $\mathscr{A}$ such that

(5.7a) $$d(x, x') \leqq \delta,$$

(5.7b) $$u(x') > u(x).$$

Using P_1 we can choose δ such that, if (5.7a) holds,

$$_1x \prec {_1x'} \equiv ({_1x_{t_0-1}}, x', {_{t_0+1}x}) \prec {_1y}.$$

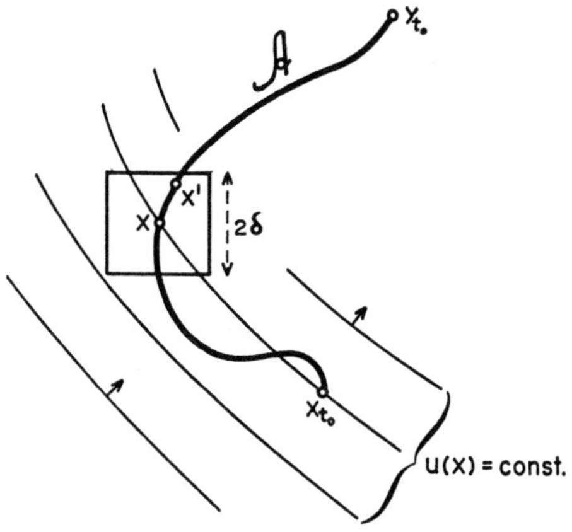

Fig. 1

But then, by (5.7b) and (5.1),

$$U({_1x'}) > U({_1x}) = U({_1y}) \text{ but } {_1x'} \prec {_1y},$$

a contradiction of (5.3). Hence (5.4) is false, and

$$U({_1x}) = U({_1y}) \text{ implies } {_1x} \sim {_1y},$$

confirming (5.1) in this case as well. Since the third case, $U({_1x}) < U({_1y})$, is symmetric to the first, the proof is now complete.

6. Concluding Remarks on the Representation of $\gtrsim$

The representations we have found show unexpectedly strong implications of the postulates used. It turns out that offsetting program changes in future periods can be determined on the basis of just two mathematical data,

(i) the function $u(x)$ which allows the comparison of "utility differences" within the same period, and

(ii) a constant discount factor α which extends that comparison to utility differences in different periods.

The representation may be called cardinal in the sense that only increasing linear transformations, applied simultaneously to $u(x)$ and to $U({}_1x)$, will preserve these simple properties.

Since $\alpha < 1$ the present postulates do not permit expression of the ethical principle of treating all future generations' utilities on a par with present utilities. A way has been found to include that limiting case in models of optimal growth by retreating to the notion of a partial ordering. VON WEIZSÄCKER (1965) has proposed to call a program ${}_1x$ better than a program ${}_1y$ if there exists a $T \geqq 1$ such that

$$\sum_{t=1}^{T'} u(x_t) > \sum_{t=1}^{T'} u(y_t) \text{ for all } T' \geqq T.$$

This criterion has been called the *overtaking criterion* by GALE (1967). Under appropriate conditions, it has permitted determination of an optimal path which turns out to be comparable with, and better than, every other feasible path (KOOPMANS (1965, 1967a)).

Returning to the case of a complete ordering, with a discount factor $\alpha < 1$, it is conceivable that the representation (5.1) can be extended on the basis of the present postulates to larger sets of programs not all bounded in utility. In Subsection 6* we allude to a reasoning from a strengthened monotonicity postulate that permits an extension to all programs for which the sum (5.1) exists.

It will be clear that, if $u(x)$ is unbounded on $\mathscr{X}$, then there exist programs for which the sum (5.1) diverges. In such cases the representation (3.2) restricted to a class of ultimately identical programs, all "divergent in utility," may still be valuable. It would permit formulating a partial optimality criterion in which a path is found to stand comparison with all other feasible paths differing from it in a finite number of future periods only. Other considerations would then have to be brought to bear on the choice of the class of ultimately identical programs.

6*. *An Alternative Monotonicity Postulate.* One might wish to strengthen P5 to

POSTULATE 5″ (Strong Monotonicity). *If* ${}_1x$, ${}_1y^{(i)}$, $i = 1, 2, \ldots$, *are programs such that*

$$\left.\begin{aligned} &{}_1y^{(i)} \precsim {}_1y^{(i+1)}, \\ &{}_1y^{(i)}_{t_i} = {}_1x_{t_i}, \quad 0 \leqq t_i < t_{i+1}, \end{aligned}\right\} \text{ for all } i = 1, 2, \ldots,$$

then, ${}_1y \precsim {}_1x$.

This postulate considers successive improvements each extending over an arbitrary number of periods, but where the set of periods affected by successive improvements becomes more and more remote in time. It allows one, for any program ${}_1x$ for which the sum (5.1) exists, to construct an equivalent constant program ${}_{\text{con}}x$ such that $U({}_1x) = U({}_{\text{con}}x)$, thus extending the representation (5.1) to all programs for which that sum exists. Conversely, for any program ${}_1x$ equivalent to a constant program, the sum (5.1) does exist.

7. Limited Independence, Time Perspective and Impatience

If instead of complete independence (P3) we postulate only limited independence (P3′), Proposition 2 is not available, and we must fall back on Result A. A study along these lines was made in two consecutive papers by KOOPMANS (1960) and by KOOPMANS, DIAMOND and WILLIAMSON (1964). The postulates of that study were the analogues of the present postulates of continuity (P1), sensitivity (P2), limited independence (P3′), stationarity (P4), and the existence of extreme programs (P5′), applied to a given utility function $U({}_1x)$ rather than to an ordering.[8]

A theorem by DIAMOND (1965, p. 173) now allows us to obtain all the results of the previous study from the present postulates P1′ (see Footnote 8), P2, P3′, P4, P5′ as applied to an ordering $\succsim$ on ${}_1\mathscr{X}$. The resulting representation $U({}_1x)$ of $\succsim$ is found to satisfy a *recursive relation*

$$U({}_1x) = V(u(x_1), U({}_2x)), \tag{7.1}$$

where $V(u, U)$ is a continuous function defined on the product of two nondegenerate intervals, which is increasing in each of its variables. This *aggregator function* indicates how the single-period utility $u(x_1)$ of the first installment x_1 of ${}_1x$ and the utility $U({}_2x)$ of the sequel ${}_2x$ (were that sequel to start immediately) are combined to form the utility of the entire program ${}_1x$. In particular, if P3 holds, $V(u, U) = u + \alpha U$.

The representation (7.1) is *ordinal* in the sense that any pair of continuous increasing functions Φ, φ with the appropriate domains will define an

[8] Apart from this difference, P1 was strengthened to make P1′, say, by adding two statements: (a) that the continuity on ${}_1\mathscr{X}$ of $U({}_1x)$ is uniform on each equivalence set, (b) that $\mathscr{X}$ is bounded and convex. The latter was used in the proof that the range $\mathscr{U}$ of $U({}_1x)$ is an interval. Alternatively, that result could have been obtained by adding to P5′ that among the extreme programs there are a best and worst constant program, or by deriving that statement in turn from a variant of P5 restricted to $\sim$.

alternative representation

$$(7.2)\qquad U^*({}_1x) \equiv \Phi(U({}_1x)) = \Phi(V(u(x_1), U({}_2x)) = V^*(u^*(x_1), U^*({}_2x)),$$

say, where

$$(7.3)\qquad u^*(x) \equiv \varphi(u(x)), \quad V^*(u^*, U^*) \equiv \Phi(V(\varphi^{-1}(u^*), \Phi^{-1}(U^*))).$$

This being so, the question arises what takes the place of the discount factor α, the existence of which was derived in Section 3 from P3. In particular, what corresponds to the inequality $\alpha<1$ crucial to convergence of the representation (5.1)?

It is readily seen from (7.2) and (7.3) (KOOPMANS (1960, Section 14*)) that, in the case of a differentiable function $V(u, U)$, the discount factor associated with a constant program ${}_{\text{con}}x = (x, x, x, \ldots)$,

$$(7.4)\qquad \alpha(x) \equiv \left(\frac{\partial V(u, U)}{\partial U}\right)_{u=u(x),\; U=U({}_{\text{con}}x)}$$

satisfies $0 \leqq \alpha(x) \leqq 1$, and is invariant under differentiable increasing scale changes for u and U. Moreover, as distinct from the representation (5.1), $\alpha(x)$ in (7.4) can vary with x. The limited independence postulate P3′ therefore allows scope for the idea already expressed by Irving FISHER (1930, Chapter IV, Sections 3 and 6) with regard to individual preferences: that the discount factor may depend on the level of present and prospective income.

As an illustration, let $\mathscr{X}$ be the closed unit interval $\mathscr{I} = (0, 1)$, let $u(x) = x$, and consider the aggregator function

$$(7.5)\qquad V(x, U) = U + (x - U)(a - bx + cU),$$

where we require that

$$(7.6)\qquad b,\ c,\ a-2b,\ a-b-c,\ 1-a-2c > 0.$$

Then, if we assign to U the same range $\mathscr{I}$, $V(x, U)$ is increasing in both variables, and

$$(7.7)\qquad V(0, 0) = 0, \qquad V(1, 1) = 1.$$

Finally, since $U({}_{\text{con}}x) = x$ is the only root U of $U = V(x, U)$ in the range $\mathscr{I}$,

$$(7.8)\qquad \alpha(x) = 1 - a + (b - c)x.$$

Hence the direction of change of $\alpha(x)$ with increasing income x is given by the sign of $(b-c)$. Following FISHER (1930, Chapter IV, Section 6), many but not all economists I have consulted regard an increasing $\alpha(x)$ as the normal case. This implies that the ratio of the marginal utility of future consumption to that of present consumption increases as the level of the constant consumption flow ${}_{\text{con}}x$ is raised. Examples where the sign of $\mathrm{d}\alpha(x)/\mathrm{d}x$ depends on x can also be constructed.

While $\alpha(x)$ is defined only for constant programs, there is a generalization[9] of the convergence condition $\alpha<1$ in (5.1) to the present case that applies in the entire range of $V(u, U)$. It is found that there exists a transformation function Φ (here one takes $\varphi(u)=u$) such that the function $V^*(u, U^*)$ in (7.3) satisfies (dropping asterisks)

$$V(u, U')-V(u, U) \leqq U'-U \text{ whenever } U'>U. \tag{7.9}$$

This inequality has been called the (*weak*) *time perspective* property of the utility scale resulting from the transformation Φ. It says that the utility difference between two programs, measured in a suitable scale, does not increase (and generally diminishes) if both programs are postponed by one or more periods, while the same consumption or the same sequence of consumptions is inserted in the gaps so created. This inequality between utility differences is satisfied by a class of scales linked by transformations that include nonlinear as well as all linear transformations. For this reason, a representation $U({}_1x)$ satisfying (7.1) where $V(u, U)$ has the property (7.9) has been called *quasi-cardinal.*

There are indications that the weak inequality sign ($\leqq$) in (7.9) can be strengthened to strict inequality ($<$), referred to as *strong time perspective,* without strengthening the postulates. If so, it follows that the function $U({}_1x)$ can be reconstructed from a pair of functions $u(x)$, $V(u, U)$ implied in it. The example (7.5), (7.6) has the strong time perspective property as it stands, without requiring a prior scale change.

Precisely because it compares utility differences between pairs of programs, the time perspective inequality, strong or weak, does not by itself predict the choice within any one pair of programs. However, by elementary steps of reasoning, (7.9) implies a second family of ordinal inequalities, of which the simplest representative is

$$\begin{cases} \text{if} \quad u=u(x)<u'=u(x'), \quad U({}_{\text{con}}x) \leqq U \leqq U({}_{\text{con}}x'), \\ \text{then } V(u', V(u, U)) \underset{(=)}{>} V(u, V(u', U)). \end{cases} \tag{7.10}$$

[9] This generalization has been derived from statement (*a*) in Footnote 8. The proof uses a variant of the theory of Haar measure.

This inequality, weak or strong depending on whether the inequality (7.9) is weak or strong, has been called an *impatience* inequality. It indicates that if the single-period utility of a vector x' exceeds that of a vector x, then any program $(x', x, {}_3x)$, in which ${}_3x$ is selected from a wide class of "continuations," is preferred (or equivalent) to the corresponding program $(x, x', {}_3x)$ in which the better item is moved from first to second place. The class of continuations ${}_3x$ permitted in (7.10) consists of all those which, if started immediately, would be ranked between ${}_{\text{con}}x$ and ${}_{\text{con}}x'$. This condition should be read in conjunction with Result E of Section 4, which holds also under the present assumptions.

The impatience inequality holds for a wider range of U-values than that indicated in (7.10), and can be generalized to the interchange of two disjoint segments ${}_tx_{t'}$, ${}_sx_{s'}$ of a program, that need not be of equal length or contiguous in time.

8. Nonstationary Orderings and Eventual Impatience

Diamond (1965) has studied the implications of postulates similar to those of this chapter, with the main difference that no explicit stationarity postulate corresponding to our P4 is present. However, a certain comparability over time is introduced by assuming, in one interpretation, that there is only a single consumption good ($\mathscr{X}$ is the closed unit interval $\mathscr{C}$), more of which is always better. In another interpretation leading to the same mathematical analysis, there is a given single-period utility function $u(x)$ mapping $\mathscr{X}$ onto $\mathscr{C}$, which is the same for all t. For simplicity, we shall adopt the notation of an ordering $\succsim$ of all programs ${}_1x$ on the denumerable product space $\mathscr{C} \times \mathscr{C} \times \ldots = {}_1\mathscr{C}$, say, that corresponds to the first interpretation. The nonstationarity then applies to the way in which the sequences ${}_1x$ of scalars x_t enter into $\succsim$.

Diamond's postulates then can be shown[10] to be equivalent to specializations, to the case $\mathscr{X} = \mathscr{C}$, of our P1, P3, supplemented by a postulate P6 implying similar specializations of P2, P5, P5'.

Postulate 6 (General Monotonicity.) *If* $x_t \geqq y_t$ *for all* t, $x_t > y_t$ *for some* t, *then* ${}_1x \succ {}_1y$.

From these assumptions he derives the following property of *eventual impatience*: For any given program ${}_1x$ and any number $\varepsilon > 0$, there exists

[10] Using the results of Gorman (1968b) referred to in Footnote 10 of Chapter 3.

a T such that

(8.1) $\quad {}_1x \succ (x_t, {}_2x_{t-1}, x_1, {}_{t+1}x)$ for all $t \geqq T$ with $x_1 \geqq x_t + \varepsilon$.

In words, the interchange with x_1 of any x_t which occurs sufficiently far into the future, and which falls short of x_1 by at least ε, diminishes the utility of the program ${}_1x$. This subtle result, which at first sight appears to miss its aim by a hair's breadth, is both vindicated and complemented by another theorem, attributed to Yaari, which hits the mark exactly (see DIAMOND (1965, p. 176)). It states that P6 and the present specialization of P1 taken together are incompatible with the statement

$$\text{for all } t \text{ and all } {}_1x \text{ in } {}_1\mathscr{X},\ {}_1x \sim (x_t, {}_2x_{t-1}, x_1, {}_{t+1}x),$$

that expresses "equal treatment of all generations."

Similar but somewhat stronger conclusions are obtained by Diamond by changing the distance function underlying P1 to

$$D^*({}_1x, {}_1y) = \sum_{t=1}^{\infty} (\tfrac{1}{2})^t d(x_t, y_t).$$

The results are stronger presumably because this modification explicitly reduces the weight attached, in the definition of continuity, to given consumption differences in a more distant future.

9. Concluding Remarks

The main results of the studies reported in this chapter appear to be two-fold.

In the first place the studies show a sequence of instances of increasing generality, in which a complete and continuous preference ordering of consumption programs for an infinite future necessarily gives a decreasing, or eventually decreasing, weight to consumption in a more distant future. Somewhat fancifully, one may say that the real numbers appear to be a sufficiently rich set of labels to accommodate in a continuous manner all infinite sequences of consumption vectors *only* if one gradually or eventually decreases the weight given to the more distant vectors in the preference ordering to be represented.

Secondly, the studies containing the stationarity postulate P4 have produced interesting special forms for the utility function $U({}_1x)$ in terms of simpler functions $u(x)$ and possibly $V(u, U)$, that facilitate the use of $U({}_1x)$ in models of optimal economic growth, and may perhaps suggest further parametrization or other specialization for econometric studies of individual consumption plans over time.

The use of substantive terms such as "consumption," "preference," "time" in what is essentially a formal mathematical analysis may hinder the perception of other possible applications in which one or more of these terms are inappropriate. The stationarity postulate, however, strongly suggests temporal or other consecutiveness in the vectors x_t, $t = 1,2, \ldots$, as a condition for meaningful application. In DIAMOND's (1965) study, where stationarity in the aggregation of single-period utilities is dropped, consecutiveness is immaterial in spite of appearances to the contrary in the formulation of some of the postulates. What is interpreted as eventual impatience if t stands for time is therefore also open to the wider interpretation that in *any* permutation of the vectors in the infinite sequence x_t, $t = 1,2, \ldots$, the weight given to vectors further up in the sequence must eventually decrease.

References [papers 4 and 5]

ARROW, K. J. (1952), "The Determination of Many-Commodity Preferences Scales by Two-Commodity Comparisons," *Metroeconomica*, *4*, 105–115.

ARROW, K. J. (1963), *Social Choice and Individual Values*, (2nd ed.), Wiley, New York.

AUMANN, R. (1964a), "Subjective Programming," Chapter 12 in SHELLY and BRYAN (eds.), *Human Judgments and Optimality*, Wiley, New York, pp. 217–242.

BLASCHKE, W. and G. BOL (1938), *Geometrie der Gewebe*, Springer, Berlin.

DEBREU, G. (1954), "Representation of a Preference Ordering by a Numerical Function," Chapter 11 in THRALL, COOMBS, and DAVIS (eds.), *Decision Processes*, Wiley, New York, pp. 159–165.

DEBREU, G. (1959), *Theory of Value*, Wiley, New York.

DEBREU, G. (1960), "Topological Methods in Cardinal Utility Theory," Chapter 2 in K. J. ARROW, S. KARLIN, and P. SUPPES (eds.), *Mathematical Methods in the Social Sciences*, Stanford University Press, Stanford, pp. 16-26.

DEBREU, G. (1964), "Continuity Properties of Paretian Utility," *International Economic Review*, *5*, 285–293.

DIAMOND, P. A. (1965), "The Evaluation of Infinite Utility Streams," *Econometrica*, *33*, 170–177.

EILENBERG, S. (1941), "Ordered Topological Spaces," *American Journal of Mathematics*, *63*, 39–45.

FISHER, I. (1930, original edition), *The Theory of Interest*, reprinted by Augustus Kelley, New York, 1961.

GALE, D. (1967), "On Optimal Development in a Multi-Sector Economy," *Review of Economic Studies*, *34*, 1–18.

GALE, D. (1968), "A Mathematical Theory of Optimal Economic Development," *Bulletin of the American Mathematical Society*, *74*, 207–223.

Goldman, S. M. and H. Uzawa (1964), "A Note on Separability in Demand Analysis," *Econometrica, 32*, 387–398.

Gorman, W. M. (1959a), "Separable Utility and Aggregation," *Econometrica, 27*, 469–481.

Gorman, W. M. (1959b), "The Empirical Implications of a Utility Tree: A Further Comment," *Econometrica, 27*, 489.

Gorman, W. M. (1965), "Conditions for Additive Preferences," (unpublished),

Gorman, W. M. (1968a), "Conditions for Additive Separability," *Econometrica, 36*, 605–609.

Gorman, W. M. (1968b), "The Structure of Utility Functions," *Review of Economic Studies, 35*, 367-390.

Koopmans, T. C. (1960), "Stationary Ordinal Utility and Impatience," *Econometrica, 28*, 287–309.

Koopmans, T. C. (1964), "On Flexibility of Future Preference," Chapter 13 in Shelly and Bryan (eds.), *Human Judgments and Optimality*, Wiley, New York, pp. 243–254.

Koopmans, T. C., P. A. Diamond, and R. E. Williamson (1964b), "Stationary Utility and Time Perspective," *Econometrica, 32*, 82–100.

Koopmans, T. C. (1965), "On the Concept of Optimal Economic Growth," in *The Econometric Approach to Development Planning*, North Holland, Amsterdam, and Rand McNally, Chicago, (a reissue of *Pontificiae Academiae Scientiarvm Scripta Varia*, Vol. XXVIII, 1965), pp. 225–300.

Koopmans, T. C. (1966), "Structure of Preference over Time," Cowles Foundation Discussion Paper No. 206.

Koopmans, T. C. (1967a), "Objectives, Constraints and Outcomes in Optimal Growth Models," *Econometrica, 35*, 1–15.

Koopmans, T. C. (1967b), "Intertemporal Distribution and 'Optimal' Aggregate Economic Growth," Chapter 5 in Fellner *et al.*, *Ten Economic Studies in the Tradition of Irving Fisher*, Wiley, New York, pp. 95–126.

Koopmans, T. C., P. A. Diamond, and R. E. Williamson (1964), "Stationary Utility and Time Perspective, "*Econometrica, 32*, 82-100.

Lancaster, K. J. (1966a), "A New Approach to Consumer Theory," *Journal of Political Economy, 74*, 132–157.

Lancaster, K. J. (1966b), "Change and Innovation in the Technology of Consumption," *American Economic Review, 56*, 14–23.

Leontief, W. (1947a), "Introduction to a Theory of the Internal Structure of Functional Relationships," *Econometrica, 15*, 361–373.

Leontief, W. (1947b), "A Note on the Interrelation of Subsets of Independent Variables of a Continuous Function with Continuous First Derivatives," *Bulletin of the American Mathematical Society, 53*, 343–350.

Rader, T. (1963), "The Existence of a Utility Function to Represent Preferences," *Review of Economic Studies, 30*, 229–232.

Samuelson, P. A. (1947), "Some Special Aspects of the Theory of Consumer's Behavior," Chapter 7 in *Foundations of Economic Analysis*, Harvard University Press, Cambridge, pp. 172–202.

Strotz, R. H. (1956), "Myopia and Inconsistency in Dynamic Utility Maximization," *Review of Economic Studies, 23*, 165–180.

STROTZ, R. H. (1957), "The Empirical Implications of a Utility Tree," *Econometrica, 25,* 269–280.

STROTZ, R. H. (1959), "The Utility Tree–A Correction and Further Appraisal," *Econometrica, 27,* 482–488.

VON WEIZSÄCKER, C. C. (1965), "Existence of Optimal Programmes of Accumulation for an Infinite Time Horizon," *Review of Economic Studies, 32,* 85–104.

WOLD, H. (1943), "A Synthesis of Pure Demand Analysis, Part II," *Skandinavisk* Aktuaritidskrift, pp. 220–263.

YAARI, M. E. (1964), "On the Consumer's Lifetime Allocation Process," *International Economic Review, 5,* 304–317.

6

On the Definition and Computation of a Capital Stock Invariant under Optimization*

Terje Hansen and Tjalling C. Koopmans*

Journal of Economic Theory 5, no. 3 (1972), pp. 487–523

1. Introduction

The objective function (maximand) most often adopted in the literature on optimal economic growth is a discounted sum of future utility flows, of the form

$$\sum_{t=1}^{\infty} \alpha^{t-1} u(y_t), \qquad 0 < \alpha < 1, \tag{1.1}$$

if we assume a discrete time variable t. Here $u(y)$ is a concave "single-period-utility" function of a consumption flow y (scalar or vector), y_t is the flow in period t, and α a discount factor applied to utility flows. This function is then maximized subject to a specified initial capital stock z_1 and a given technology and resource base. If assumed constant over time, technological constraints may be expressed by

$$(z_t, y_t, w_t, z_{t+1}) \in \mathscr{T} \qquad \text{for all } t,$$

where w_t is a scalar or vector resource input in period t, and the choice of $\mathscr{T}$ as a closed convex cone expresses the assumption of constant returns

* Research carried out under Grants from the Ford Foundation and from the National Science Foundation.

to scale. Constant resource constraints may be expressed by the inequalities[1]

$$0 \leqq w_t \leqq w \qquad \text{for all } t.$$

In this paper we are not concerned with finding the optimal growth path corresponding to any initial capital stock that is given *a priori.* We limit ourselves to the search for a capital stock $\hat{z}$ that is *invariant* under the optimization described. That is, we seek a value $z_1 = \hat{z}$ for the initial stock that gives rise to an optimal program $(\hat{y}_t, \hat{z}_t)$ such that $\hat{y}_t = \hat{y}$, $\hat{z}_t = \hat{z}$ for all t.

The simple case in which y_t, z_t are scalar and

$$\mathscr{T} = \{(z_t, y_t, z_{t+1}) \geqq 0 \mid y_t + z_{t+1} \leqq f(z_t)\}$$

has been extensively explored in the literature. (Here scarcity of the single resource, labor say, is expressed indirectly by the strict concavity of the increasing production function f with $f(0) = 0$.) In this case (e.g., see [8], where continuous time is used) $(\hat{y}, \hat{z})$ exists (with $\hat{z} > 0$, provided $f'(0) > \alpha^{-1} > \lim_{z\to\infty} f'(z)$) and is unique, and also represents the limit

$$\lim_{t\to\infty} (\hat{y}_t, \hat{z}_t) \tag{1.2}$$

for the unique optimal path that starts from any other positive initial capital stock z_1.

Sutherland [19, 20] has studied the more general case where y_t, z_t are vectors. He uses a single-period utility function $u^*(z_t, z_{t+1})$ that can be related to our $u(y_t)$ by

$$u^*(z_t, z_{t+1}) = \sup_{\substack{0 \leqq w_t \leqq w \\ (z_t, y_t, w_t, z_{t+1}) \in \mathscr{T}}} u(y_t).$$

He finds that the problem of finding an invariant optimal capital stock is equivalent to a fixed-point problem, and uses Kakutani's fixed-point theorem to prove the existence of a solution. The solution is no longer necessarily unique, even if $u^*(z_t, z_{t+1})$ is strictly concave.

Sutherland also concludes to the near-equivalence of the problem of finding an invariant optimal capital stock to a single-period problem to be described below. The present paper proves and utilizes that equivalence for an experiment in computing such a stock, or rather an approximately invariant stock. Both the equivalence proof and the computation are

[1] $a \geqq b$ for vectors a, b, denotes $a_i \geqq b_i$ for all i; $a \geq b$ denotes $a \geqq b$ and $a \neq b$; $a > b$ denotes $a_i > b_i$ for all i.

carried through in terms of a specific model developed, in ignorance of Sutherland's work, by the second author (see [9]). This model uses a von Neumann type technology of capital transformation, in which resources and consumption goods have been incorporated. The method of computation we use is a member of the class of algorithms for computing an approximately fixed point of a continuous mapping, recently developed by Scarf [14, 15, 16, 17, 18] and Hansen [4, 5], (see also Kuhn [11, 12] and Eaves [1]). The present method was developed and applied by the first author. The equivalence proof was formulated by the second author.

We shall not be concerned here with the straightforward extension of the problem to equal exponential rates of exogenous growth applicable to all resources and to the consuming population.

Sections 4 and 7 are devoted to proofs and other technical observations, and can be skipped without affecting the reading of later sections.

2. The Model

2.1. *Technology and Resource Constraints*

In line with our emphasis on computability, we consider a von Neumann type technology with L capital goods, M resources other than capital goods, K consumption goods, and I productive processes that are constant over time, and each of which is defined by a unit activity.

The following constraints connect the capital input vector $z_t \equiv (z_{t1}, z_{t2}, \ldots, z_{tL})$ of the t-th period, the capital output vector z_{t+1} for that period, the resource availability vector $w \equiv (w_1, \ldots, w_M)$ which is assumed the same for all periods, and the consumption vector $y_t \equiv (y_{t1}, \ldots, y_{tK})$ for the t-th period, with the vector of activity levels $x_t \equiv (x_{t1}, \ldots, x_{tI})$ assigned to each process, $i = 1, \ldots, I$, for that period. All these vectors are nonnegative column[2] vectors.

$$\text{(capital input)} \qquad -Ax_t \geqq -z_t, \qquad \text{(2.1A)}$$

$$\text{(capital output)} \qquad Bx_t \geqq z_{t+1}, \qquad \text{(2.1B)}$$

$$\text{(resources)} \qquad -Cx_t \geqq -w, \qquad \text{(2.1C)}$$

$$\text{(consumption)} \qquad Dx_t \geqq y_t, \qquad \text{(2.1D)}$$

$$t = 1, 2, \ldots .$$

[2] The notation (,...,) for a vector will be used without making a distinction between column and row vectors. The same notation will be used for the adjoining of column vectors, or of row vectors, into a single vector. The symbol $\equiv$ denotes equality by definition.

The constant coefficients of inputs and outputs of the various commodities that characterize the various processes have been assembled in matrices A, B, C, D of orders (L, I), (L, I), (M, I), (K, I), respectively, and are required to satisfy the following sign rules:

$$a_{li}, b_{li}, c_{mi}, d_{ki} \geqq 0 \qquad \text{for all } l, m, k, i, \tag{2.2}$$

$$\sum_i a_{li}, \sum_i b_{li}, \sum_i c_{mi}, \sum_i d_{ki} > 0 \qquad \text{for all } l, m, k, \tag{2.3, row}$$

$$\sum_l a_{li}, \sum_m c_{mi}, \sum_l b_{li} + \sum_k d_{ki} > 0 \qquad \text{for all } i. \tag{2.3, col}$$

The constraint in (2.3, row) says that each capital good and each resource is an input to at least one process, and each capital good and each consumption good is an output of at least one process. The column constraint says that each process requires the input of at least one capital good and at least one resource, and produces at least one good, capital or consumption.

A capital stock $z \geqq 0$ is called *reproducible* if the conditions (2.1A, B, C) for $t = 1$ permit $z_1 = z_2 = z$. Clearly, the null stock $z = 0$ is reproducible. To assure the existence of a positive reproducible capital stock, we impose on the technology the *viability condition*

$$Bx > Ax > 0 \qquad \text{for some} \quad x \geq 0. \tag{2.4}$$

We write $>$ rather than $\geqq$ in the first inequality in order that some positive reproducible capital stock shall have some capacity to spare for the production of consumption goods, and, if desired, for further expansion of the capital stock itself.

For sufficiently small activity levels, this interpretation of the viability condition is independent of the resource constraints (2.1C), because we require that the resource availability vector w be positive,

$$w_m > 0 \qquad \text{for all } m. \tag{2.5}$$

Therefore, the set of vectors $x = (x_{\cdot 1}, x_{\cdot 2}, \ldots, x_{\cdot I}) \geqq 0$ satisfying just (2.1C) contains a "chip" of the form

$$\mathscr{C}(\epsilon) = \left\{x \mid x \geqq 0, \sum_{i=1}^{I} x_{\cdot i} \leqq \epsilon\right\}, \qquad \epsilon > 0, \tag{2.6}$$

within which points satisfying the linear homogeneous condition (2.4) can also be found.

Depreciation of capital can be represented, as in the original presentation by von Neumann [22], by treating capital goods in different states of wear as different capital goods. In that interpretation, the statement that a process "produces" a capital good also applies to somewhat worn capital goods provided we interpret "produces" as meaning "releases from use."

A *z-feasible path*, $z \geqq 0$, is now defined as a sequence $\{(x_t, y_t, z_t), t = 1, 2, \cdots\}$ satisfying (2.1) for all t and such that $z_1 = z$. The sign restrictions (2.2), (2.3) on the elements of C and (2.5) on those of w then imply boundedness of the set of all z-feasible paths,

$$0 \leqq x_t \leqq \bar{x}, \quad 0 \leqq y_t \leqq D\bar{x} \equiv \bar{y}, \quad 0 \leqq z_t \leqq B\bar{x} \equiv \bar{z}, \quad t = 1, 2, \ldots, \quad \text{for some } \bar{x} > 0. \tag{2.7}$$

Here we have imposed on the initial capital stock $z = z_1$ the same constraint, $0 \leqq z_1 \leqq \bar{z}$, found to apply to all z_t with $t > 1$, thus making the bounds (2.7) uniform for all z_t considered. Since the null-path, $x_t = y_t = 0$, $t = 1, 2, \ldots$, $z_t = 0$, $t = 2, \ldots$, satisfies (2.1) for any $z_1 \geqq 0$, the set of z-feasible paths is also nonempty for any $z \geqq 0$.

2.2. *The Objective Function*

We adopt an objective function of the form[3] (1.1). We require that the single-period utility function $u(y)$, where $y \equiv (y_{\cdot 1}, y_{\cdot 2}, \ldots, y_{\cdot K})$ is a consumption flow (column) vector, is defined for all $y \geqq 0$, is concave, and is continuously differentiable and increasing with regard to each component $y_{\cdot j}$ of y. We shall avoid a specification, often made in optimal growth models, that instead of assuming differentiability in the origin $y = 0$ requires that $\partial u/\partial y_{\cdot k} \to \infty$ for all k as $y \to 0$, and permits $u(y) \to -\infty$ as well. We shall argue at the end of Section 3 that the simplification bought by avoiding that specification causes little loss of generality in the present context.

The assumption that $u(y)$ is increasing in each $y_{\cdot k}$ implies global non-saturation with regard to all consumption goods. Therefore, no disposal of any consumption good ever takes place in an optimal path, and we can eliminate y by defining a utility function in terms of the activity vector x,

$$v(x) \equiv u(Dx), \qquad x \geqq 0. \tag{2.8}$$

Then $v(x)$ is again concave, and $v_i'(x) \equiv \partial v/\partial x_{\cdot i} \geqq 0$ for all i and all $x \geqq 0$. The row vector of these derivatives will be denoted $v'(x) \equiv (v_1'(x), \ldots, v_I'(x))$.

[3] For a discussion deriving this form from postulates about a preference ordering on the space of consumption programs $(y_1, y_2, \ldots)$ see Koopmans [10].

2.3. *Invariant Capital Stock*

We now formally state two problems, to be denoted $P_\infty(z, \alpha)$ and $P_\infty(\alpha)$, which in combination define the topic of this paper.

$P_\infty(z, \alpha)$: *Given a reproducible initial capital stock* z *and a discount factor* α *with* $0 < \alpha < 1$, *maximize* $\sum_{t=1}^{\infty} \alpha^{t-1} v(x_t)$ *on the set of* z*-feasible paths*

A path $(\hat{x}_t, \hat{z}_t)$ that solves this problem is called *z-optimal.*

$P_\infty(\alpha)$: *Choose a value* $z = \hat{z}$ *of the initial capital stock in* $P_\infty(z, \alpha)$ *such that there exists a constant path* $(x_t, z_t) = (\hat{x}, \hat{z})$, $t = 1, 2,...,$ *that solves* $P_\infty(\hat{z}, \alpha)$.

A solution $\hat{z}$ of $P_\infty(\alpha)$ is then what we have already called an *invariant optimal capital stock*. By definition, such a capital stock must be reproducible. We shall use the expression "solution of $P_\infty(\alpha)$" also for the pair $(\hat{x}, \hat{z})$.

Obviously, $P_\infty(\alpha)$ has for all α one trivial and uninteresting solution, namely, $\hat{z} = 0$, $\hat{x} = 0$, the *null solution.*

3. An Equivalent One-Period Problem

In Section 4 we shall prove the near-equivalence between the problem of finding an invariant capital stock $\hat{z}$ with an associated activity vector $\hat{x}$, and a one-period problem now to be defined, likewise in two steps. The first step is to define the problem

$P(z)$: *Given some reproducible* z, *maximize* $v(x)$ *subject to*

$$-Ax \geqq -z, \qquad q_1 \qquad (3.1\text{A})$$

$$Bx \geqq z, \qquad q_2 \qquad (3.1\text{B})$$

$$-Cx \geqq -w, \qquad r \qquad (3.1\text{C})$$

$$x \geqq 0. \qquad (3.1\text{D})$$

This problem arbitrarily prescribes a reproducible beginning-of-period capital stock z, and imposes the stationarity requirement that the same capital stock be reproduced at the end of the single period under consideration.

By our assumptions the constraint set (3.1) is nonempty, closed, and bounded; the maximand is continuous. Hence, for every reproducible z there exists a solution $\hat{x} = \hat{x}(z)$ of $P(z)$. Since $v(x)$ is concave, by the

Kuhn–Tucker theorem [13, Section 3] any feasible vector $\hat{x}$ is a solution if and only if it has associated with it vectors q_1, q_2, r of dual variables corresponding to the constraints (3.1A, B, C), respectively, that satisfy the conditions

$$(q_1, q_2, r) \geq 0, \tag{3.2a}$$

$$v'(\hat{x}) - q_1 A + q_2 B - rC \leqq 0, \tag{3.2b}$$

$$v'(\hat{x})\hat{x} - q_1 z + q_2 z - rw = 0. \tag{3.2c}$$

The components of q_1, q_2, r can be interpreted as shadow prices, expressed in terms of "marginal utility productivity," of the initial and terminal capital goods and of the resource flows, respectively. Since the timing of availability of these goods differs as between inputs and outputs it should be clarified that these valuations are all defined as "present values" as of the same "present" point in time, say, the beginning of the period. Then (3.2b) says that the marginal shadow profits, associated with small increases in the level of each activity when starting from $x = \hat{x}$, are all nonpositive. The scalar condition (3.2c), taken together with (3.2a), (3.2b) and (3.1), then says in a concise implicit way that (i) marginal profits of all processes in use at $\hat{x}$ (i.e., with $\hat{x}_{.i} > 0$) are zero, and (ii) there is at $\hat{x}$ no disposal of any capital good or resource that has a positive shadow price (see also [21]). If in addition the q_1, q_2, r are uniquely determined by (3.2), they represent derivatives of the maximal attainable utility $v(\hat{x})$ with respect to net increases in the initial capital availabilities $z_1 = z$, decreases in the terminal capital requirements $z_2 = z$, and increases in the resource availabilities w. Finally, independently of the uniqueness of q_1, q_2, r, an opportunity to barter, for immediate or future delivery, any positive or negative amounts of initial capital goods or resources (delivered prior to production) at relative prices q_1^*, r^*, and of terminal capital or consumption goods (delivered after production) at relative "present" prices q_2^*, p^*, will not make attainment of a higher utility level possible, if and only if $v'(\hat{x}) = p^*D$, q_1^*, q_2^*, r^* satisfy the "dual constraints" (3.2) (see [7, Theorem 5.11, p. 93]).

The second step is to define the problem

$P(\alpha)$: Given a discount factor α with $0 < \alpha < 1$, choose a reproducible value $z = \hat{z}$ of the capital vector z in $P(z)$ in such a way that there exists a solution $\hat{x} \equiv \hat{x}(\hat{z})$ of $P(\hat{z})$ with associated dual variables q_1, q_2, r which, besides (3.2), *also satisfy*

$$q_2 = \alpha q_1 . \tag{3.3}$$

This condition requires that the shadow prices ("present values") of all capital goods diminish, when one changes availability from the beginning to the end of the single period considered, in the same proportion α, which in turn equals the given discount factor. If we again refer also to the pair $(\hat{x}, \hat{z})$ as a solution of $P(\alpha)$, we can now state a theorem that more fully sets out conditions under which the equivalence of $P(\alpha)$ and $P_\infty(\alpha)$ has been ascertained.

This theorem utilizes a slightly strengthened concept of reproducibility. A capital stock z is called *more-than-reproducible* if there exist vectors z', z'' satisfying $0 \leqq z' \leqq z \leqq z''$ with $z' < z''$, and a z'-feasible path z_t of finite length τ with terminal capital stock $z_{\tau+1} \geqq z''$. This condition specifies some slack in the reproducibility of all components of z without prescribing whether the slack for any particular component can be achieved in the initial or terminal capital stock, and without placing an *a priori* limit on the number of steps needed to achieve the slack. It rules out the case $z = 0$, and some other cases where z is in the boundary of the reproducible set. We give more information on these cases in Section 4.5, from which we infer that the condition of more-than-reproducibility, applied to an invariant optimal capital stock, covers all cases of practical interest in applications.

THEOREM 1. (Equivalence). *For a pair $(\hat{x}, \hat{z})$ to solve $P_\infty(\alpha)$ it is sufficient that $(\hat{x}, \hat{z})$ solve $P(\alpha)$. The latter condition is also necessary if $\hat{z}$ is more-than-reproducible.*

Note that this theorem allows us without further conditions to compute as many solutions of $P_\infty(\alpha)$ as we can compute of $P(\alpha)$. The theorem also tells us that all solutions of $P_\infty(\alpha)$ in which $\hat{z}$ is more-than-reproducible occur as solutions of $P(\alpha)$ as well.

The proof of Theorem 1 is given in Section 4. In the proof of necessity we first single out the instructive special case in which (3.2) with $z = \hat{z}$ by itself suffices to determine the prices q_1, q_2 uniquely. Next we show that a certain boundedness condition on the prices associated with the constant path $(x_t, z_t) = (\hat{x}, \hat{z})$ over any finite period guarantees the necessity asserted in Theorem 1. Finally we show that this boundedness condition is met if $\hat{z}$ is more-than-reproducible.

Theorem 1 specializes two theorems stated[4] by Sutherland [19, pp. 15, 24; 20, pp. 587–588] to the von Neumann type technology with provision for resources and for consumption. This specialization reveals interesting connections between the properties of the solution set of $P(\alpha)$ as a function of α and known properties of the strict von Neumann model, obtained from the present model by omitting (2.1C and D) from the constraint set. We return to these connections in Appendix II. In particular, Lemma 2 of

[4] We cannot follow one step in Sutherland's proof, [19], p. 20, lines 8–10.

Appendix II implies that the null solution of $P_\infty(\alpha)$, valid for all α, does not solve $P(\alpha)$ for some values of α.

Finally, we note a property of $P(\alpha)$ that enlarges the range of cases to which the present model applies. Let $(\hat{x}, \hat{z})$ solve $P(\alpha)$, and let (q_1, q_2, r) be a price vector satisfying (3.2) and (3.3). Now consider a different problem $P^*(\alpha)$, obtained from $P(\alpha)$ by substituting for $u(y)$, $v(x)$, functions

$$u^*(y) = \Phi(u(y)), \qquad v^*(x) = \Phi(v(x)),$$

obtained by an increasing and differentiable transformation $\Phi(\cdot)$ of the single-period utility scale that preserves the concavity of $u(y)$, hence of $v(x)$. Then, unless Φ is linear, the preference ordering on the space of consumption programs is no longer the same. However, the set of solutions $(\hat{x}, \hat{z})$ of $P(\alpha)$ remains unchanged. This is so because the vector $v'(\hat{x})$ is changed only proportionally,

$$v^{*\prime}(\hat{x}) = \Phi' \cdot v'(\hat{x}), \qquad \text{where} \qquad \Phi' \equiv \Phi'(v(\hat{x})) > 0.$$

and (3.2), (3.3) are satisfied again if we change the price vector correspondingly,

$$(q_1{}^*, q_2{}^*, r^*) = \Phi' \cdot (q_1, q_2, r).$$

For this reason there is for our present purpose little loss of generality in the assumption that $u(y)$ is differentiable also in the origin $y = 0$. Many (though perhaps not all) cases where $\lim_{y \to 0} u_k'(y) = \infty$ can be generated from the present case by an appropriate transformation of the scale for single-period utility.

4. Proof and Further Evaluation of Theorem 1

4.1. *Sufficiency*

Assume first that $\hat{z}$ solves $P(\alpha)$. Then there also exists a solution $\hat{x}$ of $P(\hat{z})$. Therefore, all the results cited in Section 3 apply if we substitute in (3.1) and (3.2)

$$z = \hat{z}, \qquad q_2 = \alpha q_1 \equiv \alpha q, \text{ say.} \tag{4.1}$$

Now let (x_t, z_t), $t = 1, 2, \ldots$, be any $\hat{z}$-feasible path, and consider a segment $(x_1, \ldots, x_T)$ of the path for x_t. Then, by multiplying (3.2b) by

$\sum_{t=1}^{T} \alpha^{t-1} x_t$, subtracting (3.2c) multiplied by $\sum_{t=1}^{T} \alpha^{t-1}$, using (4.1) and rearranging terms we obtain

$$q\left[(-Ax_1 + \hat{z}) + \sum_{t=2}^{T} \alpha^{t-1}(-Ax_t + Bx_{t-1}) + \alpha^T(Bx_T - \hat{z})\right]$$

$$+ r \sum_{t=1}^{T} \alpha^{t-1}(-Cx_t + w)$$

$$\leqq -v'(\hat{x}) \sum_{t=1}^{T} \alpha^{t-1}(x_t - \hat{x}) \leqq -\sum_{t=1}^{T} \alpha^{t-1}(v(x_t) - v(\hat{x})), \qquad (4.2)$$

the second inequality again being due to the concavity of $v(x)$. By (3.1) and (4.1), all expressions in parentheses in the left-hand member are nonnegative, except possibly the one occurring in the term $q\alpha^T(Bx_T - \hat{z})$, which by (2.7) tends to zero as $T \to \infty$, since $0 < \alpha < 1$. Therefore,

$$\sum_{t=1}^{\infty} \alpha^{t-1} v(x_t) \leqq \sum_{t=1}^{\infty} \alpha^{t-1} v(\hat{x}), \qquad (4.3)$$

and the constant path $(\hat{x}_t, \hat{z}_t) = (\hat{x}, \hat{z})$ for all t solves $P_\infty(\hat{z}, \alpha)$. Hence $\hat{z}$ solves $P_\infty(\alpha)$.

4.2. *Necessity if Shadow Prices are Unique*

Assume next that $\hat{z}$ solves $P_\infty(\alpha)$, and let the constant path $(\hat{x}_t, \hat{z}_t) = (\hat{x}, \hat{z})$ be $\hat{z}$-optimal. Then, in particular, for any integers T_1, T_2 with $T_1 \leqq T_2$, the path segment $\hat{x}_t = \hat{x}$, $t = T_1, \ldots, T_2$, solves

${}_{T_1}P_{T_2}(\hat{z}, \alpha)$: *Maximize* $\sum_{t=T_1}^{T_2} \alpha^{t-1} v(x_t)$ *subject to*

$$\begin{array}{llll} & -Ax_{T_1} \geqq -\hat{z}, & & q_{T_1} \\ & Bx_{t-1} - Ax_t \geqq 0, & t = T_1 + 1, \ldots, T_2, & q_t \\ & Bx_{T_2} \geqq \hat{z}, & & q_{T_2+1} \\ x_t \geqq 0, & -Cx_t \geqq -w, & t = T_1, \ldots, T_2. & r_t \end{array} \qquad (4.4)$$

This is so for $T_1 = 1$ because imposing the additional constraints $(x_t, z_t) = (\hat{x}, \hat{z})$, $t = T_2 + 1, T_2 + 2, \ldots$, in the statement of $P_\infty(\hat{z}, \alpha)$ does not constrain the solution $(\hat{x}_t, \hat{z}_t) = (\hat{x}, \hat{z})$, $t = 1, 2, \ldots$. By multiplying the maximand by α^{T_1-1} one sees readily that the same statement holds for any other segment $t = T_1, \ldots, T_2$, including those with $T_1 < 1$.

By the Kuhn–Tucker theorem there now exists for each period $[T_1, T_2]$ a vector of the form

$$(q_{T_1}, r_{T_1}, q_{T_1+1}, \ldots, q_{T_2}, r_{T_2}, q_{T_2+1}) \tag{4.5}$$

satisfying the dual constraints

$$\begin{aligned} q_t, r_t, q_{t+1} &\geqq 0 \\ \alpha^{t-1}v'(\hat{x}) - q_t A - r_t C + q_{t+1} B &\leqq 0 \\ \alpha^{t-1}v'(\hat{x})\hat{x} - q_t \hat{z} - r_t w + q_{t+1}\hat{z} &= 0 \qquad t = T_1, \ldots, T_2 . \end{aligned} \tag{4.6}$$

Consider first the case $T_1 = 1$, $T_2 = 2$. If (3.2) determines q_1, q_2 uniquely, then the two subsets of the nonhomogeneous linear conditions (4.6) labeled $t = 1$ and $t = 2$, taken separately, uniquely determine (q_1, q_2) and (q_2, q_3), respectively, on the basis of the only nonhomogeneous terms, the given vectors $\alpha^{t-1}v'(\hat{x})$ of marginal utilities for $t = 1, 2$, respectively. It follows that $q_2 = \alpha q_1$, hence $(\hat{x}, \hat{z})$ solves $P(\alpha)$.

4.3. *Necessity if Prices Referred to Delivery Time are Uniformly Bounded*

We now need to use (4.6) for $T_1 = 1$ and all $T_2 \equiv T > 1$. It will help to transform to prices quoted for payment at time of delivery,

$$(\bar{q}_t, \bar{r}_t) \equiv \alpha^{-t+1}(q_t, r_t), \qquad t = 1, 2, \ldots, \tag{4.7}$$

in terms of which (4.6) becomes

$$\begin{aligned} \bar{q}_t, \bar{r}_t, \bar{q}_{t+1} &\geqq 0 \\ v'(\hat{x}) - \bar{q}_t A - \bar{r}_t C + \alpha\bar{q}_{t+1} B &\leqq 0 \\ v'(\hat{x})\hat{x} - \bar{q}_t \hat{z} - \bar{r}_t w + \alpha\bar{q}_{t+1}\hat{z} &= 0 \qquad t = 1, \ldots, T. \end{aligned} \tag{4.8}$$

We note that the subsystems of (4.8) for specific values of t are all of the same form, defining congruent closed sets in the spaces of (q_t, r_t, q_{t+1}) for $t = 1, \ldots, T$, respectively.

Assume now that there exists for each $T \geqq 1$ a solution

$$(\bar{q}_1^{\,T}, \bar{r}_1^{\,T}, \bar{q}_2^{\,T}, \ldots, \bar{q}_T^{\,T}, \bar{r}_T^{\,T}, \bar{q}_{T+1}^{\,T}) \tag{4.9}$$

of (4.8) such that the component vectors of all these solutions are bounded uniformly in t and T,

$$\sum_l (\bar{q}_{tl}^T + \bar{q}_{t+1,l}^T) + \sum_m \bar{r}_{tm}^T \leqq P < \infty \qquad \text{for} \quad 1 \leqq t \leqq T, \quad T = 1, 2, \ldots . \tag{4.10}$$

Then the averages

$$(\bar{\bar{q}}_1{}^T, \bar{\bar{r}}_1{}^T, \bar{\bar{q}}_2{}^T) = \frac{1}{T}\sum_{t=1}^{T} (\bar{q}_t{}^T, \bar{r}_t{}^T, \bar{q}_{t+1}^T)$$

taken successively in the solutions (4.9) all satisfy (4.8) and (4.10) for $t = 1$, hence belong to a closed and bounded set, and a subsequence of these averages converges to a vector $(\bar{q}_1{}^*, \bar{r}_1{}^*, \bar{q}_2{}^*)$ satisfying (4.8) with $t = 1$. Finally, since

$$\lim_{T\to\infty} (\bar{\bar{q}}_2{}^T - \bar{\bar{q}}_1{}^T) = \lim_{T\to\infty} \frac{1}{T} (q_{T+1}^T - q_1{}^T) = 0,$$

we have $\bar{q}_2{}^* = \bar{q}_1{}^*$. By (4.7), the limit vector transforms back into a vector (q_1, r_1, q_2) satisfying (3.2) with $z = \hat{z}$, and $q_2 = \alpha q_1$.

4.4. *Proof that Prices at Time of Delivery can be Bounded Uniformly*

We first recall an inequality from concave programming under linear constraints. Let $V(X)$ be concave, differentiable, and defined for $X \geqq 0$, where X is a column vector. Let E be a fixed matrix, e a column vector which we may vary, both of orders such that

$$X \geqq 0, \qquad EX \geqq e, \tag{4.11}$$

represents a constraint set for the maximization of $V(X)$. We say that X is *e-feasible* if it satisfies (4.11), *e-optimal* if it maximizes $V(X)$ under those constraints. The maximum attained,

$$\hat{V}(e) \equiv V(\hat{X}(e)) \equiv \max\{V(X) \mid X \text{ is } e\text{-feasible}\}$$

is then defined on the set $\mathscr{E}$ of all e for which (4.11) is satisfied by at least one X. With any e-optimal vector $\hat{X} \equiv \hat{X}(e)$ for any $e \in \mathscr{E}$, the Kuhn–Tucker theorem associates a price vector Q such that

$$Q \geqq 0, \qquad V'(\hat{X}) + QE \leqq 0, \qquad V'(\hat{X})\hat{X} + Qe = 0.$$

Finally, for any $e' \in \mathscr{E}$, let X' denote any e'-feasible vector. Then, using the concavity of $V(X)$,

$$-\Delta \equiv V(X') - V(\hat{X}) \leqq V'(\hat{X})(X' - \hat{X}) \leqq -Q(EX' - e) \leqq Q(e - e'). \tag{4.12}$$

We now return to (4.6), choosing $T_1 \equiv 1 - \tau$, $T_2 \equiv T + \tau$, $T \geqq 1$, and specifying

$$X \equiv (x_{1-\tau}, \ldots, x_{T+\tau}), \qquad V(X) \equiv \sum_{t=1-\tau}^{T+\tau} \alpha^{t-1} v(x_t), \tag{4.13}$$

$$E \equiv \begin{array}{c} \\ \left[\begin{array}{ccccccc} (x_{1-\tau}) & (x_{2-\tau}) & \cdots & (x_0) & (x_1) & \cdots & (x_{T+\tau}) \\ -A & & & & & & \\ -C & & & & & & \\ B & -A & & & & & \\ & -C & & & & & \\ & B & -A & & & & \\ & & \vdots & \vdots & & & \\ & & & B & -A & & \\ & & & & -C & & \\ & & & & B & & \\ & & & & & \vdots & \\ & & & & & B & -A \\ & & & & & & -C \\ & & & & & & B \end{array}\right] \end{array} \begin{array}{l} \\ (1-\tau) \\ \\ (2-\tau) \\ \\ (3-\tau) \\ \vdots \\ (1) \\ \\ (2) \\ \vdots \\ (T+\tau) \\ \\ (T+\tau+1) \end{array},$$

$$e \equiv \begin{bmatrix} -\hat{z} \\ -w \\ 0 \\ -w \\ 0 \\ \vdots \\ 0 \\ -w \\ 0 \\ \vdots \\ 0 \\ -w \\ \hat{z} \end{bmatrix}, \qquad e' \equiv e + \begin{bmatrix} \hat{z} - z' \\ 0 \\ 0 \\ 0 \\ \\ \vdots \\ z'' - \hat{z} \\ 0 \\ 0 \\ \vdots \\ 0 \\ 0 \\ 0 \end{bmatrix} \begin{array}{l} (1-\tau) \\ \\ (2-\tau) \\ \\ \vdots \\ \\ (1) \\ \\ (2) \\ \vdots \\ (T+\tau) \\ \\ (T+\tau+1) \end{array} \tag{4.14}$$

Here τ, z', z'' are the quantities appearing in the definition of the more-than-reproducibility of $\hat{z}$. Therefore there exists a path segment $\{x_t' \mid t = 1 - \tau, \ldots, 0\}$ satisfying those of the constraints (4.11), with e' replacing e, that refer to the time periods it covers, and delivering a capital stock $Bx_0' \geqq z'' \geqq \hat{z}$ at the beginning of the period $t = 1$. By extending this path with the constant segment $\{x_t' = \hat{x} \mid t = 1, \ldots, T + \tau\}$ we obtain an

e'-feasible path. Hence $e' \in \mathscr{E}$, and (4.12) applies if for $\hat{X}$ we choose the e-optimal constant path $x_t = \hat{x}$, $t = 1 - \tau,..., T + \tau$. Therefore,

$$-\Delta \leqq -q_{1-\tau}(\hat{z} - z') - q_1(z'' - \hat{z}),$$

and, since $z' \leqq \hat{z} \leqq z''$ and $q_t \geqq 0$, we have

$$\Delta \geqq q_{1-\tau,l}(\hat{z}_l - z_l'), \qquad \Delta \geqq q_{1l}(z_l'' - \hat{z}_l), \qquad l = 1,..., L.$$

Let $\mathscr{L}'$, $\mathscr{L}''$ denote the subsets of $\mathscr{L} \equiv \{1,..., L\}$ in which $\hat{z}_l - z_l'$ and $z_l'' - \hat{z}_l$ are positive, respectively. Then each l belongs to at least one of $\mathscr{L}'$, $\mathscr{L}''$, and, if we let

$$\Delta' \equiv \Delta[\min_{l \in \mathscr{L}'} (\hat{z}_l - z_l')]^{-1}, \qquad \Delta'' \equiv \Delta[\min_{l \in \mathscr{L}''} (z_l'' - \hat{z}_l)]^{-1},$$

we have

$$q_{1-\tau,l} \leqq \Delta' \quad \text{if} \quad l \in \mathscr{L}', \qquad q_{1,l} \leqq \Delta'' \quad \text{if} \quad l \in \mathscr{L}''.$$

For each $t = 2,..., T + \tau + 1$, we repeat the above reasoning with e' changed to

$$e_t' \equiv e + (\overset{1-\tau}{0}, \overset{2-\tau}{0}, \overset{}{0},..., 0, \overset{t-\tau}{\hat{z} - z'}, 0,..., 0, \overset{t}{z'' - \hat{z}}, 0,..., 0, \overset{T+\tau+1}{0}).$$

The only difference is that the segment of the e_t'-feasible path X_t' on which X_t' differs from the e-optimal path $\hat{X}$ is deferred by one period, without other change, whenever t increases by one. Because of the form (4.13) of $V(X)$, this leads to

$$\begin{aligned} q_{t-\tau,l} &\leqq \alpha^{t-1}\Delta', \qquad l \in \mathscr{L}' \\ q_{t,l} &\leqq \alpha^{t-1}\Delta'', \qquad l \in \mathscr{L}'', \qquad t = 1,..., T + \tau + 1. \end{aligned}$$

Note that the ranges of both $t - \tau$ and t, as t ranges from 1 to $T + \tau + 1$, include the values $t = 1,..., T + 1$. Therefore, returning by (4.7) to prices timed at delivery, we have

$$0 \leqq \bar{q}_{t,l} \leqq \max\{\alpha^\tau \Delta', \Delta''\} < \infty, \qquad l \in \mathscr{L}, \qquad 1 \leqq t \leqq T + 1,$$

showing that in any sequence of solutions of (4.8) with $T = 1, 2,...$, $\bar{q}_t^T$ is bounded uniformly in t and T, where $1 \leqq t \leqq T + 1$. Since $w > 0$, the equality in (4.8) then implies that $\bar{r}_t^T$ is likewise uniformly bounded.

4.5. *Evaluation*

In conclusion, we prove a lemma indicating that the requirement that a reproducible capital stock z be more-than-reproducible is not very restrictive. We shall call a capital stock $z \geqq 0$ *prolific* (Sutherland uses the term "sufficient" for this concept) if either $z > 0$, or $z \ngtr 0$ and there exists a feasible path leading from the initial stock z to a stock $z' > 0$ in a finite number of periods. Clearly the null stock is not prolific. Also, if z is prolific so is λz for all $\lambda > 0$. Therefore, the resource constraints (2.1C) (refer also to (2.6)) do not enter into whether a given z is prolific.

LEMMA 1. *For a reproducible capital stock z to be more-than-reproducible, it is necessary that z be prolific. If that condition is met, either of the following additional conditions is sufficient:*

(i) *There exists* $x \geq 0$ *with* $Bx \geqq z > Ax, \quad Cx \leqq w$.

(ii) *There exists* $x \geq 0$ *with* $Bx \geqq z \geqq Ax, \quad Cx < w$.

The necessary condition is obvious.

The sufficient condition (i) requires some slack in reproducibility but not necessarily in resource use. The sufficiency is obvious, because the one-period feasible path given by $x_1 = x$ leads from $z_1 = z' \equiv Ax$ to $z_2 = z$, where $z' < z$. The interpretation is that z can be produced from a smaller z' by devoting all resources, or as much as proves necessary, to capital formation.

Condition (ii) places the slack in resource use, leaving a margin of the scarce resources for the production of consumption goods. To prove its sufficiency we set aside $(1 - \epsilon)z$, where $0 < \epsilon < 1$, to be reproduced through the process vector $(1 - \epsilon)x$ as often as necessary. We use ϵz to produce $\epsilon z'' > 0$ after a nonnegative number of periods, choosing ϵ small enough to stay within the available resource margin $w - (1 - \epsilon)\, Cx$ throughout the path. If necessary, we diminish $\epsilon z''$ by some disposal to obtain $\epsilon z' > 0$ where z' satisfies the viability condition

$$Bx' > z' = Ax' > 0 \qquad \text{for some} \quad x' \geq 0.$$

We then have

$$\rho \equiv \min_i((Bx')_i/(Ax')_i) > 1,$$

and it is technologically possible to increase $\epsilon z'$ by a factor ρ as often as needed (using disposal as needed), with a claim on resources given by

$$\epsilon \rho^n Cx'$$

in the n-th round. However, the number of rounds required to attain the target

$$\epsilon\rho^n z' > \epsilon z, \qquad \text{hence} \qquad z'' = (1 - \epsilon)z + \epsilon\rho^n z' > z,$$

is independent of ϵ. Therefore, the claim on resources can be kept within the positive initial resource margin $w - Cx$ until the target is attained, by choosing ϵ small enough.

Obviously, there is a great deal of overlap between cases (i) and (ii). Presumably, one could find a more general third sufficient condition allowing the required slack to be distributed in a coordinated manner between resource availability and reproducibility. However, the lemma goes far enough to indicate that there are at most two ways (that may occur separately or perhaps in combination) in which a reproducible capital stock z can fail to be more-than-reproducible. In one case, z would have a zero component or subvector which, given the technology and the other components of z, cannot be made positive. In the other, z would have a component or subvector which can be reproduced but not increased under the resource constraints, and also cannot be reached starting from a lower level. Both cases lack relevance for any applications in which a model with constant technology and constant resource availabilities constitutes a tolerable simplification. In the former case, what is the point of putting capital goods in the model which historically could not, even with present technology, have been produced from an earlier initial state in which they were absent? Likewise, in the latter case, how could the capital goods in question have originally been brought up to the levels of which the reproducibility is resource-constrained, if present technology and resource constraints do not make this possible? We conclude that, in applications of the present model, it would not hurt us if we should be unable to compute some weird solutions of $P_\infty(\alpha)$ that are not solutions of $P(\alpha)$.

5. A Combinatorial Theorem Due to Scarf

For our purposes, the importance of the Equivalence Theorem resides in that $P(\alpha)$ has a much more suitable form for the computation of an approximately invariant capital stock than $P_\infty(\alpha)$. At first sight, $P(\alpha)$ looks very similar to an ordinary nonlinear programming problem. There is one crucial characteristic of the problem, however, that distinguishes it from all ordinary nonlinear programming problems. This is the requirement that the vectors of Lagrangean multipliers q_1 and q_2 have to satisfy the additional linear constraint $q_2 = \alpha q_1$. This places the problem in the category of fixed point problems for a continuous mapping. One of us [9] has indicated two alternative, equivalent and still more condensed formulations of $P(\alpha)$ that explicitly have the form of fixed point problems, one in the space of activity levels, the other in the space of prices. The former of these equivalent formulations also provides a convenient basis for a proof of the existence of a solution of $P(\alpha)$.

In the present section we state a combinatorial theorem due to Scarf [14, 15], which has provided the starting point for the algorithms for computing an approximate competitive equilibrium mentioned in Section 1. Section 6 describes the application of this theorem to the computation of an approximately invariant optimal capital stock. As a byproduct, this application also provides a direct and constructive proof for the existence of an invariant optimal capital stock.

The combinatorial theorem is expressed in terms of the concept of a *primitive set* of vectors selected from a larger set. In order to review that concept, let $\Pi = (\pi^1, \dots, \pi^J)$ be a collection of (column) vectors in s-dimensional Euclidean space. The first s vectors of Π are assumed to have the form

$$\begin{aligned} \pi^1 &= (0, M_1, \dots, M_1) \\ \pi^2 &= (M_2, 0, M_2, \dots, M_2) \\ &\vdots \\ \pi^s &= (M_s, M_s, \dots, 0) \qquad \text{where} \quad M_1 > M_2 > \cdots > M_s > 1. \end{aligned} \tag{5.1}$$

and will be called the *slack* vectors. The remaining, *nonslack*, vectors lie on the unit simplex, i.e.,

$$\text{for all } j > s, \qquad \sum_{i=1}^{s} \pi_i^j = 1, \qquad \text{and} \qquad 0 \leqq \pi_i^j \leqq 1 \qquad \text{for all } i. \tag{5.2}$$

Finally, we make the *nondegeneracy assumption* that no two distinct vectors in Π have the same i-th coordinate for any i.

Before defining a primitive set, we define and denote the *vector minimum* for any set $\Phi \equiv \{\varphi^j \mid j = 1, \dots, s\}$ of s vectors in an s-dimensional vector space by

$$\min\{\varphi^1, \dots, \varphi^s\} \equiv (\underline{\varphi}_1, \dots, \underline{\varphi}_s),$$

where

$$\underline{\varphi}_i \equiv \min\{\varphi_i^j \mid j = 1, \dots, s\}, \qquad i = 1, \dots, s.$$

A set $\{\pi^{j_1}, \dots, \pi^{j_s}\}$ of s distinct vectors of Π is now defined to be a *primitive set* if there is no vector π^j in Π for which

$$\pi^j > \min\{\pi^{j_1}, \dots, \pi^{j_s}\}. \tag{5.3}$$

Figure 1 illustrates this concept. The large triangle encloses the simplex (5.2) in the space of $s = 3$ dimensions. The nonslack vectors π^j, $j > 3$ are represented by dots, the three slack vectors π^j, $j = 1, 2, 3$, by the sides of the large triangle on which $\pi_j^j = 0$. The three small triangles identify primitive sets with zero, one and two slack vectors, respectively. Each side of the triangle identifying a primitive set must contain a different one of the vectors π^j (if j is nonslack) or be contained in the large side representing π^j (if j is slack). The condition (5.3) specifies that the small triangle shall contain no nonslack point π^j in its interior. (Because of the nondegeneracy assumption, it can have no other such point in its boundary.) For further discussion, see [15].

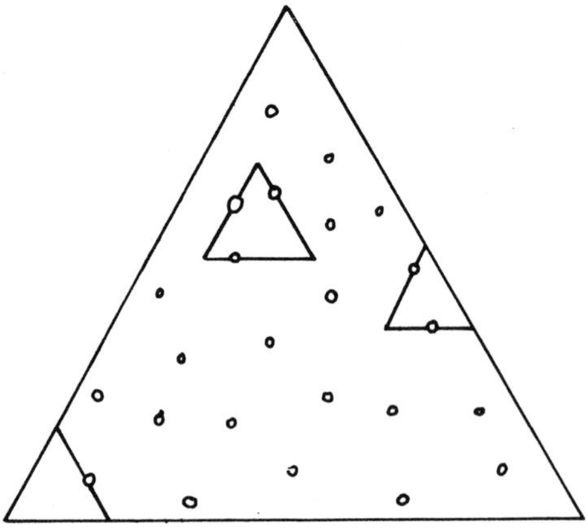

FIGURE 1

Finally, we recall from linear programming the definition of a feasible basis for a set of linear constraints on a set of nonnegative variables. Given a matrix F of order (s, J), $s < J$, and a column vector g of order s, a submatrix F^* consisting of s linearly independent columns $f^{j_1}, \ldots, f^{j_s}$ of F is called a *feasible basis* for the system of equations $F\eta = g$ if that system has a solution η in which $\eta_j \geqq 0$ for $j = j_1, \ldots, j_s$, and $\eta_j = 0$ for all other j.

The combinatorial theorem [14, Theorem 2] may now be stated:

THEOREM 2 (Combinatorial Theorem). *Let Π be a matrix of order (s, J) as described above, and let*

$$F \equiv \begin{bmatrix} 1 & 0 & \cdots & 0 & f_1^{s+1} & \cdots & f_1^J \\ 0 & 1 & \cdots & 0 & f_2^{s+1} & \cdots & f_2^J \\ \vdots & \vdots & & \vdots & \vdots & & \vdots \\ 0 & 0 & \cdots & 1 & f_s^{s+1} & \cdots & f_s^J \end{bmatrix}$$

be a matrix and $g \equiv (g_1, \ldots, g_s)$ *a nonnegative column vector such that the set of nonnegative vectors* η *satisfying* $F\eta = g$ *is bounded. Then there exists a primitive set* $\{\pi^{j_1}, \ldots, \pi^{j_s}\}$, *so that the corresponding columns* $\{f^{j_1}, \ldots, f^{j_s}\}$ *of* F *form a feasible basis for* $F\eta = g$.

The proof of the above theorem also provides us with an algorithm for finding a primitive set whose associated columns in F form a feasible basis for $F\eta = g$.

6. Design for an Algorithm for Approximate Solution of $P(\alpha)$

In this section we shall show how the combinatorial theorem stated in the preceding section may be used to compute an approximate solution of $P(\alpha)$. We use the expression "approximate solution" rather than "approximation to a solution" since the algorithm is designed to compute vectors x, z, q_1, $q_2 = \alpha q_1$, r satisfying to a high degree of accuracy the conditions (3.2), (3.3) for a solution of $P(\alpha)$ (with x substituted for $\hat{x}$).

Since time subscripts on the vector x are no longer needed, we shall change the notation for its components to $x \equiv (\xi_1, \ldots, \xi_I)$.

We shall make two additional stipulations about the model stated in Section 2. First, because of (2.5), suitable choices of the unit levels of activity for all processes will insure that

$$Cx \leqq w, \quad x \geqq 0 \text{ implies } \sum_{i=1}^{I} \xi_i \leqq \gamma < 1 \quad \text{for some } \gamma > 0. \tag{6.1}$$

The second stipulation is indeed a new assumption, to be called the *growth capability condition*. It implies the first inequality in the viability condition and strengthens it by introducing the discount factor into it:

$$\text{there exists } \bar{x} > 0 \text{ such that } (A - \alpha B)\bar{x} < 0. \tag{6.2}$$

This says that, disregarding consumption, the capital stock can be made to grow at a rate at least slightly higher than $\beta \equiv \alpha^{-1}$ per period, where of course $\beta > 1$. If we define

$$\bar{\beta} = \sup\{\beta \mid (A - \beta^{-1}B)x < 0 \text{ for some } x \geqq 0\},$$

then the viability condition (2.4) assures us that $\bar{\beta}^{-1} < 1$, hence that there is a nonempty open interval

$$\bar{\beta}^{-1} < \alpha < 1 \tag{6.3}$$

on which α satisfies both (1.1) and (6.2).

The growth capability condition derives additional plausibility from a study of the connections between the solution set of $P(\alpha)$ and the characteristics of the strict von Neumann model obtained if we delete all consumption goods and all resources from the present model. Some results of this kind are assembled in Appendix II. In any case, the growth capability condition simplifies matters by rendering services analogous to those of the constraint qualification in ordinary nonlinear programming.

Because of (2.6), we can also find an $\bar{x}$ satisfying both (6.2) and

$$C\bar{x} \leqq w, \qquad \text{hence} \quad \sum_{i=1}^{I} \bar{\xi}_i \leqq \gamma < 1 \tag{6.4}$$

by (6.1). This helps because the concept of a primitive set will now be applied to the space of vectors x of activity levels ξ_i. In order to overcome the difficulty that the activity levels bear no natural relation to the simplex $\{x \mid \xi_i \geqq 0, \xi_1 + \cdots + \xi_I = 1\}$ we introduce an additional coordinate

$$\xi_0 = 1 - \sum_{i=1}^{I} \xi_i , \tag{6.5}$$

which by (6.4) is positive for all feasible vectors x. We can therefore now define primitive sets in relation to the simplex of dimensionality I,

$$\Sigma \equiv \left\{ \xi \equiv (\xi_0, \xi_1, \ldots, \xi_I) \mid \xi_i \geqq 0 \text{ for } i = 0, \ldots, I, \sum_{i=0}^{I} \xi_i = 1 \right\}. \tag{6.6}$$

Thus ξ differs from x only by the presence of an additional component ξ_0. A primitive set will consequently consist of $I + 1$ vectors with $I + 1$ components each. A collection $\Xi \equiv \{\xi^0, \xi^1, \ldots, \xi^J\}$ of $(I + 1)$-dimensional vectors is selected, where $J > I$. The $I + 1$ slack vectors are given by

$$\begin{aligned} \xi^0 &= (0, M_0, M_0, \ldots, M_0) \\ \xi^1 &= (M_1, 0, M_1, \ldots, M_1) \\ &\vdots \\ \xi^I &= (M_I, M_I, M_I, \ldots, 0) \qquad \text{where} \quad M_0 > M_1 > \cdots > M_I > 1, \end{aligned} \tag{6.7}$$

while the $J - I$ nonslack vectors are selected so as to have a rather even distribution over Σ, and again such that no two vectors have identical i-th coordinates for any i.

Each vector ξ^j in Ξ is associated with the corresponding column f^j in a matrix F, as follows:

$$F = \begin{array}{c} \begin{matrix} \xi^0 & \xi^1 & \xi^2 & & \xi^I & \xi^{I+1} & & \xi^j & & \xi^J \end{matrix} \\ \begin{bmatrix} 1 & 0 & 0 & \cdots & 0 & f_0^{I+1} & \cdots & f_0^j & \cdots & f_0^J \\ 0 & 1 & 0 & \cdots & 0 & f_1^{I+1} & \cdots & f_1^j & \cdots & f_1^J \\ 0 & 0 & 1 & \cdots & 0 & f_2^{I+1} & \cdots & f_2^j & \cdots & f_2^J \\ \vdots & \vdots & \vdots & & \vdots & \vdots & & \vdots & & \vdots \\ 0 & 0 & 0 & \cdots & 1 & f_I^{I+1} & \cdots & f_I^j & \cdots & f_I^J \end{bmatrix} \end{array} \tag{6.8}$$

We define the columns f^j, $j = 0,\ldots, J$, of F as functions of the $\xi^j \equiv (\xi_0{}^j, x^j)$ by considering an exhaustive enumeration of possible cases, to be labeled 0_i, 1_j, 2_l, 3_m where $i = 0,\ldots, I$, $j = I + 1,\ldots, J$, $l = 1,\ldots, L$, and $m = 1,\ldots, M$. The case that applies to a particular ξ^j with $j > I$ is determined on the basis of which, if any, of the following set of $L + M$ constraints are violated by x^j,

$$(A - B)x \leqq 0,$$
$$Cx \leqq w.$$

These constraints have been obtained from the primal constraint set of $P(\alpha)$ by elimination of $\hat{z}$.

0_i. As indicated, for $i = j \leqq I$, $f^j \equiv e^j$ is the unit vector with $e_j{}^j = 1$.

All remaining cases refer to $j > I$.

1_j. If $(A - B)\, x^j \leqq 0$ and $Cx^j \leqq w$, then with ξ^j we associate

$$f^j = (1, v_1'(x^j) + 1,\ldots, v_I'(x^j) + 1). \tag{6.9}$$

2_l. If one or more of the constraints $(A - B)x \leqq 0$ are violated for $x = x^j$, and if the first of these constraints to be violated is the l-th, say, then with ξ^j we associate

$$f^j = (1, -a_{l1} + \alpha b_{l1} + 1,\ldots, -a_{lI} + \alpha b_{lI} + 1). \tag{6.10}$$

It is this stipulation that introduces the parameter α characterizing $P(\alpha)$ into the algorithm.

3_m. If $(A - B)\, x^j \leqq 0$, but one or more of the constraints $Cx \leqq w$ are violated for $x = x^j$, the first that is violated being the m-th, then with ξ^j we associate

$$f^j = (1, -c_{m1} + 1,\ldots, -c_{mI} + 1). \tag{6.11}$$

Finally, we select $g \equiv (1,\ldots, 1)$, and note that the constraint set $\mathscr{H} \equiv \{\eta \mid F\eta = g, \eta \geqq 0\}$ is bounded because $\eta \in \mathscr{H}$ implies

$$0 \leqq \eta_j, \qquad j = 0,\ldots, J; \qquad \eta_0 + \sum_{j=I+1}^{J} \eta_j = 1;$$

and (6.12)

$$\eta_i = 1 - \sum_{j=I+1}^{J} f_i{}^j \eta_j, \qquad i = 1,\ldots, I.$$

Theorem 2 consequently applies, and there exists a primitive set $\Xi^* \equiv \{\xi^{j_0},..., \xi^{j_I}\}$ whose associated columns form a feasible basis $F^* \equiv \{f^{j_0},..., f^{j_I}\}$ for $F\eta = g$. Hence

$$\begin{bmatrix} f_0^{j_0} \\ f_1^{j_0} \\ \vdots \\ f_I^{j_0} \end{bmatrix} \eta_{j_0} + \cdots + \begin{bmatrix} f_0^{j_I} \\ f_1^{j_I} \\ \vdots \\ f_I^{j_I} \end{bmatrix} \eta_{j_I} = \begin{bmatrix} 1 \\ 1 \\ \vdots \\ 1 \end{bmatrix}, \tag{6.13}$$

with the f^{j_h}, $h = 0,..., I$, linearly independent and with $\eta_{j_h} \geqq 0$ for all h.

In the next section we show

THEOREM 3 (Convergence). *For any sequence* $\{\Xi(n) \mid n = 1, 2,...\}$ *of matrices* Ξ *of which the nonslack vectors* $\xi^j, j = I + 1,..., J_n$, *are scattered with indefinitely increasing and rather uniform density over* Σ, *there exists a subsequence* $\{\Xi(n_k) \mid k = 1, 2,...]$ *with a corresponding sequence* $\{\Xi^*(n_k)\}$ *of primitive sets of which all nonslack vectors converge to a vector* $\hat{\xi} \equiv (\hat{\xi}_0, \hat{x})$. *Moreover, if for any such vector* $\hat{x}$ *we define* $\hat{z} \equiv A\hat{x}$, *then* $(\hat{x}, \hat{z})$ *is a solution of* $P(\alpha)$.

Clearly, Theorem 3 also establishes the existence of a solution $(\hat{x}, \hat{z})$ to $P(\alpha)$ under the assumptions made. Moreover, it is shown in Lemma 2 of Appendix II that the growth capability condition (6.2) precludes the existence of a trivial null solution $(\hat{x}, \hat{z}) = (0, 0)$.

It is not difficult to construct examples with only a few commodities and processes, for which more than one solution exists. In that case, the solution obtained may depend on the way in which the algorithm is started up.

Now that the construction of the matrix F has been fully specified in terms of particulars of the present problem, the steps carried out for any given pair (Ξ, F) to find a primitive set satisfying (6.13) can be laid out according to any version of the general procedure for problems of this kind. For the published versions, see Scarf [14, 15] and Hansen [4].

7. Proof of Convergence of the Algorithm

We proceed from the relation (6.13) characterizing the pair (Ξ^*, F^*) of a primitive set Ξ^* and an associated feasible basis F^* for the equation $F\eta = g$.

Let $\mathcal{G}$ denote the set of $(I + 1) + (J - I) + L + M$ indices labeling the possible cases 0_i, 1_j, 2_l, 3_m listed in the rules for assigning vectors f^j of F to vectors ξ^j of Ξ. Given Ξ^*, we denote by $\mathcal{G}^*$ the subset of $\mathcal{G}$

consisting of the labels of all cases that do arise in the assignment of vectors f^{j_h} to vectors ξ^{j_h} of Ξ^*. Then $\mathscr{G}^*$ partitions according to the four categories of cases into

$$\begin{aligned} \mathscr{G}^* &= \mathscr{I} \cup \mathscr{J} \cup \mathscr{L} \cup \mathscr{M}, \qquad \text{where} \\ \mathscr{I} &\equiv \{ i \mid i = j \leqq I,\ \xi^j \in \Xi^* \} \\ \mathscr{J} &\equiv \{ j \mid j > I,\ \xi^j \in \Xi^*,\ \xi^j \text{ is in case } 1_j \} \\ \mathscr{L} &\equiv \{ l \mid j > I,\ \xi^j \in \Xi^*,\ \xi^j \text{ is in case } 2_l \} \\ \mathscr{M} &\equiv \{ m \mid j > I,\ \xi^j \in \Xi^*,\ \xi^j \text{ is in case } 3_m \}. \end{aligned} \tag{7.1}$$

The number of elements of $\mathscr{G}^*$ is $I + 1$. We observe also that $\Xi^0 = \{\xi^0, \ldots, \xi^I\}$ is not a primitive set. Hence $\mathscr{J} \cup \mathscr{L} \cup \mathscr{M}$ is not empty.

The definitions of the columns of F^* now allow us to write (6.13) in the form

$$\text{(7.2a)} \qquad \eta_0 + \sum_{j \in \mathscr{J}} \lambda_j + \sum_{l \in \mathscr{L}} \epsilon_l + \sum_{m \in \mathscr{M}} \delta_m = 1$$

$$\text{(7.2b)} \begin{cases} \eta_i + \sum_{j \in \mathscr{J}} \lambda_j (1 + v_i'(x^j)) + \sum_{l \in \mathscr{L}} \epsilon_l (1 - a_{li} + \alpha b_{li}) \\ \qquad + \sum_{m \in \mathscr{M}} \delta_m (1 - c_{mi}) = 1, \\ i = 1, \ldots, I, \qquad \text{where} \quad \eta_i \equiv 0 \quad \text{for} \quad i \notin \mathscr{I}. \end{cases} \tag{7.2}$$

Here a_{li}, b_{li}, c_{mi} $(i = 1, \ldots, I)$ are as given in (3.1). Coefficients η_{jh} in (6.13) attached to vectors f^{jh} assigned in $\mathscr{I}$, $\mathscr{J}$, $\mathscr{L}$, or $\mathscr{M}$ recur in (7.2) as one of the η_i, λ_j, ϵ_l, or δ_m, respectively. We therefore have

$$\eta_i, \lambda_j, \epsilon_l, \delta_m \geqq 0 \qquad \text{for} \quad i \in \mathscr{I}, j \in \mathscr{J}, l \in \mathscr{L}, m \in \mathscr{M}, \tag{7.3a}$$

$$i \notin \mathscr{I} \qquad \text{for at least one} \quad i \in \{0, 1, \ldots, I\}, \tag{7.3b}$$

$$1 - \eta_0 = \sum_{j \in \mathscr{J}} \lambda_j + \sum_{l \in \mathscr{L}} \epsilon_l + \sum_{m \in \mathscr{M}} \delta_m > 0. \tag{7.3c}$$

The equality in (7.3c) arises from (7.2a). The inequality arises from (7.3b) and (7.2b).

If the number J of vectors in Ξ is large, and if the nonslack vectors ξ^j are distributed rather evenly throughout Σ, then, as Fig. 1 suggests, the nonslack vectors in the primitive set $\xi^{j_0}, \xi^{j_1}, \ldots, \xi^{j_I}$ (those for which $j_h > I$)

must be close to each other. Likewise, for any slack member ξ^j of the primitive set ($j \leqq I$) we have $\xi_j^j = 0$, and hence $\xi_j^{j_h}$ must be close to zero for all nonslack members ($j_h > I$). For otherwise, vectors $\xi^{j'}$ could be found in Ξ that have the relation (5.3) to Ξ^* that is excluded by the definition of a primitive set.

Consider now an infinite sequence

$$\{\Xi(n) \mid n = 1, 2, \ldots\} \tag{7.4}$$

of sets $\Xi(n)$ in which the "density" of nonslack vectors ξ^j (those with $j > I$) increases indefinitely in all parts of Σ. From each $\Xi(n)$ we select a primitive set $\Xi^*(n)$ such that its associated submatrix $F^*(n)$ of $F(n)$, determined as before, satisfies the relations (6.13) and therefore (7.2) and (7.3). Without continually changing notation, we select a finite sequence of subsequences of $\{\Xi(n)\}$, each subsequence being selected from the preceding sequence or subsequence, such that the following conditions are successively met:

(i) the (nonempty) sets of the nonslack vectors $\xi^j(n)$, $j > I$, of $\Xi^*(n)$ converge, as $n \to \infty$, to some single vector $\hat{\xi} \equiv (\hat{\xi}_0, \hat{x})$, say, where $\hat{\xi} \in \Sigma$;

(ii) the set of vectors $v'(x^j(n))$ for j labeling the nonslack vectors $\xi^j(n)$ of $\Xi^*(n)$ converges to $v'(\hat{x})$;

(iii) the index sets $\mathscr{I}(n)$, $\mathscr{L}(n)$, $\mathscr{M}(n)$ specifying the types of columns of $F(n)$, corresponding to cases 0_i, 2_l, 3_m, incorporated in $F^*(n)$, are independent of n (and will again be denoted $\mathscr{I}$, $\mathscr{L}$, $\mathscr{M}$);

(iv) the coefficients $\eta_i(n)$, $\epsilon_l(n)$, $\delta_m(n)$ occurring in the analog of (7.2) for each n converge to $\hat{\eta}_i$, $\hat{\epsilon}_l$, $\hat{\delta}_m$, respectively, where $i \in \mathscr{I}$, $l \in \mathscr{L}$, $m \in \mathscr{M}$. The sum $\sum_{j \in \mathscr{J}(n)} \lambda_j(n)$ of the coefficients $\lambda_j(n)$ converges to $\hat{\lambda}$.

The compactness sufficient for convergence under (i) follows from (6.6). Convergence under (ii) then follows from the continuity of $v'(x)$. The stabilization of the index sets in (iii) is made possible by the finiteness of the set $\mathscr{G}^*$ in (7.1) and of the larger set of "cases" (column types of $F(n)$) from which $F^*(n)$ is selected. The compactness sufficient for convergence under (iv) follows from (7.2) and (7.3a).

We have defined and define

$$\hat{\lambda} \equiv \lim_{n \to \infty} \lambda(n), \qquad \lambda(n) \equiv \sum_{j \in \mathscr{J}(n)} \lambda_j(n), \qquad \hat{\epsilon} \equiv \sum_{l \in \mathscr{L}} \hat{\epsilon}_l, \qquad \hat{\delta} \equiv \sum_{m \in \mathscr{M}} \hat{\delta}_m, \tag{7.5}$$

with the understanding that, if any of the index sets $\mathscr{J}(n)$, $\mathscr{L}$, $\mathscr{M}$ is empty, the corresponding sum $\lambda(n)$, $\hat{\epsilon}$, $\hat{\delta}$ equals zero. We now list some properties of $\hat{x}$, $\hat{\eta}_i$, $\hat{\lambda}$, $\hat{\epsilon}_l$, $\hat{\delta}_m$ that follow directly from the construction. From (7.3) we have, in the limit for $n \to \infty$,

$$\hat{\eta}_i, \hat{\epsilon}_l, \hat{\delta}_m, \hat{\lambda}, \hat{\epsilon}, \hat{\delta} \geqq 0 \quad \text{for} \quad i \in \mathscr{I}, \quad l \in \mathscr{L}, \quad m \in \mathscr{M},$$

$$\text{where} \quad \hat{\eta}_i = 0 \quad \text{if} \quad i \notin \mathscr{I}, \tag{7.6a}$$

$$i \notin \mathscr{I} \quad \text{for at least one} \quad i \in \{0, 1, \ldots, I\}, \tag{7.6b}$$

$$\hat{\eta}_0 + \hat{\lambda} + \hat{\epsilon} + \hat{\delta} = 1. \tag{7.6c}$$

If $i \in \mathscr{I}$, we have $\xi_i{}^i(n) = 0$ for all n, hence $\hat{\xi}_i = 0$, for the reason stated in the paragraph following (7.3). Therefore,

$$\text{for} \quad i = 0, \ldots, I, \qquad \hat{\xi}_i > 0 \ \text{ implies } \ \hat{\eta}_i = 0. \tag{7.7}$$

From the definitions of the columns of F,

$$\hat{\lambda} > 0 \quad \text{implies} \quad (A - B)\hat{x} \leqq 0 \quad \text{and} \quad C\hat{x} \leqq w, \tag{7.8}$$

$$l \in \mathscr{L}, \quad \hat{\epsilon}_l > 0 \ \text{ imply } \ (a_l - b_l)\hat{x} \equiv \sum_{i=1}^{I} (a_{li} - b_{li})\, \hat{\xi}_i \geqq 0, \tag{7.9}$$

$$m \in \mathscr{M}, \qquad \hat{\delta}_m > 0 \quad \text{imply} \quad c_m\hat{x} \equiv \sum_{i=1}^{I} c_{mi}\hat{\xi}_i \geqq w_m. \tag{7.10}$$

Before we can bring these relations to fruition, we must show that $\hat{\lambda} > 0$. To that end, we rewrite the limiting form of (7.2) as

$$\hat{\eta}_i + \hat{\lambda}(1 + v_i'(x)) + \sum_{l \in \mathscr{L}} \hat{\epsilon}_l(1 - a_{li} + \alpha b_{li}) + \sum_{m \in \mathscr{M}} \hat{\delta}_m(1 - c_{mj}) = 1,$$
$$i = 1, \ldots, I, \tag{7.11}$$

and subtract (7.6c) from (7.11), obtaining

$$\hat{\eta}_i - \hat{\eta}_0 + \hat{\lambda} v_i'(\hat{x}) + \sum_{l \in \mathscr{L}} \hat{\epsilon}_l(-a_{li} + \alpha b_{li}) - \sum_{m \in \mathscr{M}} \hat{\delta}_m c_{mi} = 0,$$
$$i = 1, \ldots, I. \tag{7.12}$$

Finally, let $\bar{x} \equiv (\bar{\xi}_1, \ldots, \bar{\xi}_I) \geq 0$ be a column vector satisfying (6.2) and (6.4), and write $\bar{\xi} \equiv (\bar{\xi}_0, \bar{x}) \in \Sigma$. Multiplying (7.12) by $\hat{\xi}_i - \bar{\xi}_i$ and summing for $i = 1, \ldots, I$ we have, since $\sum_{i=1}^{T} (\hat{\xi}_i - \bar{\xi}_i) \equiv \bar{\xi}_0 - \hat{\xi}_0$, rearranging terms,

$$\sum_{i=0}^{I} \hat{\eta}_i\hat{\xi}_i - \sum_{i=0}^{I} \hat{\eta}_i\bar{\xi}_i + \hat{\lambda} \sum_{i=1}^{I} v_i'(\hat{x})(\hat{\xi}_i - \bar{\xi}_i) + \sum_{l \in \mathscr{L}} \epsilon_l \sum_{i=1}^{I} (-a_{li} + \alpha b_{li})\, \hat{\xi}_i$$
$$+ \sum_{l \in \mathscr{L}} \hat{\epsilon}_l \sum_{i=1}^{I} (a_{li} - \alpha b_{li})\, \bar{\xi}_i - \sum_{m \in \mathscr{M}} \hat{\delta}_m \sum_{i=1}^{I} c_{mi}(\hat{\xi}_i - \bar{\xi}_i) = 0. \tag{7.13}$$

The first term vanishes by (7.7). The second, fourth, fifth and sixth terms are nonpositive, the fourth because, by (7.9),

$$\hat{\epsilon}_l > 0 \qquad \text{implies} \ \sum_{i=1}^{I} a_{li}\hat{\xi}_i \geqq \sum_{i=1}^{I} b_{li}\hat{\xi}_i \geqq \alpha \sum_{i=1}^{I} b_{li}\hat{\xi}_i$$

the fifth by (6.2), the sixth by (7.10) and (6.4). In particular, the fifth term is negative if $\hat{\epsilon}_l > 0$ for some l, the sixth if $\hat{\delta}_m > 0$ for some m. Therefore,

$$\hat{\lambda} \sum_{i=1}^{I} v'(\hat{x})(\hat{\xi}_i - \xi_i) \begin{bmatrix} > \\ \geqq \end{bmatrix} 0 \qquad \text{if} \quad \hat{\epsilon} + \hat{\delta} \begin{bmatrix} > \\ = \end{bmatrix} 0. \tag{7.14}$$

Now suppose $\hat{\lambda} = 0$. Then, by (7.14), $\hat{\epsilon} + \hat{\delta} = 0$, hence, by (7.6c), $\hat{\eta}_0 = 1$, and, by (7.11), $\hat{\eta}_i = 1$ for $i = 1,..., I$, contradicting (7.6b), (7.6a). Therefore $\hat{\lambda} > 0$.

It follows by (7.8) that, if we define $\hat{z} \equiv A\hat{x}$, the pair $(\hat{x}, \hat{z})$ satisfies the constraints (3.1A,B,C) for $P(\alpha)$. In particular, from (7.9), (7.10),

$$\begin{aligned} &\hat{\epsilon}_l > 0 \qquad \text{implies} \ \sum_{i=1}^{I} a_{li}\hat{\xi}_i = z_l = \sum_{i=1}^{I} b_{li}\hat{\xi}_i\,, \qquad l = 1,..., L, \\ &\hat{\delta}_m > 0 \qquad \text{implies} \ \sum_{i=1}^{I} c_{mi}\hat{\xi}_i = w_m\,, \qquad m = 1,..., M, \end{aligned} \tag{7.15}$$

because $\hat{\epsilon}_l \equiv 0$ for $l \notin \mathscr{L}$, $\hat{\delta}_m \equiv 0$ for $m \notin \mathscr{M}$. Moreover, (3.1C) for $x = \hat{x}$ implies $\hat{\xi}_0 > 0$ by (6.1), hence, by (7.7) and (7.6c),

$$\hat{\eta}_0 = 0, \qquad \hat{\lambda} + \hat{\epsilon} + \hat{\delta} = 1. \tag{7.16}$$

If, at last, we define row vectors q, r of orders L, M, respectively, with the components

$$q_{\cdot l} \equiv \hat{\lambda}^{-1}\hat{\epsilon}_l\,, \quad l = 1,..., L, \qquad r_{\cdot m} \equiv \hat{\lambda}^{-1}\hat{\delta}_m\,, \quad m = 1,..., M, \tag{7.17}$$

then (7.12) and (7.16) yield the Kuhn–Tucker conditions (7.18a), (7.7) and (7.15) the conditions (7.18b),

$$v'(\hat{x}) - qA + \alpha qB - rC \leqq 0, \tag{7.18a}$$

$$v'(\hat{x})\hat{x} - (1 - \alpha)\, q\hat{z} - rw = 0. \tag{7.18b}$$

The proof of Theorem 3 (convergence) is thereby complete.

8. A Numerical Example

We consider an economy with three consumption goods, two capital goods, and two resources other than capital goods (e.g., skilled and unskilled labor). Each good can be produced by two alternative processes. Thus, of the total of ten processes, processes one through six produce consumption goods.

The matrices A, B, C and D are given by

$$A = \begin{bmatrix} 2. & 2. & 2. & 2. & 2. & 2. & 2. & 2. & 2. & 2. \\ 3. & 3. & 2. & 2. & 1. & 1. & 1. & .5 & 1. & .5 \end{bmatrix}$$

$$B = \begin{bmatrix} 1.5 & 1.5 & 1.5 & 1.5 & 1.5 & 1.5 & 4. & 3. & 1.5 & 1.5 \\ 2.7 & 2.7 & 1.8 & 1.8 & .9 & .9 & .9 & .4 & 2. & 1.5 \end{bmatrix}$$

$$C = \begin{bmatrix} 1. & 1. & 1. & 1. & 1. & 1. & 1. & 1. & 1. & 1. \\ .5 & 1.5 & 1.5 & .5 & .5 & 1.5 & 1.5 & .5 & .5 & 1.5 \end{bmatrix}$$

$$D = \begin{bmatrix} 1. & 2.5 & 0. & 0. & 0. & 0. & 0. & 0. & 0. & 0. \\ 0. & 0. & 2.5 & 1. & 0. & 0. & 0. & 0. & 0. & 0. \\ 0. & 0. & 0. & 0. & 2. & 3. & 0. & 0. & 0. & 0. \end{bmatrix}$$

and the resource availabilities by

$$w = (0.8,\ 0.8).$$

The utility functions $u(y)$, $v(x)$ are

$$u(y) = y_{\cdot 1}^{0.2} y_{\cdot 2}^{0.2} y_{\cdot 3}^{0.2},$$

so

$$v(x) = (\xi_1 + 2.5\xi_2)^{0.2} (2.5\xi_3 + \xi_4)^{0.2} (2\xi_5 + 3\xi_6)^{0.2},$$

The nonslack vectors $\xi^{11}, \ldots, \xi^J$ in Ξ are selected to be all vectors of the form

$$(m_0/100,\ m_1/100, \ldots, m_{10}/100), \quad \sum_{i=1}^{10} m_i = 100, \quad m_i \text{ strictly positive integers.}$$

This particular choice of the grid has substantial appeal since it provides a uniform density throughout the simplex, and need not be stored explicitly in the memory units of the computer. It does violate the nondegeneracy assumption required in the definition of primitive sets and in the description of the algorithm. However, in the presence of degeneracy the algorithm can readily be made to retain its validity by a suitable tie breaking rule. We have used a specific tie breaking procedure which has its origins in

TABLE 1

Terminal Primitive Sets $\{\xi^{j_h} \mid h = 0, \cdots, 10\}$ for a Constructed Example

Discount factor α	0.7						0.8						0.9						
Number of iterations introducing nonslack vectors	335						420						721						
Labels j_h of slack vectors ξ^{j_h}	1	4	5	8	9		1	4	5	8	10		1	4	6	10			
Components $\xi_i^{j_h}$ of nonslack vectors ξ^{j_h}																			
$i = 0$	43	44	44	44	44	44	38	39	39	39	39	39	19	20	20	20	20	20	20
1	1	1	1	1	1	1	1	1	1	1	1	1	1	1	1	1	1	1	1
2	9	8	8	9	9	9	10	9	10	10	10	10	12	11	11	12	12	12	12
3	10	10	11	10	10	10	12	12	11	12	12	12	13	13	14	13	13	13	13
4	1	1	1	1	1	1	1	1	1	1	1	1	1	1	1	1	1	1	1
5	1	1	1	1	1	1	1	1	1	1	1	1	23	23	22	22	22	23	23
6	15	15	14	14	15	15	15	15	15	14	15	15	1	1	1	1	1	1	1
7	11	11	11	11	10	11	12	12	12	12	11	12	13	13	13	13	14	13	13
8	1	1	1	1	1	1	1	1	1	1	1	1	6	6	6	6	5	5	6
9	1	1	1	1	1	1	8	8	8	8	8	7	10	10	10	10	10	10	9
10	7	7	7	7	7	6	1	1	1	1	1	1	1	1	1	1	1	1	1
Computing time	14 Minutes on IBM-1130; equivalent to about one minute on IBM 360-50.																		

Note: All components of nonslack vectors have been multiplied by 100.

Hansen's thesis [4], and which has other computational advantages besides the saving-on-memory use already mentioned. Its relationship to primitive sets is explained in Scarf [18].

The algorithm has been run for three different values of α, namely $\alpha = 0.7, 0.8$, and 0.9. The terminal primitive sets, the number of iterations for each α and the total computing time for the three α's taken together are shown in Table 1. A preliminary approximation x^* of $\hat{x}$ was obtained from the vectors ξ^{j_h}, $h = 0,\ldots, I$, of the terminal primitive set as follows. If ξ^{j_h} is a slack member, we write $\xi^*_{j_h} = 0$. The other components of x^*

TABLE 2

Approximately Invariant Optimal Capital Stock

			0.7	0.8	0.9
Discount factor		α	0.7	0.8	0.9
One-period utility attained		$v(\tilde{x})$	0.48855	0.52216	0.55935
Activity levels for producing consumption good	1	$\tilde{\xi}_1$	0.	0.	0.
		$\tilde{\xi}_2$	0.08615	0.10528	0.12621
	2	$\tilde{\xi}_3$	0.11086	0.12581	0.13986
		$\tilde{\xi}_4$	0.	0.	0.
	3	$\tilde{\xi}_5$	0.	0.	0.24817
		$\tilde{\xi}_6$	0.15544	0.15630	0.
capital good	1	$\tilde{\xi}_7$	0.10667	0.11789	0.13393
		$\tilde{\xi}_8$	0.	0.	0.04345
	2	$\tilde{\xi}_9$	0.	0.08416	0.10839
		$\tilde{\xi}_{10}$	0.07423	0.	0.
Capital stock		$\tilde{z}_{\cdot 1} = (A\tilde{x})_1$	1.06667	1.17889	1.60000
		$\tilde{z}_{\cdot 2} = (A\tilde{x})_2$	0.77937	0.92581	1.17055
Unused resources		$(w - C\tilde{x})_1$	0.26667	0.21056	0.
		$(w - C\tilde{x})_2$	0.	0.	0.
Shadow prices, capital goods		$q_{\cdot 1}$	0.35921	0.33408	0.31705
		$q_{\cdot 2}$	0.68327	0.57821	0.45534
resources		$r_{\cdot 1}$	0.	0.	0.02690
		$r_{\cdot 2}$	0.02304	0.15933	0.26258

Notes: 1. All subscripts refer to processes or commodities, none to time. 2. The numbers given satisfy $(A - B)\tilde{x} = 0$ and (7.18). 3. An expression is interpreted as 0 if it differs from 0 by less than 10^{-7} in absolute value.

are arithmetic averages of the corresponding components of the nonslack vectors ξ^{j_h} in the set. A preliminary approximation q^*, r^* of the shadow prices is obtained as follows:

(1) calculating the η_{j_h} of (6.13) and the sum $\lambda = \sum_{j \in \mathscr{J}} \eta_j$ of those η_{j_h}, denoted λ_j in (7.2), that correspond to the weights of the partial derivatives of $v(x)$;

(2) dividing the other η_{j_h}, denoted η_i, ϵ_l, δ_m in (7.2), by λ.

If, for example, η_{j_h} for some h is equal to 0.2 and $\lambda = 0.4$ and if further $f^{j_h} = (1, -a_{l1} + \alpha b_{l1} + 1, \dots, -a_{ln} + \alpha b_{ln} + 1)$, this means that a preliminary approximation for the l-th component q_{1l} of q_1 is given by $q_{1l} = 0.2/0.4 = 0.5$ and for that of q_2 by $q_{2l} = \alpha q_{1l} = 0.5\alpha$. If some l does not occur in $\mathscr{L}$, we put $q_{1l} = q_{2l} = 0$, and similarly for r_m.

Finally, the function $v(x)$ was locally linearized and a set of specific linear programming problems were solved to yield the final approximation $\tilde{x}$, which is given in Table 2. Details of this computation are given in an Appendix.

Note that in this example, as α increases, utility attained, the optimal capital stock and, to the extent possible, resource use increase, and that such shifts in processes as occur all economize on resource use.

APPENDIX I: Final Approximation Procedure

The purpose of this appendix is to describe the sequence of linear programming problems used in obtaining the final approximation $\tilde{x} = (\tilde{\xi}_1, \dots, \tilde{\xi}_I)$ given in Table 2.

Let $x^*(0)$ denote the preliminary approximation of $\hat{x}$ and $q^*(0) = (q^*_{\cdot 1}(0), \dots, q^*_{\cdot L}(0))$, $\alpha q^*(0)$ and $r^*(0)$ the preliminary approximations of the shadow price vectors. Let $s = 1, \dots, S$ label the programming problem within the sequence and let $x^*(s)$ denote the approximation of $\hat{x}$ resulting from the s-th programming problem. Finally let $q^*(s)$, $\alpha q^*(s)$ and $r^*(s)$ denote the associated approximations to the shadow price vectors resulting from the s-th programming problem.

Define the linear functions $V_i(x, q, r)$, $i = 1, \dots, I$, as follows:

$$V_i(x, q, r) \equiv v_i'(x^*(s-1)) - \sum_{l=1}^{L} q_l(a_{li} - \alpha b_{li}) - \sum_{m=1}^{M} r_m c_{mi}$$
$$+ \sum_{j=1}^{I} v''_{ij}(x^*(s-1))(\xi_j - \xi_j^*(s-1)),$$

where the $v''_{ij}(x^*)$ denote second derivatives of $v(x)$ at x^*. The s-th programming problem is then given by the following.

Minimize u by choice of $x \equiv (\xi_1, \ldots, \xi_I)$, q, r, subject to $x, q, r \geqq 0$ and

$$|V_i(x, q, r)| \leq u \qquad \text{for all } i \text{ with } \xi_i^*(s-1) > 0,$$

$$V_i(x, q, r) \leq 0 \qquad \text{for all } i \text{ with } \xi_i^*(s-1) = 0,$$

$$\left|\sum_i (a_{li} - b_{li})\, \xi_i\right| \leq u \qquad \text{for all } l \text{ with } q^*_{\cdot l}(s-1) > 0,$$

$$\sum_i (a_{li} - b_{li})\, \xi_i \leq 0 \qquad \text{for all } l \text{ with } q^*_{\cdot l}(s-1) = 0,$$

$$\left|\sum_i c_{mi}\xi_i - w_m\right| \leq u \qquad \text{for all } m \text{ with } r^*_{\cdot m}(s-1) > 0,$$

$$\sum_i c_{mi}\xi_i - w_m \leq 0 \qquad \text{for all } m \text{ with } r^*_{\cdot m}(s-1) = 0,$$

$$|\xi_i - \xi_i^*(s-1)| \leq 0.1\xi_i^*(s-1) \qquad \text{for all } i,$$

$$|q_{\cdot l} - q^*_{\cdot l}(s-1)| \leq 0.1 q^*_{\cdot l}(s-1) \qquad \text{for all } l,$$

$$|r_{\cdot m} - r^*_{\cdot m}(s-1)| \leq 0.1 r^*_{\cdot m}(s-1) \qquad \text{for all } m.$$

where all summations extend from $i = 1$ to I.

The optimal solution of the s-th linear programming problem is denoted $x^*(s)$, $q^*(s)$, $r^*(s)$. Observe that if an activity is operated at a zero level in the preliminary approximation $x^*(0)$ it stays at a zero level through the sequence of linear programming problems. Similarly if a shadow price is 0 in the preliminary approximation it is not changed through the linear programming problems.

The reader should have no difficulty in convincing himself that if the value of the objective function of the linear programming problem at the S-th iteration is 0 and in addition $x^*(S) = x^*(S-1)$ then the desired final approximation is obtained by setting

$$(\tilde{x}, \tilde{y}, \tilde{z}, \tilde{q}_1, \tilde{r}, \tilde{q}_2) \equiv (x^*(S), Dx^*(S), Ax^*(S), q^*(S), r^*(S), \alpha q^*(S)).$$

For each of the problems described in Section 8 the linear programming problem above needed to be applied three times.

To illustrate the approximation the preliminary as well as the final approximation for $\alpha = 0.7$ is given in Table 3.

TABLE 3

Preliminary and Final Approximation of an Invariant Optimal Capital Stock for the Case $\alpha = 0.7$

			Preliminary (x^*)	Final ($\tilde{x}$)
One-period utility attained		$v(x)$	0.47520	0.48855
Activity levels for producing				
Consumption good	1	ξ_1	0.	0.
		ξ_2	0.08666	0.08615
	2	ξ_3	0.10166	0.11086
		ξ_4	0.	0.
	3	ξ_5	0.	0.
		ξ_6	0.14666	0.15544
Capital good	1	ξ_7	0.10833	0.10667
		ξ_8	0.	0.
	2	ξ_9	0.	0.
		ξ_{10}	0.06833	0.07423
Capital stock		$z_{\cdot 1} = (Ax)_1$	1.02333	1.06667
		$z_{\cdot 2} = (Ax)_2$	0.75250	0.77937
Unused resources		$(w - Cx)_1$	0.28834	0.26667
		$(w - Cx)_2$	0.03251	0.
Shadow prices, capital goods		$q_{\cdot 1}$	0.36271	0.35921
		$q_{\cdot 2}$	0.68995	0.68327
Resources		$r_{\cdot 1}$	0.	0.
		$r_{\cdot 2}$	0.02326	0.02304

APPENDIX II: CONNECTIONS WITH THE VON NEUMANN MODEL

We first prove a lemma, alluded to at the end of Section 6, which states that the growth capability condition permits only solutions of $P(\alpha)$ in which at least one resource is in full use. It follows, in particular, that the growth capability condition excludes a null solution of $P(\alpha)$.

LEMMA 2. *If the growth capability condition* (6.2) *holds, then any solution* $(\hat{x}, \hat{z})$ *of* $P(\alpha)$ *satisfies* $(C\hat{x})_m = w_m$ *for at least one* m.

Proof. Suppose (6.2) holds but $C\hat{x} < w$ for a solution $(\hat{x}, \hat{z})$ of $P(\alpha)$. Then (3.2) and (3.3) are satisfied by a vector $(q_1, q_2, r) = (q, \alpha q, 0)$, and from (3.2a) and (3.2b) we have

$$q \geq 0, \qquad q(A - \alpha B) \geqq v'(\hat{x}) \geq 0,$$

respectively, of which the second in turn implies

$$q(A - \alpha B)x > 0 \qquad \text{for all} \quad x > 0.$$

But this is contradicted by the particular $\bar{x} > 0$ occurring in (6.2), for which, since $q \geq 0$, we have $q(A - \alpha B)\bar{x} < 0$. It follows that $(C\hat{x})_m = w_m$ for at least one m. (This holds also with $\leqq$ replacing $<$ in (6.2).)

There are interesting connections between the growth capability condition, the existence of a null solution to $P(\alpha)$, and the properties of the von Neumann model obtained by deleting resources and consumption from the present model. The technological constraint set for a single period then takes the form

$$\begin{aligned} -Ax &\geqq -z_1, && \text{(capital input)} \\ Bx &\geqq z_2, && \text{(capital output)} \\ x &\geqq 0. \end{aligned} \tag{II.1}$$

We first summarize the pertinent properties of this model (see [2, 6]).

A growth factor $\beta > 0$ is achievable if there exist vectors x, z_1, z_2 satisfying (II.1) with $z_2 \geqq \beta z_1 \geq 0$. Eliminating z_1 and z_2, the problem of fastest growth is the following.

$\bar{P}$: *Maximize* β *subject to* $(B - \beta A)x \geqq 0$ *for some* $x \geq 0$.

If $\bar{\beta}$, $\bar{x}$ solve $\bar{P}$ then there exists a vector $\bar{q}$ such that

$$(B - \beta A)x \geqq 0, \qquad x \geq 0, \tag{II.2a}$$

$$q(B - \beta A) \leqq 0, \qquad q \geq 0, \tag{II.2b}$$

$$q(B - \beta A)x = 0, \tag{II.2c}$$

holds with $\beta = \bar{\beta}$, $x = \bar{x}$, $q = \bar{q}$. One can interpret $\bar{q}$ as a price vector $\bar{q}_t$ referred to time t of availability, which in the present model can be taken to be independent of t. Then $\rho = \bar{\beta} - 1$ becomes an interest rate to be used in adding $\rho\bar{q}A$ to the cost vector $\bar{q}A$ of capital inputs for the unit of activity of each process at the beginning of the period before subtracting it from the vector $\bar{q}B$ of proceeds from capital outputs at the end of the period. The unit profit vector then is $\bar{q}(B - \bar{\beta}A)$, and (II.2b) says that no process yields a positive profit. Furthermore, the addition of (II.2c) to the other constraints forces a zero rate of profit on all processes in use ($\bar{x}_i > 0$), and a zero price on all capital goods produced in excess, i.e., for which

$$(B\bar{x})_l > \bar{\beta}(A\bar{x})_l \,.$$

Dual to $\bar{P}$ is the following problem.

$\underline{P}$: *Minimize* β *subject to* $q(B - \beta A) \leqq 0$ *for some* $q \geq 0$.

If $\underline{\beta}$, $\underline{q}$ solve $\underline{P}$ then there exists a vector $\underline{x}$ such that (II.2) holds with $\beta = \underline{\beta}$, $x = \underline{x}$, $q = \underline{q}$.

Clearly, $\underline{\beta} \leqq \bar{\beta}$. One has $\underline{\beta} = \bar{\beta}$ if the model is regular, that is (see Gale [2]), if $B\bar{x} > 0$ for all $\bar{x}$ such that $\bar{\beta}$, $\bar{x}$ solve $\bar{P}$. This is the case, in particular, if the indefinitely continued production of *each* good in the model requires, either as a direct input, or (indirectly) as an input to the production of a direct or indirect input, the continued production of *every* good in the model.

We now prove a lemma linking the growth capability condition with $\underline{\beta}$ and $\bar{\beta}$.

LEMMA 3. *The growth capability condition* (6.2) (i) *implies* $\alpha > \bar{\beta}^{-1}$ *and* (ii) *is implied by* $\alpha > \underline{\beta}^{-1}$.

Proof of Lemma 3(i). Let (6.2) hold. Then there exists $\bar{x} > 0$ such that $(B - \alpha^{-1}A)\bar{x} > 0$, hence $(B - (\alpha^{-1} + \epsilon)A)\bar{x} \geqq 0$ for some $\epsilon > 0$. Therefore (using $\bar{P}$) $\alpha^{-1} + \epsilon \leqq \bar{\beta}$, so $\alpha > \bar{\beta}^{-1}$ (and $\alpha \geqq \bar{\beta}^{-1}$ for $\leqq$ in (6.2)).

Proof of Lemma 3(ii). Assume now that (6.2) does not hold. Then, for all $x > 0$, we must have $(B - \alpha^{-1}A)x \ngtr 0$. This means that the cone $\mathscr{B}^0(\alpha^{-1}) \equiv \{(B - \alpha^{-1}A)x \mid x > 0\}$ in L-dimensional space, spanned by the columns of $(B - \alpha^{-1}A)$ does not intersect the interior $\mathscr{X}_L{}^0 \equiv \{z \mid z > 0\}$ of the positive orthant of that space. By the separation theorem of convex sets, there then exists a vector $q \neq 0$ with

$$q(B - \alpha^{-1}A)x \leqq 0 \quad \text{for all } x > 0, \qquad qz \geqq 0 \quad \text{for all } z > 0.$$

Therefore $q(B - \alpha^{-1}A) \leqq 0$, $q \geq 0$, and, using $\underline{P}$, $\alpha^{-1} \geqq \underline{\beta}$, hence $\alpha \leqq \underline{\beta}^{-1}$. Therefore $\alpha > \underline{\beta}^{-1}$ implies (6.2).

Lemmas 2 and 3(ii) together imply that $\alpha > \underline{\beta}^{-1}$ precludes $C\hat{x} < w$, and in particular $\hat{x} = 0$, in any solution of $P(\alpha)$. We conclude by proving a complementary statement.

LEMMA 4. *The solution set of* $P(\alpha)$ *contains the null solution* $(\hat{x}, \hat{z}) = (0, 0)$ *if* $\alpha < \bar{\beta}^{-1}$.

Proof of Lemma 4. Let $\alpha < \bar{\beta}^{-1}$, hence $\alpha^{-1} > \bar{\beta}$. Then, using $\bar{P}$, there exists no $x \geq 0$ with $(B - \alpha^{-1}A)x \geqq 0$, and, as in the proof of Lemma 3(ii), the (this time closed) cone

$$\mathscr{B}(\alpha^{-1}) \equiv \{(B - \alpha^{-1}A)x \mid x \geqq 0\}$$

intersects the (closed) positive orthant $\mathscr{Z}_L \equiv \{z \mid z \geqq 0\}$ only in the origin. We use the theory of polar cones (we shall cite theorems from Gerstenhaber [3]) to obtain a somewhat stronger separation statement for this case. If in Gerstenhaber's Theorem 12(1)(e) we substitute our $\mathscr{Z}_L$ for his A, and our $\mathscr{B}(\alpha^{-1})$ for his B, we obtain that the vector sum of the polar

$$\mathscr{Z}_L^+ \equiv \{q \mid qz \geqq 0 \quad \text{for all} \quad z \in \mathscr{Z}_L\} \equiv \{q \mid q \geqq 0\}$$

of $\mathscr{Z}_L$ and the polar

$$\mathscr{B}^+(\alpha^{-1}) \equiv \{q \mid qz \geqq 0 \quad \text{for all} \quad z \in \mathscr{B}(\alpha^{-1})\}$$

of $\mathscr{B}(\alpha^{-1})$ is the entire L-dimensional space, $\mathscr{R}_L$, say,

$$\mathscr{Z}_L^+ + \mathscr{B}^+(\alpha^{-1}) = \mathscr{R}_L .$$

Now $\mathscr{Z}_L^+$ is L-dimensional. To show that the same holds for $\mathscr{B}^+(\alpha^{-1})$ we use $\bar{P}$ once more, writing $x = x' + x''$, to conclude that there exist no $x' \geq 0$, $x'' \geq 0$, such that

$$(B - \alpha^{-1}A)x' = -(B - \alpha^{-1}A)x''.$$

Therefore $\mathscr{B}(\alpha^{-1})$ does not contain an entire line, hence, by Theorem 12(2), $\mathscr{B}^+(\alpha^{-1})$ is L-dimensional.

Finally, substituting in Gerstenhaber's Theorem 13 our $\mathscr{Z}_L^+$ for his A and our $-\mathscr{B}^+(\alpha^{-1})$ for his B, we obtain that the intersection of the interiors of $\mathscr{Z}_L^+$ and $-\mathscr{B}^+(\alpha^{-1})$ is not empty. Therefore, there exists q such that

$$q > 0, \qquad q(B - \alpha^{-1}A)x < 0 \qquad \text{for all} \quad x \geq 0,$$

hence $q(B - \alpha^{-1}A) < 0$. This allows (3.2), (3.3) to be satisfied for $\hat{x} = 0$, $z = 0$, by choosing $r = 0$, $q_1 = \lambda q$, $q_2 = \alpha\lambda q$ with λ sufficiently large to have $v'(0) \leqq \lambda q(A - \alpha B)$.

Note that we have not answered the question whether $\alpha < \bar{\beta}^{-1}$ permits *only* the null solution. We are hopeful that further light can be thrown on this question if we impose additional restrictions on the signs of the elements of A, B, C, D, which are plausible for many applications.

In the example of Section 8, $\underline{\beta} = \bar{\beta} = \beta^* = 1.468$, $\alpha^* \equiv \beta^{*-1} = .6812$.

Acknowledgments

We are indebted to Herbert Scarf, to Alexander Schmidt and to the referee for highly valuable comments. The referee supplied the idea and proof now incorporated in Lemma 2 of Appendix II.

References

1. B. C. Eaves, Computing Kakutani Fixed Points, *SIAM J. Appl. Math.* (1970), in press.
2. D. Gale, The Closed Linear Model of Production, "Linear Inequalities and Related Systems," *in* (H. W. Kuhn and A. W. Tucker, Eds.), pp.285–303, Princeton Univ. Press, 1956.
3. M. Gerstenhaber, Theory of Convex Polyhedral Cones, *in* "Activity Analysis of Production and Allocation" (T. C. Koopmans, Ed.), Chap. 18, pp. 298–316. Wiley, New York, 1951 (reprinted by Yale Univ. Press, 1971).
4. T. Hansen, On the Approximation of a Competitive Equilibrium, Ph.D. Thesis, Yale University, 1968.
5. T. Hansen, A Fixed Point Algorithm for Approximating the Optimal Solution of a Concave Programming Problem, Cowles Foundation Discussion Paper No. 277, June, 1969, mimeographed, 17 pp.
6. J. G. Kemeny, O. Morgenstern and G. L. Thompson, A Generalization of the von Neumann Model of an Expanding Economy, *Econometrica*, **24** (1956), 115–135.
7. T. C. Koopmans, (1951). Analysis of Production as an Efficient Combination of Activities, *in* "Activity Analysis of Production and Allocation" (T. C. Koopmans, Ed.), Chap. 3, pp. 33–97, Wiley, New York, 1951 (reprinted by Yale Univ. Press, 1971).
8. T. C. Koopmans, On the Concept of Optimal Economic Growth, *in* "The Econometric Approach to Development Planning," North Holland Publishing Co. and Rand McNally, 1966 (a reissue of *Pontificiae Academiae Scientiarum Scripta Varia*, **28** (1965), 225–300).
9. T. C. Koopmans, A Model of a Continuing State with Scarce Capital, *in* "Contributions to the von Neumann Growth Model" (G. Bruckmann and W. Weber, Eds.), *Zeitschrift für Nationalökonomie*, Suppl. 1, 1971 and Springer, 1971, 11–22.
10. T. C. Koopmans, Representation of Preference Orderings Over Time, *in* "Decision and Organization," (C. B. McGuire and R. Radner, Eds.), Chap. 4, 79–100, North Holland Publishing Co., 1972.
11. H. W. Kuhn, Simplicial Approximation of Fixed Points, *Proc. Nat. Acad. Sci.* **65** (1968), 1238–1242.
12. H. W. Kuhn, Approximate Search for Fixed Points, *in* "Computing Methods in Optimization Problems," Academic Press, New York, 1969, 199–211.

13. H. W. KUHN AND A. W. TUCKER, Nonlinear Programming, "Proceedings of the Second Berkeley Symposium on Mathematical Statistics and Probability" (J. Neyman, Ed.), University of California Press, Berkeley, Cal., 1950, 481–492 (reprinted *in* "Readings in Mathematical Economics" (P. Newman, Ed.), Vol. I, Johns Hopkins Press, Baltimore, 1968).
14. H. E. SCARF, The Core of an *n* Person Game, *Econometrica*, **35** (1967), 50–69.
15. H. E. SCARF, The Approximation of Fixed Points of a Continuous Mapping, *SIAM J. Appl. Math.* (15) (1967), 1328–1343.
16. H. E. SCARF, On the Computation of Equilibrium Prices, *in* "Ten Economic Studies in the Tradition of Irving Fisher," (W. Fellner *et al.*,) Chap. 8, Wiley, New York, 1967, 207–230.
17. H. E. SCARF, An Example of Calculating General Equilibrium Prices, *Amer. Econ. Rev.* **59** (1969), 669–677.
18. H. E. SCARF, (with the collaboration of T. Hansen), "The Computation of Economic Equilibria," Cowles Foundation Monograph, Yale Univ. Press, forthcoming.
19. W. R. S. SUTHERLAND, "On Optimal Development Programs when Future Utility is Discounted," Ph.D. Thesis, Brown University, June, 1967, University Microfilms, Ann Arbor, Michigan.
20. W. R. S. SUTHERLAND, On Optimal Development in a Multi-Sectoral Economy: The Discounted Case, *Rev. Econ. Studies*, **37** (4), (1970), 585–589.
21. A. W. TUCKER, Linear and Nonlinear Programming, *Operations Research*, **5** (1957), 244–257.
22. J. VON NEUMANN, A Model of General Equilibrium, *Rev. of Econ. Studies*, **13** (1945–46), 10–18 (translated from the German original in "Ergebnisse eines Mathematischen Kolloquiums" (Karl Menger, Ed.), **8** (1935–36), published 1937).

7

Some Observations on 'Optimal' Economic Growth and Exhaustible Resources*

Tjalling C. Koopmans**

Economic Structure and Development: Essays in Honour of Jan Tinbergen, ed. H. C. Bos, H. Linnemann, and P. de Wolff (Amsterdam: North-Holland, 1973), pp. 239–255

1. Introduction

It is a principal theme of Irving Fisher's [1] classical work 'The Theory of Interest' that, in a competitive market over time, the real rate of interest is determined by the interacting forces of consumers' intertemporal preferences and of the opportunities to shift goods across time offered by technology and resource supply. It will serve as an introduction to the present paper to recall his illustrations (in chapter VIII) of the effects of technology and of resource availability by a few striking examples, of which I cite two. In the 'sheep example', the flock of sheep has a natural annual rate of increase of 10%. Assuming other inputs to be abundant and costless, the rate of interest (with sheep as numéraire at all times) then also equals 10% p.a. In contrast, in the 'hardtack example', a group of sailors is stranded on a barren island, each with a supply of nonperishable hardtack. In that numéraire, the rate of interest is zero. In these simple settings, the statements describe the outcome of competitive trades between owners of sheep or of hardtack, regardless of the intertemporal preferences of the trading parties.

In the models of optimal growth theory a social intertemporal preference structure is specified exogenously in the form of a social welfare functional. In many models this is taken to be of the form

$$U = \int_0^T e^{-\rho t}\, u(c_t)\, dt\,, \qquad (1.1)$$

* The research described in this paper is supported by grants from the National Science Foundation and from the Ford Foundation.

** Cowles Foundation for Research in Economics, Yale University. I am indebted to Robert Dorfman, William Nordhaus and Herbert Scarf for valuable comments.

where c_t denotes consumption at time t, $u(c)$ a strictly increasing and strictly concave function giving the utility flow arising from a consumption flow c, ρ a nonnegative continuous-time discount *rate* applied to *utility*, and $e^{-\rho t}$ the corresponding discount *factor* for time t. Then we can again take the consumption good as numéraire. Denoting the path optimal under given constraints by $\hat{c}_t$, the corresponding discount factor for *consumption* is

$$e^{-\rho t} \frac{u'(\hat{c}_t)}{u'(\hat{c}_0)}, \tag{1.2}$$

which in turn implies a continuous-time interest rate i_t as a function of time, defined likewise with the consumption good as the numéraire. It follows that any constraint on that interest rate i_t arising from technology or resource availability must give rise also to a condition on the optimal path $\hat{c}_t$.

In this note I wish to contrast the optimal paths obtained for the hardtack example, to be renamed the *exhaustible resource model,* and for a slight generalization of the sheep example, renamed the *capital model.* We shall make this comparison both for $\rho = 0$, and for positive ρ. We occasionally place the word 'optimal' in quotes as a reminder that the optimality concept is relative to a particular choice of ρ, of $u(\cdot)$, and indeed of all other specifications of the models examined.

In these inferences the rate of interest i_t will not occur explicitly. It was brought up in the foregoing remarks only to point out that the contrast we are examining – like so much else in capital theory – was already noted and analyzed in a market context in Fisher's work.

2. *The capital model*

For this, Ramsey's [2] model with discounting, we can be very brief because it has been thoroughly examined and discussed in the literature. An additional variable, the capital stock k_t, is introduced, and output $g(k_t)$ from that capital stock is at all times to be optimally divided between consumption c_t and net investment $\dot{k}_t$. The horizon is extended to $T = \infty$. The problem then becomes that of maximizing the welfare functional

$$U = \int_0^\infty e^{-\rho t} u(c_t)\, dt, \tag{2.1}$$

subject to

$$c_t, k_t \geqq 0, \quad c_t + \dot{k}_t = g(k_t) \ \text{ for } \ t \geqq 0, \quad 0 < k_0 \text{ (given)}. \tag{2.2}$$

The utility and production functions are independent of time and satisfy

$$u'(c) > 0\,, \quad u''(c) < 0 \quad \text{for} \quad c > 0\,, \tag{2.3}$$

$$g(0) = 0\,, \quad g'(k) > 0\,, \quad g'(\hat{k}) = 0\,, \quad g''(k) < 0$$
$$\text{for all} \quad k \geqq 0 \quad \text{and some} \quad \hat{k} > 0\,. \tag{2.4}$$

While neither resources nor labor appear explicitly, their presence in the background is implicit in the strict concavity of $g(\cdot)$ and in the assumption of a finite saturation level $\hat{k}$ for capital. The sheep fit into this model both as capital and as a source of food and clothing, provided labor and land are limited and, indeed, constant over time.

The well-known characteristics of the unique optimal path in this model are exhibited in figure 1, which is more fully explained in Koopmans.[3] In the case of a low initial capital stock k_0, the optimal capital path $\hat{k}_t$ climbs monotonically (starting up more steeply the smaller ρ is) and approaches an asymptotic level $\hat{k}(\rho)$, which is higher as ρ is smaller. Initially optimal consumption $\hat{c}_t$ is higher as ρ is larger, but the asymptotic level $\hat{c}(\rho)$ (which can be read from the diagram at left) is again higher as ρ is smaller. For $\rho = 0$ the asymptotic capital stock $\hat{k}(0) \equiv \hat{k}$ achieves the highest sustainable consump-

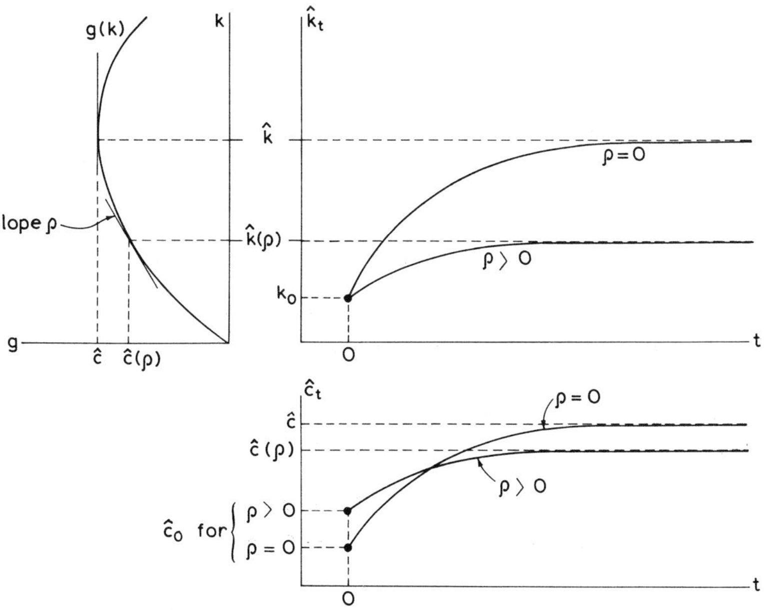

Figure 1

tion flow $\hat{c}(0) \equiv \hat{c}$. *Hence, in the capital model, discounting of future utilities as compared with no discounting favors consumers in a nearby future. It also levels off consumption over the rest of the future sooner, and at a level lower than what would ultimately be attainable by greater and longer initial sacrifice of consumption. These effects are stronger, the higher is* ρ.

The construct of capital saturation, so outside the range of experience, helps overcome a mathematical difficulty connected with the assumption of a constant population. An alternative but ultimately unsatisfactory assumption of exogenous exponential population growth at a rate λ allows $g(k)$ to be interpreted as the per capita output from a per capita capital stock k minus an allowance λk for the per capita investment needed just to make the total capital stock grow in proportion to the population.

3. *The exhaustible resource model*

Hotelling's [4] classic is for the theory of the optimal rate of utilization of exhaustible resources what Ramsey's paper is for the theory of optimal capital growth. Hotelling's context is that of a given demand function for a mineral resource. Separate sections deal with the allocation of the resource over time resulting from free competition, from a monopoly of supply, and from a consideration of the social optimum.

The optimal growth literature that has sprung up in the last two decades consists preponderantly of wide ramifications and generalizations of the Ramsey model. The attention given to the problem of best allocation of exhaustible resources over time has been much sparser. While resources have been introduced in an optimizing context in papers by Malinvaud,[5] Radner [6,7] and Hansen and Koopmans,[8] it has been the resource flows rather than the total stocks that have been assumed exogenously given. This misses the main characteristic of exhaustible resources: that extraction and use can be shifted between future periods, subject to a *finite* (though usually uncertain) upper bound on cumulative extraction over an infinite future. This stands in striking contrast to the fact that shiftability over time of consumption and capital formation is in the focus of the optimal growth literature.

A small step toward the recognition of exhaustible resources in optimal growth theory occurs in an article by Gale [9] otherwise entirely in the Ramsey framework. On page 4 of that article there is a brief 'example 2' of the optimizing cake eater. Each day he can eat a piece of a size he chooses from a nonperishable cake of finite size, until it is exhausted. If his current utility from cake consumption r is an increasing and strictly concave function $v(r)$ of r, he seeks to maximize (using discrete time)

$$V \equiv \sum_{t=1}^{\infty} v(r_t), \tag{3.1}$$

subject to

$$r_t \geqq 0, \qquad \sum_{t=1}^{\infty} r_t \leqq R, \quad \text{say, where} \quad R > 0. \tag{3.2}$$

Gale points out that no optimal program exists, because,

(1) if, for any t', t'' with $t' \neq t''$, we have $r_{t'} \neq r_{t''}$ in a given program $(r_t) = \{r_t | t = 1, 2, ...\}$, then the program $(\bar{r}_t)$ with

$$\begin{cases} \bar{r}_t = \frac{1}{2}(r_{t'} + r_{t''}), & \text{for} \quad t = t', t'' \\ \bar{r}_t = r_t, & \text{otherwise} \end{cases}$$

is better than (r_t) because of the strict concavity of $v(r)$,

(2) the only feasible program with $r_t = r_1$ for all t has $r_1 = 0$, which is clearly nonoptimal.

Hence in this problem a zero discount rate paralyzes the 'optimizing' decision maker. (This may, but need not be the case with discounting at a positive rate, depending on the behavior of $v(r)$ as r approaches zero.)

Let us apply this simple model to Fisher's stranded sailors, with two modifications. First, rather than trading from private hoards, the sailors have pooled their resources and, having heard of Ramsey, wish their pooled stock R of hardtack to be allocated over time by maximization of a utility integral. Secondly, they are aware of the existence of a bare subsistance level $\underline{r}$ of consumption, at which survival is just possible, but below which all life ceases instantly. By instantly tightening the belt to a consumption level of $\underline{r}$, the group can assure itself a painful survival for $\overline{T} = R/\underline{r}$ days, but no longer. The paralysis of Gale's cake eater has now been avoided, but a new problem needs to be faced. It is possible to attain a higher level of daily consumption for the duration of survival by accepting a shorter period T of survival. Population P_t can therefore follow any of the following paths

$$\begin{cases} P_t = P_0, & 0 \leqq t \leqq T, \\ P_t = 0, & T < t, \end{cases}$$

where T is a decision variable constrained by $0 < T \leqq \overline{T}$.

This formulation raises a new question in the interpretation of the objective functional (1.1) of much optimal growth theory. As long as population change is treated as exogenously given, the ranking of feasible paths, and therefore the choice of an optimal path, are not changed if one adds a constant to the utility function, say

$$v^*(r) = v(r) + \varphi .$$

As soon as the number of people is no longer exogenously given for all times, $v(r)$ is pressed into the additional role of an *absolute* valuation placed on one day of life (group life in the present case) at the consumption level r. As a consequence, the addition of a constant to $v(r)$ will in general change the ranking of paths, hence also the optimal path. To simplify matters, we shall somewhat arbitrarily assign to life at the bare subsistence level $\underline{r}$ an intrinsic value of zero,

$$v(\underline{r}) = 0 , \tag{3.3}$$

although arguments for another number, positive or even negative, could be advanced. We now regard $v(r)$ as defined only for $r \geqq \underline{r}$.

Reverting to continuous time but still rejecting the discounting of future utilities we must then maximize

$$\int_0^T v(r_t)\,\mathrm{d}t \tag{3.4}$$

with respect to (T, r_t), subject to

$$0 < T \leqq \bar{T} , \qquad \int_0^T r_t\,\mathrm{d}t = R , \qquad r_t \geqq \underline{r} . \tag{3.5}$$

Maintaining strict concavity of $v(r)$, optimality again requires constancy of r_t during survival, so that

$$r_t = r = R/T \quad \text{for} \quad 0 \leqq t \leqq T , \qquad r_t = 0 \quad \text{for} \quad T < t .$$

Adopting r rather than $T = R/r$ as the remaining decision variable, we must now maximize

$$\int_0^T v(r_t)\,\mathrm{d}t = \frac{R}{r}\, v(r)$$

over the domain of definition of $v(r)$. Since $v(r) > v(\underline{r}) = 0$ for $r > \underline{r}$, optimality requires $r > \underline{r}$, and $0 = (\mathrm{d}/\mathrm{d}r) \log(v(r)/r) = (v'(r)/v(r)) - (1/r)$, so

$$v'(r) = \frac{v(r)}{r} . \tag{3.6}$$

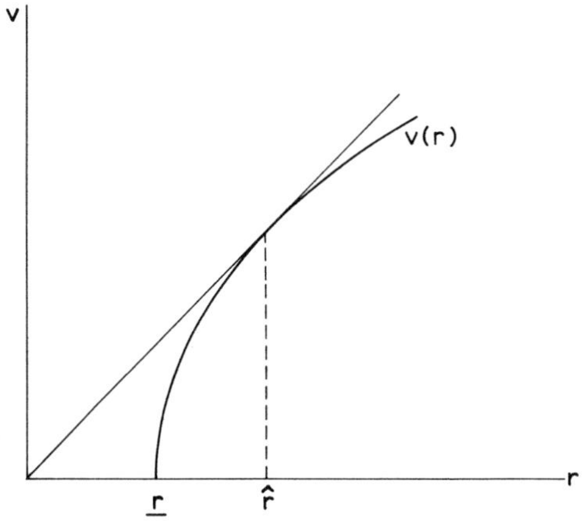

Figure 2

Figure 2 shows the construction of a unique optimal $\hat{r}$ by drawing a tangent from the origin to the curve $v = v(r)$. This construction leads to a unique and finite $\hat{r}$ if $v(\cdot)$ is bounded, and also if $\lim_{r\to\infty} v'(r) = 0$. (Functions $v(\cdot)$ for which no such $\hat{r}$ exists imply that the value of the maximand is higher the shorter the survival period – a case of little interest.) The 'optimal' survival time is $\hat{T} = R/\hat{r}$, which, of course, falls short of the maximum survival time $\overline{T} = R/\underline{r}$.

What happens if we discount future utilities at the rate ρ, maximizing the welfare functional

$$\int_0^T e^{-\rho t} v(r_t)\, dt\,, \tag{3.7}$$

with respect to (T, r_t), under the constraints

$$r_t \geqq \underline{r} \quad \text{for} \quad 0 \leqq t \leqq T, \qquad \int_0^T r_t\, dt = R\,. \tag{3.8}$$

We give an intuitive argument, illustrated in figure 3, suggesting that the optimal path is uniquely determined by three conditions. *

As a first step, hold T fixed at some arbitrarily chosen value with $0 < T < \overline{T}$, and maximize first only with respect to r_t. We must then have as the first, *myopic*, condition of 'T-optimality' of r_t that

* Reserving a rigorous proof for publication elsewhere.

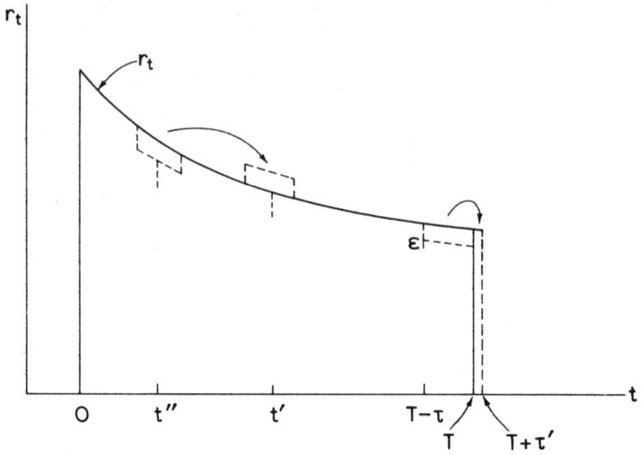

Figure 3

$$\varphi_t \equiv e^{-\rho t} v'(r_t) = \text{constant} \quad \text{for} \quad 0 \leqq t \leqq T. \tag{3.9}$$

This is so because, if $\varphi_{t'} > \varphi_{t''}$, say, for some t', t'' with $0 \leqq t', t'' \leqq T$, one could (see figure 3) increase (3.7) by shifting a small amount of consumption from a neighborhood in $[0,T]$ of t'' to one of t'. (A proviso for this reasoning is that $r_t \geqq \underline{r} + \epsilon > \underline{r}$ for all t with $0 \leqq t \leqq T$.)

Since $v''(r) < 0$, the condition (3.9) requires r_t to be a segment of a curve that is one of a family of descending curves. Any curve in this family can be identified by specifying the value of r_t for some suitable value of t. The second, *terminal*, condition* chooses the point $t = T$ for this purpose. Figure 3 shows another 'small' modification of the path r_t that reduces the consumption flow on a short terminal interval $[T-\tau, T]$ by an amount ϵ and uses the amount $\tau\epsilon$ thus saved to extend the survival period by a flow at the constant level $r_t = r_T$ continuing for the period $[T, T+\tau']$, where $\tau' = \tau\epsilon / r_T$. The first order effect on the utility integral (3.7) is

$$\left(-v'(r_T) + \frac{v(r_T)}{r_T}\right) \tau\epsilon\, e^{-\rho T},$$

where ϵ though small can be given either sign. ** It follows that the segment r_t, $0 \leqq t \leqq T$, is anchored by the terminal condition

$$r_T = \hat{r}, \tag{3.10}$$

* The form of this condition was suggested to me by William Nordhaus.

** For $\epsilon < 0$, one adds $|\epsilon|$ to r_t for $T' - \tau \leqq t \leqq T'$, where T' is just enough below T to again satisfy (3.8) with T' replacing T.

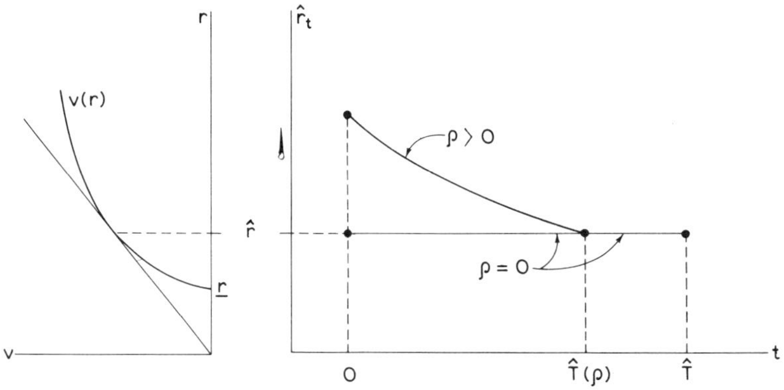

Figure 4

where $\hat{r}$ is the optimal consumption for $\rho = 0$ defined by (3.6). (Note that due to this construction the T-optimal path r_t satisfies the proviso stated above.)

Finally, the third, *length of survival,* condition uniquely determines the optimal survival time $T = \hat{T}(\rho)$ from the requirement that the segment $r_t = \hat{r}_t$ so selected shall just exhaust the given stock R.

Figure 4 indicates the nature of the optimal path $\hat{r}_t$, its connection with the utility function $v(\cdot)$, and its dependence on the discount rate ρ. The path $\hat{r}_t$ starts higher, descends faster, and ends sooner, the larger is ρ. *In the exhaustible resources model, discounting of future utilities favors an earlier generation over any surviving later generation, and shortens the period of survival. These effects are stronger the higher the discount rate.*

4. A comparative discussion

We shall now seek to interpret the contrasts in the solutions of the two models considered, and speculate about the empirical relevance of the various traits of the models.

Since the welfare functional is constructed along the same lines in the two cases, the contrast in the solutions must be due to the difference in supply conditions. In the capital model decision makers can at any time arrange to reap the prospective consumption-increasing benefits of a larger future capital stock only through net investment at points in time in a more nearby future. The future benefit to be derived from an extra unit of investment is smaller the larger the capital stock already attained. The optimal capital build-up therefore slows down as it proceeds, and stops at the point where the discounted cost of further investment balances the more strongly discounted benefit. The optimal rate of consumption therefore also increases with time, and slows down to a stop at a stationary consumption point corresponding to the stationary capital stock. The higher the discount rate, the lower both the stationary optimal stock and the associated consumption flow.

In contrast, in our simplified model * of resource exhaustion, consumption of an extra unit of the resource can at any time be decided on and implemented instantly, without having to go through a process of prior investment. Moreover, the opportunity cost of this instant benefit is incurred later, by an equal curtailment of consumption within the survival period, or by a shortening of that period. Finally, the analysis leading to (3.6) shows that even in the absence of discounting a reduction in the rate of consumption below $\hat{r}$ is deemed too high a price for the extension of the survival period it could buy. Discounting can thus only lift earlier generations above the resource consumption levels of later ones, along a path that stops when the level $\hat{r}$ is reached.

Let us now consider the question whether there is anything in the long-range outlook for resource supply that gives a tinge of realism to the model of possibly slow but inexorable and ultimately catastrophic exhaustion.

This issue is the subject of a protracted and continuing debate between economists and conservationists. The view prevailing among economists is that technological change has kept enlarging the aggregate size and diversity of the economically accessible resource base faster than extraction has diminished the resource base. This enlargement has come about through reductions in the cost of extraction of a given material, and through substitution of more abundant materials for increasingly scarce ones, including the scientific discovery of entirely new, often plentiful, kinds of resources. These substitutions within the resources category may be accompanied by increased capital inputs needed for the utilization of the newer more abundant resources. In aggregate accounts comparing quantity indices of total output, resource inputs and capital use inputs (all weighted by base-year prices), such substitutions may therefore show up as an aggregate substitution of capital for 'resources', where the resource flow at the same time changes its composition. In contrast, within the resource sector, the chain of events wereby technological change dominates the effect of continuing specific resource extraction shows up in a gradual decrease in the labor and capital input cost per unit of extractive output, relative to that same cost per unit of net output in the rest of the economy. A similar decrease is found in the market price of minerals relative to that of nonextractive goods, even though the price includes the element of scarcity rent not included in the cost measure.

* Professor Richard Gordon has kindly pointed out that the statements of this paragraph need to be modified if one recognizes the fact that capital is used also in the extraction of minerals.

This interpretation of events * is persuasively summarized in chapter 1 of Barnett and Morse [11] and statistically documented in chapters 8 and 9. A more recent study by Nordhaus and Tobin (reference 12, pp. 14–17) extends their work by ingenious simulations (reference 12, Appendix B, pp. 60–70) in which neoclassical aggregate production functions are employed to show that elasticities of substitution in excess of 1 between resources and 'capital plus labor' best fit observed characteristics of aggregate economic growth in the period 1909–1958.

The forward-looking relevance of the empirical observations made by the Barnett–Morse and Nordhaus–Tobin teams depends on an extrapolation into the future of the observed resource saving or augmenting effects of technological change. Two observations are pertinent here.

The first concerns the protection of the environment, through suitable choices of new technology, and through the modification of existing technology especially when applied on a larger scale. Particular problems arise in the extraction of resources from deposits of increasing depths or lower grades. Regarded itself as a resource, the environment is exhaustible if subjected to irreversible damage, renewable if the damage is temporary or restorable at a cost. An aggregate evaluation of the cost of protection of the environment must await further experience in the study and application of protective policies for many specific environmental problems. I shall here assume that a satisfactory level of protection can be attained over time at a reasonable cost.

The second observation concerns the need for looking behind the observed predominance of resource saving or augmenting technological change over resource extraction to seek to perceive the underlying causes. The first impression here is one of a huge reserve of detailed physical, chemical, geological and physiological relationships: known, suspected but not yet known, or even as yet unsuspected. The veil is gradually drawn away by a process of discovery, partly or initially accidental, gradually resulting from a more systematic search which is never assured of specific successes until these are actually achieved. Why should this process permit extrapolation of past aggregate relationships?

If present knowledge permits an answer to this question, the principal contributions should come from natural scientists and engineers. As long as there are many independent lines of advance for research and development, it is perhaps not unreasonable to assume that the proportion of successes will continue to fluctuate around the level of past experience, and a statistical aggregative approach would appear justified. The crucial question is whether

* An optimization model incorporating some of the traits of this interpretation was recently discussed by Kent Anderson. [10]

perhaps there is at least one Achilles heel of resource supply, a specific resource that is in limited supply, essential to life and welfare, used dissipatively, and with no substitute in greater supply.

My rather casual inquiries and reading of scientific periodicals have not revealed a clear and present case of such an Achilles heel. The claim by Goeller [13] that the phosphorus–fertilizer–food chain might become an example if world population levels off only at a multiple of its present size has been contested by others on the basis (among other reasons) of the considerable abundance of phosphorus (see, for example, Wells [14]). Another example might just possibly arise with regard to energy in the unlikely contingency that none of a substantial number of current or future largely independent R&D projects to widen the supply base of energy is really successful. *If* the nuclear breeder should turn out not to be safe or otherwise not environmentally acceptable, *if* controlled nuclear fusion should not be found workable on an industrial scale, *if* both geothermal and solar energy use should turn out to remain limited to special and local situations, and *if* no other new sources of energy are discovered and developed, ... only *then* could our present stock of fossil and nuclear fuels become such an Achilles heel – though even then oil shale might extend the period of availability quite substantially.

An interesting case (though not an Achilles heel) brought out by Goeller is that of helium. Its cost of extraction is expected to go up by a large factor (Goeller mentions the number 100) when natural gas is exhausted and extraction shifts to the atmosphere as the source. While not regarded as essential to life, helium may well become more important than it is now if cryogenic power transmission is successfully developed, with important savings in transmission losses of energy.

If we were compelled to choose between the capital model and the exhaustible resource model, therefore, the former would seem as yet to have the greater relevance. In the next section we experiment with combinations of the two models.

5. *Two models combining capital and an exhaustible resource*

We conclude by briefly considering two alternative models that combine the essential traits of the capital and resource models. The very simple form given to this combination will allow conclusions to be drawn almost directly from the results obtained for the two models in sections 2 and 3 above.

In both models the welfare functional has the form

$$W = \int_0^T e^{-\rho t} [u(c_t)+v(r_t)]\, dt\,. \tag{5.1}$$

The constraints common in form to both models are

$$c_t + \dot{k}_t = g(k_t)\,, \qquad c_t, k_t \geqq 0, \quad 0 \leqq t \leqq T, \quad 0 < k_0 \text{ (given)}\,, \tag{5.2}$$

$$\int_0^T r_t \, dt = R > 0\,, \quad r_t \geqq \underline{r}, \text{ where } \underline{r} \geqq 0. \tag{5.3}$$

Thus the total utility flow is obtained additively from a flow $u(c_t)$ due to consumption c_t of a good produced with the use of a capital stock k_t and a constant labor force, along the lines of the Ramsey model, and a flow $v(r_t)$ arising from the rate of depletion r_t of a resource stock R. (We neglect any capital and labor inputs involved in the extraction or consumption of the resource.) $u(\cdot)$ and $v(\cdot)$ are again increasing and strictly concave.

The two models differ only in regard to the specifications with regard to the horizon T and the resource flow utility function $v(\cdot)$. In the first model consumption of the resource is not essential to life. We can therefore take $T = \infty$, and specify that $\underline{r} = 0$, $v(0) = 0, v'(0) < \infty$. This model has some of the traits of the helium problem.

The problem now breaks up into two independent maximizations, of

$$U = \int_0^\infty e^{-\rho t} u(c_t)\, dt\,, \qquad V = \int_0^\infty e^{-\rho t} v(r_t)\, dt\,, \tag{5.4}$$

respectively. The maximization of U leads to the same optimal path $\hat{c}_t$ as before, while that of V has a somewhat different outcome only because now $\underline{r} = 0$, whereas survival can continue on the basis of the consumption flow c_t alone. The modification of figure 2 thus needed is obvious. For the reasons given by Gale there is no optimal path for $\rho = 0$. For $\rho > 0$ there is an optimal path $r_t = \hat{r}_t$ defined by

$$\begin{cases} e^{-\rho t} v'(r_t) = e^{-\rho T} v'(0)\,, & \text{for } 0 \leqq t \leqq T, \\ r_t = 0\,, \ \text{hence } v(r_t) = 0\,, & \text{for } t \geqq T, \end{cases} \tag{5.5}$$

where we must again choose $T = \hat{T}(\rho)$ so that the resource constraint (5.3) is satisfied. Thus the resource flow diminishes over time, the more steeply the larger is ρ, and reaches zero at the time of exhaustion of the resource stock. The path $\hat{c}_t$ is not affected by these events, and is therefore independent of the resource stock R.

In the second model the resource is essential to life, and consumption of both c_t and r_t ceases at the time $t = T$ of exhaustion of the resource. Now, as in section 3, $v(r)$ is defined only for $r \geqq \underline{r}$, where the minimum resource flow $\underline{r}$ required for survival satisfies $\underline{r} > 0$. Therefore, T in (5.1) is now a number such that $0 < T \leqq \overline{T} = R/\underline{r}$. We also specify $v(\underline{r}) = 0$, $\lim_{r \to \underline{r}} v'(r) = \infty$, as a further expression of the essential character of the resource. Finally, we set $u(0) = 0, \lim_{c \to 0} u'(c) = \infty$.

In this model we need to maximize $W = U_T + V_T$, where

$$U_T = \int_0^T e^{-\rho t}\, u(c_t)\, dt, \qquad V_T = \int_0^T e^{-\rho t}\, v(r_t)\, dt, \tag{5.6}$$

with respect to the triple (T, c_t, r_t), subject to the constraints (5.2), (5.3). The new element is that the same as yet unknown value of T has to occur in both U_T and V_T.

Figure 5 illustrates the nature of the unique optimal paths $\hat{c}_t, \hat{r}_t$ for $\rho > 0$. The resource use path $\hat{r}_t$ now dips below the value $\hat{r}$ near the end point $\hat{T}^*(\rho)$ of the survival period. This occurs because continued enjoyment of a high

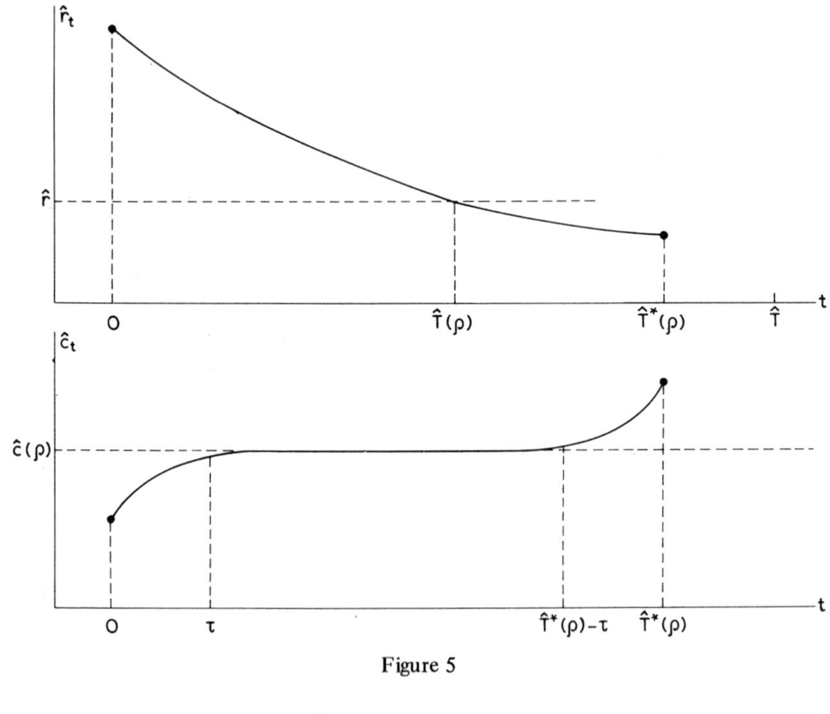

Figure 5

level $\hat{c}_t$ of general consumption compensates for what otherwise would have been an unacceptably low level of resource consumption $\hat{r}_t$. In an Appendix we give a list of intuitively plausible statements from which a proof of the assertions of this paragraph can be built up.

An interesting implication of these findings is the behavior of the ratio q_t/p_t of the shadow prices

$$q_t \equiv e^{-\rho t} v'(\hat{r}_t) = v'(\hat{r}_0), \qquad p_t \equiv e^{-\rho t} u'(\hat{c}_t), \tag{5.7}$$

of the resource and the consumption good on the long middle interval $[\tau, \hat{T}^*(\rho)-\tau]$ in the second model, and on the long interval $[\tau, \hat{T}(\rho)]$ in the first. In both cases we have

$$p_t \approx e^{-\rho t} u'(\hat{c}(\rho)), \quad \text{hence} \quad q_t/p_t \approx \text{const. } e^{\rho t}. \tag{5.8}$$

Thus, the combination of discounting of future utilities at a positive rate and the costless storage in nature of the resource prior to extraction leads to an exponential increase in the shadow price of the resource relative to that of the consumption good. In a monetary system with the latter good as the numéraire, an ideal competitive market with indefinitely long foresight would therefore exhibit a sustained exponential increase in the scarcity price of the resource. The extent to which actual markets reflect this effect has been discussed by Nordhaus.[15]

Appendix

Statements supporting the solution of the second model of section 5

As in section 3, we consider again first a prescribed survival period T, which allows provisional independent maximizations of U_T and V_T for that period. The following intuitively plausible statements will not be sharpened and proved here. Those relating to U_T follow from the work of Brock [16] and earlier work of Cass [17] or Koopmans.[18] Those relating to V_T are implied in the results of section 3. Regarding U_T, writing $c_t = c_t^T$ for the T-optimal consumption path and $\hat{U}_T$ for the maximal value of U_T attained on that path, we have for sufficiently large T that

(i) c_t^T increases with t for $0 \leqq t \leqq T$;

(ii) c_0^T is practically independent of T and $\lim_{T\to\infty} c_0^T \equiv c_0^\infty > 0$;

(iii) c_t^T is close to $\hat{c}(\rho)$ during a long middle segment $[\tau, T-\tau]$, $0 < \tau \ll T$, of the survival period;

(iv) for t approaching T, c_t^T rises further while the associated capital stock k_t^T falls to $k_T^T = 0$;

(v) $\mathrm{d}\hat{U}_T/\mathrm{d}T > 0$ (for *all* $T > 0$);

(vi) $0 \leqq \lim_{T\to\infty} \mathrm{e}^{\rho T} (\mathrm{d}\hat{U}_T/\mathrm{d}T) < \infty$ for all $\rho > 0$.

Regarding V_T, writing $r_t = r_t^T$ for the T-optimal path, $\hat{V}_T$ for the maximum attained, we have for $0 < T < \bar{T}$ that

(vii) r_t^T satisfies (3.9), hence r_t^T decreases as t increases and $r_t^T > \underline{r}$ for all $\rho > 0$ and $0 \leqq t \leqq T$;

(viii) $\mathrm{e}^{\rho T} (\mathrm{d}\hat{V}_T/\mathrm{d}T) = v(r_T^T) - r_T^T v'(r_T^T) \left\{\begin{smallmatrix}\geq\\=\\<\end{smallmatrix}\right\} 0$ for $T \left\{\begin{smallmatrix}\leq\\=\\>\end{smallmatrix}\right\} \hat{T}(\rho)$ as defined following (3.10) and $\mathrm{e}^{\rho T} (\mathrm{d}\hat{V}_T/\mathrm{d}T)$ decreases as T increases for $0 < T < \bar{T}$;

(ix) as $T \to \bar{T}$, $r_t^T \to \underline{r}$ uniformly in t for each ρ, hence $\lim_{T\to\bar{T}} \mathrm{e}^{\rho T} (\mathrm{d}\hat{V}_T/\mathrm{d}T) = -\infty$.

Assuming smooth approaches to the limits in (vi), (ix), it follows from (v), (vi), (viii), (ix) that for any given $\rho > 0$, if the resource stock R and hence $\bar{T}$ are sufficiently large, W reaches a unique maximum for a survival period $T = \hat{T}^*(\rho)$, determined from the condition

$$\mathrm{e}^{\rho T} \frac{\mathrm{d}}{\mathrm{d}T} (\hat{U}_T + \hat{V}_T) = 0\,, \tag{A1}$$

and located in the open interval

$$\hat{T}(\rho) < \hat{T}^*(\rho) < \bar{T}\,. \tag{A2}$$

Note added in proof

Shortly after the submission of this paper, an article by Vousden[19] appeared with in part overlapping results. Since the latter paper uses Pontryagin's Maximum Principle, the present paper offers an exposition of the overlapping results with simpler, more intuitive, though less rigorous mathematical methods.

References

[1] I. Fisher, The theory of interest (Macmillan, New York, 1930); reprinted (Augustus Kelley, New York, 1961).

[2] F.P. Ramsey, A mathematical theory of saving, Economic Journal 38 (Dec. 1928) pp. 543–559.

[3] T.C. Koopmans, Intertemporal distribution and 'optimal' aggregate economic growth, in: Ten economic studies in the tradition of Irving Fisher (Wiley, New York, 1967) pp. 95–126.

[4] H. Hotelling, The economics of exhaustible resources, Journal of Political Economy 39 (April 1931) pp. 137–175.

[5] E. Malinvaud, Capital accumulation and efficient allocation of resources, Econometrica 21 (April 1953) pp. 233–268.

[6] R. Radner, Optimal growth in a linear-logarithmic economy, International Economic Review 7 (Jan. 1966) pp. 1–33.

[7] R. Radner, Dynamic programming of economic growth, in: E. Malinvaud and M.O.L. Bacharach, eds., Activity analysis in the theory of growth and planning (St. Martin's Press, New York, 1967) ch. 4, pp. 111–141.

[8] T. Hansen and T.C. Koopmans, On the definition and computation of a capital stock invariant under optimization, Journal of Economic Theory 5 (Dec. 1972) pp. 487–523.

[9] D. Gale, On optimal development in a multi-sector economy, Review of Economic Studies 34 (Jan. 1967) pp. 1–18.

[10] K. Anderson, Optimal growth when the stock of resources is finite and depletable, Journal of Economic Theory 4 (April 1972) pp. 256–267.

[11] H.J. Barnett and C. Morse, Scarcity and growth, the economics of natural resource availability (Johns Hopkins Press, Baltimore, 1963).

[12] W.D. Nordhaus and J. Tobin, Is growth obsolete?, in: Economic growth, Fiftieth Anniversary Colloquium V (National Bureau of Economic Research, 1972) pp. 1–80.

[13] H.E. Goeller, The ultimate mineral resource situation – An optimistic view, Proceedings, National Academy of Sciences, U.S.A. 69 (Oct. 1972) pp. 2991–2992.

[14] F. Wells, The long run availability of phosphorus, unpublished manuscript (Feb. 14, 1973).

[15] W.D. Nordhaus, Markets and appropriable resources, unpublished manuscript (1973), abstract in: M.S. Macrakis, ed., Energy: demand, conservation and institutional problems (MIT Press, Cambridge, Mass., 1973).

[16] W.A. Brock, Sensitivity of optimal growth paths with respect to a change in target stocks, in: G. Bruckman and W. Weber, eds., Contributions to the Von Neumann growth model (Zeitschrift für National-Ökonomie and Springer Verlag, New York and Vienna, 1971) pp. 73–89.

[17] D. Cass, Optimum growth in an aggregate model of capital accumulation: A turnpike theorem, Econometrica 34 (Oct. 1966) pp. 833–850.

[18] T.C. Koopmans, On the concept of optimal economic growth, in: The econometric approach to development planning (North-Holland Publishing Co., Amsterdam, and Rand McNally, 1966); Pontificiae Academiae Scientiarum Scripta Varia 28 (1965) pp. 225–300.

[19] N. Vousden, Basic theoretical issues of resource depletion, Journal of Economic Theory 6 (April 1973) pp. 126–143.

8

Is the Theory of Competitive Equilibrium With It?

Tjalling C. Koopmans

American Economic Review 64, no. 2 (1974), pp. 325–329

Recent discussions in the literature have raised serious challenges to the theory of competitive equilibrium. Looking at the debate, I perceive two main issues. I put them in the form of two questions to which, by way of advance summary of my remarks, my own tentative answers are attached.

One. Does the model of competitive equilibrium (the "*CE* model") in its simplest form represent one useful pure and special case, one valuable foothold for a steep climb? My answer: Yes.

Two. Can we as yet evaluate the merit or promise of the various ramifications of the theory in recent literature? My answer: I find it hard to assess this fascinating blend of high achievements, challenging starts and possible dead-ends.

I shall mix the motivation of my answers in with comments on some recent criticisms. I am thinking in particular of John Kenneth Galbraith, Nicholas Kaldor, Janos Kornai and Martin Shubik. Since Professor Galbraith is with us, I shall not try to anticipate him.

Beginning with question one, I think the issue does not lie in the mathematical form of the theory. The contributions made by mathematical reasoning were necessary if the problems put were to be answered. The issue is the problems put. I do not hesitate about my "yes" to question one, because of the great value to economic theory of a fully worked out special case. I entirely agree with Kornai about the many aspects of reality ignored in the *CE* model which are brought out in his book: the importance of the control system in all existing economies, the role in that system of information about quantities as well as prices, the importance of increasing returns to scale, etc. I differ only on what to do from here on. Kornai's "revolutionary" proposal is now to start afresh with entirely new approaches embodying other aspects of reality, which he enumerates with care and perception. The "reformist" alternative, which Kornai rejects, is to amend and extend the given special case by grafting other important aspects on to it. I think *both* should be attempted.

Kaldor also calls for "a major act of demolition" of the basic conceptual framework of equilibrium theory, without which "it is impossible to make any real progress." The case for the reform approach can be illustrated by what seems to me Kaldor's gravest charge: that equilibrium theory ignores the pervasiveness and inexhaustibility of increasing returns to scale. I think that this important point can be met at least half-way, by introducing further assumptions that bear on the way time and space enter into the problem. As to time, the construction of the next generation of capital goods for larger scales of processing requires time. Kaldor recognizes that the allocation of the existing capital stock and other factors to current production can meanwhile be administered by short-run equilibrium prices. A recent paper by M. L. Weitzman for a two-sector model leads me to expect that an efficient stringing together of a sequence of such temporary equilibria is mathematically feasible in the presence of increasing returns, at least in terms of an "optimal growth" model. If so, this would support an allocation scheme on the "Hungarian plan," in which investment in large capital units is centralized, while capital utilization decisions are decentralized in a price-guided way. However, extension to a complete intertemporal market model might be subject to the same realistic limitation as that noted by Kaldor in regard to exhaustible resources: Firms might not exercise foresight long enough ahead for the time scale required by the problem. A relevant spatial factor is the cost of transporting the product from producer to user. This will slow down the increase in scale, and may even balance it out in an ultimate equilibrium for a number of goods.

Both Kornai and Shubik stress the need for a more detailed modelling of the circumstances and constraints under which suppliers and demanders obtain access to each other and conclude their trades. In particular, Shubik is concerned with constraints on credit that are expressed by a liquidity requirement constraining an agent at every moment of time. This is in contrast to a budget constraint applicable just to the sum of expenditures minus receipts over an accounting period. It will require modelling the economy as a process, a sequence over time of moves fully feasible to the individual acting by himself. In the presence of uncertainty this should include bankruptcy proceedings as a possible outcome for the agent. Shubik may well be right in his claim that this model cannot be accommodated within the framework of the *CE* model. However, logical links are undoubtedly present.

The asperity of some of the criticisms seems to me in part provoked by the spillover into mathematical economics of attitudes and traditions imparted by training in mathematics. Mathematical economics, while long on rigor, has generally been short on interpretation and practically silent on motivation for its choice of problems. Thus, the sheer volume of work expended on the theory of equilibrium is taken by the general economist as evidence of a strong belief in the explanatory reach of the model. I think the explanation is different. While I was searching for words to express the phenomenon, the precise words were presented to me by David Freedman, mathematician, probabilist and statistician, in a recent seminar at Yale: "Mathematicians are incapable of leaving well enough alone." In other words, any particular problem or model should be plumbed to its full depth and given its most general formulation. As a result, the shifts of focus, the breaking out of molds needed from time to time in any empirical science, take longer to come about.

The counterweight to this element of mathematical style must and has come from economists with a more pragmatic outlook. There is a continuing need for general and critical discussion of the choice of problems to be examined in economic theory. By its nature, rigor has no hold on this question. While the criticism takes shape, substantial further progress has been and is being made within the *CE* model, due also to its great flexibility of interpretation. I shall expand on my answer to question two in a brief discussion of this work. The task is facilitated by the important recent book by Kenneth J. Arrow and F. H. Hahn. It breaks a tradition by being generous with interpretation and by providing in the preface a motivation that is specific, frank and subtle. Important to the general economist is its careful discussion of present knowledge about the uniqueness and stability of equilibrium. The validity of the widely used method of policy analysis by "comparative statics" is found to be as yet subject to qualifications.

Another innovative recent book, by Herbert Scarf (with the collaboration of T. Hansen), enables us to make such applications with greater precision and to cases involving more variables and relationships. The algorithm approximates an equilibrium as a fixed point of a continuous mapping. An application to a problem of taxation has been made by John B. Shoven and John Whalley.

Two earlier developments are in the nature of magnificent *tours de force*, enriching our insight, but with a somewhat strained relation to reality. One of these, originated by Arrow (1953) and extended by Gerard Debreu (ch. 7), introduces uncertainty by considering trade in commodities contingent on the "state of nature." The approach is a heroic attempt to stretch the *CE* model as far as it will go. Roy Radner (1967, 1968) examines the limitations of the attempt connected with the different information requirements placed on the agents.

The other *tour de force* concerns the connection between the set of competitive equilibria and the game-theoretical concept of the core of an economy when the number of agents increases without limit. Roughly, an allocation is in the core if no coalition of any number of agents can do better for its members by coordinated quantitative bargaining. The principal result, suggested or proved with increasing generality by Shubik, Scarf, Debreu and Scarf, and Arrow and Hahn (ch. 8), is that the larger the number of agents, the closer any outcome of core-type bargaining comes to some competitive (price-guided) equilibrium. A fanciful extension by R. J. Aumann (1964, 1966), Karl Vind, Debreu, W. Hildebrand, Arrow and Hahn (see ch. 8) and others utilizes the concept of an economy with an infinity of agents, whose characteristics are continuously distributed in a measure space.

The interpretative weakness of both *tours de force* lies in the information handling requirements implicitly placed on the agents without regard to cost or even feasibility. In the case of contingent trading, these requirements go up in proportion to the number of states of nature, hence much more steeply than the number of future periods beset with uncertainty. With regard to the concept of the core, they go up in proportion to the number of coalitions containing a given member, that is, much more steeply than the number of members. It seems to me that these two lines of work will either remain standing as essentially unused but brilliant interpretational or mathematical feats—or one or both may possibly be the beginning of a long development in which institutional detail is introduced piece by piece, to represent the limitations of markets that deal with the future, or the various barriers on coalition formation existing in society.

I conclude with a few remarks about the finite competitive economy that assumes objective certainty about the outcome of given actions by all agents. There has been an increasing concern in the recent literature with fitting adjustment processes into that model. I attribute this concern to a weakness in the model—not a logical but an interpretative weakness. Optimizing responses of economic agents are simultaneously feasible only if the proper prices are already known to them. But these prices must somehow themselves be the result of these same responses. Thus there is something circular in the description of events. The market participants must be endowed with extrasensory perception (if acting simultaneously) or with supernatural premonition (if acting successively). One is thus led to think in terms of a process in which information flows, the individually feasible actions they induce, and the new flows generated by the actions, etc., are spelled out sequentially. I believe (with Kornai and Shubik) that such processes are now the more challenging objects of research, for the following reasons:

1. The notion of a process does not presuppose the approach to an equilibrium.
2. A process that does not approach an equilibrium (under constant technology and preferences) can be of great interest in itself.
3. An equilibrium that is not approached by any process that starts from a different initial state is of no interest in itself.
4. With the process notion, one can relieve the strain on our credulity and experiment with diminished degrees of individual rationality, perception, foresight, capacity for computation, and formalization of states of uncertainty. We could then at least ask how much of such relaxing of rationality still allows an equilibrium with some optimality properties to be approached.
5. In a world of continuing but only dimly foreseeable change in technology and in preferences, the notion of equilibrium disappears, but that of an adjustment process remains.

Possible connections between processes and equilibrium can be glimpsed from some recent work in "optimal growth" theory. One can look at the study of optimal growth as a scouting device that suggests useful conjectures for more complicated market processes which do approach an optimizing equilibrium. Some pointers of this kind are contained in work on many-sector models by W. R. S. Sutherland and by T. Hansen and Koopmans, and in analogies with known properties of one- and two-sector models. The "invariant capital stock," which generalizes to n dimensions the "golden rule stock (modified by discounting)," has a mathematical structure similar to that of a competitive equilibrium. It is a "fixed point" of a mapping and can be computed by fixed-point methods. This approach may therefore allow a reconnaissance of the problem of distinguishing interesting equilibria from uninteresting ones.

REFERENCES

K. J. Arrow, "Le Rôle des Valeurs Boursières pour la Répartition la Meilleure des Risques," *Econométrie*, 1953, 41–48, repr. in Eng. trans., as "The Role of Securities in the Optimal Allocation of Risk-Bearing," *Rev. Econ. Stud.*, 1963–64, *31*, 91–96.

——— **and F. H. Hahn**, *General Competitive Analysis*, San Francisco and Edinburgh 1971.

R. J. Aumann, "Markets with a Continuum of Traders," *Econometrica*, Jan. 1964, *32*, 39–50.

———, "Existence of Competitive Equilibria in Markets with a Continuum of Traders," *Econometrica*, Jan. 1966, *34*, 1–17.

G. Debreu, *Theory of Value*, New York 1959.

——— **and H. Scarf**, "A Central Limit Theorem on the Core of an Economy," *Int. Econ. Rev.*, 1963, *4*, 235–246.

J. K. Galbraith, *Economics and the Public Purpose*, Boston 1973.

T. Hansen and T. C. Koopmans, "On the Definition and Computation of a Capital Stock Invariant Under Optimization," *J. Econ. Theory*, Dec. 1972, *5*, 487–523.

W. Hildebrand, "On Economies with Many Agents," *J. Econ. Theory*, 1970, *2*, 161–188.

N. Kaldor, "The Irrelevance of Equilibrium Economics," *Econ. J.*, Dec. 1972, *82*, 1237–1255.

J. Kornai, *Anti-Equilibrium*, Amsterdam 1971.

R. Radner, "Equilibre des Marchés a Terme et au Comptant en Cas d'Incertitude," *Cahiers d'Econometrie*, Nov. 1967, *12*, 35–52.

———, "Competitive Equilibrium under Uncertainty," *Econometrica*, Jan. 1968, *36*, 31–58.

H. Scarf, with the collaboration of T. Han-

sen, *The Computation of Economic Equilibria,* New Haven 1973.

J. B. Shoven and J. Whalley, "A General Equilibrium Calculation of the Effects of Differential Taxation of Income from Capital in the U.S.," *J. Pub. Econ.*, 1972, *1.*

——— **and** ———, "General Equilibrium with Taxes: A Computational Procedure and an Existence Proof," *Rev. Econ. Stud.*, Oct. 1973, *40,* 475–490.

M. Shubik, "Commodity Money, Oligopoly, Credit and Bankruptcy in a General Equilibrium Model," *West. Econ. J.*, Mar. 1973, *11,* 24–38.

W. R. S. Sutherland, "On Optimal Development in a Multi-Sectoral Economy: The Discounted Case," *Rev. Econ. Stud.*, Oct. 1970, *37,* 585–589.

K. Vind, "Edgeworth Allocations in an Exchange Economy with Many Traders," *Int. Econ. Rev.*, 1964, *5,* 165–177.

9

Proof for a Case where Discounting Advances the Doomsday

Tjalling C. Koopmans

Review of Economic Studies, Symposium on the Economics of Exhaustible Resources, 1974, pp. 117–120

In a previous paper (Koopmans [1]) I considered some problems of " optimal " consumption $\hat{r}_t$ over time of an exhaustible resource of known finite total availability R. In one of the cases studied, consumption of a minimum amount of the resource is assumed to be essential to human life, in such a way that all life ceases upon its exhaustion at time T. Assuming a constant population until that time, and denoting by $\underline{r}$ the positive minimum consumption level needed for survival of that population, the survival period T is constrained by

$$0<T \leqq R/\underline{r} \equiv \bar{T}. \tag{1}$$

Here equality ($T = \bar{T}$) can be attained only by consuming at the minimum level ($r_t = \underline{r}$) at all times, $0 \leqq t \leqq \bar{T}$.

However, optimality is defined in terms of maximization of the integral over time of discounted future utility levels,

$$V(\rho, T, (r_t)) \equiv \int_0^T e^{-\rho t} v(r_t) dt, \qquad \text{...(2)}$$

where ρ is a discount rate, $\rho \geqq 0$, applied in continuous time to the utility flow $v(r_t)$ arising at any time t from a consumption flow r_t of the resource. The utility flow function $v(r)$ is defined for $r \geqq \underline{r}$, is twice continuously differentiable and satisfies

$$v'(r)>0, \qquad \text{...(3a)}$$

$$v''(r)<0 \text{ for } r>\underline{r}, \qquad \text{...(3b)}$$

$$v(\underline{r}) = 0, \qquad \text{...(3c)}$$

$$\lim_{r\to\underline{r}} v'(r) = \infty. \qquad \text{...(3d)}$$

That is, $v(r)$ is (*a*) strictly increasing and (*b*) strictly concave. The stipulation (*c*) anchors the utility scale. Some such anchoring, though not necessarily the given one, is needed whenever population size is a decision variable. The last requirement (*d*) simplifies a step in the proof, and can be secured if needed by a distortion of $v(r)$ in a neighbourhood of $\underline{r}$ that does not affect the solution.

This research was started at the Cowles Foundation for Research in Economics at Yale University, New Haven, Conn., USA, with the support of the National Science Foundation and the Ford Foundation, and completed at the International Institute for Applied Systems Analysis in Laxenburg, Austria. I am indebted to John Casti for valuable comments.

The paper referred to gives an intuitive argument for the following

Theorem. *For each* $\rho \geqq 0$ *there exists a unique optimal path* $r_t = \hat{r}_t$, $0 \leqq t \leqq \hat{T}_\rho$, *maximizing* (2) *subject to*

$$r_t \text{ is a continuous function on } [0, T], \qquad \text{...(4a)}$$

$$\int_0^T r_t dt \leqq R,\ r_t \geqq \underline{r},\ 0 \leqq t \leqq T. \qquad \text{...(4b)}$$

For $\rho = 0$, *the optimal path* $(\hat{r}_t \mid 0 \leqq t \leqq \hat{T}_0)$ *is defined by*

$$\hat{r}_t = \hat{r}, \text{ a constant, for } 0 \leqq t \leqq \hat{T}_0, \qquad \text{...(5a)}$$

$$v(\hat{r}) = \hat{r}v'(\hat{r}), \qquad \text{...(5b)}$$

$$\hat{r}\hat{T}_0 = R. \qquad \text{...(5c)}$$

For $\rho > 0$ *it is defined by*

$$e^{-\rho t}v'(\hat{r}_t) = e^{-\rho \hat{T}_\rho}v'(\hat{r}),\quad 0 \leqq t \leqq \hat{T}_\rho,\quad \hat{r} \text{ as in (5b)}, \qquad \text{...(6a)}$$

$$\int_0^{\hat{T}_\rho} \hat{r}_t dt = R. \qquad \text{...(6b)}$$

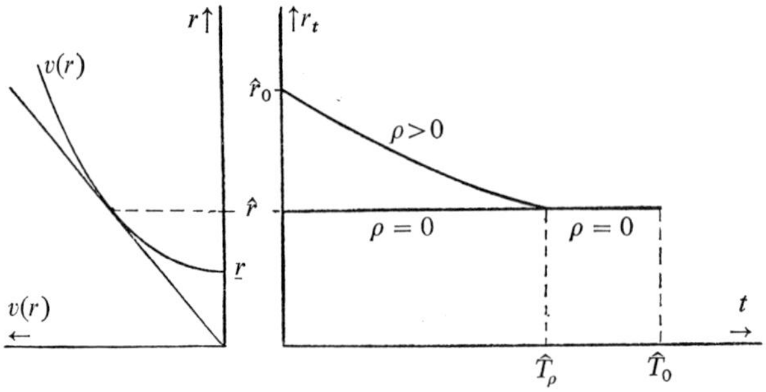

FIGURE 1

Figure 1 illustrates the solution. For $\rho = 0$, (6) implies (5), and consumption of the resource is constant during survival. Its optimal level $\hat{r}$ is obtained in (5*b*, *c*) by balancing the number of years of survival against the constant level of utility flow that the total resource stock makes possible during survival. Since $\hat{r} > \underline{r}$, the optimum survival period $\hat{T}_0$ is shorter than the maximum $\overline{T}$ defined by (1).

For $\rho > 0$, the optimal path $\hat{r}_t$ follows a declining curve given by (6*a*), which starts from a level $\hat{r}_0$ such that, when resource exhaustion brings life to a stop at time $t = \hat{T}_\rho$, the level $\hat{r}_{\hat{T}_\rho} = \hat{r}$ is just reached. Since the decline is steeper when ρ is larger, the survival period is shorter, the larger is ρ—which explains the title of this note.

The intuitive argument already referred to gives insight into the theorem; the following proof establishes its validity.

Proof. We first consider paths optimal under the added constraint of some arbitrarily fixed value $T = T^*$ of T satisfying $0 < T^* < \overline{T}$. Assume that such a "T^*-optimal" path r_t^* exists and that

$$r_t^* \geqq \underline{r} + \delta \text{ for } 0 \leqq t \leqq T^* \text{ and some } \delta > 0. \qquad \text{...(7)}$$

Then, if s_t is a continuous function defined for $0 \leqq t \leqq T^*$ such that

$$| s_t | \leqq \delta, \quad \int_0^{T^*} s_t dt = 0, \qquad \ldots(8)$$

the path

$$r_t = r_t^* + \varepsilon s_t, \quad 0 \leqq t \leqq T^*, \qquad \ldots(9)$$

is T^*-feasible for $| \varepsilon | \leqq 1$ and satisfies

$$V(\rho, T^*, (r_t)) - V(\rho, T^*_, (r_t^*)) = \int_0^{T^*} e^{-\rho t}(v(r_t) - v(r_t^*))dt \qquad \ldots(10a)$$

$$= \varepsilon \int_0^{T^*} e^{-\rho t} v'(r_t^*) s_t dt + R(\varepsilon), \qquad \ldots(10b)$$

where the remainder $R(\varepsilon)$ is of second order in ε. It is therefore a necessary condition for the T^*-optimality of r_t^* that

$$p_t \equiv e^{-\rho t} v'(r_t^*) = \text{constant} = e^{-\rho T^*} v'(r_{T^*}^*), \text{ say,} \qquad \ldots(11)$$

because, if we had $p_{t'} \neq p_{t''}$, $0 \leqq t', t'' \leqq T^*$, we could by choosing s_t of one sign in a neighbourhood in $[0, T^*]$ of t', s_t of the opposite sign in one of t'' and zero elsewhere while preserving (8) make the last member of (10) positive for some ε with $| \varepsilon | \leqq 1$.

In the light of (3*a*, *b*), (11) justifies our assumption that r_t^* is a continuous function of t. We now find that r_t^* is constant for $\rho = 0$, strictly decreasing for $\rho > 0$. Given $r_{T^*}^*$, say, the solution r_t^* of (11) is uniquely determined, and, for each t, r_t^* is a strictly increasing differentiable function of the given $r_{T^*}^*$. Also, by (3*d*),

$$\lim_{r_{T^*}^* \to \underline{r}} \int_0^{T^*} r_t^* dt = \int_0^{T^*} \underline{r} dt = T^* \underline{r} < \bar{T} \underline{r} = R,$$

whereas, for sufficiently large $r_{T^*}^*$,

$$\int_0^{T^*} r_t^* dt > R.$$

Therefore there is a unique number $\alpha^* > \underline{r}$ such that the unique solution r_t^* of (11) with $r_{T^*}^* = \alpha^*$ satisfies

$$\int_0^{T^*} r_t^* dt = R. \qquad \ldots(12)$$

From here on r_t^* will denote that path for the chosen T^*. Note that this path satisfies (7)

To prove the unique T^*-optimality of r_t^*, let r_t be any T^*-feasible path such that $r_{t_0} \neq r_{t_0}^*$ for some $t_0 \in [0, T]$. Then, by the continuity of r_t, r_t^*, $r_t \neq r_t^*$ for all t in some neighbourhood τ of t_0 in $[0, T^*]$. By (3*b*), for all $t \in [0, T^*]$,

$$v(r_t) - v(r_t^*) \begin{bmatrix} < \\ \leqq \end{bmatrix} (r_t - r_t^*) v'(r_t^*) \text{ for } t \in \begin{bmatrix} \tau \\ \tau^* \end{bmatrix}, \qquad \ldots(13)$$

where $\tau^* = [0, T^*]-\tau$. Therefore, we have from (10*a*), (11), (4*b*) with $T = T^*$, and (12) that

$$V(\rho, T^*, (r_t))-V(\rho, T^*, (r_t^*)) = \left(\int_\tau + \int_{\tau^*}\right) e^{-\rho t}(v(r_t)-v(r_t^*))dt$$

$$< \int_0^{T^*} (r_t-r_t^*)e^{-\rho t}v'(r_t^*)dt$$

$$= e^{-\rho T^*}v'(r_{T^*}^*) \int_0^{T^*} (r_t-r_t^*)dt \leqq 0.$$

Hence r_t^* is uniquely T^*-optimal.

We now make T^* a variable, writing T instead of T^* and r_t^T instead of r_t^*. Note that, for each t, $0 \leqq t<\bar{T}$, r_t^T is a differentiable function of T for $t \leqq T<\bar{T}$. Therefore

$$V_T \equiv V(\rho, T, (r_t^T)) = \int_0^T e^{-\rho t}v(r_t^T)dt$$

is a differentiable function of T for $0 \leqq T<\bar{T}$, and

$$\frac{dV_T}{dT} = e^{-\rho T}v(r_T^T)+ \int_0^T e^{-\rho t}v'(r_t^T)\frac{dr_t^T}{dT}\,dt$$

$$= e^{-\rho T}v(r_T^T)+e^{-\rho T}v'(r_T^T)\int_0^T \frac{dr_t^T}{dT}\,dt$$

by (11). But, by (12),

$$0 = \frac{dR}{dT} = r_T^T + \int_0^T \frac{dr_t^T}{dT}\,dt.$$

Therefore,

$$e^{\rho T}\frac{dV_T}{dT} = v(r_T^T)-r_T^T v'(r_T^T).$$

But then, from (5*b*), since $d(v(r)-rv'(r))/dr = -rv''(r)>0$ for $r>\underline{r}>0$, by (3*b*),

$$\frac{dV_T}{dT}\begin{bmatrix}<\\=\\>\end{bmatrix} 0 \quad\text{for}\quad r_T^T\begin{bmatrix}<\\=\\>\end{bmatrix}\hat{r}.$$

Finally, since $0<T<T'<\bar{T}$ implies $r_{T'}^{T'} \leqq r_T^{T'}<r_T^T$,

$$\frac{dV_T}{dT}\begin{bmatrix}<\\=\\>\end{bmatrix} 0 \quad\text{for}\quad T\begin{bmatrix}>\\=\\<\end{bmatrix}\hat{T}_\rho.$$

Thus, V_T reaches its unique maximum for that value $\hat{T}_\rho$ of T for which $r_T^T = \hat{r}$.

This establishes the second part of the theorem. The first part follows by specialization when $\rho = 0$.

REFERENCE

1. Koopmans, "Some Observations on 'Optimal' Economic Growth and Exhaustible Resources" [paper 7 in present volume].

10

Concepts of Optimality and Their Uses

Nobel Memorial Lecture, December 11, 1975

Tjalling C. Koopmans

Les Prix Nobel en 1975 (Stockholm: Nobel Foundation, 1976)

According to a frequently cited definition, economics is the study of "best use of scarce resources." The definition is incomplete. "Second best" use of resources, and outright wasteful uses, have equal claim to attention. They are the other side of the coin.

For our present purpose the phrase "best use of scarce resources" will suffice. However, each of the two nouns and two adjectives in this phrase needs further definition. These definitions in turn need to be varied and adjusted to fit the specific circumstances in which the various kinds of optimizing economic decisions are to be taken.

I will assume that the main interest of this gathering is in the range of applications of the idea of best use of scarce resources, and in the ways in which the main categories of applications differ from each other. I shall therefore describe mathematical ideas and techniques only to an extent helpful for the exploration of that range of applications.

A good place to start is with the *production programs of the individual plant or enterprise* for a short period ahead. The "resources" then include the capacities of the various available pieces of equipment. In a centrally directed economy they may also include the allotments of nationally allocated primary inputs such as fuels, raw materials, labor services. In a market economy with some capital rationing one single allotment of working capital available for the purchase of primary inputs at given market prices would take the place of most of the primary input allotments.

In either institutional framework, an especially simple prototype problem is obtained if one fixes the quantity of required output of the product or products made by the enterprise, while prices for the primary products are given. Then the term "use" of resources stands for a choice of a technical process or a combination of processes that meets that requirement within the given constraints. "Best" use is a, or if unique, that choice that meets the requirement at minimum cost of primary inputs.

Economists have differed as to whether this problem belongs in economics. In the twenties the British economist A. C. Pigou stated

> . . . it is not the business of economists to teach woolen manufacturers how to make and sell wool, or brewers how to make and sell beer . . .

This was not the attitude of economists in several other European countries. In particular, there was in the thirties a lively discussion among Scandinavian and German economists concerning models of production possibilities and their use in achieving efficiency within the enterprise. The Nordisk Tidsskrift for Teknisk Økonomi provided an important medium for these discussions.

Significant contributions[1] were made by Carlson, Frisch, Gloerfelt Tarp, Schmidt, Schneider, Stackelberg, and Zeuthen.

Thus the situation at the end of the thirties was one in which important practical problems in the best use of resources within the enterprise had been neglected by economists in several countries, and had been taken up by only a handful of economists in a few other countries. In addition, the problems were of a kind in which special knowledge possessed by other professions, mathematicians, engineers, managers, was pertinent. One could therefore have expected important new contributions to come from these neighboring professions.

This is precisely what happened, and several times over. Chronologically first was the publication by the mathematician Leonid V. Kantorovich (1939, in Russia) of a 68-page booklet entitled, in translation (1960), "Mathematical Methods of Organizing and Planning of Production." The importance of this publication is due to the simultaneous presence of several ideas or elements, some of which had also been present in earlier writings in different parts of economics or mathematics. I enumerate the elements.

(1) *A model of production* in terms of a finite number of distinct production processes, each characterized by constant ratios between the inputs and outputs specific to the process.

This element has a long history in economics. It is found in Walras (1874, Leçon 41; 1954, Lesson 20), Cassel (1919, Ch. IV), the mathematician von Neumann (1936), Leontief (1936, 1941), all dealing with models of the productive system as a whole. However, the feature most important for our purpose was present only in the classical writers in the theory of international trade[2] and in the models of von Neumann and of Kantorovich. This feature is that the output of one-and-the-same required commodity can in general be achieved by more than one process. The same specified vector of outputs of all required commodities can therefore in general be obtained as the outcome of many different combinations of processes. Two such combinations may differ in the list of processes included—and in the levels of activity assigned to the processes they both use. It is due to this element of choice between alternative ways of achieving the same end result that a genuine optimization problem arises. It is true that Walras also optimized (1954, Lesson 36) on the choice of processes, but from an infinite collection defined by a differentiable production function. It is precisely this choice of a more general collection of processes that delayed the recognition by economists of the applications that are our present topic:

(2) The perception of a wide range of *practical applications* of the model to industries that themselves are sources for the data required by these applications.

[1] For references to these authors and to the Pigou quotation, see Koopmans (1957), p. 185.

[2] See the references to Torrens (1815), Ricardo (1817), Mill (1852), Graham (1923), and others in the survey article by Chipman (1965).

These included the transportation problem to be discussed below, an agricultural problem, and various industrial applications. The definition and collection of available data of a different, more aggregative, kind was also an important element in Leontief's input-output analysis.

(3) The demonstration that with an optimal solution of the given problem, whether of cost minimization or output maximization, one can associate what in Western literature has been called *shadow prices*, one for each resource, intermediate commodity or end-product.

Kantorovich's term in 1939 was "resolving multipliers", which he changed to "objectively determined valuations"[3] in his book of 1959. In general, these valuations are equal to the first derivatives, of the negative of the cost minimum, with respect to the specified availabilities of the goods in question. In mathematical terminology these valuations have also been called "dual variables", in contrast with the activity levels assigned to the processes, which are then called "primal variables". Analogous dual variables occur also in von Neumann's model of proportional growth, with an interpretation as prices in competitive markets.

(4) The identification of a *separation theorem* for convex sets due to Minkowski as a mathematical basis for the existence of the dual variables[4].

(5) The *computation* of optimal values of the primal and associated dual variables for illustrative examples, and some indications toward calculating such solutions in more complex cases.

Finally, brief but precise explanations of

(6) The interpretation of the dual variables as defining equivalence ratios (*rates of substitution*) between different primary inputs and/or different required outputs, and

(7) the additional interpretation of the dual variables as *guides for* the coordination of *allocative decisions* made in different departments or organizations.

I shall return to (7) below.

Kantorovich's work of 1939 did not become known in the West until the late fifties or early sixties. Meanwhile the transportation model was redeveloped in the West without knowledge of the work on this topic by Kantorovich (1942, reprinted 1958) and Kantorovich and Gavurin (1940, 1949). The Western contributions were made by Hitchcock (1941), Koopmans (memo dated 1942, published 1970; articles of 1949 and 1951 (with Reiter)), Dantzig (Ch. XXIII in Koopmans, ed., 1951).

The general linear model was rediscovered and developed by George B. Dantzig and others associated with him, under the initial stimulus of the scheduling problems of the United States Air Force. The term "linear programming" came into use for the mathematical analysis and computational procedures associated with this model. A compact early publication of this

[3] Ob'ektivno obuslovlennye otsenki.

[4] For this purpose von Neumann had used the heavier tool of a topological fixed-point theorem. The dispensibility of this for his purpose was shown later by Gale (1956) and by Koopmans and Bausch (1959, Topic 5).

work can be found in a volume entitled "Activity Analysis of Production and Allocation", edited by Koopmans (1951). Substantial further developments appeared in such journals as Econometrica, Management Science, Operations Research, and were brought together in Dantzig's "Linear Programming and Extensions" (1963), a book that was many years in the making. These developments, in which many mathematicians and economists took part, went substantially beyond the earlier work of Kantorovich, in several directions. I note only a few of the extensions to the elements listed above.

(2') *Extension of the range of applications* to animal feeding problems, inventory and warehousing problems, oil refinery operations, electric power investments[5] and many other problems.

(3', 4') Further clarification of the *mathematical relations between primal and dual variables* and their extension to *nonlinear programming* by[6] Tucker, Gale, Kuhn and others.

This work also traced additional mathematical origins or precursors for the duality theory of linear programming in the work on game theory by von Neumann (1928 and, with Morgenstern, 1944) and by Ville (1938), and in work on linear inequalities by Gordan (1873), Farkas (1902), Stiemke (1915), Motzkin (1936) and others.[7]

(5') The development by Dantzig of the *simplex method* for maximizing a linear function under linear constraints (including inequalities) and the further improvements to this method by Dantzig and others.

The simplex method has become the principal starting point for a family of algorithms dealing with linear and convex nonlinear allocation problems. These methods can be set up so as to compute optimal values of both primal and dual variables.

Most important to economic theory as well as application was a further extension of (7) into

(7') analysis of the *role or use of prices* toward best allocation of resources, either through the operation of competitive markets, or as an instrument of national planning.

These ideas, again, have a long history in economics. In regard to competitive markets, they go back at least as far as Adam Smith (1776), and were eloquently restated and developed by Hayek (1945). Important writers on the use of prices in socialist planning were Barone (1908), Lange (1936), and Lerner (1937, 1938). The new element in the work by Koopmans (1949, 1951) and Samuelson (1949, 1966) was the use of the linear model and, in my own case, the attempt to develop what may be called a *pre*-institutional theory of allocation of resources. It was already foreshadowed in the work of Lange and Lerner that hypothetical perfect competition and hypothetical perfect planning both imply efficient allocation of resources—although neither occurs in reality.

[5] See, for instance, Massé and Gibrat (1957).

[6] See Gale, Kuhn and Tucker (1951), Kuhn and Tucker (1950), and, for a summary, Tucker (1957).

[7] For references see Dantzig (1963), Ch. 2–3.

It therefore seemed useful to turn the problem around, and just postulate allocative efficiency as a model for abstract, pre-institutional study. Thereafter, one can go on to explore alternative institutional arrangements for approximating that model.

I believe that the linear model offers a good foothold for this purpose. First, it makes a rigorous discussion easier. Secondly, the most challenging *non*-linearity—that connected with increasing returns to scale—in fact undermines competition. It also greatly escalates the mathematical and computational requirements for good planning. The linear model, therefore, makes a natural first chapter in the theory of best allocation of resources. In its simplest form it leads to the following symmetric relationships between activity levels of the processes and the (shadow) prices of the resources and goods produced:

(7'') (a) Every process in use makes a zero profit,
(b) No process in the technology makes a positive profit,
(c) Every good used below the limit of its availability has a zero price,
(d) No good has a negative price.

These same relationships are a recurrent theme in the first two chapters of Kantorovich's (1959) book, which also was many years in the making prior to publication. It was subsequently translated into French and English, the latter under the title "The Best Use of Economic Resources." The gist of the book's recommendations is that socialist planning can achieve best attainment of the goal set by the planning body through calculations that ensure the fulfillment of these or similar conditions for optimality.

Kantorovich did not go much beyond his earlier remarks on the questions concerning possible use of a price system for decentralization of decisions. This became a major theme, however, in the abstract work of Koopmans (1951, Sec. 5.12), in the work on two-level planning by Kornai and Lipták (1962, 1963, 1965) in relation to planning in Hungary, and in that by Malinvaud (1967) stimulated by experiences with planning in France. The principal computational counterpart of this work was developed by Dantzig and Wolfe (1960, 1961) under the name "the decomposition principle."

The third chapter of Kantorovich's book deals with the problem of investment planning to enlarge the production base. The principal emphasis is on the concept of the *normal effectiveness of capital investment*. This is a discount rate applied to future returns and to contemplated investments and other future costs, in the evaluation and selection of investment projects. This idea had been proposed earlier by Novozhilov (1939). The point emphasized by Kantorovich is that the prices to be used in calculating returns and costs should be the objectively determined valuations determined by his methods, for the selection to have an optimal result. These proposals were at the time new to the practice of Soviet economic planning. I believe that the principle of the normal effectiveness of capital investment has gained increasing acceptance in Soviet theory and practice since that time. There is an obvious formal analogy with the profitability criterion for investment planning used by the firm in a market economy, using anticipated market prices and the appropriate market rate of interest. The institutional framework contemplated is, of course, fundamentally different. I believe that the underlying pre-institutional optimizing theory is the same.

Summing up, I see two principal merits in the developments I have reviewed so far. One is their initially pre-institutional character. Technology and human needs are universal. To start with just these elements has facilitated and intensified professional contacts and interactions between economists from market and socialist countries. The other merit is the combination and merging of economic theory, mathematical modeling, data collection, and computational methods and algorithms made possible by the modern computer. A genuine amalgam of different professional contributions!

The linear model, followed by the convex nonlinear model, have provided the proving ground for these developments—and—their most conspicuous limitation: The nonconvex nonlinearities associated with increasing returns to scale—i.e., with the greater productivity of large-scale production in many industries—require quite different methods of analysis, and also raise different problems of institutional frameworks conducive to best allocation.

I now proceed to a rather different class of applications of the idea of best allocation of scarce resources. This field is usually referred to as the *theory of optimal economic growth.* In most studies of this kind made in the countries with market economies there is not an identifiable client to whom the findings are submitted as policy recommendations. Nor is there an obvious choice of objective function, such as cost minimization or profit maximization in the studies addressed to individual enterprises. The field has more of a speculative character. The models studied usually contain only a few highly aggregated variables. One considers alternative objective functions that incorporate or emphasize various strands of ethical, political, or social thought. These objectives are then tried out to see what future paths of the economy they imply under equally simplified assumptions of technology or resource availability. The principal customers aimed for are other economists or members of other professions, who are somewhat closer to the making of policy recommendations. These may be those engaged in making more disaggregated optimizing models of growth that incorporate numerical estimates of technological or behavioral parameters. (I shall return to this field of "development programming" below.) Or the hoped-for customers may be policy economists who may find it useful to have the more abstract ideas of this field in the back of their mind when coping with the day-to-day pressures for outcomes rather than criteria.

The question of the clientèle is even more baffling when the problem concerns growth paths for time spans covering several generations. What can at best be recommended in that case is the signal the present generation gives, the tradition it seeks to strengthen or establish, for succeeding generations to take off from.

The classic in the optimal growth field is a paper published in 1928 by Frank Ramsey, known also as the author of equally fundamental papers on the foundations of mathematics and on subjective probability. His definition of "best" involves the maximization of a sum (or integral) of utility flows to be derived from future consumption. Using a continuous time variable, Ramsey's choice of objective function is a limiting case of a broader class of functions which I shall consider first,

$$U = \int_0^\infty e^{-\varrho t} u(c_t)dt,\ 0 < \rho, \quad \left\{ \begin{array}{l} \text{the objective function} \\ \text{representing generations.} \end{array} \right.$$

Here c_t denotes the aggregate consumption flow as of time t, and $u(c)$ is a utility flow serving as an evaluating score for the consumption flow c. One chooses the function $u(c)$ so as to increase with c but at a decreasing rate $\frac{du}{dc}$ as c increases. This expresses that at all times "more is better", but less so if much is already being enjoyed (see Figure 1). The effect on the allocation of consumption goods between generations is similar to the effect of a progressive income tax on spendable incomes among contemporaries.

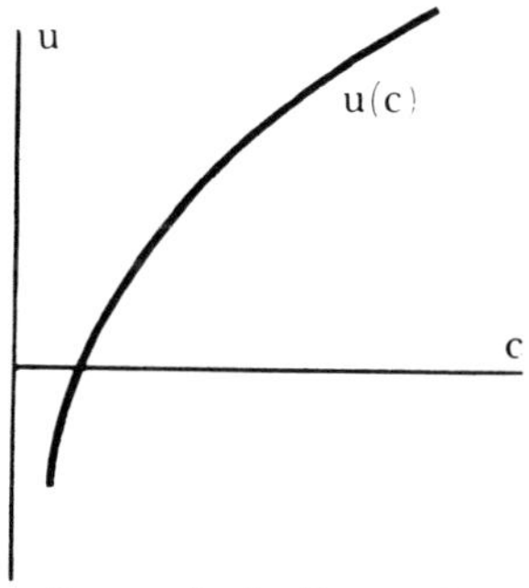

Fig. 1

We shall call the exponentially decaying factor $e^{-\varrho t}$, $\varrho > 0$, *the discount factor for utility*. It diminishes the weight given to future utility flows in the summation of the entire utility flow over all the future to form a total score U. The weight is smaller the larger the *discount rate for utility*, ϱ, and the further one looks into the future. On ethical grounds Ramsey would have none of this. I shall take the view that the important question of discounting utility—or for that matter any other aspect of the choice of the objective function—should not be settled entirely on a priori grounds. Most decision makers will first want to know what a given objective function will make them do in given circumstances. I shall therefore hold $\varrho > 0$ for this first exploration,[8] and turn to the mathematical modeling of the "circumstances" in terms of technological and resource constraints on the consumption and capital variables.

One "resource" is the labor force. It need not enter the formulae because it will be assumed to remain inexorably constant over time. The only other resource is an initial capital stock denoted k_0, historically given as of time $t = 0$. The "use" at any time t of labor and of the then capital stock k_t consists

[8] For an objective function implying a variable discount rate that depends on the path contemplated see Koopmans (1960), Koopmans, Diamond and Williamson (1964) and Beals and Koopmans (1969).

of two steps. The first and obvious step is to achieve at all times the highest net output flow $f(k_t)$ that can be produced by the labor force, using the capital stock fully and to best effect. The form given to the function $f(k)$ summarizes and simplifies broad technological experience. It specifies $f(0) = 0$ ("without capital no output"), $f(k)$ initially increasing with k but at a diminishing rate $\frac{df}{dk}$, in such a way that from some point $\hat{k}$ of capital saturation on, $f(k)$ decreases because depreciation rises more steeply than gross output. (See Figure 2.)

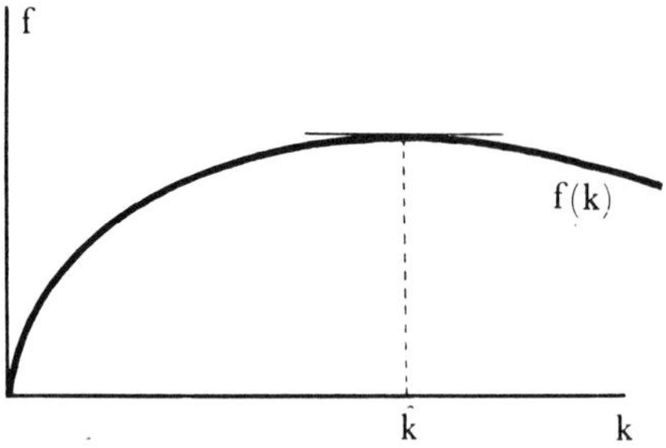

Fig. 2

In all this the product flow $f(k)$ is regarded as consisting of a single good, which can be used as desired for consumption or for adding to the capital stock,

$$f(k_t) = c_t + \frac{dk_t}{dt}, \quad \text{the allocation constraint.}$$

To determine this allocation for all t is the second step. This is done "best" at all future points of time if the total score U is thereby maximized.

It might seem as if this constrained maximization problem is quite different in mathematical structure from those discussed before. This is not the case. The main difference is that the discussion has shifted from a vector space to a function space, using conventional notations not designed to reveal the common structure of the two problems. In particular, as long as the crucial convexity assumptions are maintained, interpretations in terms of shadow prices remain valid.

The problem for $\varrho > 0$ was solved independently by Cass (1966), Koopmans (1965, 1967), Malinvaud (1965, 1967), thirty-five years after Ramsey. Without proof I indicate the nature of the solution in Figure 3. In the diagram on the left, the *abscissa* k is set out along the *vertical* half-axis, the *ordinate* $y = f(k)$ along the *horizontal* half-axis pointing left. For given $\rho > 0$, find the unique point $\hat{k}(\rho)$ on the curve $y = f(k)$ in which the slope $\frac{df}{dk}$ equals ρ. Then, if the initial capital stock k_0 should happen to equal $\hat{k}(\rho)$, the optimal capital path remains constant, $k_t = \hat{k}(\rho)$, over all the future. For any initial stock k_0 less than or larger than $\hat{k}(\rho)$, the optimal path shows a monotonic and asymptotic approach to $\hat{k}(\rho)$. All this is illustrated in solid lines in the top right diagram in Figure 3. The lower right diagram shows the corresponding optimal consumption path c_t, which approaches the asymptotic level $\hat{c}(\rho) = f(\hat{k}(\rho))$.

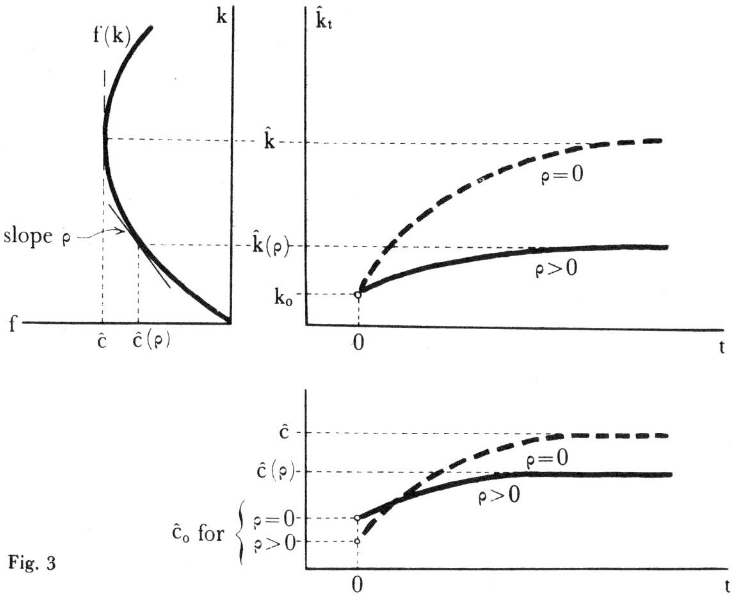

Fig. 3

The differential equation which, together with the allocation constraint given above, governs the approaches of k_t and c_t to their asymptotes is subject to an interesting interpretation in terms of shadow prices. Define such prices, p_t for the consumption good and q_t for the use of a unit of the capital stock, by

$$p_t = e^{-\varrho t}\left(\frac{du}{dc}\right)_{c=c_t}, \quad q_t = p_t\left(\frac{df}{dk}\right)_{k=k_t}.$$

Then p_t is the marginal utility of consumption, $\frac{du}{dc}$, at the level c_t of consumption flow reached at time t, discounted back to time zero. In turn, q_t is the marginal productivity of capital, $\frac{df}{dk}$, at the level k_t reached at time t, multiplied by the shadow price p_t of the product, already defined. This makes q_t the marginal productivity of capital in terms of discounted utility.

In these terms the differential equation is

$$q_t = -\frac{dp_t}{dt}, \quad \text{the allocation principle.}$$

If p_t and q_t were to be market prices for the capital good and for its use in production, this equality would state that the returns on two alternative dispositions for the capital good would be equal: One is to sell the good now, the other is to sell first only its use for a short period, and thereafter to sell the good itself. That this principle is necessary for optimality is intuitively plausible. Its sufficiency can be proved from the convexity assumptions about the functions $-u(\cdot)$ and $-f(\cdot)$, plus the boundary condition that $\lim_{t\to\infty} k_t = \hat{k}(\varrho)$.

What is the effect of choosing different values of the discount rate ϱ? Figure 3 suggests the answer for the realistic case that the initial capital stock k_0 is well below its ultimate level $\hat{k}(\varrho)$. In that case, as ϱ is *de*creased, that is, as the present valuation of consumption in a distant future is *in*creased, then the asymptotic levels of the capital stock and of consumption are both *in*creased. However, to accumulate the additional capital that makes this feasible, consumption in the present and the near future is further *de*creased. Thus, the impatience expressed by a positive discount rate merely denies to uncounted distant generations a permanently higher level of consumption because that would necessitate a substantially smaller present consumption. Perhaps a pity, but not a sin.

Ramsey showed that the effect of a decrease in ϱ goes right down to but not beyond the limiting case of no discounting, $\varrho = 0$. The optimal paths for that case are shown by dashed lines in Figure 3. Ramsey used an ingenious mathematical device that gets around the nonconvergence of the utility integral for $\varrho = 0$, and also leads to a proof simpler than the one for positive ϱ.

This narrow escape for virtue is blocked off by some quite plausible modifications of the model toward greater realism. For instance, one may introduce a population (= labor force) L_t that changes with time and, for interpersonal equity, modify the objective function to read

$$V = \int_0^\infty e^{\varrho - t} L_t u(c_t)\,dt, \quad \begin{cases} \text{the objective function} \\ \text{representing individuals,} \end{cases}$$

where c_t is now interpreted as *per capita* consumption, k_t as ditto capital. The thought here is to give equal weight (apart from discounting) to all future individuals rather than generations. Assume further that L_t cannot be influenced but is subject to an exogenous exponential growth

$$L_t = L_0 e^{\lambda t}, \quad \lambda > 0,$$

over time. By way of example, let λ correspond to a growth by 3 % per year. Then, for mathematical reasons alone, the discount rate ϱ has to correspond to at least 3 % per year for an optimal path to exist. If one tries to keep ϱ at zero and force existence by imposing a *finite* time horizon of one century, say, then the "optimization" produces an irrational and arbitrary pile-up of consumption toward the end of that century while the capital stock runs down to zero—or to any other prescribed level that still leaves room for a terminal splurge.

The model discussed so far leaves out important aspects of the modern economy. I shall comment briefly on the incorporation into the model of

(1) exhaustible resources,
(2) technological change,
(3) population as a policy variable.

With regard to *exhaustible resources*, I shall only consider the extreme case of an *essential* resource. By this I mean a resource that is essential to sustaining life, is not capable of complete recycling, and has no substitute either now or later within the remaining period of its availability.

I have constructed a highly simplified model (Koopmans, 1973) of an essential resource which leads to conclusions quite different from those reached for the preceding *capital model*. The only process in the technology consists of costless extraction of the resource combined with its immediate and direct consumption. This process is available at all times until the time T at which the resource is exhausted. Population is assumed given and constant for the *survival period* $0 \leqslant t \leqslant T$. At time T it falls to zero. In these circumstances, higher per capita consumption by those living early enough to share in the available resource shortens the survival period, hence reduces the total number sharing. Thus the survival period is now a policy variable, and thereby so is population in some part of the future.

We now adopt again the objective function of the Ramsey model with discounting, except that the integration extends only over the period of survival. Then, unlike in the capital model, the optimal path now depends on where one places the zero point in the utility scale in which the function $u(\cdot)$ is expressed. Let us set this zero point somewhat arbitrarily at the utility flow level, $u(\underline{r}) = 0$, of the resource consumption level $\underline{r}$ below which life cannot be sustained. The resulting function $u(r)$ is shown (again sideways) on the left in Figure 4.

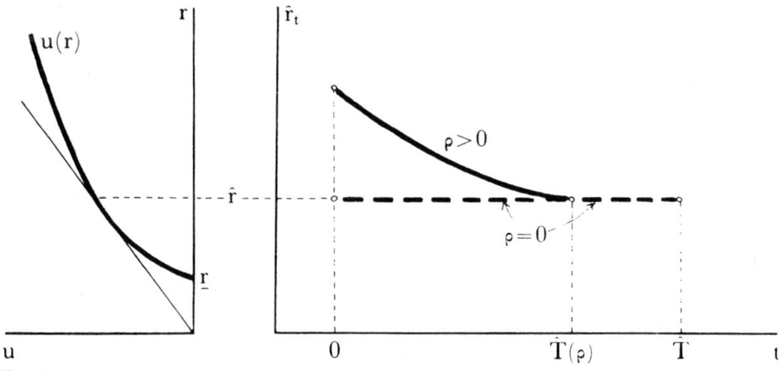

Fig. 4

In the absence of discounting ($\varrho = 0$), time now enters only as a scale on which the fatal cut-off point T is determined. Among those so admitted equal sharing is clearly optimal, hence optimal consumption stays at a constant level over time. Figure 4 shows (dashed lines) how this level, and therewith the survival period, are determined: All included claimants consume optimally at that unique per capita level $\hat{r}$ that maximizes the utility flow per unit of resource flow consumed. Note that this consumption level is well above the subsistence minimum $\underline{r}$. This result is to be expected from an objective function that places value not on the number of included people as such, but only on the "number of utils" enjoyed by all alive taken together.

Discounting ($\varrho > 0$) now introduces unequal weights, decreasing as time goes on, between people with equal technological opportunities. The result is (solid line) that the consumption of earlier claimants is raised over that of later ones, with the last claimants no better off than before. Of necessity, the cut-off point arrives sooner, and some of those included for $\varrho = 0$ will not be there to press their claim if $\varrho > 0$.

I hold no brief for the realism of this model. I have brought it up only as a stark demonstration of the point that the problem of whether and how much to discount future utilities cannot be equitably resolved a priori and in the abstract. One needs to take into account the opportunities expected to be available to the various consumers now and later, for the given technology and resource base.

Does there exist an essential resource, as defined above, exhaustible in less than astronomical or even geological time? I have argued elsewhere (Koopmans, 1973) that the best available answer to this question must come from those natural scientists and engineers most able to assess what future technology may do, or be made to do, to find substitute materials or fuels for those now within sight of exhaustion. I should add that geologists may well develop ways to pin down further the best estimates of ultimate availability. Economists could bring up the rear with methods for integrating the diverse pieces of information so obtained.

This leads to a few remarks on models that recognize *technological change*, and the uncertainty by which it is inevitably surrounded. A conceptual step forward in this direction has been made recently by Dasgupta and Heal (1974). Their model postulates an exhaustible resource for which a substitute will or may become available at an uncertain future date. The uncertainty is described by a subjectively estimated probability distribution. Capital accumulation is also represented in the model. The objective function is the mean value of the distribution of the sum of discounted utilities over an infinite future period. The optimal path to be found consists of two successive segments. One is the path to be followed from $t = 0$ up to the as yet unknown time $t = T$ of the availability of the substitute. The other is the path to be followed from time T on, which of course depends on the situation in which the advent of the substitute finds the economy.

In one interesting sub-case, the effect of uncertainty can be represented by an equivalent addition to the discount rate—until the substitute is available. This is the case in which the technological change is expected to be so incisive that the old capital stock will lose all its value as a result of the availability of the new technology.

Deep problems of choice of optimality criterion arise in models in which *population size is a decision variable*, or is affected by decision variables. I shall contrast only two distinct alternative criteria. One, used in a population context by Meade (1955), Dasgupta (1969) and others, is given by the "objective function representing individuals" already discussed. This function multiplies the utility of per capita consumption by the number of consumers before forming the discounted sum. The other criterion, the "function representing generations", sums just the per capita utilities.

The argument by Arrow and Kurz (1970, I. 4) in favor of the former criterion uses the analogy of two contemporaneous island populations under one government. It shows convincingly that per capita utilities for the two islands must before their addition be multiplied by the respective populations if one wants to avoid discrimination between people of the two groups.

Does this argument carry over to generations that succeed each other in time? One might well argue this on the same grounds if population increase is a truly exogenous function of time, unalterable by any policy, but fortunately one that permits a feasible path. One such case was already considered above. But in fact population *can* be influenced, directly by persuasion and provision of information, or indirectly through other economic variables. I submit that this makes a difference.

A distinction should be made here between concern for the welfare of those already alive and of those as yet unborn whose numbers are still undecided. Current social ethic urges recognition of the needs and desires of living persons, within nations, and between nations—even though practice differs from norm. But there is something open-ended about the same concern for our descendants. How many descendants?

The answer to that question is different for the two criteria we are now comparing. On the basis of indications in a recent paper of Pitchford (1975, p. 21) I conjecture:[9] that the criterion representing individuals will, under constraints like those considered above, recommend a smaller per capita utility for all generations, present and future, than does the criterion representing generations. This is to be expected because the criterion representing individuals attaches value to numbers as such. Specifically it would rate the combination of a given per capita utility level and population size below another combination with a 5% lower utility, say, and a more than 5% larger population.

So the issue appears to be one of quantity versus quality. Again, one would want to try out the two criteria, and other ones, under a variety of constraints before a fully considered judgment can be made. But the simple idea of adding up individual utilities does not seem to me compelling in itself. Those already born are committed to their existence by the instinct of selfpreservation. Choosing a criterion that limits births so as to allow a good existence to an indefinitely continuing sequence of generations appears sufficient as an end in itself. Why more people at the expense of each of them?

The foregoing discussion tacitly assumes that net population increase can be controlled without much delay, within the range recommended by optimization. In reality, neither the techniques nor the acceptance of birth control are such as to support that assumption. On the other hand it is not so that population increase can be regarded as entirely exogenous. This suggests refinement of the models in two directions.

[9] For this conjecture to be well defined, the criterion must again specify the zero point in the utility scale. I set it again at the subsistence minimum, because associating a zero utility with any higher consumption level would imply a preference for the phasing out of human life in some adverse circumstances in which a very low consumption level permitting survival remains feasible.

First, a more realistic model should incorporate estimates of the relations describing the response of reproductive behavior to levels of income, education, housing, medical care, and other causative variables. In circumstances where the resulting path of population does not seriously reduce per capita income below what could be achieved by a more direct population policy, no further action would be required. Where this is not the case, the processes whereby reproductive behavior can be influenced, and in particular the relation between resource inputs into these processes and the responses to them (prompt and delayed) need to be incorporated in the model. Considerations of this kind have been introduced into optimal population models by Pitchford (1974).

The second refinement concerns the optimality criterion. Situations occur in which what can be achieved by population policies can only diminish but not prevent a lowering of the per capita consumption sustained by domestic resources, for an extended period ahead. In such cases a realistic view will recognize a degree of exogeneity in the future path of population for some time to come. One may then want to explore optimality criteria that extend to those as yet unborn children whose birth had better, but cannot, be prevented the same consideration as to those already born.

We have considered two broad fields of application for optimization models. One comprises the detailed and data-oriented optimization of the decisions of the enterprise or public agency—and also the coordination of such decisions through a price system, through centralized planning and management, or both. The other is the more speculative study of alternative aggregate future growth paths for an entire economy.

In conclusion I want to make some remarks about the growing field of *development programming*, in which the two strands of thought are being combined and merged. One early step in this development was the construction of a mathematical programming model for an economy as of some future year, including investments and the flow of aid in the intervening period as decision variables. An example is the study of the economy of Southern Italy by Chenery, writing with Kretschmer (1956) and with Uzawa (1958). An evaluative description of experiences with Hungarian economic planning along these lines was written by Kornai (1967). Later studies, such as that of the Mexican economy by Goreux, Manne and coauthors (1973), envisaged a sequence of future years. In most of these studies data availabilities determined the use of Leontief's input-output framework for representing the production possibilities of the economy as a whole. Policy choices and optimization were introduced where data so permitted. One example is the choice between domestic production versus imports paid for by exports in the Southern Italy study. Others are the sectoral detail in the Hungarian studies, and concentration on the energy and especially electric energy sectors in the Mexican one.

A weakness in the treatment of consumption in optimal growth models, noted by Chakravarty (1969), is the lack of continuity between consumption levels in the past and those recommended by otherwise reasonable looking optimality criteria for the near future. One remedy proposed by Manne

(1970) has been to constrain future consumption paths to a family of smooth paths all anchored on the most recent observed level of consumption.

Econometric studies have been used to estimate consumption, production and investment relations describing decisions not or only partly controlled by the policy maker. In some cases the studies have gone beyond the convexity assumptions of most optimal growth models to recognize economies of scale in production. Examples are studies by Chenery (1952) of investment in pipelines in the United States, and by Manne (1967) and coauthors of plant size, location and timing of availability in four industries in India.

A substantial part of the work in this field may have escaped the general reader of economic journals, because much of the work has been published in collective volumes. Examples of these, not already mentioned, are Manne and Markowitz (1963), Adelman and Thorbecke (1966), Chenery (1971), Blitzer, Clark and Taylor (1975).

One final remark. The economist as such does not advocate criteria of optimality. He may invent them. He will discuss their pros and cons, sometimes before but preferably after trying out their implications. He may also draw attention to situations where allover objectives, such as productive efficiency, can be served in a decentralized manner by particularized criteria, such as profit maximization. But thc ultimate choice is made, usually only implicitly and not always consistently, by the procedures of decision making inherent in the institutions, laws and customs of society. A wide range of professional competences enters into the preparation and deliberation of these decisions. To the extent that the economist takes part in this decisive phase, he does so in a double role, as economist, and as a citizen of his polity: local polity, national polity, or world polity.

REFERENCES:

Adelman, I. and E. Thorbecke, eds. (1966), *The Theory and Design of Economic Development*. Baltimore, Johns Hopkins Press.

Arrow, K. J. and M. Kurz (1970), *Public Investment, the Rate of Return and Optimal Fiscal Policy*. Baltimore, Johns Hopkins Press.

Barone, E. (1908), "Il Ministro della Produzione nello Stato Collettivista," *Giorn. degli Econ.;* English Translation in F. A. Hayek, ed., *Collectivist Economic Planning*, London, 1935.

Beals, R. and T. C. Koopmans (1969), "Maximizing Stationary Utility in a Constant Technology," *SIAM Journal of Applied Mathematics* 17, 5, pp. 1001—1015.

Blitzer, C. R., P. C. Clark and L. Taylor, eds. (1975), *Economy-Wide Models and Development Planning*. Oxford U. Press.

Cass, D. (1966), "Optimum Growth in an Aggregate Model of Capital Accumulation: A Turnpike Theorem," *Econometrica* 34, 4, pp. 833—850.

Cassel, Gustav (1918), *The Theory of Social Economy*. London, 1923. Originally published in German, 1918.

Chakravarty, S. (1969), *Capital and Development Planning*. Cambridge, Mass., M.I.T. Press.

Chenery, H. B. (1952), "Overcapacity and the Acceleration Principle," *Econometrica* 20, 1. pp. 1—28.

Chenery, H. B. and K. Kretschmer (1956), "Resource Allocation for Economic Development," *Econometrica* 24, 4, pp. 365—399.

Chenery, H. B. and H. Uzawa (1958), "Non-Linear Programming in Economic Development" in Arrow, K. J., L. Hurwicz and H. Uzawa, eds., *Studies in Linear and Non-Linear Programming.* Stanford. U. Press.

Chenery, H. B., ed. (1971), *Studies in Development Planning.* Cambridge, Mass., Harvard U. Press.

Chipman, J. S. (1965), "A Survey of the Theory of International Trade: Part I, The Classical Theory," *Econometrica,* 33, 3 pp. 477—519.

Dantzig, G. B. (1951), "Application of the Simplex Method to a Transportation problem" in Koopmans, T. C., ed., *Activity Analysis* . . . (see below), pp. 359—373.

Dantzig, G. B. and P. Wolfe (1960), "The Decomposition Principle for Linear Programming," *Operations Research* 8, 1, pp. 101—111.

Dantzig, G. B. and P. Wolfe (1961), "The Decomposition Algorithm for Linear Programs," *Econometrica* 29, 4, pp. 767—778.

Dantzig, G. B. (1963), *Linear Programming and Extensions.* Princeton U. Press.

Dasgupta, P. S. (1969), "On the Concept of Optimum Population," *Review of Econ. Studies,* 36, 1, pp. 295—318.

Dasgupta, P. S. and G. Heal (1974), "The Optimal Depletion of Exhaustible Resources," *Review of Econ. Studies, Symposium,* pp. 3—28.

Gale, D. (1956), "The Closed Linear Model of Production," Paper 18, Kuhn, H., and A. W. Tucker, eds., *Linear Inequalities and Related Systems.* Princeton U. Press.

Gale, D., H. W. Kuhn and A. W. Tucker (1951), "Linear Programming and the Theory of Games," Ch. XIX of Koopmans, T.C., ed., *Activity Analysis* . . . (see below), pp. 317—329.

Goreux, L. M., A. S. Manne and coauthors (1973), *Multi-Level Planning: Case Studies in Mexico.* Amsterdam, North-Holland Publ.

Hayek, F. A. (1945), "The Use of Knowledge in Society," *Am. Ecom. Rev.,* 35, 4, pp. 519—30.

Hitchcock, F. L. (1941), "The Distribution of a Product from Several Sources to Numerous Localities," *Journal of Mathematics and Physics,* 20, pp. 224—230.

Kantorovich, L. V. (1939), *Mathematicheskie Metody Organizatsii i Planirovania Proizvodstva,* Leningrad State University Publishers, translated as "Mathematical Methods in the Organization and Planning of Production" (1960) in *Management Science* 6, 4, pp. 366—422.

Kantorovich, L. V. and M. K. Gavurin (first version 1940, publ. 1949), "Primenenie matematicheskikh metodov v voprosakh analiza gruzopotokov," in *Problemy povysheniia effektivnosti raboty transporta* (The Use of Mathematical Methods in Analyzing Problems of Goods Transport, in *Problems of Increasing the Efficiency in the Transport Industry,* pp. 110—138). Academy of Sciences, U.S.S.R.

Kantorovich, L. V. (1942), "On the Translocation of Masses," *Comptes Rendus (Doklady) de l'Académie des Sciences de l'URSS,* 37, nos. 7—8. Reprinted (1958) in *Management Science,* 5, 1, pp. 1—4.

Kantorovich, L. V. (1959), Ekonomicheskii raschët nailichshego ispolzovania resursov, Acad. of Sc., USSR (translated (1965), *The Best Use of Economic Resources.* Cambridge, Mass., Harvard U. Press.)

Koopmans, T. C. (memo dated 1942, publ. 1970), "Exchange Ratios between Cargoes on Various Routes," in *Scientific Papers of Tjalling C. Koopmans.* Berlin, Springer Verlag.

Koopmans, T. C. (1949) (conference paper, publ. 1951), "Optimum Utilization of the Transportation System," in *Proceedings of the International Statistical Conferences,* 5, pp. 136—145.

Koopmans, T. C., ed., (1951), *Activity Analysis of Production and Allocation.* New York, Wiley.

Koopmans, T. C. (1951), "Analysis of Production as an Efficient Combination of Activities," in Koopmans, T. C., ed., *Activity Analysis . . ., op. cit.*

Koopmans, T. C. and S. Reiter (1951), "A Model of Transportation," in Koopmans, T. C., ed., *Activity Analysis . . . , op. cit.*, pp. 222—259.
Koopmans, T. C. (1957), *Three Essays on the State of Economic Science.* New York, McGraw-Hill.
Koopmans, T. C. and A. F. Bausch (1959), "Selected Topics in Economics Involving Mathematical Reasoning," *SIAM Review*, 1, 2, pp. 79—148.
Koopmans, T. C. (1960), "Stationary Ordinal Utility and Impatience," *Econometrica* 28, 2, pp. 287—309.
Koopmans, T. C., P. A. Diamond, and R. E. Williamson (1964), "Stationary Utility and Time Perspective," *Econometrica,* 32, 1—2, pp. 82—100.
Koopmans, T. C. (1965), "On the Concept of Optimal Economic Growth," in *The Econometric Approach to Development Planning,* Pontif. Acad. Sc. Scripta Varia 28, pp. 225—300; reissued North-Holland Publ. (1966).
Koopmans, T. C. (1967), "Intertemporal Distribution and 'Optimal' Aggregate Economic Growth," in Fellner *et al., Ten Economic Studies in the Tradition of Irving Fisher,* pp. 95—126. New York, Wiley.
Koopmans, T. C. (1973), "Economic Growth and Exhaustible Resources," in Bos, H. C., H. Linneman, and P. de Wolff, eds., *Economic Structure and Development,* Essays in Honour of Jan Tinbergen, pp. 239—255. Amsterdam, North Holland Publ.
Kornai, J. and Th. Liptak (1962, 1965), "Two-Level Planning," 'duplicated', in Hungarian; *Econometrica,* 33, 1, pp. 141—169.
Kornai, J. (1967), *Mathematical Planning of Structural Decisions.* Budapest, Hungarian Academy of Sciences.
Kuhn, H. W. and A. W. Tucker (1959), "Nonlinear Programming," in Neyman, J., ed., *Proc. Second Berkely Symposium on Math. Stat. and Probability,* Berkeley, pp. 481—492.
Lange, O. (1936), "On the Economic Theory of Socialism," *Review of Econ. Studies,* 4, 1 and 2, pp. 53—71, 123—142. Repr. in Lippincott, B., ed., *On the Economic Theory of Socialism* (1938). Minneapolis, U. of Minnesota Press.
Leontief, W. W. (1936), "Quantitative Input and Output Relations in the Economic System of the United States," *Review of Econ. Statistics,* 18, 3, pp. 105—125.
Leontief, W.W. (1941), *The Structure of American Economy, 1919—1939.* Oxford U. Press.
Lerner, A. P. (1937), "Statics and Dynamics in Socialist Economics," *Economic Journal,* 47, 2, pp. 253—270.
Lerner, A. P. (1938), "Theory and Practice in Socialist Economics," *Review of Econ. Studies,* 6, 1, pp. 71—75.
Malinvaud, E. (1965), "Croissances optimales dans un modèle macroéconomique," in *The Econometric Approach . . . ,* see Koopmans (1965).
Malinvaud, E. (1967), "Decentralized Procedures for Planning," in Malinvaud, E. and M. O. L. Bacharach, eds., *Activity Analysis in the Theory of Growth and Planning.* London, Macmillan; New York, St. Martin's Press.
Manne, A. S. and H. Markowitz, eds. (1963), *Studies in Process Analysis,* New York, Wiley.
Manne, A. S. and coauthors (1967), *Investments for Capacity Expansion: Size, Location, and Time-Phasing.* Cambridge, Mass., M.I.T. Press.
Manne, A. S. (1970), "Sufficient Conditions for Optimality in an Infinite Hirozon Development Plan," *Econometrica* 38, 1, pp. 18—38.
Massé, P. and R. Gibrat (1957), "Application of Linear Programming to Investments in the Eletric Power Industry," *Management Science* 3, 2, pp. 149—166.
Meade, J. E. (1955), *Trade and Welfare,* Oxford U. Press.
von Neumann, J. (1936), "Über ein ökonomisches Gleichungsystem und eine Verallgemeinerung des Brouwerschen Fixpunktsatzes," in Menger, K., ed., *Ergebnisse eines mathematischen Kolloquiums,* no 8. Translated as "A Model of General Equilibrium," *Review of Econ. Studies* 13, 1. pp. 1—9 (1945).

Novozhilov, V. V. (1939), "Metody soizmerenia narodnokhaziaistvennoi effektivnosti planovikh i proiektnikh variantov" ("Methods of Comparison of the National Economic Efficiency of Plan- and Project-Variants"). *Transactions of the Leningrad Industrial Institute,* 4.

Pitchford, J. D. (1974), *Population in Economic Growth.* Amsterdam, North-Holland Publ.

Pitchford, J. D. (1975), "Population and Economic Growth: Macroeconomics," paper presented at the Econometric Society, Third World Congress, Toronto, Canada.

Ramsey, F. P. (1928), "A Mathematical Theory of Saving," *Economic Journal,* 38, 4, pp. 543—559.

Samuelson, P. A. (1949, 1966), "Market Mechanisms and Maximization," Rand Corporation, 1949. Reprinted in *The Collected Scientific Papers of Paul A. Samuelson* Cambridge, Mass. M.I.T. Press, pp. 425—493.

Smith, Adam (1776), *The Wealth of Nations.*

Tucker, A. W. (1957), "Linear and Nonlinear Programming," *Operations Research,* 5, 2, pp. 244—257.

Walras, L. (1874), *Eléments d'économie politique pure,* Lausanne; translated (1954) by W. Jaffé as *Elements of Pure Economics,* London.

11

Examples of Production Relations Based on Microdata
Tjalling C. Koopmans

The Microeconomic Foundations of Macroeconomics: Proceedings of a Conference held by the International Economic Association at S'Agaro, Spain, ed. G. C. Harcourt (London: Macmillan, 1977), pp. 144–178

I INTRODUCTION

The view has been expressed by many that a meaningful capital theory can and should be developed without ever defining an aggregate capital index. A fine prototype of this approach is Malinvaud's now classical paper of 1953. The same banner has been unfurled, though not with full identity of views, in Cambridge, England and in Cambridge, Massachusetts.

With princely unconcern econometricians have continued to fit aggregate production functions approximating an aggregate output index, for an economy or a sector, by a function $F(L, K)$ of aggregate labour (L) and capital (K) input indices. When the matter of the logical foundations for such a construct is raised, words such as 'parable' or 'metaphor' are pressed into service.

Coexistence of logically unconnected or even incompatible approaches makes for a rich science. Part of this richness lies in the challenge to find points of view that may tie together what appear to be competing approaches. This paper does not attempt to arrive at a definite stand on the issue of capital aggregation. Its more modest purpose is to select a few pieces of work in the literature that have a bearing on the problem, to describe their principal ideas in a summarising way, and to comment on such insights as they may give in the problem of aggregating production relations. The selection is avowedly subjective, and leaves out some important contributions already extensively discussed in the literature.

There are two other self-imposed constraints. One is the acceptance of that shadowy notion of perfect allocation that is subject to two seemingly opposite interpretations: that of perfect markets guided by complete information and perfect foresight, and that of perfect planning possibly guided by appropriate shadow prices. This constraint is adopted on the hunch that aggregation is simpler within it than without it, while what is learned in this way may still be a worthwhile starting point for the study of more complicated situations. The constraint is applied to that part of the economy whose aggregation is under discussion, and not necessarily to the rest of the economy. It may also

Research supported by grants from the National Science Foundation and the Ford Foundation. I am indebted to Katsuhito Iwai and Herbert Scarf for valuable comments.

Note: The numbering of the figures reflects the chapter number in the original volume.

be applied to the future under conditions showing that it could not have held in the past.

The second constraint arises from a preference for the notion of elementary processes as the building blocks from which production relations are constructed. In the simplest case each process is defined merely by the ratios of inputs to outputs in any utilisation of the process. Use of this simple linear case implies an assumption of constant returns to scale within any one process, possibly subject to an upper bound set by a capacity limit. The assumption of a finite number of processes has the advantage that the micro-data that describe technology in detail often are of this nature. Also, algorithms for marshalling such data to answer broader questions are available. Finally, cases of joint production can readily be included in this way. Generally speaking, however, the discrete representation of processes is more suited for the industrial sector than for agriculture. In the latter case, the differentiable production function normally employed for aggregate relations may well be the appropriate form to represent a family of elementary processes that allows continuous substitution of one factor of production for another. Production relations in which the two forms are combined may, of course, be most appropriate in some cases.

In Section II we reason from a given size and composition of the capital stock available to each productive unit and held constant during the single period considered. The object of the analysis is to derive the production function in the space of current inputs and outputs implicit in efficient utilisation of its 'own' capital stock by each unit. The characteristics of these stocks find expression in the shape of the production locus, but do not explicitly appear as variables. In this context, therefore, the term aggregation refers only to the fact that one production relation for the whole is derived from a number of simpler relations for the parts. There is no attempt yet to reduce the number of variables by the formation of suitable index numbers. Rather, the number of relations is reduced to one, using the assumption of internally efficient utilisation (or in some cases non-use) of the individually controlled parts of the capital stock.

In Section III the size and composition of the total capital stock do explicitly appear in the model, and can change over time. However, the attention concentrates on the search for a capital stock that if initially given does not change (is 'invariant') as a result of optimisation of the production path for capital goods and consumption goods over an infinite horizon. Implied in this optimisation is that not only the use of individually controlled parts of the capital stock, but indeed the size, composition, allocation and use of the total stock are optimally chosen in a sense to be defined in Section III. The ideas of Section III are presented with the help of a simple example.

Section IV discusses how such an invariant capital stock may depend on the discount factor for future utility flows that enter into the optimality criterion for paths over time. While normally a larger discount factor (a smaller discount rate) is associated with a larger invariant capital stock, a simple example of the reverse relationship is given.

Section V is an Addendum following the S'Agaro conference, in order to elaborate on statements made in the discussion in response to comments and questions by a number of participants. In particular, the Addendum indicates that, in a counter-intuitive example of an invariant capital stock that is larger when the discount factor is smaller, that invariant stock is not unique, is not stable under small changes in the initial capital stock, and is bracketed by two other invariant stocks each of which is stable.

II ONE-PERIOD PRODUCTION RELATIONS

Consider a period short enough so that the size and composition of the stock of fixed capital can be regarded as given and constant within the period. The discussion concerns itself with an aggregate or *whole* that may be interpreted as a branch of industry, a sector of the production economy, or the entire production system of an economy. We are looking for a procedure that derives the 'short-run' production function for the whole from production possibility data associated with the *parts* (pieces of equipment, departments, plants, firms, or branches of industry) that together make up the whole. In keeping with the short-run point of view, we allow (but do not insist on) an interpretation in which the possibility of transfers of capital goods between parts during the period is ruled out.

The *locus classicus* is a beautiful brief paper by Houthakker (1955). Variants of his procedure were developed by Levhari (1968) and K. Sato (1969). A fuller and more systematic treatment is given by Johansen (1972) in an important book in which the various production function and supply function concepts are defined, are related to each other, and to empirical data.

Houthakker, Johansen and Levhari represent the production possibilities inherent in the capital stock of any given part by a *process vector* in the space of input and output commodity flows. Besides indicating the ratios of inputs and outputs by the ratios of its components, the process vector is given a length expressing the absolute inputs and outputs corresponding to full-capacity use of the capital stock for that part. Then, as long as the capital stock is held constant, the collection of process vectors, one for each part, is all one requires for the derivation of the short-run production function for the whole. Information about the physical composition of the capital stock available to each part and the processes involved in its production are needed only at a later stage of analysis, where changes in the capital stock are introduced.

We have argued above that, in regard to industrial production, it seems more suitable to treat the number of parts represented by process vectors as finite, but often large. Houthakker, Levhari and, in his Chapters 3, 4, 5, Johansen, approximate this discrete collection of vectors by an infinite number of process vectors arranged in a smooth frequency distribution over the entire space of inputs and outputs, or over some sub-set of this space that may be of lower dimensionality. This has the advantage that each individual process may be thought of as operating only at a level of 1 or 0.

Here I shall use a finite number of process vectors, as is done by Johansen in his first exposition of the short-run production function (Section 2.4) and in his applications to the Swedish wood pulp industry (Section 8.7) and the Norwegian tanker fleet (Chapter 9). As already explained, let in this case the *capacitated* process vector $a^j \equiv (a^j_1, a^j_2, \ldots, a^j_n)$ represent inputs and outputs under full utilisation of the capital stock of that part. A scalar *utilisation factor* x_j can then be applied to the process vector a^j to represent the input and output flows at feasible activity levels by the scalar product

$$x_j a^j \equiv (x_j a^j_1, x_j a^j_2, \ldots, x_j a^j_n), \qquad 0 \leqslant x_i \leqslant 1.$$

Figure 5:1 illustrates the construction of the short-run production function in the simplest case of one input and one output. This case could serve as a first approximation for a collection of base-load power plants burning clean coal (if we include labour with the capital stock). Process vectors a^1, a^2, a^3, a^4 might represent plants of increasing age with decreasing 'efficiency' of conversion of fuel into electric energy. In this simple case the

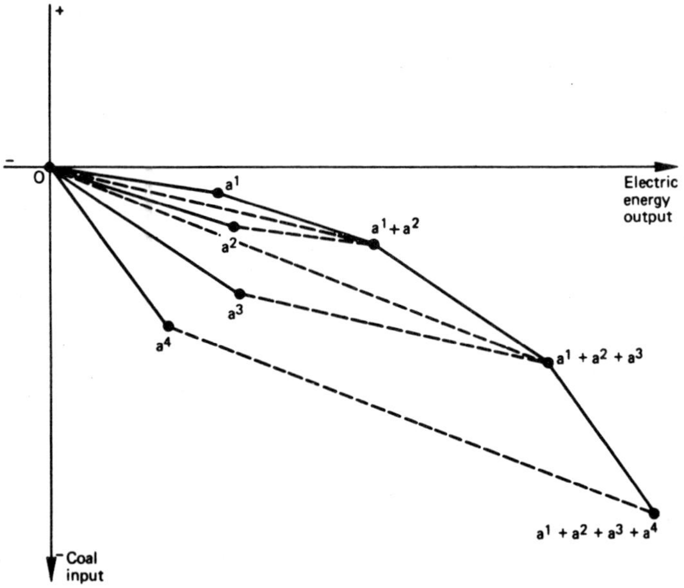

Fig. 5:1 Short-run aggregated production function for four electric power plants

short-run production function is represented by the broken straight line connecting the successive partial sums $0, a^1, a^1 + a^2, \ldots,$ of the given process vectors taken in order of decreasing 'efficiency' of conversion. Under a regime of maximisation of net revenue from current operations of the whole, a gradual increase of the ratio of the output price to the input price will trace out the production function. Intervals on the relative price axis will correspond to points $a_1, a_1 + a_2, \ldots,$ where the production function has a kink, and relative prices characteristic of successively less efficient pieces of capital will correspond to segments on which these pieces are taken into use in the same order.

If there are $m > 2$ inputs and outputs and n processes, there is no natural linear order of the subsets of processes successively taken into use, and there are price vectors which permit more than one process to be efficiently taken into partial use simultaneously. The construction then is as follows.

Let T (for 'technology') denote the set $\{a^j \mid j = 0, 1, \ldots, n\}$ of all capacitated process vectors a^j, where $a^0 \equiv 0$ (the origin). For any subset T' of T (including T itself but excluding the empty set) let $a(T')$ be the sum

$$a(T') \equiv \sum_{a^j \in T'} a^j$$

of all process vectors of T'. Then the feasible set in the space of commodity flows is the convex hull H of the set of vectors $a(T')$ for all T'; that is,

$$H \equiv \left\{ \sum_{T' \subset T} x(T')\, a(T') \mid \sum_{T' \subset T} x(T') = 1, x(T') \geqslant 0 \text{ for all } T' \subset T \right\},$$

the set of all convex-linear combinations of all the partial sums $a(T')$. Finally, the graph F of the production function is the efficient boundary of H; that is, the set of those points h of H such that the only point $h + \epsilon$ of H with $\epsilon \geqslant 0$ is the point h with $\epsilon = 0$.

In this case, as output prices increase and/or input prices decrease, the order in which additional processes are started up under current net revenue maximisation depends on the path in the price space followed.

A diagram illustrating this construction in the case of three processes and three goods (two outputs, one input) is given here as Figure 5:2. A similar diagram for the case of two inputs and one output is given by Johansen (1972, p. 17) in projection on the input space, with isoquants drawn in to indicate increasing output levels.

III A CAPITAL STOCK INVARIANT UNDER OPTIMIZATION OVER TIME

In Section II simplicity was bought by the assumption of a fixed capital stock and a fixed technology for its utilisation. In the present section, in which we

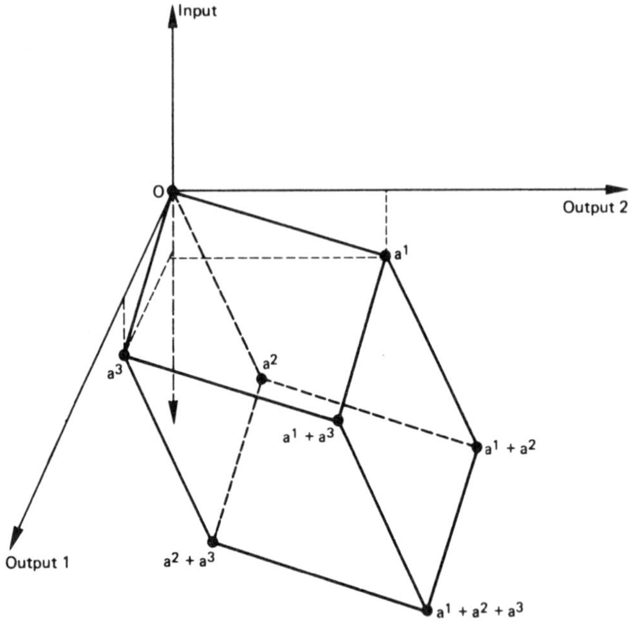

Fig. 5:2 Short-run aggregated production function for three plants with one input and two outputs. (a^2 is not on the efficient production locus.)

consider an intertemporal model of an entire economy, we shall continue to assume a fixed technology, not only in the utilisation of capital goods in production, but also in the production of the capital goods themselves. However, we shall treat changes over time in the capital stock as entirely feasible. We also assume absence of institutional barriers to the transfer of capital goods from one control to another. The process notion therefore no longer implies allocative control over a fixed capital stock associated with each part. The process thus becomes a more purely technological concept, in which capital goods are now represented by coefficients for capital inputs required by the process.

We shall also strengthen the assumption of efficient use of resources to one of intertemporal optimality, defined by specifying some suitable social objective function over time. As explained already, this construct can be regarded as a simulation that yields a first approximation either to a centrally planned and managed economy, or to the course over time of a market economy that manages to sustain reasonably full employment. In the latter case the interpretation of the assumed intertemporal preferences is an implicit rather than an explicit one. In both cases, the simulation takes a rosy view of the working of the simulated economy.

We shall utilise an objective function of the form

$$U \equiv \sum_{t=1}^{\infty} (\alpha)^{t-1} u(y^t), \quad 0 < \alpha < 1.$$

Here y^t denotes a vector of final consumption flows of the various consumables in period t, $u(y)$ the utility flow associated with a consumption flow of y per unit period,[1] and α a discount factor[2] per unit of time, applied to future utilities and assumed given and constant. Consumption goods as well as capital goods are produced using processes selected from a finite collection of processes. The inputs to these processes include the utilisation of capital goods and the consumptive use of resource flows such as labour, minerals, clean air. Total available flows of resources in each period are again assumed fixed over time (for simplification though not realism).

The grand and difficult problem posed by this model is to associate with any (historically) given initial capital stock an optimal path (if one exists); that is, a path that maximises the objective function U among all feasible paths over an infinite time period.

However, some further provisional simplification can again be bought by first asking only the following question: *Does there exist a capital stock which, if put in the place of the given initial stock, will be reproduced precisely at the end of each period as a result of the optimisation?* If so, such a capital stock can be regarded as being in equilibrium with the technology, the resource constraints, and the preferences, both intertemporal as given by α, and within each period as given by $u(\cdot)$. We shall refer to such a stock as an *invariant optimal capital stock.*

For the basic case of a single good in the double role of capital good and consumption good, our question has been fully answered by Ramsey (1928) and his followers.[3] If the output flow of that good produced by a fixed labour force is a strictly concave function of the available capital stock, then there is a *unique* invariant optimal capital stock. It has been called the golden rule stock modified by discounting. Its dependence on the discount *factor* α is also well known: As α increases (hence the discount *rate* $\rho = (1-\alpha)/\alpha$ decreases), the invariant stock increases and approaches the golden rule stock proper as $\alpha \rightarrow 1$, hence $\rho \rightarrow 0$. It is readily computed from the value of α and the form of the production function, by requiring the marginal productivity of the good as capital in terms of the good as an output flow to be equal to ρ. Hence, it does not depend on the shape of the utility function. Finally, for any α, $0 < \alpha < 1$, and any positive initial capital stock, a unique optimal

[1] $u(y)$ is assumed differentiable and concave.

[2] $(\alpha)^t$ denotes α raised to the power t, in contrast with the use of superscripts t as time labels in y^t, and in x^t, z^t below.

[3] For a more recent exposition see Koopmans (1967), in which other literature is also cited.

capital path exists which approaches the modified golden rule stock as time proceeds.

Matters are more complicated for an arbitrary number of commodities. An analysis of the general case involving any finite numbers of processes and of the three types of goods (i.e., capital, consumption, resources) is given by Hansen and Koopmans (1972) from both the theoretical and computational points of view, with references to earlier work. Here we consider in some detail an example with *one* capital good, *one* resource and *two* consumption goods. It is hoped that such an exploration will bring out some of the economic content and implications of the concept of an invariant optimal capital stock more vividly than can the theorems and algorithms regarding the general case. While the presentation is self-contained and uses only elementary calculus, some unproved statements are supported by the reference cited.

We shall assume that the single-period utility function $u(y_1, y_2)$ is defined for all $y_1 \geqslant 0, y_2 \geqslant 0$, increases strictly with each of the two consumption flows, y_1, y_2 (nonsaturation), is strictly concave and continuously differentiable. As to the constraints, Table 5:1 gives the input and output coefficients

TABLE 5:1

Technology Matrix for an Intertemporal Model of Production

Notations for coefficient vectors				*Activity levels x_i and technical coefficients*			*Availabilities and total 'outputs'*	
				x_1	x_2	x_3	$\geqslant$	
f_1	f_2	f_3	=	$-a_1$	$-a_2$	$-a_3$	$-z^1$	capital input
				b_1	b_2	b_3	z^2	capital 'output'
-1	-1	-1	=	-1	-1	-1	-1	labour
d_1	d_2	0	=	1	0	0	y_1	cons. good '1'
				0	1	0	y_2	cons. good '2'

for the four goods for each of three processes. The symbols a_j, b_j, x_j, y_i, z^t represent non-negative scalars. The technical coefficients a_j, b_j are independent of time by assumption. The coefficient vectors are normalised so as to specify a unit input of the single resource (labour, say) for the unit activity level of each process. Also, the units of the two consumption goods are chosen so that one unit of labour is required to produce one unit of either good. As to timing, labour and consumption can be regarded as flows during the period. In those parts of the reasoning in which we consider only one period at a time, no time label will be attached to the x_j, y_i. Capital input is required to be available at the beginning of each period for use during that period. Capital output becomes available at the end of each period. Since capital input and output for a given period may differ, a time superscript t is attached to the symbol z whenever needed.

Capital 'output' represents the sum of (already used) capital released for possible use in the next period and new capital goods produced during the period. In principle one should consider two capital goods constructed from the same blueprint but with different lengths of prior use as different capital goods. For simplicity, for the processes $j = 1, 2$, interpreted as producing consumption goods only, we specify $a_j > b_j$ to simulate loss of effectiveness of the capital good by a constant geometric decline per period in its quantity, regardless of the rate of use. In this case the specification $a_3 < b_3$ is essential for an increase or even constancy over time of the capital stock to be compatible with a positive level of consumption. The symbols f_j, d_j are abbreviated notations for the corresponding column vectors of order two for the coefficients of capital goods and consumption goods, respectively. These symbols are used mostly in the diagrams.

The first line of the table expresses the feasibility constraint

$$-a_1x_1 - a_2x_2 - a_3x_3 \geqslant -z^1$$

which says that capital in use during the period cannot exceed the amount available at its beginning. The other constraints can be read off accordingly. The entire set of constraints remains the same at all times, and can be read as applying either to the first period, or to any nameless future period. To apply it to a specific period, say the tth, superscripts t are attached to the x_j and y_i, and $t - 1$ is added to the superscripts of z^1, z^2.

Note that the only variable occurring in the constraints for two successive periods, say those with labels $t, t + 1$, is the variable z^{t+1}. This, together with the additive form of the objective function, makes it possible to carry out the optimisation of the entire future path (starting with any prescribed initial stock z^1) in two stages. In the first stage all values z^t for $t = 1, 2, \ldots,$ are held fixed at arbitrary jointly attainable levels, and the attention is directed towards maximising the term $\alpha^{t-1}u(y^t)$ within each period by choice of the x_j^t, y_i^t, subject only to the constraints for that period. The result is a value

$$\max_{x^t, y^t} \alpha^{t-1}u(y_1^t, y_2^t) \equiv \alpha^{t-1}\,\psi(-z^t, z^{t+1}), \text{ say},$$

that depends only on the initial and terminal capital stocks of that period. The second stage then consists in maximising

$$\bar{U} \equiv \sum_{t=1}^{\infty} \alpha^{t-1}\psi(-z^t, z^{t+1})$$

subject to the given initial stock z^1 and such constraints on the pairs (z^t, z^{t+1}), $t = 1, 2, \ldots$, as are implicit in those of Table 5:1.

While our focus is on initial stocks z^1 that in the second stage yield constant optimal paths $z^t = z^1$, $t = 2, 3, \ldots$, it will help if we do not yet specify $z^t = z^{t+1}$ in describing the first stage. Reverting to the nameless-period notation of Table 5:1 we therefore now take both z^1 and z^2 as given and possibly different, and drop the factor α^{t-1}. The first observation then is that optimality requires

$$y_1 = x_1, \quad y_2 = x_2,$$

because any slack in the consumption of either good would unnecessarily diminish the utility $u(y_1, y_2)$.

Our procedure for analysing stage one will be to compare the maximal utility flow, $\psi(-z^1, z^2)$, for the given z^1, z^2, with that attainable flow, to be denoted $\varphi(-z^1, z^2)$, that results if each of the three other constraints is tentatively required also to hold with strict equality,

$$\begin{aligned} -a_1x_1 - a_2x_2 - a_3x_3 &= -z^1 \\ b_1x_1 + b_2x_2 + b_3x_3 &= z^2 \\ -x_1 - x_2 - x_3 &= -1. \end{aligned}$$

We shall call these the no-slack constraints for capital input, capital output and labour, respectively. The domain of definition of $\varphi(-z^1, z^2)$ then is that set of points $(-z^1, z^2)$, to be denoted $\mathscr{Z}$ below, for which a non-negative solution (x_1, x_2, x_3) of the no-slack constraints exists.

We choose our example such that the 3 x 3 matrix of coefficients of the x_j is non-singular, solve for x_3 from the third equation and substitute the resulting expression in the other two equations, obtaining

$$\begin{aligned} -(a_1 - a_3)\,x_1 - (a_2 - a_3)\,x_2 - a_3 &= -z^1 \\ (b_1 - b_3)\,x_1 + (b_2 - b_3)\,x_2 + b_3 &= z^2, \end{aligned}$$

with a non-singular 2 x 2 matrix. Ignoring non-negativity constraints, these equations define a 1:1 linear mapping from the points (x_1, x_2) to the points $(-z^1, z^2)$.

The non-negativity of the activity levels x_j, $j = 1, 2, 3,$[1] and the identity of the x_j and y_j allow us to enter the level curves (indifference curves) of $u(y_1, y_2)$ in the closed positive quadrant of the (x_1, x_2)-plane (see Figure 5:3). We recall for later use some elementary mathematical verities. Since the derivatives

$$u_1(x_1, x_2) \equiv \frac{\partial u}{\partial x_1}, \quad u_2(x_1, x_2) \equiv \frac{\partial u}{\partial x_2},$$

[1] For $j = 3$ the constraint now takes the form $x_1 + x_2 \leqslant 1$.

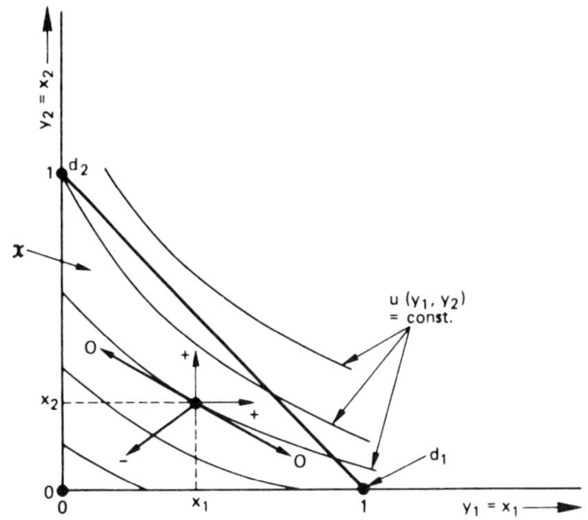

Fig. 5:3 Level curves of the single-period utility function

are positive in all points of the quadrant, there is in each point (x_1, x_2) a tangent to the level curve of negative finite[1] slope. This tangent partitions the set of all directions out of the point (x_1, x_2) into three sub-sets. As illustrated by arrows labelled +, 0, or − in Figure 5:3, in all directions (δ_1, δ_2) leading from (x_1, x_2) to points 'above' the tangent the directional derivative

$$\left(\frac{du(x_1 + \lambda\delta_1, x_2 + \lambda\delta_2)}{d\lambda}\right)_{\lambda = 0}$$

of u is positive; in the two directions along the tangent that derivative is zero; in all directions to points 'below' the tangent the derivative is negative. The origin is 'below' the tangent.[2] Finally, an implication of the strict concavity of u should be noted. Proceeding from (x_1, x_2) along a straight line in any direction with a non-positive directional derivative in (x_1, x_2), the function will monotonically decrease along the entire feasible segment of that line. In particular, the maximum of $u(x_1', x_2')$ among points (x_1', x_2') of the tangent in (x_1, x_2) is reached uniquely in (x_1, x_2).

The no-slack constraints for labour allow us to represent the set of attainable activity vectors (x_1, x_2, x_3) by the closed triangle $\mathcal{X} \equiv \mathcal{X}(0, d_1, d_2)$ with vertices $0, d_1, d_2$ in the space of (x_1, x_2) only, since $x_3 = 1 - x_1 - x_2$. The mapping $(x_1, x_2) \leftrightarrow (-z^1, z^2)$ in turn transforms this triangle into the triangle $\mathcal{Z} \equiv \mathcal{Z}(f_1, f_2, f_3)$ in the space of $(-z^1, z^2)$ – see Figure 5:4. The triangle $\mathcal{Z}$ represents the set of all those pairs $(-z^1, z^2)$ that are both attainable

[1] Our assumptions about $u(., .)$ imply that the axes are not tangent to any level curve.
[2] Whenever $(x_1, x_2) \neq (0, 0)$.

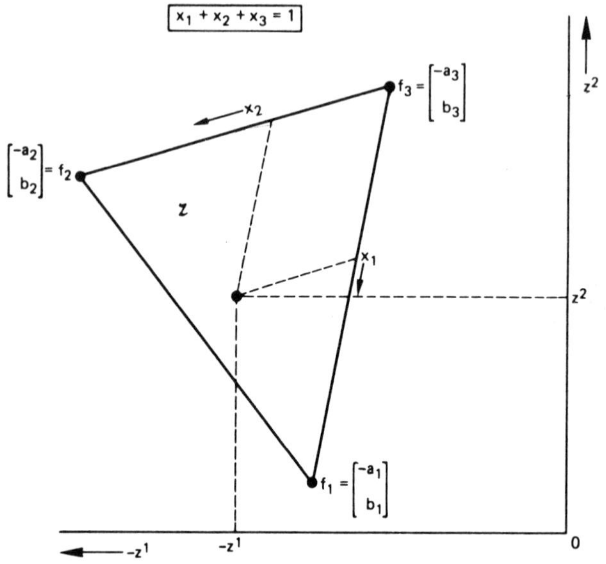

Fig. 5:4 Attainable set $\mathscr{Z}$ in the capital input and output

and consistent with the added no-slack constraints. Any point in this triangle simultaneously represents the pair $(-z^1, z^2)$ by reference to the rectangular co-ordinate axes of $-z^1$ and z^2, and the pair (x_1, x_2) by reference to a skew co-ordinate system defined within the triangle by placing the origin in f_3 and unit points on the two axes in f_1 and f_2. Transferred to the new (x_1, x_2)-co-ordinates defined on $\mathscr{Z}$, the level curves of $u(x_1, x_2)$ now also serve as level curves for the function $\varphi(-z^1, z^2)$ mentioned above (see Figure 5:5). This function is then defined on $\mathscr{Z}$ by

$$\varphi(-z^1, z^2) \equiv u(x_1, x_2) \quad \text{whenever } (x_1, x_2) \leftrightarrow (-z^1, z^2).$$

It represents the utility attained in the given period with initial and terminal capital specifications $(-z^1, z^2)$ if each of the five constraints is forced to hold with equality. Because of the linearity of the mapping φ inherits the continuous differentiability and the strict concavity of u.

The function $\varphi(-z^1, z^2)$ so defined in $\mathscr{Z}$ is not necessarily the same, even within $\mathscr{Z}$, as the function $\psi(-z^1, z^2)$ defined earlier in the entire set of feasible $(-z^1, z^2)$. The difference within $\mathscr{Z}$ is that $\psi(-z^1, z^2)$ is the maximum attainable utility under constraints permitting slacks, whereas $\varphi(-z^1, z^2)$ is the unique utility level that is attainable – hence optimal – under constraints that rule out all slacks. Since narrowing the constraint set cannot increase the maximum attainable utility we must have

$$\psi(-z^1, z^2) \geqslant \varphi(-z^1, z^2)$$

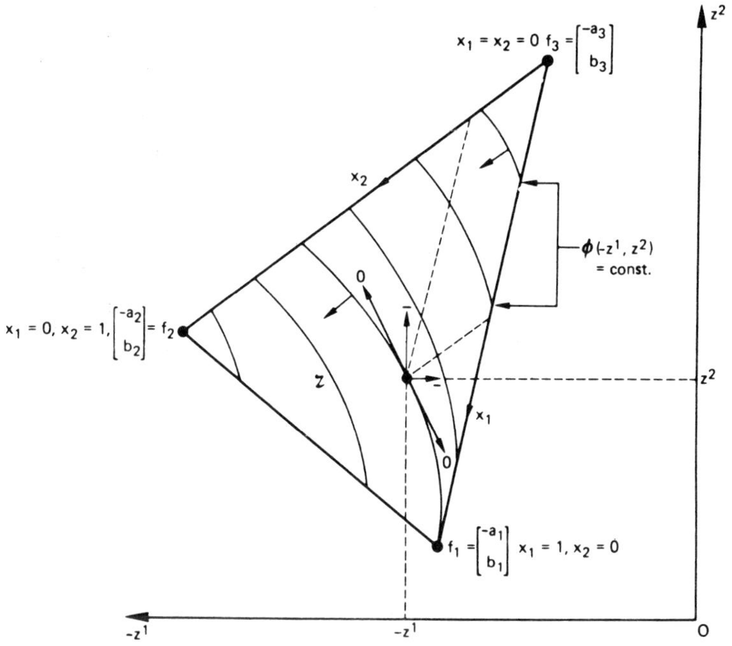

Fig. 5:5 Test of no-slack constraints for capital input and output

in all points $(-z^1, z^2)$ of $\mathscr{X}$. On the other hand, we must have

$$\psi(-z^1, z^2) = \varphi(-z^1, z^2)$$

in all those points $(-z^1, z^2)$ of $\mathscr{X}$ in which the maximum utility attainable under constraints permitting slacks is in fact attained for the unique no-slack activity vector $(x_1, x_2) \leftrightarrow$ the given $(-z^1, z^2)$. We shall now examine for each of the three constraints under what conditions this is the case.

Let $(-z^1, z^2)$ be a point in the interior of $\mathscr{X}$. Taking first the two capital constraints, we assume that the no-slack constraint for labour is satisfied. Then a slack of $\delta^1 > 0$ in capital input would mean that out of a stock z^1 made available only $z^1 - \delta^1$ is used in production. Similarly, a slack of $\delta^2 > 0$ in capital output would be to produce $z^2 + \delta^2$ but hand on only z^2. For either of these and any combination of them to decrease utility, it is sufficient[1] for

[1] In the configuration of Figure 5:5, where the new origin f_3 for the (x_1, x_2)-coordinate system is 'above' and 'to the right of' the point $(-z^1, z^2)$, it is necessary and sufficient that these derivatives are non-positive (not both can be zero), thus allowing a vertical or a horizontal tangent. See the implication of strict concavity of u discussed above.

the two derivatives

$$\varphi_1(-z^1, z^2) \equiv \frac{\partial\varphi}{\partial(-z^1)}, \qquad \varphi_2(-z^1, z^2) \equiv \frac{\partial\varphi}{\partial z^2},$$

to be negative. Figure 5:5 illustrates that this implies a finite negative slope

$$s \equiv -\frac{\varphi_1(-z^1, z^2)}{\varphi_2(-z^1, z^2)} = \left(\frac{dz^2}{d(-z^1)}\right)_{\varphi = \text{const.}}$$

for the tangent to the level curve of φ in the point $(-z^1, z^2)$.

We now turn to the no-slack constraint for labour, which we examine assuming the no-slack constraints for capital to be satisfied. Let the amount of labour in use be changed from 1 to

$$x_1 + x_2 + x_3 = 1 - \epsilon, \qquad 0 < \epsilon \leqslant 1$$

allowing a slack of ϵ. We choose a particular small value of ϵ and treat the above equation as defining a new experimental equality constraint on labour. This defines a new mapping between the new activity levels $\tilde{x}_1, \tilde{x}_2$ and the capital specifications z^1, z^2, according to the equations

$$-(a_1 - a_3)\tilde{x}_1 - (a_2 - a_3)\tilde{x}_2 - a_3(1 - \epsilon) = -z^1$$
$$(b_1 - b_3)\tilde{x}_1 + (b_2 - b_3)\tilde{x}_2 + b_3(1 - \epsilon) = z^2.$$

But then those values $\tilde{z}^1, \tilde{z}^2$ of the capital stocks that would have produced the present consumption flows $\tilde{x}_1, \tilde{x}_2$ in the absence of any labour or capital disposals are related to the specified flows z^1, z^2 by

$$-\tilde{z}^1 = -z^1 - \epsilon a_3, \qquad \tilde{z}^2 = z^2 + \epsilon b_3.$$

It is these values that are to be tested in relation to the level curves of the function φ in Figure 5:5. This is done in Figure 5:6, where the dashed line connecting the interior point $(-z^1, z^2)$ of $\mathscr{Z}$ with $(-\tilde{z}^1, \tilde{z}^2)$ is drawn so as to be parallel, in slope and direction, to the line $0f_3$ connecting the origin of the $(-z^1, z^2)$-plane with the point $f_3 = (-a_3, b_3)$ representing the capital-producing process. Therefore, for any slack in labour use to be non-optimal, the following condition on the directional derivative in the direction $(-a_3, b_3)$ is both necessary[1] and sufficient,

$$\left(\frac{d\varphi(-z^1 - \lambda a_3, z^2 + \lambda b_3)}{d\lambda}\right)_{\lambda = 0} = -a_3\varphi_1(-z^1, z^2) + b_3\varphi_2(-z^1, z^2) \leqslant 0.$$

Since we assume capital slacks to be non-optimal, φ_1 and φ_2 must be non-positive, which precludes $\varphi_2 = 0$. Therefore the condition just obtained is

[1] The necessity is achieved by the inclusion of the = sign, on the strength of the strict concavity of φ.

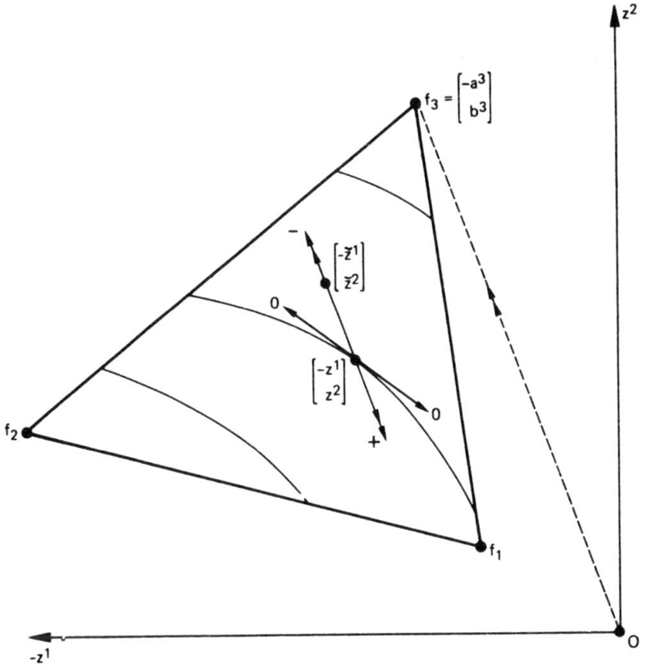

Fig. 5:6 Test of the no-slack constraint for labour

equivalent to the slope condition

$$s(-z^1, z^2) \equiv -\frac{\varphi_1(-z^1, z^2)}{\varphi_2(-z^1, z^2)} \geqslant -\frac{b_3}{a_3},$$

as illustrated in Figure 5:6.

We have now derived condtiions on the non-optimality of slacks by testing the effect of the no-slack constraints one or two at a time while assuming the other(s) to be satisfied. Due to the differentiability and strict concavity of φ, the conditions so obtained can be combined to form one condition on the non-optimality of any combination of non-negative slacks in the three constraints with $\delta^1 + \delta^2 + \epsilon > 0$, that leaves the resulting point $(-z^1 + \delta^1 - \epsilon a_3, z^2 + \delta^2 + \epsilon b_3)$ in $\mathscr{Z}$. In terms of the slope $s \equiv s(-z^1, z^2)$ of the tangent to the level curve of φ in $(-z^1, z^2)$ that comprehensive sufficient (necessary)[1] condition then is

$$-\frac{b_3}{a_3} \leqslant s(-z^1, z^2) < (\leqslant)\ 0.$$

[1] See footnote [on p. 221].

Finally, in all interior points $(-z^1, z^2)$ of $\mathscr{Z}$ in which the comprehensive sufficient condition is satisfied we must have, as explained above,

$$\varphi(-z^1, z^2) = \psi(-z^1, z^2).$$

Therefore, the level curves of φ and ψ coincide in that part of $\mathscr{Z}$ in which the sufficient slope condition is satisfied. Moreover, in those points, we can look upon the negatives

$$q^1 \equiv -\varphi_1(-z^1, z^2), q^2 \equiv -\varphi_2(-z^1, z^2), r \equiv a_3\varphi_1(-z^1, z^2) - b_3\varphi_2(-z^1, z^2),$$

of the directional derivatives used in testing for the tightness of the capital and labour constraints as non-negative shadow prices associated with the corresponding inputs and outputs. These prices are expressed in units of marginal utility discounted to time $t = 1$.

For all points $(-z^1, z^2)$ of $\mathscr{Z}$ for which the no-slack conditions are met, stage one, the discussion of optimisation within single periods for which $(-z^1, z^2)$ is given, has now been completed. It will turn out that the stage one analysis for this subset of $\mathscr{Z}$ is sufficient for our present exploratory purpose.

We are therefore now ready for stage two, the search for invariant optimal capital stocks. We now want to examine points $(-z^1, z^2)$ for which $z^1 = z^2 = z$, say. In the diagrams these points are denoted

$$f = (-z, z) = z \cdot (-1, 1) \equiv z \cdot e,$$

that is (see Figure 5:7), points of the line $\mathcal{L}$ through the origin and of slope -1. Again, we first limit our search to points $(-z, z)$ in which the reproduction of $z^2 = z$ from $z^1 = z$ is achieved optimally without slacks. This limits the search first of all to points of the segment $\mathscr{S}$ in which $\mathcal{L}$ intersects $\mathscr{Z}$. Since by previous assumptions about the a_j, b_j the points f_1, f_2 are 'below' $\mathcal{L}$, f_3 'above' $\mathcal{L}$, the segment $\mathscr{S}$ intersects $\mathscr{Z}$ in its interior. It is the segment $\mathscr{S}$ minus its end points in which we shall now search.

Secondly, we shall at first use the slightly more restrictive sufficient slope condition

$$-\frac{b_3}{a_3} < s(-z, z) < 0.$$

for the within-period optimality of the no-slack activity vector $(x_1, x_2) \leftrightarrow (-z, z)$.

Assuming that such a point $(-z, z)$ exists we must now find a test whether the maximisation of

$$U = \sum_{t=1}^{\infty} \alpha^{t-1} \psi(-z^t, z^{t+1})$$

subject to $z^1 = z$ and the within-period constraints for each period is achieved by $z^t = z$ for all $t > 1$. Trimming our sails once more, we shall first study a

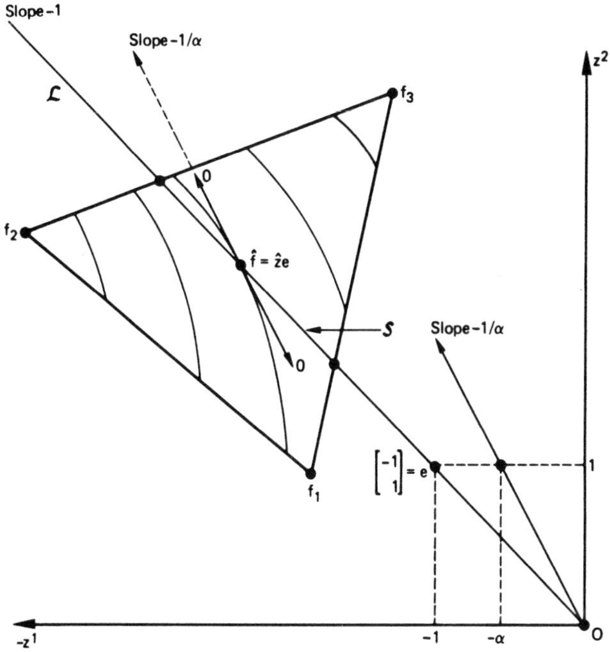

Fig. 5:7 Condition for an invariant optimal capital stock in an interior point of $\mathscr{Z}$

weaker test, necessary but perhaps not sufficient, obtained by specifying

$$z^1 = z = z^3 = z^4 = \ldots,$$

which leaves only z^2 free to vary. We then need to consider only the maximisation of

$$V \equiv \psi(-z, z^2) + \alpha\psi(-z^2, z)$$

with respect to z^2. Finally, since u and therefore φ have continuous first derivatives, the present slope condition is satisfied also in a neighbourhood $\mathscr{N}$ within $\mathscr{Z}$ of the point $(-z, z)$. Therefore, restricting z^2 further such that both $(-z, z^2)$ and $(-z^2, z)$ are in $\mathscr{N}$, we are in fact maximising

$$W \equiv \varphi(-z, z^2) + \alpha\varphi(-z^2, z).$$

The test then is whether the maximum of W within $\mathscr{N}$ is attained for $z^2 = z$. For this to occur, it is necessary that

$$0 = \left(\frac{dW}{dz^2}\right)_{z^2 = z} = \varphi_2(-z, z) - \alpha\varphi_1(-z, z),$$

or, equivalently,[1]

$$s(-z, z) = -\frac{\varphi_1(-z, z)}{\varphi_2(-z, z)} = -\frac{1}{\alpha}.$$

It has been proved elsewhere[2] that this necessary condition for the maximality of U in the constant programme $z^t = z$ is also sufficient. Figure 5:7 illustrates the construction. *One scans the points of* $\mathcal{S}$ *to find one or more points where the slope of the level curve of* φ *has the value* $-1/\alpha$ *for the given* α. *Any point in the interior of* $\mathcal{Z}$ *satisfying this 'slope condition' represents an invariant optimal capital stock, to be denoted* $\hat{z}$, *provided* the prescribed slope $-1/\alpha$ itself meets our present 'no-slack' slope constraint[3]

$$-\frac{b_3}{a_3} < -\frac{1}{\alpha} = s(-\hat{z}, \hat{z}).$$

The 'slope condition' for an invariant capital stock we have found has a natural interpretation in terms of the shadow prices q^t, r^t associated with the constant programme $z^t = \hat{z}$. The condition specifies

$$q^2 = \alpha q^1, q^3 = \alpha q^2, \ldots, \text{so } q^t = (\alpha)^{t-1} q^1, t = 2, 3, \ldots,$$

a geometric decline in marginal utility of the invariant capital stock $z^t = \hat{z}$, in the ratio α per period equal to the discount factor prescribed by the objective function U.

The condition $q^2 = \alpha q^1$ extends to the end points of $\mathcal{S}$ and to points of $\mathcal{L}$ for which an associated optimal activity vector involves slacks. It also generalises to similar models with any number of capital goods, resources and consumption goods. In these cases, q^1, q^2 are to be regarded as vectors of shadow prices (dual variables). Where these vectors are not uniquely determined, the condition $q^2 = \alpha q^1$ requires only that one can find values q^1, q^2 within the permissible joint range of (q^1, q^2) that meet the condition.

IV THE RELATION BETWEEN THE DISCOUNT FACTOR AND AN INVARIANT OPTIMAL CAPITAL STOCK

In the preceding Section III, the element of intertemporal preferences was introduced by a discount factor α applicable to future *utilities.* At the end of the Section it was found that, if an invariant capital stock is indefinitely maintained, that same factor α also applies in the definition of shadow prices of *goods.* The reason is simple. As long as the capital stock, the consumption vector, and the one-period utility function $u(\cdot, \cdot)$ do not change over time, the same holds for the *marginal utilities of the goods* in question. Therefore the discount factor for utilities equals that for goods in this case.

[1] Since not both, hence neither, of φ_1, φ_2 can vanish in $(-z. z)$.

[2] Hansen and Koopmans (1972).

[3] We do not need to reiterate the constraint $s < 0$ because the specification $0 < \alpha < 1$ requires that $s < -1$.

It is of interest to study the relation between the discount factor α and the associated value or values of the invariant capital stock $\hat{z}(\alpha)$. This may be defined as the set of compatible pairs $(\alpha, \hat{z}(\alpha))$. This notion is applicable equally to the perfect market interpretation and to the perfect planning model. Its principal weakness in either case is the disregard of technical change. A second weakness is the circumstance that for a historically given initial capital stock, even without further technical change, continued growth towards an attractive invariant capital stock is likely to be, in most if not all existing economies, the first recommendation of the criterion U on which the concept rests. For most policy problems knowledge of the characteristics of the near-future segment of that path is the most urgent requirement.

However, we have to crawl before we can walk, and walk before we can run. It is hoped that an analysis of the relation between α and $\hat{z}(\alpha)$ may add precision to intuitions and ideas with a long history in economic theory. It may also turn out to be a useful preparation for the more difficult problems associated with a path that chases a capital stock which itself is in a moving equilibrium over time with changing technology, changing resource availability, and changing momentary and intertemporal preferences.

Figure 5:8 illustrates that there can easily be more than one invariant capital stock for a given value of α. The diagram exhibits two distinct points of $\mathscr{S}$, both labelled $\hat{f}(\alpha)$, with identical slopes $-1/\alpha$, and between them a third

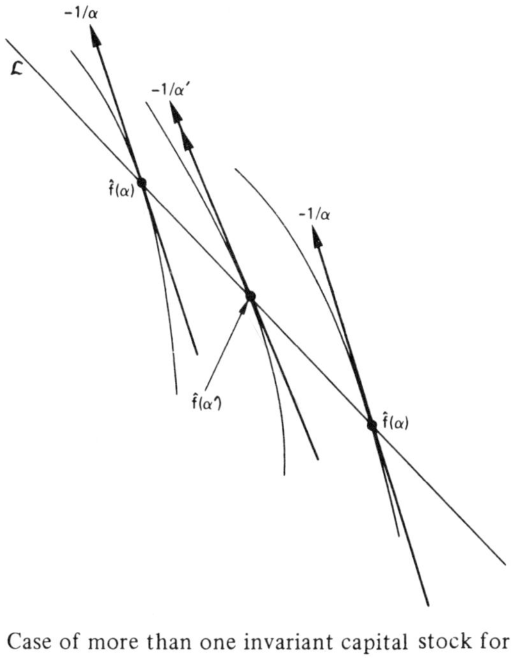

Fig. 5:8 Case of more than one invariant capital stock for a given α

point $\hat{f}(\alpha')$ with a different slope $-1/\alpha'$, where $\alpha' > \alpha$. Such a pattern is entirely compatible with strict concavity of the function $\varphi(-z^1, z^2)$.

Figures 5:9 and 5:10 illustrate that this cannot occur if the two consumption goods are *normal* goods. By this I mean that, for any fixed positive relative prices p_1, p_2, the utility-maximising consumption pair y_1, y_2 attainable within a given budget b at those prices increases strictly in both components as b increases. In that case the absolute value of the slope

$$| s^*(y_1, y_2) | \equiv \frac{u_1(y_1, y_2)}{u_2(y_1, y_2)}$$

of the level curve of u in the point (y_1, y_2) increases if y_2 increases with y_1 held constant and decreases if y_1 increases with y_2 constant. Therefore, if one follows any straight line with negative slope such as $\overline{d_1'd_2'}$ in Figure 5:9, the absolute slope of the level curve increases as y_2 increases (and hence y_1 decreases at the same time). Choosing $\overline{d_1'd_2'}$ in such a way that by the mapping $(y_1, y_2) = (x_1, x_2) \leftrightarrow (-z^1, z^2)$ it transforms into the segment $\mathscr{S}$ in Figure 5:10, we find that $\hat{z}(\alpha)$ increases as α increases. The interpretation is that a higher discount factor (a lower real interest rate) is associated both with a higher equilibrium capital stock per worker and with a proportionately higher consumption of the good '2', which is more capital-intensive in its production than good '1'. In contrast, in Section V we shall consider the counter-intuitive case of decreasing $\hat{z}(\alpha)$, where a higher discount factor is associated with a smaller invariant capital stock and, indeed, a lower utility level in each period.

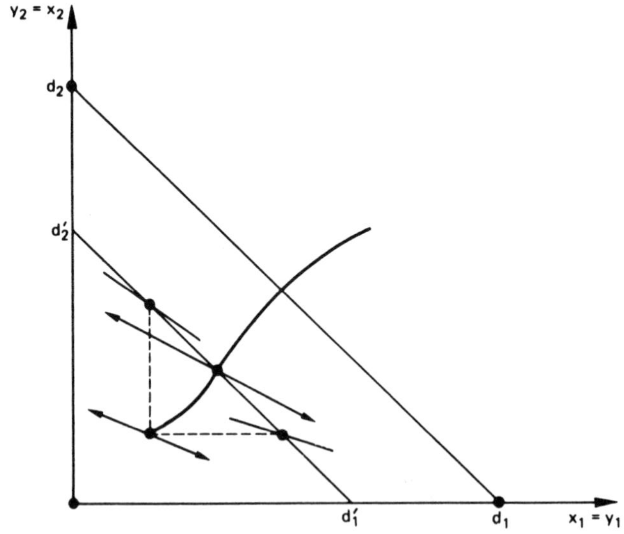

Fig. 5:9 Slopes of level curves of the utility function for normal consumption goods

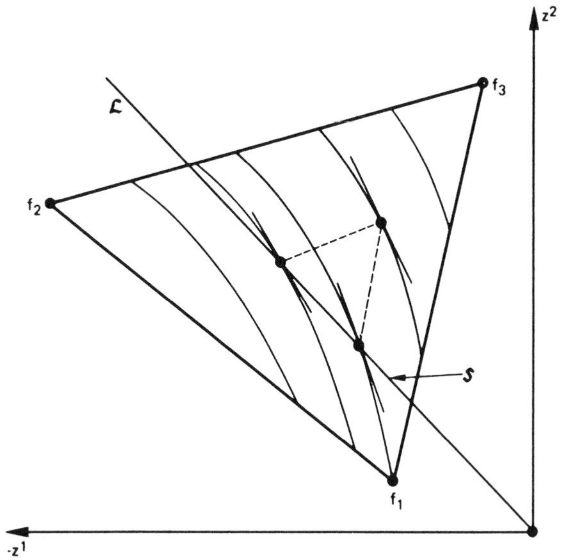

Fig. 5:10 The invariant stock increases with α when both consumption goods are normal

In that case the more capital-intensive good '2' is superior[1] to good '1'.

For the present case of normal consumption goods, we shall describe without full proof the $(\alpha, \hat{z}(\alpha))$ pairs for α and/or z at the end points of their permitted ranges. If, as in Figure 5:11 on p. 165 $s(-z, z)$ reaches its algebraic upper bound -1 in some point $(-\hat{z}(1), \hat{z}(1))$ of $\mathcal{S}$ interior to $\mathcal{Z}$, then

$$\hat{z}(1) \equiv \lim_{\alpha \to 1} \hat{z}(\alpha)$$

is an analogue of the (undiscounted) golden rule capital stock of the one-sector model. Values $z > \hat{z}(1)$ then cannot occur as invariant capital stocks for any permitted value of α. If as in Figure 5:12 the slope $-1/\bar{\alpha}$ of φ at the (boundary) point $(-\bar{z}, \bar{z})$ of $\mathcal{Z}$ with the highest attainable value $\bar{z}$ of z satisfies

$$-\frac{b_3}{a_3} < s(-\bar{z}, \bar{z}) \equiv -\frac{1}{\bar{\alpha}} \leqslant -1,$$

then $\bar{z}$ is an invariant stock for the following set of values of α,

$$\hat{z}(\alpha) = \bar{z} \quad \text{for} \quad \bar{\alpha} \leqslant \alpha \leqslant 1.$$

[1] At least in a neighbourhood of the set of consumption vectors $\hat{y}_1(\alpha), \hat{y}_2(\alpha)$ associated with the pairs $(\alpha, \hat{z}(\alpha))$ in question.

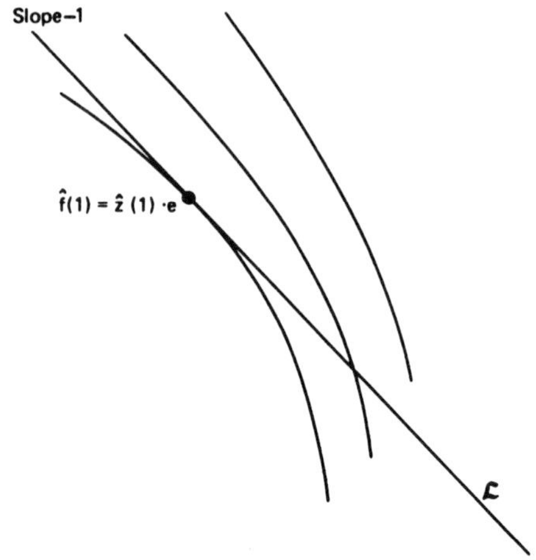

Fig. 5:11 Limiting invariant stock for $\alpha \to 1$

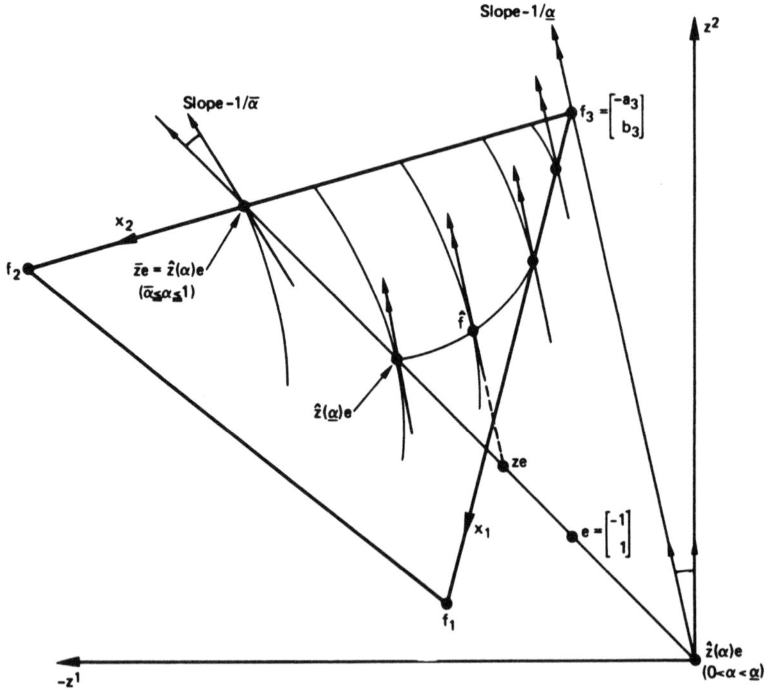

Fig. 5:12 Locus of the invariant capital stock for $1 > \alpha > 0$

Most intriguing is the situation for the lowest value

$$\alpha = \underline{\alpha} \equiv \frac{a_3}{b_3}$$

of α permitting within-period optimality without labour slack in combination with the corresponding invariant stock of $\hat{z}(\alpha)$, if a stock satisfying the 'slope condition' exists for that $\underline{\alpha}$. In Figure 5:12, this $\hat{z}(\underline{\alpha})$ is in the interior of $\mathscr{Z}$. It could also be the lower end point z of $\mathscr{S}$. In either case, the same value $\alpha = \underline{\alpha}$ can also be associated with any stock z in the range

$$0 \leqslant z \leqslant \hat{z}(\underline{\alpha})$$

in the role of an invariant stock for that $\underline{\alpha}$, with unemployment increasing as z decreases.

Figure 5:12 shows for any given such z the determination of the *unemployment* $\epsilon = 1 - x$, say, where $x = x_1 + x_2 + x_3$ is the remaining *employment*, both measured in a total-labour-force unit. It is now preferable to give up the principle underlying Figure 5:4, the representation of (x_1, x_2) and $(-z^1, z^2)$ by a single point referred to two different co-ordinate systems. If we were to insist on maintaining this principle in the presence of unemployment, we would have to use a co-ordinate system of (x_1, x_2) that moves, level curves and all, with the axes remaining parallel to themselves but the origin in the point $(-a_3 x, b_3 x)$ sliding along $\overline{0f_3}$ in step with the employment x. It is simpler to retain the old origin f_3 for the co-ordinate system of (x_1, x_2). Using z as a parameter, and denoting the corresponding employment and activity levels by

$$\hat{x}(z), \hat{x}_1(z), \hat{x}_2(z), \qquad 0 \leqslant z \leqslant \hat{z}(\underline{\alpha}),$$

these quantities are determined with the help of a displaced vector

$$(-\tilde{z}^1, \tilde{z}^2) \equiv (-z, z) + (1 - x)(-a_3, b_3)$$

similar to that used in the tightness test for the labour constraint. For given z and variable x, the point so defined moves from $(-z, z)$ along a straight line of slope $-b_3/a_3 = -1/\underline{\alpha}$. To determine the value $x = \hat{x}(z)$ of x corresponding to the given z one extends this line, if possible, until it is tangent to an (undisplaced) level curve of $\varphi(-z^1, z^2)$. The value of x at the point of tangency $\hat{f} \equiv \hat{f}(z) \equiv (-\tilde{z}^1(z), \tilde{z}^2(z))$, say, is the desired $\hat{x}(z)$. The values of $\hat{x}_1(z), \hat{x}_2(z)$ are read off from the mapping relation

$$(\hat{x}_1(z), \hat{x}_2(z)) \leftrightarrow (-\tilde{z}^1(z), \tilde{z}^2(z)),$$

taken in the reverse direction. If no tangency points exists, $(-\tilde{z}^1(z), \tilde{z}^2(z))$ is a boundary point of $\mathscr{Z}$. Which one it is, is determined by rules similar to those applicable in the end points of $\mathscr{S}$. As to the latter, if in no point of $\mathscr{S}$ interior to $\mathscr{Z}$ there is a tangent to $\varphi(z^1, z^2)$ of slope $-1/\underline{\alpha}$, then the boundary point $(-\underline{z}, \underline{z})$ of $\mathscr{Z}$ on $\mathscr{S}$ nearest to the origin will take the place of $(-\hat{z}(\underline{\alpha}), \hat{z}(\underline{\alpha}))$ in the above description, and will also serve as a no-slack invariant capital stock for all α such that

$$-\frac{1}{\bar{\alpha}} \leqslant -\frac{1}{\alpha} \leqslant s(-z, z).$$

How does the ratio a_3/b_3 come to have such an important role as a critical value $\underline{\alpha}$ of the discount factor in the present problem? The answer lies in a connection between the present model and the von Neumann model obtained from Table 5:1 by discarding all but the first two constraints. Since process '3' has the highest ratio b_j/a_j of capital output to input among the three processes, the requirement of fastest capital growth implicit in the von Neumann model can be met only by shifting all labour from the production of consumption goods to that of capital goods – a feat easier in the so truncated model than in reality. A counterpiece to this observation arises in the present model. If impatience rises, hence the discount factor sinks, below the critical value $\underline{\alpha}$,

$$0 < \alpha < \underline{\alpha} \equiv a_3/b_3,$$

then the only invariant capital stock in existence is the null stock,

$$\hat{z}(\alpha) = 0, \quad \text{with } \hat{x}_j(\alpha) = 0, \quad j = 1, 2, 3.$$

At the precise point $\alpha = \underline{\alpha}$, a whole family of invariant capital stocks z, $0 \leqslant z \leqslant \hat{z}(\alpha)$, and associated employment levels $\hat{x}(z)$ varying continuously from 0 to 1, maintains the connectedness of the set of all points $(\alpha, \hat{z}(\alpha), \hat{x}_j(\alpha), j = 1, 2, 3)$ in 5-dimensional space.

Figure 5:12 illustrates the dependence of $\hat{z}(\alpha)$ on α and shows one particular possible geometrical form for the family of $\hat{x}(\underline{\alpha})$ associated with $\alpha = \underline{\alpha}$. Figure 5:13 exhibits a corresponding curve for the dependence of the $\hat{x}_j(\alpha), j = 1, 2,$

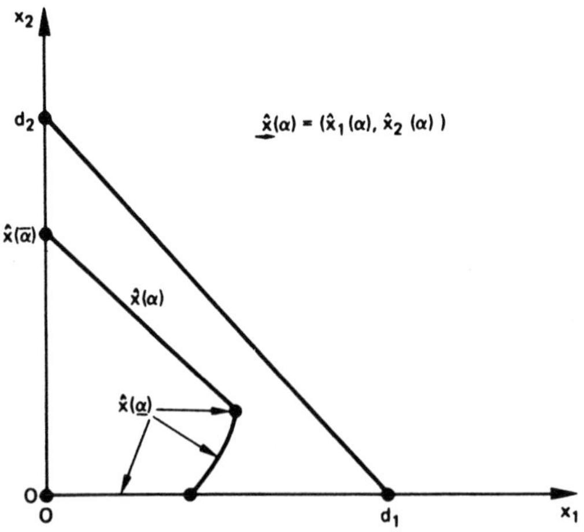

Fig. 5:13 Locus of the associated consumption vector for $1 > \alpha > 0$

on α in the (x_1, x_2)-plane, again with a one-parameter family of points for the value $\alpha = \underset{\sim}{\alpha}$.

V ADDENDUM:[1] *INSTABILITY OF THE INVARIANT CAPITAL STOCK IN THE COUNTER-INTUITIVE CASE*

So far we have only asked for a capital stock *invariant* under optimisation. We now raise the question of *stability* of an invariant capital stock under small perturbations of the initial stock. An invariant optimal capital stock will be called *stable* (under optimisation) if optimal paths starting from initial stocks in some neighbourhood of the invariant stock will converge over time to that invariant stock.

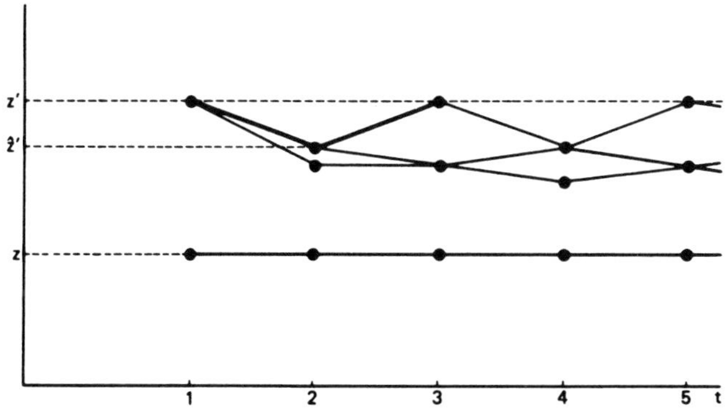

Fig. 5:14 Stability test for invariant capital stock z

Figure 5:14 illustrates a simple heuristic (non-rigorous) test of the stability of an invariant optimal (scalar) capital stock in one important case. It is based on properties of the function

$$W \equiv W(z^1, z^2, z^3; \alpha) \equiv \varphi(-z^1, z^2) + \alpha\varphi(-z^2, z^3)$$

that go beyond those studied above in connection with the test of invariance of an initial stock $z = z^1 = z^3$. Recall that the latter test confirms the invariance of such a z if the maximum of W with respect to z^2 is attained when also $z^2 = z$. Let this be the case.

The heuristic test of stability then applies in the case where, for all z^1 and z^3 in a neighbourhood $(z - \epsilon, z + \epsilon)$ of z, the value $\hat{z}^2$ of z^2 that maximises W is a strictly increasing function both of z^1 and of z^3. While this, let us say, *strong smoothness* condition on W may seem arbitrary, it becomes more natural if we think in terms of a class of functions W which, in the limit for smaller and smaller time units, permits a smooth transition to a continuous time variable.

[1] As indicated at the end of Section I, this Addendum was added after the Conference.

To apply the stability test to the invariant stock z, let $z < z' < z + \epsilon$, and now take $z^1 = z' = z^3$ and write $\hat{z}'$ for the value of z^2 maximising $W(z', z^2, z')$. The strong smoothness condition then requires that $\hat{z}' > z$. The stability test then says that,

$$\left.\begin{array}{l} z \text{ is stable if } z < \hat{z}' < z' \\ \\ z \text{ is unstable if } \quad z' < \hat{z}' \end{array}\right\} \text{ whenever } z < z' < z + \epsilon.$$

To be conclusive the test would also need to be applied symmetrically to all z' with $z - \epsilon < z' < z$.

Figure 5:14 illustrates by heavy lines a case where the stability test is met by a z' with $z < z' < z + \epsilon$. The thin lines give plausibility to the test by suggesting a limiting process converging to the optimal path from an initial stock $z^1 = z'$ by alternately holding the capital stocks constant in odd-numbered and even-numbered points of time while optimising at all other points. The convergence follows from the strong smoothness condition.

So far the discussion has been concerned with the stability of a capital stock $z \equiv \hat{z}(\alpha)$ invariant for a given value of the discount factor α. We shall now show that the sàme test also answers the question whether, for a discount factor α' slightly larger (or smaller) than α, we have the intuitive case where the corresponding invariant stock $z' \equiv \hat{z}(\alpha')$ is also larger (smaller) than z, or the counterintuitive case where $z' < (>)\, z$.

The conditions defining z and z' are

$$W(z^2) \equiv \varphi(-z, z^2) + \alpha\varphi(-z^2, z) \text{ is maximal for } z^2 = z,$$

$$W'(z^2) \equiv \varphi(-z', z^2) + \alpha'\varphi(-z^2, z') \text{ is maximal for } z^2 = z'.$$

Necessary and sufficient conditions for these to hold are, respectively,

$$\varphi_2(-z, z) - \alpha\varphi_1(-z, z) \qquad = 0,$$

$$\varphi_2(-z', z') - \alpha'\varphi_1(-z', z') = 0.$$

The stability test involves a third function of a W-type, viz.,

$$W^{(\prime)} \equiv \varphi(-z', z^2) + \alpha\varphi(-z^2, z'),$$

and, is, on account of the strict concavity of $W^{(\prime)}$, equivalent to

$$z \text{ is } \begin{bmatrix} \text{stable} \\ \text{unstable} \end{bmatrix} \text{ if } \left(\frac{dW^{(\prime)}}{dz^2}\right)_{z^2 = z'} = \varphi_2(-z', z') - \alpha\varphi_1(-z', z') \begin{bmatrix} < \\ > \end{bmatrix} 0$$

for $|z - z'| < \epsilon$. But then, since this expression vanishes if α is replaced by α', and since φ_1 is positive, we find that z is stable if $\alpha < \alpha'$, unstable if $\alpha > \alpha'$. Note that these are precisely the intuitive and the counter-intuitive case, respectively, with regard to the direction of change of the invariant capital stock when the discount factor is changed.

To illustrate the implications of this finding (see Figure 5:15), assume that the counter-intuitive behaviour of $\hat{z}(\alpha)$ applies throughout the interval $\mathcal{S}$ of Figure 5:7. Let as before $\underline{z}, \bar{z}$ denote the capital stocks corresponding to the lower and upper end points of $\mathcal{S}$, and $\bar{\alpha}$, $\underline{\underline{\alpha}}$, respectively, the corresponding discount factors. Then $\underline{z} < \bar{z}$, $\underline{\underline{\alpha}} < \bar{\alpha}$, and $\underline{z} = \hat{z}(\bar{\alpha})$, $\bar{z} = \hat{z}(\underline{\underline{\alpha}})$ are invariant capital stocks for the discount factors shown, provided $\underline{\underline{\alpha}} \geqslant \underline{\alpha} \equiv b_3/a_3$. Now take an α with $\underline{\underline{\alpha}} < \alpha < \bar{\alpha}$, and study the dependence of the optimal path z^t on the prescribed initial value z^1. Then, if by chance $z^1 = \hat{z}(\alpha)$, the path z^t continues on the constant level of the unstable invariant capital stock $\hat{z}(\alpha)$. If $\underline{z} < z^1 < \hat{z}(\alpha)$, by however little, z^t decreases until the level $\underline{z}$ is reached, whereupon the path continues at that level. Likewise, if $\hat{z}(\alpha) < z^1 < \bar{z}$, the path increases until it becomes constant at the level $\bar{z}$. In fact, $\underline{z}$ is a stable invariant stock $\hat{z}(\alpha')$ for all α' such that $\underline{\underline{\alpha}} \leqslant \alpha' < \bar{\alpha}$, and $\bar{z}$ is a stable stock for all α' such that $\underline{\alpha} < \alpha' \leqslant 1$. Hence, under the present assumptions, the end-points $\underline{z}, \bar{z}$ are prototypes of empirically meaningful invariant capital stocks, while $\hat{z}(\alpha)$ is a freak, a knife-edge occurrence. Its only conceivable empirical significance is a signal that for z^1 in a neighbourhood of $\hat{z}(\alpha)$ the many features of reality not expressed in an otherwise acceptable model will influence the outcome of the toss of a coin.

Iwai (1975) has confirmed the heuristic reasoning of this Addendum by a rigorous application of stability analysis that examines the behaviour of

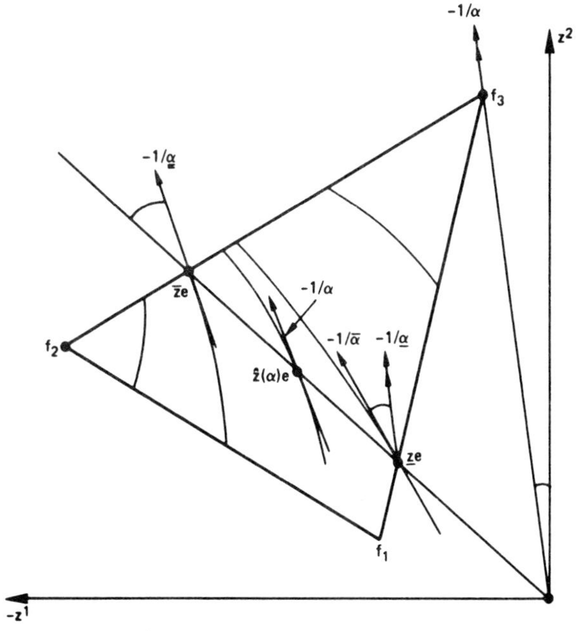

Fig. 5:15 An unstable invariant stock $\hat{z}(\alpha)$

second derivatives of the function $W(z^1, z^2, z^3; \alpha)$ for the z^t in a neighbourhood of an invariant capital stock $\hat{z}(\alpha)$. His analysis also includes the case where strong smoothness of W is not assumed. It can then happen that, for some $z^1, z^3 > \hat{z}(\alpha)$, the value of z^2 maximising W satisfies $z^2 < \hat{z}(\alpha)$. In such a case optimal paths can oscillate between values above and below $\hat{z}(\alpha)$, with stability not governed by the criterion found above.

REFERENCES

T. Hansen and T. C. Koopmans, 'Definition and Computation of a Capital Stock Invariant under Optimization,' *Journal of Economic Theory*, Vol. 5, No 3 (December 1972) pp. 487–523.

H. S. Houthakker, 'The Pareto Distribution and the Cobb-Douglas Production Function in Activity Analysis,' *Review of Economic Studies*, Vol. XXIII, No 1, (1955–56) pp. 27–31.

K. Iwai, Unpublished memorandum (1975).

L. Johansen, *Production Functions* (Amsterdam-London: North Holland Publishing Co., 1972).

T. C. Koopmans, 'Intertemporal Distribution and "Optimal" Aggregate Economic Growth,' Chapter 5 in W. Fellner, *et al.*, *Ten Economic Studies in the Tradition of Irving Fisher* (New York: Wiley, 1967) pp. 95–126.

D. Levhari, 'A Note on Houthakker's Aggregate Production Function in a Multifirm Industry,' *Econometrica*, Vol. 30, No 1 (January 1968) pp. 151–4.

E. Malinvaud, 'Capital Accumulation and the Efficient Allocation of Resources,' *Econometrica*, Vol. 21, No 2 (April 1953) pp. 233–68.

F. Ramsey, 'A Mathematical Theory of Saving,' *Economic Journal*, Vol. 38, No 152 (December 1928) pp. 534–59.

K. Sato, 'Micro and Macro Constant-Elasticity-of-Substitution Production Functions in a Multifirm Industry,' *Journal of Economic Theory* Vol. 1, No 4 (December 1969) pp. 438–53.

12

Economics Among the Sciences

Tjalling C. Koopmans

American Economic Review 69, no. 1 (1979), pp. 1–13

The title of my address implicitly assumes that economics is itself one of the sciences. I believe that to be so, and intend as I go on to indicate more fully in what sense I hold that view. However, my principal aim in choosing my topic is not that of claiming any particular status for economic analysis. Rather, I want to share with you some observations I have made over the last six years as a result of involvement in various interdisciplinary studies, through reading the reports of other such studies, or discussing them with colleagues in various fields of science.

With increasing frequency natural and social scientists are indeed finding themselves thrown together in the study of new problems that are of great practical importance for society, and essentially interdisciplinary in character. Prominent among these are problems of environmental policy, such as the protection of air and water quality. Another class of problems concerns a desirable long-range mix of technologies of energy supply, conversion and use. These two classes of problems overlap, for instance, with respect to the disposal of nuclear wastes, heat rejection to the environment, and—in the case of fossil fuels—the as yet poorly understood global and regional effects of sustained large releases of carbon dioxide into the atmosphere.

Assembled in pursuit of such studies, our interdisciplinary group soon finds that its diverse participants ask different questions; use different concepts; use different terms for the same concept and the same term with different meanings; explicitly or implicitly make different assumptions; and perceive different opportunities for empirical verification—which may lead them to apply different methods to that end. The result can be politely concealed bewilderment, possibly a suppressed surge of "we-and-they" feeling, in the worst case a growing mistrust that only time and sustained interaction can overcome.

I shall try to illustrate the difficulties of such interaction by a few examples from recent studies involving, besides economics, mostly the natural sciences and engineering. Limitations of experience, background, and time have compelled me to omit examples involving a strong participation from the other social sciences. Had my guide, mentor, and dear friend Jacob Marschak lived to give this address, and had he chosen a similar topic, the social sciences would have received an emphasis reflecting their importance to the problems of contemporary society. The writings Marschak left us, and the program and the *Proceedings* of last year's meeting of the American Economic Association, stand together as a monument to his awareness and vision of the actual and potential contributions of the social and behavioral sciences.

To prepare for the task I have set myself, I have requested and obtained interviews with a somewhat casually selected sample of natural scientists and engineers, and with a few colleagues in economics. Their responses have been drawn on in the preparation of this address, without attribution by name. I here express my, and indeed our, indebtedness for the help we have been given. Later on, I will cite some statements verbatim.

Table 1 can serve as a two-dimensional table of contents for my discussion. Three topics of study are listed on the left. On each of the three topics a recent study has

Presidential address delivered at the ninety-first meeting of the American Economic Association, August 30, 1978, Chicago, Illinois. I am indebted to Asger Aaboe, William C. Brainard, Kenneth C. Hoffman, Alan S. Manne, William D. Nordhaus, Paul C. Nordine, Guy H. Orcutt, James Tobin, and Charles A. Walker for information, ideas, and suggestions used in writing this address. All errors are mine.

TABLE 1—ISSUES AND METHODS IN ESTIMATING BENEFITS AND COSTS

	Measures of Value			Estimation From			
Illustrative Decision Problems	*GNP* (a)	Health and Life (b)	Energy (c)	Production Process and other Technical Data (d)	Market Behavior (e)	Discounting (f)	Uncertainty (g)
(1) Helium Conservation	√		√	√		√	√
(2) Technology Mix of Future Energy Supply and Use	√	√		√	√	√	√
(3) Automobile Emission Control					√		

Note: Check marks designate issues or methods discussed or mentioned for each illustrative problem.

been made by or for the National Research Council. I will draw mostly on the first two studies and briefly mention the third.

My principal intent is not that of criticizing these studies or of evaluating their findings. I want merely to identify some of the issues that arise in their formulation, contrast responses to these issues in different professions, and comment on the methods that have been or might have been proposed or applied by the respective collaborating professions. Those issues and methods that I shall have time to refer to are set out along the top of the table. Each check mark in a cell of the table indicates that a reference is made to that issue or method in my discussion of that topic of study.

I. The Case for Helium Conservation

This study is described in the preface to the report of the Helium Study Committee as "a task that had to be undertaken quickly and completed with great speed." Likewise, on the concluding page (40), it is called a "preliminary analysis."

The principal current source of helium is as an optional by-product of the production of natural gas, in which it may occur in concentrations ranging (by volume) from 10 percent on down with increasing costs of separation. Present demand for various industrial and space uses falls below present supply, and a program of storage in the partially depleted Cliffside gas field near Amarillo, Texas, is in operation. The study is motivated by the anticipation of a substantially higher future demand.

The report of the Helium Study Committee lists, on pages 35–36, five steps that can be taken for the purpose of increasing the rate of storage. I paraphrase:

Step i: Stop the current venting of helium which has been separated from natural gas allocated as a feedstock to petro-chemical industries. Store the helium instead.

Step ii: Designate helium currently stored in Cliffside a "national strategic reserve" for possible major technical changes that may greatly expand future demand.

Step iii: Reactivate presently idle separation plants to reduce the release of helium resulting from productive combustion of the host gas, and store the helium instead.

Step iv: Build new helium separation plants on helium-rich gas streams. Store the helium.

Step v: Delay the use of helium-rich gas fields, undeveloped, and already producing.

Ultimate Step: Extract helium from the atmosphere.

The ultimate step is not included in the report of the Committee, but is mentioned in the transcript, page 135, of the Public Forum held as part of the study. It involves a process that by present technology costs a large multiple of the cost of extraction from natural gas containing .3 to .5 percent helium.

Steps i, iii, iv, and the "ultimate step" consist of successive technical process choices. Taken in that order, they correspond to the economist's notion of a long-run supply curve, indicating how the cost of each additional unit of supply is a rising step function of the cumulative supply up to that point—assuming a constant state of the technology of extraction. These steps need to be carried out only according as the expectation of demand growth becomes larger and firmer. Steps ii and v are steps whose timing should depend on additional factors besides the separation cost sequence already mentioned.

The expectation of a much larger demand well into the twenty-first century is documented, in the report and in the Forum, by a fascinating enumeration of anticipated future technologies. Many of these are based on or may utilize superconductivity, so far attained best by cryogenic techniques for which helium is the working fluid. The superconductivity is in turn expected to be applicable to a number of uses, such as power transmission with low energy loss, energy storage, and a number of applications of strong magnetic fields. Among the latter are several "technologies that either do not now exist or are in early stages of development" (pp. 13–18), such as magnetic containment for nuclear fusion reactors. Another possible application is magnetohydrodynamic (*MHD*) power generation that converts some of the energy contained in a high temperature gas stream from either a coal-fired burner or a nuclear fission reactor directly into electricity, instead of routing all the energy through a conventional steam cycle. The *MHD* development is further along in the Soviet Union. There also is a development—furthest along in West Germany and Japan—of magnetically levitated low-noise high-speed trains.

It should be added that research is in progress on the use of aluminum and possibly other materials reaching low resistivity at temperatures of 20–30° K, a range reachable using liquid hydrogen as a coolant. (See L. A. Hall, National Bureau of Standards Report, and E. B. Forsyth et al.)

From the economic point of view, the case for the helium storage program is not convincingly made either in the report or in the Forum. I have not found either cost or benefit estimates for the program. Actually, because of the importance of energy supply processes among the increased uses of helium listed above, the benefits cannot be estimated without comparable cost and fuel availability estimates for alternative energy supply and use technologies which have low or zero helium requirements. In other words, to assess the helium storage program, one also needs a long-run model of the energy sector of the economy that addresses the second decision problem of Table 1. One will, of course, also need to consider other important helium uses that are not directly energy related.

Before turning to problem (2), I draw attention to a few passages in the Helium Report that will provide background for Sections III and IV below, where I shall discuss the choice of measures of value in which to express benefits and costs. The report (p. 23) contains an important piece of information bearing on cost comparisons, to the effect that the energy requirements for extracting helium from the atmosphere are about 1,000 times those for extracting it from natural gas containing .3 to .5 percent of helium. Large as that figure is, I shall describe later the economist's case (Section III) for including in the calculation inputs other than energy, such as that for plant and equipment, and (Section IV) for taking into account that the costs of all kinds in any required future extraction from the atmosphere will not be incurred until much later.

In fact, one statement in the report reads as a rejection of the idea that the time at which capital cost is incurred is at all pertinent. In a description of the possible role of the government in implementing the five steps, the report says: "The burden of the discount rate as a criterion of performance could be eliminated and the present debt to the U.S. Treasury written off" (p. 38). I shall explain in Section IV why I think not many economists will support the proposal to eliminate the criterion of the discount rate. Meanwhile, the statement leads one to infer that the capital cost component is not negligible as a factor in the decision.

II. Technology Mixes of Future Energy Supply and Use

My second illustration is a study that was carried out as an input to the deliberations of the Committee on Nuclear and Alternative Energy Systems (*CONAES*, in short), and of its Synthesis Panel. It is entitled "Energy Modeling for an Uncertain Future." As explained in the preface, it is a "supporting paper" published without having gone through the customary report review procedure of the Academy. While for the other illustrations I have not named authors or committee chairpersons, I should not conceal that I was the chairman of the group, called the Modeling Resource Group (*MRG*), which collectively did the work described in its Report. The group consisted mostly of economists and operations researchers, two somewhat like-minded professions. My comments on interdisciplinary interactions about the ideas and findings of the group will therefore draw on discussions with members of other professions within and outside *CONAES*.

For that purpose it may suffice to give only the briefest description of the questions addressed, the assumptions made, and the methods used. One important question arises from the fact that several competing objectives enter into the choice of a long-run energy technology mix. The net economic effect (economic benefit minus cost) of the development of a given technology mix can be estimated in a crude way, as suggested in Table 1, column (a), by its effect on the Gross National Product (*GNP*). In addition, one will also want to register risks of adverse effects such as mining accidents, air pollution, acid rain, oil spills, possible leakage from nuclear waste disposal, or diversion or proliferation of weapons-grade nuclear materials. For brevity, all such effects will be called "environmental" effects. The place in Table 1 for these impacts is column (b), tersely dubbed "health and life."

The Risk/Impact Panel of *CONAES* decided not to try to estimate money equivalents for such adverse impacts of various magnitudes. Were such estimates possible and available, then one could also define and find a balance between desired benefits and adverse "environmental" impacts that remain after scrubbers, inspectors, Civex and the like have done their jobs. Not having such estimates, the *MRG* turned the question around: Assume that tentatively chosen upper bounds are imposed on the use of technologies that have such impacts. Estimate the loss in *GNP* associated with these bounds. Then that number also places a price tag on the reduction in "environmental" impacts achieved by those bounds. Thus, even if an a priori valuation of the reduction in impacts is not available, then such a valuation is still implicit in any decision actually taken. It may help the decision makers to know these implicit price tags.

I will list only the principal assumptions made for this purpose. Numerical values were assigned to three sets of variables. As principal exogenous, also called "realization," variables we chose:

R1. The growth rate of real *GNP*, out to 2010, in the absence of new environmental bounds on energy technologies.
R2. Capital cost levels of present and potential future energy technologies.
R3. Availabilities of oil, gas, uranium, at various costs of extraction.
R4. Long-run price and income elasticities of demand for end-use energy forms.

The "policy" variables represent the hypothetical bounds already described,

P1. Moratoria on new nuclear construction.
P2. Limits placed on output of coal and shale oil.

Forming a third category, the "blend" variables have traits of both realization and policy variables,

B1. Discount rates applied to future benefits and costs.
B2. Oil import price or quantity ceilings.

The method applied was to compare the already specified projection of a rising future *GNP* in which no bounds have been imposed on the use of energy technologies (the *base case*), with other projections in which such a bound or bounds were imposed. This procedure was carried out for each of three long-run models of the *U.S.* energy sector. The numerical inputs into the three models were the same for almost all realization and blend variables, except for the price and income elasticities of demand, which were specific to each model. Two ideas central to current economic analysis entered into this procedure. One is the use of an optimization algorithm to simulate the behavior of a competitive market economy, in any one year, and through time. The other is the use of long-run elasticities of demand. For demand by end-use consumers, these are to be based on econometric analysis of time-series and/or cross sections of income, prices, and quantities consumed. For industrial demand, a process analysis of alternative industrial energy-using processes may add valuable information.

The principal finding was the proportionally small effect on *GNP* of sizable cuts in energy use below its base case growth path. In interpreting this finding, note that the optimization procedure implies an assumption whereby the economy responds to anticipated changes by minimizing the cost of adaptation. The principal means of adaptation are changes in the type and composition of the capital equipment for the extraction, conversion, transport, and use of energy—at the regular time for replacement or earlier.

Table 2 shows the numerical results. For two models, with price elasticities of –.25 and –.4, respectively, policies entailing percentage cuts in energy use out of the base case that gradually increase to between 10 and 20 percent in the year 2010, were found to cut not more than 2 percent out of the discounted sum of annual real *GNP*, 1975–2010, and a comparably small percentage out of *GNP* for the single year 2010. The instruments of the curtailment of growth in energy use were, in row (1) of the table, the placement of bounds on specific energy supply technologies described above. In row (2), a zero-energy-growth path is simulated by the imposition of a hypothetical "conservation tax" on primary energy flows. The rate of this fictitious tax must increase as the *GNP* continues to grow in spite of the downward pull from the zero-energy-growth path.

Another finding, reported in row (2), was that for the effects of the larger cuts in energy use, the value of the long-run price elasticity of demand for energy becomes crucial. In a sensitivity analysis made with one model, a zero-energy-growth policy from 1975 on, leading to a 60 percent cut in energy use out of the base case in 2010, was found to induce only a 2 percent cut in cumulative discounted *GNP* if that price elasticity is –.5, but a 30 percent cut if it is

TABLE 2—ESTIMATED FEEDBACK FROM CURTAILED GROWTH OF ENERGY USE TO *GNP*, 1975–2010, UNITED STATES

	Reduction out of the Base Case in		
Policies	Energy Use in 2010	Discounted[a] Sum of *GNP* 1975–2010	Price Elasticity of Demand for Energy
(1) Bounds on Specific Technologies	Up to 20%	1 to 2%	−.25 or −.4
(2) Zero Energy Growth through Conservation Tax	60%	1 to 2% up to 30%	−.5 −.25

Source: *MRG* report, Tables III.22 and III.23.
[a]Discount Rate: 6 percent per annum.

−.25. I shall come back later to the estimation of the elasticity parameters found to have been very important.

III. Interdisciplinary Differences in Outlook

We have now assembled enough reference material for us to make a start with our main topic—the way in which differences in outlook between the disciplines affect the conduct and evaluation of joint studies.

The most significant difference between economics and the natural sciences lies in the opportunities for testing and verification of hypotheses. Jacob Marschak used to say that economists carry the combined burdens of meteorologists and engineers. Like the meteorologists, they are expected to predict the future course of important variables in their field of study. Just as engineers design more and more efficient machines, economists are also expected to improve the design of society where it affects good use of resources. But, like the meteorologist, the economist has traditionally been confined to drawing inferences from passive observations, records of data generated by the turbulence of the atmosphere or the fluctuations and trends of economic life. Finally—a very important difference—meteorologists and engineers have all the laws and measurements established by physics and chemistry available to them, fully documented by experimental tests and results.

Traditionally, economists have not searched for similar inputs from experimental or observational research of a psychological or sociological nature. In the 1950's and early 1960's they have engaged in some experimentation of their own on behavior under uncertainty and in bargaining and gaming situations. However, the findings of this work have not been put to use as premises for modeling an entire economy. For that purpose, over a few articulate protests, many economists have been satisfied to postulate simple rules of behavior by consumers and business firms. The terms "introspection" and "casual empiricism" have been used to describe the cognitive sources of these premises. In the version of the currently dominant "neoclassical" school of thought, these premises express optimizing responses of demand and supply to a uniform price system: satisfaction maximizing by consumers, profit maximizing by firms.

These premises have a certain intuitive plausibility about them. Undoubtedly, their widespread adoption has also been aided by the richness of the body of inferences one can draw from them. In fact, the premises form the logical foundation for the paradigm of neoclassical economics: the concept of an equilibrium of prices and quantities that in some way ties together the economic decisions taken by all seemingly independent agents. Conceptually the prices and the quantity responses may describe a stationary state over an extended period of time. More realistically, they may be dated variables and thus also link decisions that vary over successive periods, to sustain a moving intertemporal equilibrium.

Parenthetically, use of the term equilibrium does not imply an assumption that the real economy actually is at any time "in equilibrium." Rather, the notion of equilibrium is a first approximation, a reference point or path, like the cycles of Ptolemy without the epicycles and the eccentricity.

If the market were to extend to all pertinent economic decisions over the entire period considered, the result of an intertemporal equilibrium would be an "efficient" path of the economy in the limited sense that no one can be made better off at any time without someone being made worse off at some time. Where market power interferes with competition, or where important economic decisions are made at government levels, the instinct of the neoclassical economist is to recommend that legislation, regulation, the use of suitable incentives, or direct government decision either restore or mimic the operation of the competitive market.

In the present context, an important trait of the neoclassical model is that it does not postulate one sole primary resource, be it labor, energy or any other, whose scarcity controls that of all other goods, and which thereby becomes a natural unit of value for all other goods. The model of production is such that—not by logical necessity, but as an empirical fact—any primary input to production can be substituted to some extent for any other. If such substitution does not take place within one-and-the-same production process, then it can still come about through suitable changes in the levels of several processes and in the inputs to these. In this view "the energy problem" is not one of just "saving energy," regardless of the cost in other resources. It is rather one of seeing to it that the increasing real cost of domestic energy extraction and supply, and the increased market power of *OPEC*, are—over time—reflected in the real prices of primary energy forms relative to other primary inputs, and thereby in different degrees in the prices of all other goods and services. In the projections described above, the energy prices are calculated so as to be in balance with an efficient path of the technology mix into the future, and thereby to induce the right amount of energy saving. In particular if, as projected by *MRG*, real prices of primary energy rise in this path, then energy use is projected to grow less than proportionally to *GNP*.

The contrary doctrine—that regardless of prices there is a persistent relationship between energy use and *GNP*—has frequently been expressed in the engineering literature. In line with this observation, the *MRG* finding of a possible small impact on *GNP* of incisive bounds on specific energy technologies led to lively correspondence and discussions with members of *CONAES*, and of its Supply/Delivery Panel, an engineering-oriented group. I should add that the *MRG* study was not the first modeling study to cast doubt on the doctrine referred to. By my knowledge the first was a study by Edward Hudson and Dale Jorgenson.

IV. Discounting Future Benefits and Costs

We are now ready for a closer look at the discounting of future benefits and costs. This practice reflects a simple technological fact combined with the paradigm of equilibrium over time. The simple fact is that—short of capital saturation—society can temporarily curtail the production of current consumption goods by transferring some factors of production to the formation of additional suitable capital goods, in such a way as to return a multiple (>1) of the same unit bundle of consumption goods in the future. Efficient intertemporal equilibrium then demands that the present value of the goods returned to consumption be equal to that of the goods not now consumed. The quantity of the future bundle being larger, its *per-unit* present value must be correspondingly lower. In a projection that gives to one unit of the future bundle a future real market price numerically equal to its current price, a discount factor $d < 1$ must be applied to the future market price to obtain the present value, per unit of the future bundle. Given competitive markets for capital, present goods and future goods, and ignoring differences in risk, different investments bearing fruit in the same future year t will tend to give rise to the same discount factor

$$d_t = \left(\frac{1}{1 + r_t}\right)^t$$

where r_t is the annual discount rate applicable to the period from year zero to year t. The usual practice in cost-benefit analyses is to assume also that r_t is independent of t, $r_t = r$, say.

This reasoning simply registers the economic accounting implications of assumed intertemporal efficiency with capital nonsaturation. To many highly educated people, there is something ethically offensive about it.

A difficult practical problem on which economists still differ among themselves is how to read a good estimate for r from capital market and other data. Different tax rates on corporate and individual incomes complicate the problem. Considering this and various market imperfections, the precluded alternative use of funds drawn upon for a public project also enters into the choice of r. I will not venture into these questions here.

Coming back to helium storage, the discounting criterion would lead most economists to recommend that those steps of the storage program be implemented for which the rate of return on the total investment (not that on energy alone) exceeds or equals the discount rate appropriate to the problem. Step i, storing helium currently vented, is likely to meet the test. The problem is to estimate which of the four or six steps would.

Two final remarks, the first added as an afterthought since August 30.

The two issues we have discussed—whether to count only energy costs or all costs, and whether or not to discount future benefits and costs—are logically distinct implications of the notion of intertemporal equilibrium. However, psychologically they are related. If one counts only energy costs, everything is expressible in equivalent Btu's, and to the physicist, steeped in the law of conservation of energy, Btu's are the same everywhere and at all times. To discount future Btu's therefore seems not just strange but outright wrong. So it is. But the economist does not discount quantities of any kind. He discounts only real values, that is, quantities (including energy) multiplied by real prices that reflect the expected balance of cost and preference as of a specified future time and beyond. It is to these prices that the discount factor is applied. I am hoping that this simple distinction may help to reduce misunderstanding between the professions.

Secondly, our reasoning has proceeded blandly as if there were no uncertainty about the outcome of the development of processes expected to be substantial users of helium. If there is considerable uncertainty, economists may want to add an allowance for risk to the discount rate. They may also wish to experiment with models in which judgmental probabilities are attached to these uncertain outcomes. This device may produce insights even if the conclusions depend on admittedly uncertain premises. A study of this kind is included as chapter IV in the *MRG* report.

V. Attaching Values to Health and Life

The question of estimating the value of health and the value of life arises mostly in contexts where either public decisions, or public monitoring of private decisions, can be shaped so as to improve health and prolong life. One example is the investment of public funds to diminish physical risks to traffic by the design of roads, bridges, turnouts, and crossings. Another is regular expenditures for traffic police, building inspectors, and other law enforcers who restrain some people from killing or hurting themselves or others by recklessness or neglect.

A common trait of these decisions is that from good experience records one may be able to estimate the years of lives saved, perhaps also of health and limbs preserved, per dollar spent on efficiently run projects or activities of this kind. Such calculations make it possible to spot discrepancies between different projects in regard to "health and life benefits" bought per dollar spent. The ideal of equilibrium then suggests redistributing expenditures, if needed, in order to maximize total benefits from the given expenditure for protection. Valuations of health or life that have a modicum of public approval could result from such redistribution. Note that these valuations, also called *shadow prices*, are in effect set by the budgetary decision makers, whether they are aware of it or not.

After such redistribution if called for, the calculation of money values of health and life registers what in good practice we consistently spend to save a life. The process recognizes that, disturbing as it is to our sensibilities, society is being compelled by the facts of technology and behavior to set up equivalences between lives of unidentified people and bundles of goods and services implicitly of the same market or shadow value—thus bracketing contemporary lives together with current goods and services in the same category of exchangeables.

The examples given so far concern small to moderate risks affecting small to moderate numbers of people, less than 100 at a time, say. Moreover, the time intervals between the decision to commit funds for the reduction of risks, the actual expenditure of these funds, and the reaping of benefits therefrom are moderate, less than twenty years, say. Finally, the problems are mostly local or national, not international in scope.

The long-run choices between energy technology mixes are different in these respects. By a gradual shift from oil and gas to coal, fossil fuels can remain a principal source of energy for countries with abundant resources of coal, especially the United States, the *USSR*, and China, for a long time to come. Intensive current discussion with regard to this option concerns the possible climatic effects of the increase in the atmospheric concentration of carbon dioxide caused by continued large-scale combustion of fossil fuels or their derivatives, alongside with world-wide deforestation. Among the large-scale effects held possible are an increase in average global temperature, entailing dislocation of agriculture depending on how each region is affected, and an increase in the level of the oceans due to the melting of polar ice not previously floating. The present state of knowledge is not such as to be ready for an assessment of these risks. New hypotheses and observations appear regularly in the pages of *Science* and other journals. So I would describe this problem as involving an unknown risk to a large number of people.

If current estimates of the capital cost of central station solar power are realistic, the principal alternative to fossil fuels for bulk power generation is nuclear power. I am not qualified to even comment on the reactor safety and waste disposal problems. I assume, however, that the developers of these technologies would classify these problems in terms of very small risks to substantial numbers of people. Perhaps this leaves as the principal concern the difficulty of keeping industrial and weapons use of nuclear materials apart. Since on this one we are all groping in the dark, I feel I should describe this aspect of nuclear technology as an unknown risk to a very large number of people.

I cannot see my way through to a calculus of the value of human lives in large numbers, that would help clarify issues of the scope of those just discussed—although estimates of numbers of lives at risk are and will remain important. These are basically problems for judgment, even though the need for making these judgments will weigh hard on the people called upon to make them. But supposing I should be wrong, let me point to one apparent paradox to be faced in any attempt to bring a calculus of the shadow price of human life to bear on problems with a long time span.

Suppose one accepts as an ethical principle that, in balancing risks to human life in the present and in the future, equal numbers of lives should receive equal weight. This would make the present value of the future human life independent of the time at which it is lived. However, we have seen that as long as capital saturation is not attained, the present value of a standard bundle of goods in the future decreases as that future time recedes. Hence the present value of future life relative to that of future goods will be much higher than the value of present life in relation to present goods. It should not be inferred from this that future decision makers are assumed or advised to devote greater resources to safety and health than the present decision makers, although the future ones may well want to do this for reasons of their own. The inference is rather, I submit, that the present values I have described reflect a curious mixture of three ingredients: one intertemporal ethical rule, present preferences between consumption and protection, and an assumption about savings behavior of all generations within the next fifty years, say. Under these assumptions, sets of "present values" formed at successive points in time need not, and generally will not, be consistent with each other.

VI. The Empirical Basis of Quantitative Economics

I now go on to a discussion of the empirical basis for some of the quantitative statements that economics contributes to interdisciplinary studies. I will again illustrate this question with reference to the few studies I have chosen as examples. At the same time I will emphasize the role that the premises underlying the concept of equilibrium play in this process.

The premise of profit maximization implies a subpremise of cost minimization. I regard that subpremise as fitting reality more closely than the entire premise. It underlies the supply side of the *MRG* study of future energy technology mixes I have described.

The premise of maximization of satisfaction by the consumer can be made more plausible and more applicable by a further specification. Applied to energy, it says that successive equal additions to a consumer's annual energy end-use budget are worth less and less to him. Operationally, how much each successive addition is worth to him can be measured, for instance, by that increase in the expenditure for the rest of his consumption that he would have regarded as equivalent to each next addition to his energy consumption.

This specification implies the existence of a household demand function for energy, in which per capita demand for energy decreases as its price increases, and increases as per capita real income increases. The *MRG* extended this concept to the sum of direct and indirect demand for energy, the latter being the energy used as input to the production of all nonenergy goods, including capital goods as well. Another extension distinguishes demand for individual fuels, where the demand for one fuel increases if the price of another competing fuel goes up.

These functions are then estimated from empirical data. In the procedure followed in the model with the estimated long-run price elasticity of −.4 mentioned above, a parametric form of these functions was fitted to cross-section and time-series data for seven *OECD* countries, including the United States, for the period 1955–72. In the model with price elasticity −.25 the estimation procedure was not stated with comparable explicitness. In both models the estimated long-run demand functions, written with price as a function of quantity, were then integrated to estimate the benefit from the consumption of energy in all forms.

By comparison, the empirical basis for the production side is more direct. Each of the various competing energy producing, converting, and using processes is represented by constant ratios of inputs to outputs, reflecting operating experience where available, or based on estimates of such ratios and of future availability dates for processes not yet developed. For instance, process estimates for the years 1985 and 2000 were drawn upon in estimating the elasticity of substitution between electric and nonelectric energy in the second of the two models just discussed. This did constrain but not by itself imply numerical estimates of the elasticities of demand for energy, whether in toto (given as −.25), or for the two components.

This completes my description of the empirical basis for the *MRG* procedures and the premises on which they rest. I want, in passing, to draw attention at this point to the econometric aspects of another study, designed to estimate perceived benefits of air quality improvements from residential property values in areas with different air quality. The study is entitled "The Costs and Benefits of Automobile Emission Controls." It draws on a body of econometric work in which property values are related to various characteristics of the site and the neighborhood, including air quality and other environmental amenities, and the income of the household.

The foregoing examples lead me to some broader remarks on the empirical basis of quantitative economic knowledge in general, not limited to the type of studies we are here mostly concerned with.

In all formal procedures involving statistical testing or estimation, there are explicitly stated but untested hypotheses, often called "maintained" hypotheses by statisticians. In the econometric studies we have here considered, the "premises" already discussed play that role. More in general, any statement resulting from such studies retains the form of an "if ... then ..." statement. The set of "ifs," sometimes called "the model," is crucial to the meaning of the "thens," usually but somewhat inaccurately called the "findings." For instance, in fitting demand relations, the principal maintained hypotheses specify the variables entering into these relations, and possibly other variables with which these variables are in turn linked in other pertinent relations.

The "if ... then ..." statements are similar to those in the formal sciences. They read like logical or mathematical reasoning in the case of economic theory, and like applications of statistical methods in the case of econometric estimation or testing. The heart of substantive economics is what can be learned about the validity of the "ifs" themselves, including the "premises" discussed above. "Thens" contradicted by observation call, as time goes on, for modification of the list of "ifs" used. Absence of such contradiction gradually conveys survivor status to the "ifs" in question. So I do think a certain record of noncontradiction gradually becomes one of tentative confirmation. But the process of confirmation is slow and diffuse.

For some purposes, and at considerable expense, short cuts can be made to diminish the dependence on untested "ifs." I am speaking of systematic experiments such as the so-called negative income tax experiment conducted in New Jersey over the period 1968–72, and followed by similar income maintenance experiments in other areas of the United States. If one wants to know whether income maintenance payments to families near the poverty line have a disincentive effect, or no effect, or even a positive incentive effect on labor supply, one does not need to have a pretested theory as to what, if anything, the family is maximizing. Instead, one can make such payments to a sample of families and compare its behavior with that of an unaided control group. This is what the New Jersey experiment did. In one category of families where the numbers spoke rather clearly—white husband-and-wife whole families—the effect on labor supply was found to be negative, moderate but statistically significant, and with the effect on the husband's labor supply smaller than that on the wife's. In addition, much was learned about the design, conduct, and evaluation of such experiments for use in later studies.

There have not been many such experiments on a scale needed to obtain statistically significant outcomes. Moreover, they have been limited to questions of great and urgent policy importance. Meanwhile, we do need to find ways in which verification of the premises of economics, through cumulative econometric analyses and through experiments that find a sponsor, can be pursued.

I have not found in the literature a persuasive account of how such confirmation of premises can be perceived and documented. How do we keep track of the contradictions and confirmations? How do we keep the score of surviving hypotheses? And what are we doing in those directions? The same questions have been raised before, among others by my predecessors, Wassily Leontief and Robert Aaron Gordon, and good and bad examples of concern and unconcern were referred to by both of them. Meanwhile, unresolved issues, sometimes important ones from the policy point of view, and mostly quantitative ones, drag on and remain unresolved. Do they have to?

With one exception I am aware of, even our best college-level introductory texts of economics do not press these questions. They teach good reasoning, and describe the views of leading minds and schools of thought, present and past, in the field. Texts in econometrics teach with great care how to test assumptions and to estimate parameters, duly emphasizing the crucial role of the models. What is also needed is to teach the tested and confirmed statements.

VII. Aphorisms on Interactions

After all I have said about the need for empirical validation, I owe you a brief report on my own casual-empirical sample study of the difficulties of interaction between scientists, engineers, and economists, as seen by participants in joint studies. Rather than classifying and tabulating the views expressed, I shall let the respondents speak for themselves. The following is a selection (by me) of statements, drawn from my notes, that carried the most punch.

A physical scientist: "Economists are technological radicals. They assume everything can be done."

A geologist: "Economists have been too enthusiastic about deep sea mining. They think there is more than there is, that it is easier to get up than it is, and easier to process than it is."

A development economist: "Scientists think big. Economists are marginalists. Scientists don't think in terms of opportunity cost."

An engineer: "Economics is not dismal but incomplete. The things missed are very important."[1]

A life scientist: "Market imperfection is more widespread than economists care to admit."

An economist: "Where economists see the invisible hand guiding the market place to produce pretty good outcomes, scientists see only chaos."

An engineer: "The economic motive is overrated."

A psychologist: "All the conclusions that are drawn from the assumption of rationality can also be drawn from assumptions of adaptive behavior."

A life scientist: "Economists have great skill in handling data. However, they tend to ask only for data, not for concepts and ideas. Drawing up a model is an interdisciplinary task."

An engineer: "Economists often use smooth production functions even when engineers might be reluctant to do so."

A life scientist: "Many scientists do not understand discounting."

An engineer: "Economics is the Thermodynamics of the Social Sciences. Everything is deduced from a few simple postulates without the necessity for knowing detailed mechanisms."

VIII. Final Remarks

After this instructive intermezzo, allow me a few final words. I will not be able to match the brevity and incisiveness we just savored. However, I do look on the collaboration of the diverse professions involved in the newly discovered joint problems as an important development. To economists it is a new challenge and a new frontier. Among the problems themselves are some of great importance, nationally and internationally. They deserve the best effort and talent that can be brought to bear, within and across the disciplines.

An important talent requiring cultivation is skill in communication between dis-

[1]The reference is to the need to fit environmental protection into economic analysis.

ciplines. We should begin with the defusing of jargon. Perhaps some terms should be explained at first use. To the physicist who has used calculus on problems going back to Isaac Newton, it is unexpected to learn that everything called "marginal" is a first derivative of something. It appears natural to him, however, to learn that an "elasticity" is the dimensionless slope of a curve plotted on double-log paper. There is more trouble lying in wait with "externalities," an institutional concept presupposing private property, or at least an accountability for private or public production or household decisions that is dispersed over individuals and organizations. If we will be more forthcoming with explanations of our cherished terms, our science colleagues may be more inclined to help us out with "entropy," which to me is a more difficult concept than anything economics has to offer.

A more serious problem is that, while our universities are the principal training ground for future scientists of all kinds, they do not seem to be the best place for gaining experience in interdisciplinary interaction. I believe that the root of the difficulty lies in the procedures for academic appointment and promotion. The initiative, the decisive first step, is usually taken in the department of one's own discipline. Young faculty members must prove their worth first to their senior colleagues in the field they are identified with. A joint appointment holds somewhat less promise as a stepping stone to tenure. Even our graduate students are already aware of these factors.

The increasing demand for the contributions of interdisciplinarians may gradually break the barriers down. Progress will be slow unless university faculties and administrations perceive the problem. Once they do, the irrepressible curiosity and venturesomeness of our undergraduates will provide a point at which to start and from which to build up.

REFERENCES

E. B. Forsyth et al., *Underground Power Transmission by Superconducting Cable*, Brookhaven National Laboratory 50325, Mar. 1972, esp. ch. IV.

L. A. Hall, "Survey of Electrical Resistivity Measurements on 16 Pure Metals in the Temperature Range 0 to 273°K," Nat. Bur. of Standards, Tech. Note 365, Feb. 1968, esp. p. 20.

E. A. Hudson and D. W. Jorgenson, "Economic Analysis of Alternative Energy Growth Patterns, 1975–2000," Appendix F, pp. 493–511, in *A Time to Choose*, report by the Energy Policy Project of the Ford Foundation, Cambridge, Mass. 1974.

Helium Study Committee, "Helium: A Public Policy Problem," National Resource Council, 1978.

Modeling Resource Group, "Energy Modeling for an Uncertain Future," report prepared for the Committee on Nuclear and Alternative Energy Systems, National Academy of Sciences, 1978.

Report prepared for the Committee on Public Works, U.S. Senate, "The Costs and Benefits of Automobile Emission Controls," a report by a committee for the National Academies of Sciences, and of Engineering, Sept 1974, serial no. 93-24, ch. IV.

13

Alternative Futures With or Without Constraints on the Energy Technology Mix

Tjalling C. Koopmans

Directions in Energy Policy: A Comprehensive Approach to Energy Resource Decision-Making, ed. B. Kurşunoğlu and A. Perlmutter (Cambridge, Mass.: Ballinger, 1979), pp. 103–113

As moderator of this session I shall make a few introductory remarks. After that, I shall temporarily assume the role of "dissertator."

Energy modeling has taken its stride in the last six or eight years. Its intellectual roots lie in earlier work at the Electricité de France and in more general econometric model building in the Netherlands, in the United States, and thereafter in many other countries. Particular recent flowering of energy-economic modeling has occurred in the United States and at the International Institute for Applied Systems Analysis in Austria. Similar work has also been done in India, Mexico, and several European countries.

The aim of energy modeling is to visualize alternative energy futures in a quantitative way. The information inputs to the models are drawn from various fields of knowledge and of informed speculation. The technological information is drawn from the sciences and engineering. The behavioral information is drawn from economics in regard to consumers' and producers' behavior and, where appropriate, from the other social sciences. Resource availability and cost data are drawn from geology and from mining engineering economics. This is not a complete list, but those are perhaps the principal founts of information and data.

The speculative element is inevitable in any modeling activity that looks forward into an extended future. But the words to avoid are "prediction" or "forecast." What the new modeling profession produces is neither predictions nor forecasts. I prefer to call them *projections*. They are statements of the form: If such and such, then so and so follows. The findings are not limited to stating the "thens." They take the form of a collection of "if . . . then . . . " statements.

Paper presented to the Second International Scientific Forum on an Acceptable World Energy Future, held at the University of Miami, November 27–December 1, 1978.

Note: The numbering of the figures and tables reflects the chapter numbering in the original volume.

The modeler's expertise and responsibility concern the statements so formed. The modelers should also be ready to defend their choices of alternative ifs just looked at by themselves and to explain why, where, and how they obtained them. But the ultimate responsibility for assessing the "ifs" is with the fields of knowledge that are drawn upon in their formulation.

The first paper of this session puts one and the same question to three different models and compares the answers obtained. This question concerns the effects of given constraints that for whatever reason may be imposed on the supply or the use of energy. The principal effect explored is that on the total output of the economy.*

The second paper has a conceptual intent. It looks at various ways in which that question can be formulated and examined.†

The third paper was written independently of the second and conversely.‡ It combines a so-called process model of the energy sector with an econometric model of the rest of the economy, in order to obtain or refine empirically based answers to the same question. All three papers have one important set of assumptions in common; they presuppose the underlying model of a competitive market economy, and they study the impacts of specific hypothetical interventions on the part of the government in such an economy. In other respects and in other assumptions, these three formulations will differ from each other, to give us the benefit of a variety of conceptual and empirical approaches.

This paper is concerned with the impacts of various constraints on energy supply as seen by different models. It is mostly a report on one component of a recent energy modeling study that was undertaken for the Committee for Nuclear and Alternative Energy Systems (CONAES). This in turn is a committee of the National Research Council engaged in a study of long-run energy problems for the two national academies (of sciences and of engineering). As part of the work of its "synthesis panel," a "modeling resource group" (MRG) was set up. Several members of that group, for which I served as chairman, are in the program of the present Forum. I mention Kenneth Hoffman, and William Hogan, Alan Manne, Robert Litan. My remarks here consist mostly of a summary of the work of the group as a whole. If my own opinions enter in, I may be unaware of it.

Figure 7-1 gives a compressed listing of the ifs used whenever possible in all models compared. I will not give the numerical values in all cases. The *ifs* fall into three categories. The first category is called *realization variables.* It consists of assumptions about variables that, in first approximation, are generated by processes independent of the energy policies under consideration. First comes an assumption about the GNP growth rate from 1975 to 2010. While this is assumed to vary somewhat over time, it averages 3.2 percent per annum over

**Energy Modeling for an Uncertain Future* 1978.
†Sweeney 1979.
‡Hudson and Jorgensen 1979.

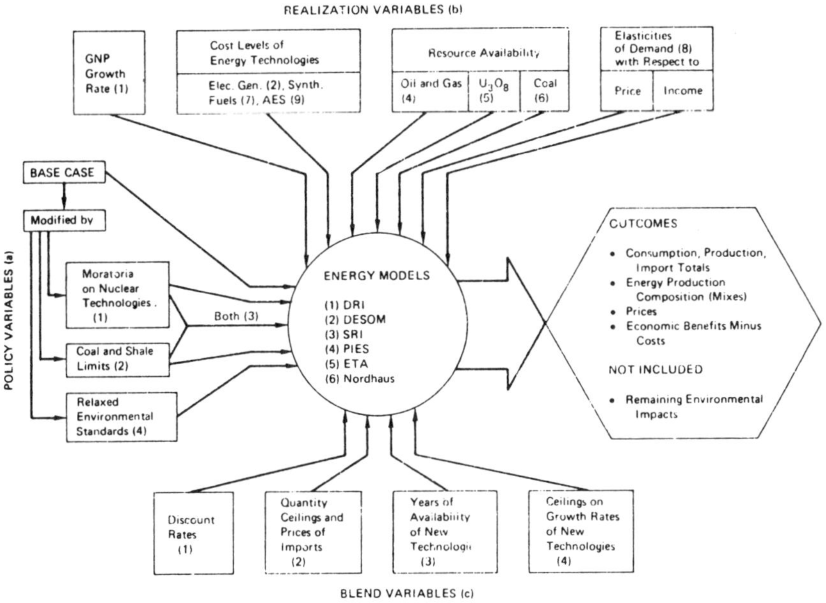

Figure 7-1. Compressed View of Driving Variables, Energy Models, and Their Outcomes.

that period. Second are the cost levels of energy technologies, with particular emphasis on the capital cost of electricity generation. All costs are expressed in real dollars as of 1975: coal-fired stations at \$520 per kilowatt-electric of capacity, light water reactors at \$650; advanced converter reactors at \$715; liquid metal fast breeder reactors at \$810; and solar central station at \$1,730, more than twice the highest cost of the other technologies. The next category of realization variables estimates resource availability with regard to oil, gas, uranium, and coal. An important additional realization variable is the price elasticity of demand for energy. This parameter is defined in absolute value as the percentage decrease in demand divided by the percentage increase in price that calls forth that decrease in demand. It is represented by a negative number. While it can be affected by energy policies, this is not assumed to be the case for the policies here considered.

On the left is a listing of what I shall call *policy variables.* First of all there is the base case. This is defined as an energy policy regime not different from what was in force in 1975. Three variants of this case are considered, which I will spell out later on. The motivation for looking at these cases is to provide estimates of what would happen if alternative policies that might be considered are in fact put in place. It is not claimed, assumed, or denied that any of these policies is desirable. To answer such questions is not a modeler's job. Of the alternatives considered, the first set specifies nuclear moratoria—that is, decisions whereby for certain classes of reactors no new construction will be started after the date from which the moratorium is initiated. The second set, coal and shale limits, is considered in recognition of concerns about the environmental impacts of coal mining, such as mining accidents, acid rain, or increases in the concentration of CO_2 in the atmosphere. The latter, a consequence of increased use of any fossil fuels, is still uncertain in its effects. However, enough worries have been expressed to make it of interest also to consider a possible limitation on this account. The last one is a relaxation of environmental standards.

The third category consists of *blend variables*—that is, variables that have both a realization aspect and a policy aspect. As an example, discount rates reflect both the actual rates of return earned in the capital market and policy decisions as to how to relate the discount rates used for evaluation of benefits and costs to the readings of the market. As a matter of, if you like, innovation in methods, the MRG has used two different discount rates in different parts of its calculations. One rate, the pre-corporation-tax rate estimated at 13 percent, was assumed to apply to actual future business decisions on investment and pricing. The other, a 6 percent posttax discount rate, was assumed to determine the balance of contemporary and future consumption flows that the consumer has open to him when he makes his savings decisions. This rate was used to reduce future benefits and costs to the reference point of 1975 in estimating the net social benefit from alternative energy policies.

Other blend variables included import ceilings and import prices, particularly on petroleum and liquefied natural gas, as well as the assumed year of commercial availability of the various technologies, put at a uniform year 2000 for the nuclear breeder reactor; the advanced converters; and the solar electricity-generating station.

The questions of the effect of the policies listed on the left were then asked of a number of models. To this end the study projected a number of items in our list of outcomes: energy consumption, production, imports, prices. The emphasis in this chapter is on the aggregate net economic effects from technology choices or constraints.

I have already mentioned one further assumption that is not recorded in this diagram—that of a competitive market system, which in modeling technique is simulated by an optimization. This goes back to Adam Smith, who spoke of the invisible hand acting through the price incentives to bring about what we now call an efficient use of resources. This idea is here extended into the future. It is implicitly assumed—I do not know to what extent Adam Smith speculated along these lines—that there is a great deal of correct foresight on the part of decisionmakers. For instance, if an energy R&D policy is announced for the long run, the model assumes that all investors in future technologies correctly estimate the totals that will be invested by the energy industry and fit their own plans into that estimate.

Three of the six models listed in the center of Figure 7-1 were used. All of these were both long-range and optimization models. The first of these was DESOM (evolved at Brookhaven Laboratory from BESOM, originally developed by Kenneth Hoffman; since then, William Marcuse has been in charge of the application and further development of that model). DESOM distinguishes itself from the other models in that it postulates an exogenously given time path of the vector of energy end uses. There is, of course, in reality a dependence of end use on price, but for reasons connected with the original purpose of the model, this assumption was made. The second was ETA (Energy Technology Assessment), modeled by Alan Manne of Stanford University; and the third, a model developed by William Nordhaus, then of Yale University, but at present on the Council of Economic Advisors to the President.

I have also mentioned that the elasticities of demand for energy, particularly the price elasticity of demand, turned out to be quite important to the results (see Table 7-1). For the DESOM model we do not have a numerical price elasticity of demand. Its authors may have estimated one, but for our purposes it is sufficient to note that it is quite small, because the only price response of demand for primary energy that can occur in that model is the application of more capital or of ingenuity in order to save energy by greater efficiency in the various conversions and other steps from primary energy extraction to energy end use. The ETA and Nordhaus estimates (shown in the second and fourth columns in the table) are rather different numerically. That fact, though puzzling in itself, was of quite some help in tracing the effect of the price elasticities. In any case, these elasticities came with the models, and therefore are inherent in all the projections made with these two models, except that Dr. Manne also made available some alternative projections based on a price elasticity indicated in the third column by −0.5. And that, again, was very useful and informative.

Table 7-2 gives a list of policies in more detail. Two separate definitions of moratoria are considered. The first is on all advanced converter reactors and fast breeder reactors (and this is, again, a moratorium only on starting new construction, not in regard to construction already underway). The second policy is a moratorium on all nuclear technologies, including construction of new light

Table 7-1. Estimated Price and Income Elasticities of Demand for Aggregate Energy in Three Models.

	DESOM	*ETA*	*ETA (−0.5)*	*Nordhaus*
Elasticity of demand for aggregate energy with respect to:				
Price	small	−0.25	−0.50	−0.40
Income	0.75	1	1	0.90

For further explanations see Table III.22 of the MRG report.

Table 7-2. Estimated Differences in Net Economic Benefits from Six Technology Mixes, Also Equal to the Net Economic Costs of Five Alternative Policies to Reduce Environmental Impacts[a] (unit: billions of 1975 dollars).

	DESOM (costs only)	*ETA*	*Nordhaus*
Shortfall below base case of benefits minus costs in six policy scenarios			
1. Base case	(0)	0	0
2. Moratorium on all ACRs and the FBR[b]	(43)	8	2
3. Moratorium on all nuclear technologies	(105)	46	136
4. Coal and shale limits	(914)	159	64
5. Moratorium on all ACRs and the FBR and coal and shale limits	(1,012)	181	72
6. Nuclear moratorium and coal and shale limits	(2,325)	358	457

[a]In all policy scenarios, total benefits and costs are the sums of year-by-year benefits and costs, discounted to 1975 at 6 percent per annum. DESOM computes only discounted costs, through 2025; ETA computes discounted benefits and costs through 2050; and Nordhaus through 2060. For each year, benefits estimate the value to the consumer of total amounts of energy consumed, on an incremental basis. For further explanations, see Section III.8 of the MRG report.

[b]For ETA this policy includes a moratorium on the LWR with plutonium recycle; for the other models it does not.

Note: Costs of R&D are excluded.

water reactors. The third policy imposes limits (that increase with time) on the production and processing of coal and oil shale. The last two policies are combinations of the preceding ones. They contain the coal and shale limits together with one or the other of these moratoria.

With regard to the numbers in Table 7-2, the economic benefit is estimated from the consumer's response to the price of energy. This is where the price elasticity of demand for energy comes in. If price is decreased just a little bit, then correspondingly demand, given enough time for the response, will stabilize at a level just a little bit higher. Take that price as per unit valuation of the small slice of demand added. If the price decrease is larger in extent, then a mathematical integration to evaluate an area under the demand curve is needed to estimate the economic benefits from a decrease in price, say, or the economic losses from a policy-induced increase in price. That is the method used in estimating the benefits. The costs were estimated from the cost data that I have already described.

Now let me explain the two titles of the table. The expression "differences in net economic benefits from six technology mixes" assumes that we speak of technologies that are not yet in opeation. For instance, entry 2. in the table estimates what economic benefit can be obtained from availability of the reactors in question. (It is not prejudged whether one or more than one reactor type will actually be used in that case.) Alternatively you can interpret the entries in the table as net economic costs of denying yourself the use of these technologies—the economic cost then being due to a higher energy price and correspondingly less consumption. The same numbers in the table are subject to both interpretations. The DESOM figures are cost figures only because, as explained, DESOM does not have an end use demand response to price. The ETA and Nordhaus figures do reflect such a response. For various reasons explained in the report of the MRG, the ETA and Nordhaus estimates don't agree in the specific numbers too well. However, some patterns stand out in all three columns. One is a certain nonadditivity. In the ETA column the all-nuclear moratorium shows $46 billion as the economic cost figure, whereas the coal and shale limits by themselves show $159 billion as the economic cost. If you impose both sets of constraints, you obtain $358 billion, which is much more than the sum of the other two numbers. This superadditivity has to do with the mathematical fact that the production side is represented, in geometric terms, by a convex body in the output and input space, while the preference side is represented by a concave utility (or preference) function. Similar effects are found in the DESOM and the Nordhaus numbers.

Another important finding for the two models that recognize a response of demand to price again stands out in spite of the differences between corresponding specific entries for these two models. This is the smallness of the effects of the various policies relative to the GNP projection as a whole—even though in absolute terms the impacts are very large sums in dollars of 1975. This is shown in Figure 7-2 where, on the horizontal axis, we set off the ratio of energy use projected for 2010 under the policy in question divided by energy use projected for the base case (primary energy equivalents in both cases). On the vertical axis we set off a similar ratio of projected GNP for 2010 in the case of the policy in question, divided by that in the base case.* Thus the base case itself is represented by the vertex point *B* of the unit square. All but one of the other ETA and Nordhaus points hug the upper side of the unit square to such an extent that the differences between points are hard to see. In order to show the details at all, we give in Figure 7-3(a) a variant of Figure 7-2 in which the unit of the vertical scale is stretched by a factor of 4.

The one exception in Figure 7-2 arises from a policy not included in the list in Table 7-2, but recorded in Section A of Table 7-3. Both the ETA and Nordhaus models were also used for experiments with another fictitious policy, that of placing various upper bounds on the rate of growth of energy use ranging from 0 to 1.5 percent per annum, out to 2010. Such a policy could be implemented, for instance, by means of a conservation tax on primary energy use.

* Or, more precisely, of the discounted sum of GNP projected year to year until 2010 in the case of the policy in question, divided by that same sum in the base year. The underlying calculations are recorded in Table 7-3(b).

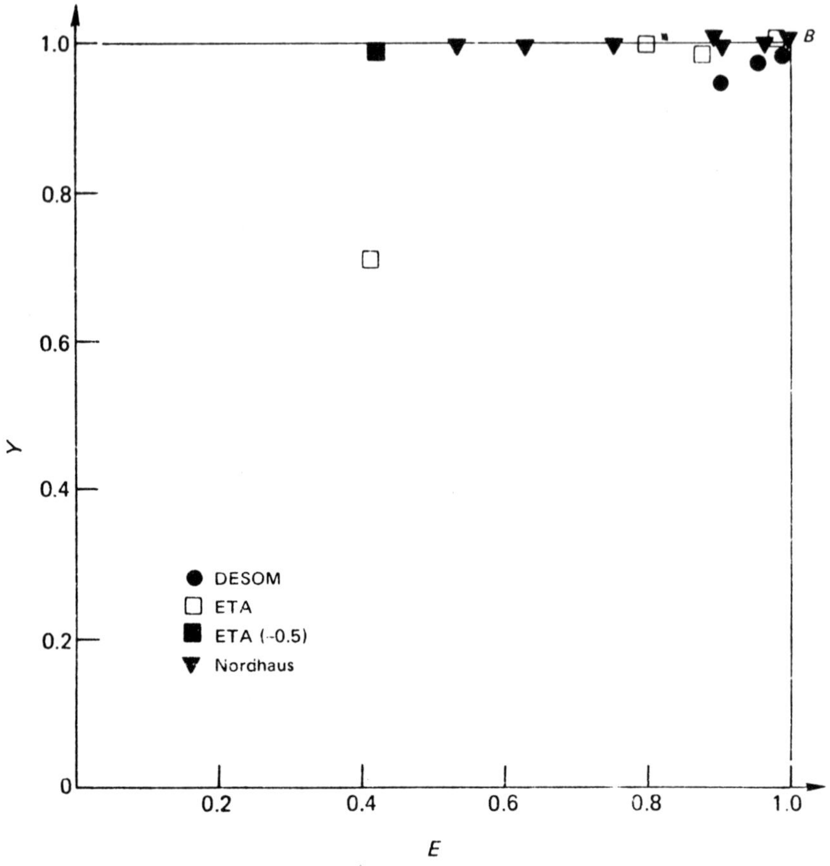

Key:

E on Horizontal Axis: Ratio of aggregate energy consumption in 2010 projected for each policy to that for the base case.

Y on Vertical Axis: Ratio of cumulative discounted GNP, 1975–2010, projected for each policy to that for the base case.

Symbols for Models are shown in the legend. Projections for DESOM extend to 2025, for ETA to 2050, for Nordhaus to 2010. ETA and ETA (-0.5) have price elasticities of -0.25 and -0.5, respectively.

Symbols for Policies: B = Base case for all models; for the lowest energy ETA and ETA (-0.5) points the policy constraints energy use to 70 quads throughout; for all other points see Figure 7-3(a).

Figure 7-2. Estimates of the Long-run Feedback from Aggregate Energy Consumption on Cumulative Discounted Real GNP.

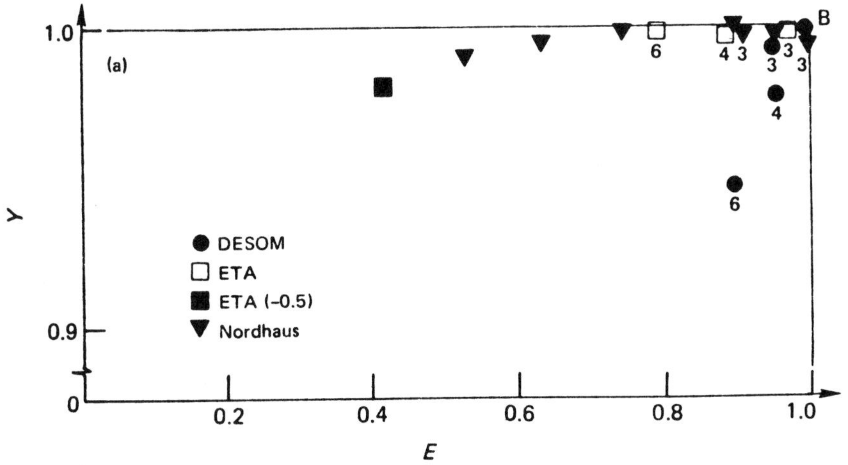

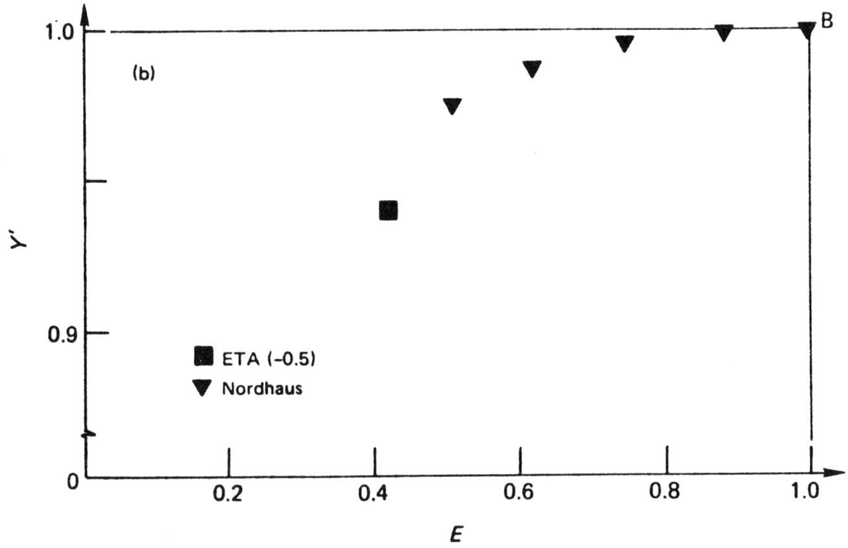

Symbols for Policies: Numbered points in (a) refer to policies 3, 4, and 6 listed in Table 7-2; the string of unnumbered Nordhaus points in both figures represents policies of successive curtailments of the growth rate of energy use, see Table 7-3; the lowest-energy ETA point has run off the scale.

Y' on Vertical Axis of (b): Ratio of undiscounted GNP in 2010 for each policy to that for the base case.

Other symbols as in Figure 7-2.

Figure 7-3. Estimates of the Long-run Feedback from Aggregate Energy Consumption on (a) Cumulative Discounted GNP, 1975-2010, and (b) Undiscounted GNP for 2010.

Table 7-3. Estimates of the Long-run Feedback from Aggregate Energy Consumption on Cumulative Discounted Real GNP.

Scenarios (policies)	Implied Conservation Tax in 2010	Nordhaus A (35.0) B (50.0)		ETA (49.4) Price Elasticity = −0.25		ETA (49.4) Price Elasticity = −0.50		DESOM (43.0)	
		$\overline{E}^a$	$\overline{Y}^a$	$\overline{E}^a$	$\overline{Y}^a$	$\overline{E}^a$	$\overline{Y}^a$	$\overline{E}^a$	$\overline{Y}^a$
A. Upper limits on growth rate of energy consumption, percent per annum	\$ (75)/ 10^6 Btu								
None	0	1.000	1.000	1.000	1.000	1.000	1.000	--	--
1.5	0.34	0.893	0.999	--	--	--	--	--	--
1.0	1.02	0.751	0.997	--	--	--	--	--	--
0.5	1.98	0.631	0.995	--	--	--	--	--	--
0.0	3.19	0.531	0.991	--	--	--	--	--	--
Upper bound of 70 Quads	b	--	--	0.419	0.711	0.419	0.982	--	--
B. MRG scenario (see Table 7-2)									
1. Base case	--	1.000	1.000	1.000	1.000	--	--	1.000	1.000
3. Nuclear moratorium	--	0.968	0.997	0.980	0.999	--	--	0.984	0.998
4. Coal and shale limits	--	1.000	0.999	0.894	0.997	--	--	0.952	0.979
6. Nuclear moratorium and coal and shale limits	--	0.901	0.991	0.795	0.993	--	--	0.900	0.946

[a] $\overline{E}$ = ratio of aggregate energy consumption in 2010 in the indicated scenario to that of the base case;
$\overline{Y}$ = ratio of cumulative discounted GNP in the indicated scenario to that of the base case.

[b] Price elasticity, −0.50 only, tax of electricity, 126 mills/kWh; oil and gas, 8.9 \$/10^6 Btu.

Note: Number in parentheses after name of model indicates total discounted GNP, in trillions of 1975 dollars, calculated over the horizon of the model.

Points representing the outcomes of these calculations were also plotted in Figures 7-2 and 7-3. In particular, Figure 7-2 shows for the ETA model two different estimates for the zero energy growth policy, with the price elasticities of demand of −0.25 and −0.50, respectively. The absolutely lower elasticity figure of −0.25 leads to a curtailment of GNP (out of the base case) larger by almost three-fifths than the figure −0.50 does–so much larger that in Figure 7-3 the corresponding point has run off the scale. Another indication of the effect of an (absolutely) small estimate of the price elasticity of demand is given by the DESOM points in Figure 7-3(a). These points already turn away from the base case GNP level for much smaller curtailments of energy use.

All these indications emphasize the importance of as accurate econometric estimates of the price elasticity of demand for energy as can be made.

References

Energy Modeling for an Uncertain Future. Report of the Modeling Resource Group of the Committee on Nuclear and Alternative Energy Systems of The National Research Council. Washington, D.C.: National Academy of Sciences, 1978.

Hudson, Edward A., and Dale W. Jorgensen. "The Economic Impact of Policies to Reduce U.S. Energy Growth." In B. Kurşunoğlu and A. Perlmutter, eds., *Directions in Energy Policy*. Cambridge, Mass.: Ballinger, 1979.

Sweeney, James L. "Energy and Economic Growth: A Conceptual Framework." In B. Kurşunoğlu and A. Perlmutter, eds., *Directions in Energy Policy*. Cambridge, Mass.: Ballinger, 1979.

14

The Transition from Exhaustible to Renewable or Inexhaustible Resources

Tjalling C. Koopmans

Economic Growth and Resources, volume 3: Natural Resources (Proceedings of the Fifth World Congress of the International Economic Association held inTokyo, Japan), ed. C. Bliss and M. Boserup (London: Macmillan, 1980), pp. 3–11

I. INTRODUCTION

Allow me to begin with some simple and rather obvious remarks on the nature of the transition problem from exhaustible to renewable or inexhaustible resource use. First, a shift in resource use means also a shift in technology, because in this age resources go together with technologies that process them and put them to use. Secondly, while I have used the word 'exhaustible', the term 'depletion' is a more suitable word, in that it suggests a more gradual process. The later stages of depletion will then whenever possible call forth a substitute resource that allows society to meet the same or a similar need to that met by the resource being depleted. Finally, I will follow the model of price as a regulator that will touch off the substitution, smoothly if the degree and rate of depletion are foreseen sufficiently in advance.

This means that the transition problem is one of phasing out the technology associated with the resource being depleted and phasing in one or more technologies associated with possible substitutes. This process requires research and development for the new technology, if not already known, and a turn-over of the capital stock and retraining of the labour force as needed. Therefore the transition problem is a long-run problem, involving, I would say, something of the nature of 50 to 100 years. Examples of this substitution process abound in the field of energy; the paper by Sassin and Häfele (1980) contains several of these.

Another important characteristic of the transition problem is its interdisciplinary nature. It involves technology and engineering; it involves geology whenever resource availability estimates are important; it involves ecology and environmental science to assess and estimate adverse impacts on the environment; and it involves economics to face up to the problem of best use of resources, whether in a market or a planning context or in a mixture of the two regimes. Also, where uncertainty about resource availabilities or future technologies is important, decision theory under uncertainty has an important role. Last but not least, the problem of transition involves ethical considerations in regard to the balancing of the interests of present and future generations. Thus the problem is by its very nature interdisciplinary in character.

Moreover, with regard to the implementation of possible solutions, the problem has international as well as national aspects. As regards the possible effect of fossil fuel combustion on CO_2 in the atmosphere, which may in turn affect climates and crops in various regions – that is undoubtedly a world problem; as regards the transition from coal to nuclear energy (or conversely), that is in part national, in part international.

I tend to regard the communication difficulties arising from the interdisciplinary character of the problem as deserving as much attention as the international aspects. Between the disciplines involved, there is need for more exchange of information, translation of jargon, and debate, interdisciplinary as well as intradisciplinary, to remove the misunderstandings in one profession about the other's terminology and its choices of problems. This difficulty is not one-way, but mutual and universal.

As a modest preparation for these interactions and debates, I will describe and comment on three approaches to the transition problem that are professionally somewhat different, and cite some examples of each without intending this to be regarded as a survey. My examples are illustrations, rarely statements of results, but where they are the latter they are results reached by others.

II. THREE APPROACHES TO THE TRANSITION PROBLEM

What was to have been my *first example*, Hotelling's seminal article on the theory of depletion of resources through competitive markets, under monopoly, and in optimal planning, has already been fully covered elsewhere.

My *second example* is a landmark paper by Dasgupta and Heal, 'The Optimal Depletion of Exhaustible Resources'. I want to comment on some parts of that paper to add substance to the foregoing general observations. The paper has two sections. In each section an optimal allocation problem is considered. In the first one, there is just one resource which is gradually being depleted, and the optimality criterion (or 'objective function') is an integral of the utility of the flow of consumption of that resource over time, discounted with a fixed discount rate δ,

$$U = \int_0^\infty e^{-\delta t}\, U(C)dt, \quad \text{where } \delta > 0. \tag{1}$$

The consumption flow is

$$C_t = F(K_t, R_t) - \dot{K}_t; \tag{2}$$

that is, the output flow of the single finished good minus the flow allocated to capital formation, as in the Ramsey model. Next, the production function $F(K, R)$ is a function of the capital stock and of the resource flow, i.e., the rate of resource depletion. Finally, the latter flow integrated over time cannot exceed the total available, S,

$$\int_0^\infty R_t \, dt \leqq S, \quad \text{where } S > 0. \tag{3}$$

The problem thus is to maximise (1) subject to (2), (3), and given an initial capital stock K_0.

The first section of the paper describes the solution of this problem in rich detail. The second section constitutes, I presume, in the authors' intent the main purpose of the paper. It considers a case where an economy starts out in the circumstances of the first section, but in addition to that it may have the good luck of discovering and developing a substitute technology, to become available at some future date which is as yet uncertain. To my knowledge the second section contains the first theoretical model of this kind that expresses the idea of an uncertain ultimate transition to a durable solution. It assumes that at some moment in the future a constant resource flow becomes available. As an example, imagine that the solar flux can suddenly be tapped cheaply and on a large scale – the moment at which this happens being subject to a probability distribution.

I want to make two comments on the two parts of the paper. First, there is an interesting connection between the solution of the first problem and that of the second problem. To state that connection requires a long sentence: *If* the new technology in the second problem is so superior that, at the moment of its appearance it destroys the value of both the then existing capital stock and the then remaining resource stock, *then* the segment of the optimal path of the second problem, up to the appearance of the new technology, coincides with the corresponding segment in a suitably modified version of the first problem. The modification requires that the discount rate in the first problem vary over time in a particular way that depends on the probability distribution of the time of appearance of the new technology in the second problem. This is a case of a valid modification of a discount rate to allow for uncertainties – something that is often done with much less motivation.

My second remark concerns the first problem taken by itself. The tail-end of the optimal path in that problem should not be taken, I submit, too seriously. In the case of a Cobb–Douglas production function, as T goes to infinity the optimal path has consumption going to zero, the capital stock going to zero, the resource flow going to zero. All of that is to be expected. However, the ratio of the capital stock to the resource flow goes to infinity. I want to make two comments on that. *First*, as all these variables go to zero, one puts a great deal of strain on the assumption of constant returns to scale if one uses that same Cobb–Douglas function deeply into that corner. *Secondly*, even if one were to be adamant about that and say 'I believe that constant returns to scale holds at all scales', then one still has the difficulty that the ratio of capital to resource use goes to infinity. This places that ratio in an area in which we could not possibly have observations from which the validity of that Cobb–Douglas function in that area could have been tested econometrically. The authors point out that the difficulty I have referred to is even worse with the so-called CES (constant elasticity of substitution) function. For this type of production function, an inessential resource (i.e. a resource whose absence still allows positive production to take place) has, as T tends to infinity, a shadow price relative to capital that also becomes infinite. On the other hand an essential resource (one without which you cannot produce) has a shadow price that remains finite. As the authors point out, this is hard to accept as a trait of the real world.

I have mentioned both of these puzzles as examples of a difficulty that recurs in many modelling studies: on the basis of econometric practice one uses a constant elasticity of substitution, or a constant price elasticity of demand, or any other parameter of a behaviour relationship. Then somehow the optimising model carries you out of the area where the observations are found. I want to press a certain warning for the interpretation of these cases. They give theoretical insight, as long as they are not mistaken as being empirically validated by the econometric estimation of a function of that particular parametric form. Fortunately, in the case in hand, and due to the introduction of the second problem, the authors end up with the questionable tail-end of the optimal path in the first problem being amputated by the occurrence of the new technology.

My *third example* has to do with the young field of energy modelling. As far as participating professions are concerned, that field is still very much a concern of economists, but with equal participation by mathematical programmers, operations researchers and engineers. The professional basis widens as we proceed to this example. In particular, production possibilities are now best represented by the use of the process model and the techniques of mathematical programming. The empirical basis is the representation of production processes by fixed ratios of inputs to outputs for each process. That model is, I would say, squarely in the area of economic theory and of econometrics, but it has not penetrated as much as for instance the input–output model of Professor Leontief – which is that special case of the process model in which any one good can be produced only on its own, and that by only one process. In contrast, the energy sector has access to many alternative processes by which a given good or service can be produced, alone, or with one or more by-products. To generate electricity you can burn coal, burn oil, or have a nuclear plant, and it is hoped in due course you will be able to catch the solar flux – there are several alternatives. To my belief, a model consisting of a set of alternative processes is a more appropriate way of expressing production possibilities for the transition problem than either the input–output model or the smooth production function of longer standing in the economic textbooks and in the teaching of Econ 100. In this connection I would like to relate a conversation I had with a friend of mine who is working in this field. I expressed to him some puzzlement over the fact that I find it much easier to communicate with engineers about the process model of production than with economists. He said ‘That is simple: engineers have never heard of a production function’.

The basic idea is that you have the individual processes represented. Any production function should be constructable from these processes if there is a need to. The programming model allows several resources and technologies to compete side by side. The optimisation suggests the best technology mix and its change over time. In a planning context, the planners would be customers for that type of analysis. In a market context, to the extent that the market process approximates a situation that in economic theory we label as perfect foresight and perfect competition, the model would simulate the market outcomes.

III. THREE MODELS OF THE UNITED STATES ENERGY SECTOR

I will refer to three long-term models of the US energy sector that apply optimisation in this role of a simulation device. One is essentially a supply model, developed in stages at Brookhaven National Laboratory by Kenneth Hoffman, William Marcuse and their associates. Now called 'DESOM', it treats final demand for energy services as an exogenously given vector path, and solves for the vector path of primary extraction, conversion and utilisation of energy by minimisation of the sum of discounted costs over time.

Two other models, 'ETA' by Alan Manne and what I will call 'Nordhaus' by William Nordhaus, while also treating the supply side by a process model, represent consumers' demand by utility maximisation. Here the utility function is derived by integration from an estimated demand function.[1] The optimisation then maximises the discounted sum of future utilities derived from consumption of energy services minus the cost of supplying them.

I will give one example of the application of these procedures to a much debated problem in which different professions have had quite different expectations about the answer. This is the question of the feedback from constraints on the growth of energy use to the growth of GNP over a particular future period in the United States. Since I cannot take time to describe the models more fully, it is more the nature of the problem that I want to place before you rather than to claim that the information supplied here is sufficient to present the conclusion as fully established – although I, myself, think it is a significant finding.

Table 1.1 summarises two sets of projections, in which the role of cause (shown in square brackets) and of effect (no brackets) is interchanged between the principal variables. Rows (0) and (1) report on 'base case' projections in which the growth rate of GNP is assumed to be a driving variable (exogenous), that of energy use a dependent variable. The principal finding is that if GNP grows at an average of 3.2 per cent p.a. over the period 1975–2010, then, depending on the model used, the energy use would grow somewhere between 1.7 and 2.9 per cent. Here capital and operating cost and resource availability parameters are the same for the various models, but inter model differences in price and income elasticities of demand could not be removed.

[1]An econometric basis of these estimates is provided in one case (WN) and claimed in another (AM).

TABLE 1.1 FEEDBACK FROM CURTAILED GROWTH OF ENERGY USE TO GNP, 1975–2010, US

	(0)	(1)	(2)
(0)	[Driving][a] and effect variables	[GNP $\equiv G_t$]	Energy use $\equiv E_t$
(1)	Growth rates in base case	[3.2% p.a.]	1.7 to 2.9% p.a.
(2)	Gauge of effect and [policy] variable	$G \equiv \sum_{t=0}^{35} \frac{G_{1975+t}}{1.06^t}$	[E_{2010}]
(3)	Curtailment fraction [specific policies]	1 to 2%	[up to 20%]
(4)	Curtailment fraction [zero-energy-growth through conservation tax]	1 to 2% if[b] $\eta = -0.5$ up to 30% if $\eta = -0.25$	[about 50%]

[a]In each set of projections causal or 'driving' variables and their values are marked by square brackets. Effect variables are without marking.
[b]η = constant price elasticity of demand for energy.

SOURCE *Energy Modeling for an Uncertain Future*: Report of the 'Modeling Resource Group' of the Committee on Nuclear and Alternative Energy Systems, Tables III.0, III.22, Charts III.11, III.12, National Academy of Sciences, 1978.

Rows (2), (3) and (4) summarise a policy analysis in which policies constraining energy use are assumed to be imposed. In Row (3), various policies curtailing the growth rate of specific forms of energy supply are assumed to be imposed for reasons of environmental protection (coal, shale oil), or from a concern with the risks of various nuclear technologies. The cause of the departure from the base case now lies in the constraint on energy use over a 35-year period (represented in the table only by the percentage curtailment of the use figure for the year 2010). Note that now the percentage figure does not stand for per cent per annum, but for the fraction of curtailment out of the base case, in column (2) of the energy use in 2010 (representing the cause), in column (1) of the sum of discounted GNP over the 35-year period (a gauge for measuring the effect).

I want to emphasise the implicit assumptions that (a) the way in which the constraining policies are imposed is gradual as well as foreseeable, and that (b) there is a reasonably full employment policy consistently and successfully applied. Therefore we do not in this discussion deal with such matters as the effect of a sudden OPEC type embargo and the shooting up of the price of oil that might be connected with that. If such events occur, they are not covered or foreseen by this analysis. Then the up-to-20 per cent curtailment of energy use imposed by these particular policies or combinations thereof still affects aggregated discounted GNP by a moderate 1 or 2 per cent. The basic reason for this outcome is that in time the technology mix can be shifted. If coal is curtailed because of the environmental effect of the dust and the sulphur it releases or because of the risk or damage from the mining, then, the constraint being foreseen and carried out gradually, nuclear fission can be called into a higher growth rate, and in that way the effect on GNP growth can be diminished. Actually, the feedback effect is due to the fact that the constraint of one technology (that is deemed harmful) to a value below the *strictly economic* 'optimum' will be not quite compensated by the gain from shifting to another technology (that is deemed less objectionable), just because you are moving away from the economic 'optimum', for non-economic reasons.

In Row (4) a much more drastic curtailment is imposed on *all* energy use, merely for analytical purposes, and in no way implying that sensible policies might lead to such a measure. This is the imposition of a low or a zero energy use growth rate brought about by an imagined conservation tax on all primary energy, where the tax rate grows fast enough to hold the energy use down to a low or zero growth rate – still making the same assumption about gradualness of the imposition. Then two new things happen – the effect turns out to be more than proportional to the curtailment, and also depends strongly on the price-elasticity of demand for energy. If that price elasticity (the parameter η) is one-half in absolute value then even the no-growth energy use policy still leaves GNP under these assumptions affected by not more than 1 or 2 per cent. But if the price elasticity of demand is only one-fourth, then, in the ETA model in which this assumption is used, the GNP is curtailed very remarkably by up to 30 per cent. So we also have a non-linearity here in the dependence of the effect of a severe policy on the price elasticity of demand for energy – assuming that elasticity to be a constant all along the demand curve.

Here is another case where our econometric practice leads us to work with a constant parameter, because we have not yet refined econometric methods to face up to a situation away from what the available data represent. However, on reflection, the price elasticity of demand cannot be a constant in the whole space. In fact, there is a theorem that has been in the folklore for some time, and of which the best proof known to me was given by Professor Hirofumi Uzawa in 1974 while at IIASA. I do not know whether he has published it, but I have a copy of his notes. Again, the theorem requires a long sentence. It says that if you consider the demand for a number of commodities as a vector function of the prices of all these commodities, and if for all prices the budget constraint is satisfied – total consumers' income is spent – and finally if you assume that all the cross- and own-price elasticities are constant, even only in a small neighbourhood of a point in the price space, then the only possible constant values of these elasticities are –1 for all own-price elasticities, and zero for all cross-elasticities. Any other set of values cannot stay constant. This theorem is rather upsetting for our econometric practice, but perhaps it does help us in further exploration of a situation in which a constant price elasticity is found to have so large an effect.

The findings summarised in Table 1.1 are the work of a modelling group that forms one of many parts of a joint study committee of the two US National Academies, of Sciences and of Engineering, that is still continuing its work. I have been involved in the work of the modelling group as its chairman, but the work that has been drawn on in Table 1.1, while leaning mostly on DESOM, ETA and Nordhaus, cannot be attributed in detail because the specific findings have been combined in the aggregation and compression into one brief table.

IV. A FOURTH SUBSTITUTABILITY MODEL

My *fourth* and last *example* contemplates a still longer time horizon. It describes a contribution from the physical sciences, by Harold E. Goeller and Alvin M. Weinberg in an article entitled *The Age of Substitutability*. The approach is still more explicitly empirical than that in the previous models I have just discussed. This is not my field. I am impressed by the work the authors have done but I cannot claim that I can evaluate it. They have gone through the entire periodic system examining all the elements plus some important compounds, to determine the flow of their extraction in 1968, and estimate for each the total resources potentially available according to a rather generous definition of potential sources – the atmosphere, the ocean and a mile-thick crust of the earth. That may be a little more justified if one takes a very long-run view, but I would have liked to see a discussion also of costs of extraction and processing, and of how these costs would evolve in the race between depletion and technical advances. In any case, the ratio of total resources to demand in that year is expressed in years to go until exhaustion at the constant 1968 rate of extraction – a simple signal of relative abundance or scarcity. In that list the most serious case, to worry about in the very long run, appears to be phosphate – 1300 years supply at the 1968 rate of use. Next come coal, oil and gas, taken together in the symbol CH_x, where x is zero for coal and positive for oil and gas. Because of the coal component this aggregate would still have 2500 years at constant use. Then manganese (13,000 years) and everything else comes out at more than a million years.

Through the entire list and in the cases where there is a clear indication of a finite life time, the authors trace the important uses and possible substitutes in these uses. Their proposal is akin to building up, for the entire list of resources, the type of process model that I have spoken of previously.

On the basis of their scrutiny of these geological and technological data, Goeller and Weinberg pronounce the principle of infinite substitutability: with the exception of phosphorus and some trace elements for agriculture, mainly cobalt, copper and zinc, and finally the CH_x (coal, oil and gas), society can exist on near-inexhaustible resources for an indefinite period. This extends into the future the thesis of Barnet and Morse that in the past a new substitute for a dwindling resource was always found. They do not say much more about the case of phosphorus except that at some point that element may have to be recycled, and emphasise its essentiality to sustaining life. Similarly with the trace elements, but on the hydrocarbons they have a very interesting observation. It is related to the doctrine of energy as the crucial resource, with which Weinberg has been strongly associated. The remark is that carbon and hydrogen are abundant, that both are tied to oxygen in nature, that it takes energy to detach the oxygen, and that there are a number of technical processes that do just that, putting in energy and obtaining the various hydrocarbons needed by industry or transport. For this to work, of course, the energy source has to be non-fossil and abundant. Among the various possibilities are solar, geothermal, the nuclear breeder reactor, and nuclear fusion. Each of those has difficulties associated with it. Solar on a central power station basis is expensive by present projections. Geothermal is still very much untried except in special situations. Perhaps the principal problem with the various nuclear breeder reactors is the difficulty that the by-products can, if so desired, be processed and diverted to become nuclear weapons-grade materials. And I understand that the technical feasibility and commercial viability of nuclear fusion reactors is still an open question. At least one of these options would have to work to make the doctrine of energy as the crucial resource a reality.

I have already said that I cannot evaluate these ideas, but I wanted you to be acquainted with this line of thought and be aware that when you look very far into the future quite a different type of information becomes important. Traditional econometrics doesn't help us here. There is a type of thinking here that draws on basic scientific notions and knowledge, and that economists should take note of.

REFERENCES

Barnett, H. J. and C. Morse, *Scarcity and Growth* (Johns Hopkins Press, 1963).

Dasgupta, P. and G. Heal, 'The Optimal Depletion of Exhaustible Resources', *Rev. of Econ. Stud., Symposium* (1974), 3–28.

Goeller, H. E. and A. M. Weinberg, 'The Age of Substitutability,' *Science* (20 Feb 1976), 683–9.

Hoffman, K. and E. Cherniavsky, 'A Model for Interfuel Substitution and Technological Change', (Brookhaven Nat. Lab., June 1974).

Hotelling, H., 'The Economics of Exhaustible Resources', *Jn. of Pol. Econ.* 39 (April 1931), 137–75.

Manne, A. S., 'Waiting for the Breeder', *Rev. Econ. Stud., Symposium* (1974), 47–66.

———, 'ETA: A Model for Technology Assessment', *Bell Jn. of Econ.* (Autumn, 1976), 379–406.

Marcuse, W. *et al.*, 'A Dynamic Time Dependent Model for the Analysis of Alternative Energy Policies', BNL-19406 (Brookhaven Nat. Lab., July 1975).

Nordhaus, W. D., 'The Allocation of Energy Resources', *Brookings Papers*, (1973), 4, 429–570.

———, 'The Demand for Energy: An International Perspective', in Nordhaus (Ed.), *Proceedings of the Workshop on Energy Demand*, CP-76-1, Int'l Inst. for Appl. Syst. An., Austria (1976), 511–87.

Ramsey, F. R., 'A Mathematical Theory of Savings', *Econ. Jn.* (Dec. 1928), 543–59.

Sassin, W., and W. Häfele, 'Energy and Future Economic Growth', in Bliss and Boserup (Eds.), *Economic Growth and Resources* (London: Macmillan, 1980).

15

Additively Decomposed Quasiconvex Functions

Gerard Debreu and Tjalling C. Koopmans

Mathematical Programming 24, no. 1 (1982), pp. 1–38

Let f be a real-valued function defined on the product of m finite-dimensional open convex sets $X_1, \dots, X_m$.

Assume that f is quasiconvex and is the sum of nonconstant functions $f_1, \dots, f_m$ defined on the respective factor sets. Then every f_i is continuous; with at most one exception every function f_i is convex; if the exception arises, all the other functions have a strict convexity property and the nonconvex function has several of the differentiability properties of a convex function.

We define the convexity index of a function f_i appearing as a term in an additive decomposition of a quasiconvex function, and we study the properties of that index. In particular, in the case of two one-dimensional factor sets, we characterize the quasiconvexity of an additively decomposed function f either in terms of the nonnegativity of the sum of the convexity indices of f_1 and f_2, or, equivalently, in terms of the separation of the graphs of f_1 and f_2 by means of a logarithmic function. We investigate the extension of these results to the case of m factor sets of arbitrary finite dimensions. The introduction discusses applications to economic theory.

1. Introduction

Let $X_1, \dots, X_m$ be m sets, and let X be their Cartesian product. We say that a real-valued function f on X is *additively decomposed according to the factorization* $\times_{i=1}^m X_i$ *of* X if there are m real-valued functions $f_1, \dots, f_m$ respectively on the factor sets $X_1, \dots, X_m$ such that for every element $x = (x_1, \dots, x_m)$ of $X = \times_{i=1}^m X_i$, one has $f(x) = \sum_{i=1}^m f_i(x_i)$. If in addition for every $i = 1, \dots, m$, X_i is a convex subset of a real vector space, the condition that f be quasiconvex is meaningful. This article is concerned with the conjunction of the two properties of additive decomposition and of quasiconvexity of the function f.

That conjunction has remarkably strong implications that we summarize here. Assume that the sets X_i are open convex subsets of finite-dimensional real vector spaces, that $m \geq 2$, and that the functions f_i are not constant. Then (1) every function f_i is continuous (Theorems 1 and 9); (2) with at most one exception every function f_i is actually convex (Theorems 2 and 10); (3) if the exception arises and the function f_j is not convex, then all the other functions f_i $(i \neq j)$ have a strict-convexity property (Theorems 2 and 10), and the function f_j itself has several of the main differentiability properties of a convex function (Theorem 3); (4) for any i, and any oriented straight line L intersecting X_i, if g denotes the restriction of f_i to L, then

(a) g is a continuous real-valued function defined on a non-empty real interval; the domain of g is partitioned into three intervals[1] $D < C < I$ (some of which may be empty) such that g is strictly decreasing in D, constant in C, and strictly increasing in I.

In Section 3 we associate with every function g satisfying (a) an extended real number $c(g)$, the convexity index of g. One of the main properties of the convexity index is stated in Theorem 6: in the case of two factors X_1, X_2 that are open real intervals and of two non-constant real-valued functions f_1, f_2 defined on X_1, X_2 respectively, the function f defined by $x = (x_1, x_2) \mapsto f(x) = f_1(x_1) + f_2(x_2)$ is quasiconvex if and only if f_1 and f_2 satisfy (a), have finite left- and right-derivatives everywhere, and $c(f_1) + c(f_2) \geq 0$. In Section 3 we also introduce a class of logarithmic functions h_θ depending on a real parameter θ, and whose domain is an open real interval Z_θ. With the notation and the assumptions of the next to last sentence, we show (Theorem 7) that the function f is quasiconvex if and only if for every $x_1^0 \in X_1$ and $x_2^0 \in X_2$, there is a function h_θ whose graph locally separates suitable linear transforms of the graphs of f_1 and f_2. In Section 4 we extend the concept of the convexity index to a real-valued function g defined on a non-empty convex subset Y of a finite-dimensional real vector space and such that for every oriented stright line L intersecting Y, the restriction g_L of g to L satisfies (a). By definition, $c(g) = \operatorname{Inf}_L c(g_L)$. In the case of two factors X_1 and X_2, and of two C^2 real-valued functions f_1 and f_2, Theorem 11 gives the expression of $c(f)$ in terms of $c(f_1)$ and $c(f_2)$. We conclude Section 4 with a characterization, by means of convexity indices, of the quasiconvexity of a C^2 real-valued function additively decomposed into a finite number (at least equal to two) of nonconstant functions defined on finite-dimensional open convex sets.

Because of our particular backgrounds, we give examples of possible applications of these results only in economic theory, pertaining to two areas of that field. We would appreciate reader responses with regard to other fields of application of mathematics.

Utility theory. Consider the case in which the set C of the commodities of an economy is partitioned into m subsets $C_1, \ldots, C_m$. For instance the commodities in set C_i are the goods and services available in the ith period. Alternatively in a study of economic uncertainty, the commodities in set C_i are the goods and

[1] The notation $D < C < I$ means that for every x, y, z in D, C, I respectively, one has $x < y < z$.

services whose availability is contingent on the occurrence of the ith state of the world. Still another example is the partitioning of the set C of commodities into groups of goods or services with related physical characteristics. The consumption of a given consumer in the economy is described by a vector x listing the quantities of the various commodities that he consumes. Corresponding to the partition of C into the sets $C_1, \dots, C_m$, there is a partition $(x_1, \dots, x_m)$ of the components of x. The vector x_i belongs to a subset X_i of the commodity space associated with the commodities in C_i and x belongs to the Cartesian product $X = \times_{i=1}^m X_i$. The preferences of the given consumer are represented mathematically by a complete preorder, i.e., by a complete, reflexive, transitive binary relation, $\lesssim$ on X where $x \lesssim x'$ is read as "x' is at least as desired as x". If the space X and the relation $\lesssim$ satisfy mild topological properties (e.g. X is connected and separable and $\{(x, x') \in X \times X \mid x \lesssim x'\}$ is closed), then the preference relation $\lesssim$ can be represented by a continuous real-valued utility function u in the sense that $x \lesssim x'$ is equivalent to $u(x) \leq u(x')$. Denoting the set of factor spaces of X by $I = \{1, \dots, m\}$ we consider a subset J of I and we fix the values of all the components of x for $i \notin J$ equal to $(x_i^0)_{i \notin J}$. Assume now that the preorder induced by $\lesssim$ on $\times_{i \in J} X_i$ given the values $(x_i^0)_{i \notin J}$ is independent of those particular values, and denote that induced preorder by $\lesssim_J$. Assume also that there are at least three factor spaces and that for every $i \in I$, the induced preorder $\lesssim_i$ is not trivial in the sense that one does not have $x \lesssim_i x'$ for every pair (x, x') of elements of X_i. Then (Debreu, 1960) there are m real-valued continuous functions u_i on X_i $(i = 1, \dots, m)$ such that the preference preorder $\lesssim$ is represented by the function u defined on X by $u(x) = \sum_{i=1}^m u_i(x_i)$. If in this situation the standard assumption of convexity of preferences is made, i.e., if the set X is convex (open and finite-dimensional) and if for every x' in X, the set $\{x \in X \mid x \gtrsim x'\}$ is convex, then the function u is quasiconcave and the results of this article apply. In particular every function u_i, with at most one exception, is concave. This observation was made for additively decomposed quasiconcave and *twice continuously differentiable* utility functions in Slutsky's classic paper of 1915, in Green (1961), Gorman (1970), and Rader (1972). It was also made by Arrow and Enthoven (1961) in the context of twice continuously differentiable production functions that we discuss below. In unpublished notes of 1971, Koopmans showed that the assumptions of differentiability and even of continuity could be dispensed with. In a paper independently written at about the same time and eventually published in 1977, Yaari established the concavity of every function u_i with at most one exception dispensing with the assumption of differentiability but retaining the assumption of continuity. (An interesting sequel of this work is Yaari (1978).)

The assumption of independence for the preorder induced by $\lesssim$ on $\times_{i \in J} X_i$ is of special interest in two interpretations in which it is assumed that the spaces X_i are identical with the same list of physical goods or services, and that the conditions of Theorem 3 of Grodal (1978) are satisfied. For $m \geq 3$, the preference relation $\lesssim$ can then be represented by a utility function v of the form

$$v(x) = \sum_{i \in I} \alpha_i u(x_i), \quad \alpha_i > 0, i \in I.$$

Moreover, if $\lesssim$ is convex, i.e., if v is quasiconcave, then every function $\alpha_i u$, with at most one exception, is concave. Hence u is concave.

The first interpretation, which gave rise to Koopmans' initial work, is that in which the values $i = 1, 2, \dots, m$ refer to successive periods in time, and $\alpha_i = \alpha^i$, $0 < \alpha < 1$, represent successive powers of a discount factor α.

In the second interpretation the values $i = 1, 2, \dots, m$ refer to different states of the world, and α_i is the judgmental probability of the ith state of the world for the decision-maker (Arrow, 1953; Hirschleifer, 1965; Cox, 1973; Blackorby et al., 1977).)

Production theory. As in Arrow and Enthoven (1961), we consider a set C of commodities used as inputs in the production of a single output and we assume that C is partitioned into m sets $C_1, \dots, C_m$. For every $i = 1, \dots, m$, there is an elementary production process transforming the input-vector x_i, whose components pertain to the commodities in C_i, into $f_i(x_i)$ units of output. Thus the input-vector $x = (x_1, \dots, x_m)$ is transformed into $f(x) = \sum_{i=1}^{m} f_i(x_i)$ units of output. In an attempt to relax the standard condition of convexity of the set of feasible input–output vectors, i.e. of concavity of the function f, Shephard (1953), Aoki (1971), Laffont (1972), Fourgeaud et al. (1974), Guesnerie (1975), Dierker et al. (1976) use the condition of convexity of the sets of input-vectors required to attain a certain level of output, i.e. of quasiconcavity of the function f. If the assumptions that we listed earlier are satisfied, namely if the domains of the functions f_i are open convex subsets of finite-dimensional real vector spaces, $m \geq 2$, and the functions f_i are not constant, then all of them, with at most one exception, are actually concave. In other words every elementary production process, with at most one exception, has a convex set of feasible input–output vectors.

2. Two factor spaces of dimension one

A real-valued function h on a convex subset C of a real vector space is said to be *quasiconvex* if for every real number k the set $\{x \in C \mid h(x) \leq k\}$ is convex. Considering *a quasiconvex function f on a nonempty open real interval X*, we define the intervals X^d and X^i as follows. (The next six paragraphs slightly extend Stoer and Witzgall (1970, Theorem 4.9.11).)

For every k in $f(X)$, the set $\{x \in X \mid f(x) \leq k\}$ is a nonempty real interval with endpoints $a(k)$ and $b(k)$ where $a(k) \leq b(k)$. The intervals $[a(k), b(k)]$ for $k \in f(X)$ are nested since $k_2 \leq k_1$ implies $a(k_1) \leq a(k_2) \leq b(k_2) \leq b(k_1)$. We define

$$\underline{x} = \operatorname*{Sup}_{k \in f(X)} a(k) \quad \text{and} \quad \bar{x} = \operatorname*{Inf}_{k \in f(X)} b(k).$$

The function f is weakly decreasing in the interval (Inf X, $\bar{x}$). To see this, consider x' and x'' such that Inf $X < x' < x'' < \bar{x}$. Let $k = f(x')$. Then $a(k) \leq x'$ and $\bar{x} \leq b(k)$. Therefore x'' belongs to the interval $(a(k), b(k))$ hence $f(x'') \leq f(x')$. We define X^d as (Inf X, $\bar{x}$] if f is weakly decreasing in that interval, and as (Inf X, $\bar{x}$) otherwise. Similarly, f is weakly increasing in the interval ($\underline{x}$, Sup X). We define X^i as [$\underline{x}$, Sup X) if f is weakly increasing in that interval, and as ($\underline{x}$, Sup X) otherwise.

We note that X^d and X^i together cover X, for if x in X belonged neither to X^d nor to X^i, one would necessarily have $x = \underline{x} = \bar{x}$, $f(x) > \text{Inf}\, f(X^d)$, and $f(x) > \text{Inf}\, f(X^i)$. However, the last two inequalities contradict the quasiconvexity of f.

Thus, X partitions into the three intervals $X^d \smallsetminus X^i$, $X^d \cap X^i$, and $X^i \smallsetminus X^d$, of which at most two may be empty. In $X^d \cap X^i$, which is a proper interval only if $\underline{x} < \bar{x}$, f takes on the constant value Inf $f(X)$. Finally if $x \in X^d \smallsetminus X^i$ and $x' \in X^i \smallsetminus X^d$, then $x < x'$.

Clearly, if X^d is not empty, then f is not weakly decreasing in any interval strictly containing X^d, and if X^i is not empty, then f is not weakly increasing in any interval strictly containing X^i.

Also note that if f is nonconstant on X, it is not possible for f to take on different constant values $f(X^d)$ and $f(X^i)$ on X^d and X^i respectively. This would require X^d and X^i to be disjoint. But then $f(X^d) < f(X^i)$ would imply $X^d \subset X^i = X$ and $f(X^i) < f(X^d)$ would imply $X^i \subset X^d = X$, contradicting the disjointness.

In the remainder of this section we always make the assumptions:

A.1. *X and Y are open real intervals. f and g are nonconstant real-valued functions on X and Y, respectively. The function $F: X \times Y \to R$ defined by $F(x, y) = f(x) + g(y)$ is quasiconvex.*

Clearly, the two functions f and g are quasiconvex. We associate with f the two intervals X^d, X^i defined earlier, and with g the corresponding intervals Y^d, Y^i.

In the sequel, we will often appeal to the following remarks. Let the function $\hat{f}$ on $\hat{X} = -X$ be defined by $\hat{f}(x) = f(-x)$, and let the function $\hat{g}$ on $\hat{Y} = -Y$ be defined by $\hat{g}(y) = g(-y)$. The three functions defined respectively on $\hat{X} \times Y$, $X \times \hat{Y}$, and $\hat{X} \times \hat{Y}$ by $(x, y) \mapsto \hat{f}(x) + g(y)$, $f(x) + \hat{g}(y)$, and $\hat{f}(x) + \hat{g}(y)$ are also quasiconvex and one has $\hat{X}^d = -X^i$, $\hat{X}^i = -X^d$, $\hat{Y}^d = -Y^i$, and $\hat{Y}^i = -Y^d$. Now consider a point (x, y) in $X \times Y$. As we noticed earlier, x belongs to X^d and/or to X^i, and y belongs to Y^d and/or to Y^i. The preceding remarks will often enable us to assume without loss of generality that x belongs to X^d or that x belongs to X^i, and that y belongs to Y^d or that y belongs to Y^i.

Theorem 1. *Under Assumptions* A.1, *the functions f and g are continuous.*

Proof. Since g is nonconstant on Y^d and/or on Y^i, we can assume without loss of generality that g is not constant on Y^i.

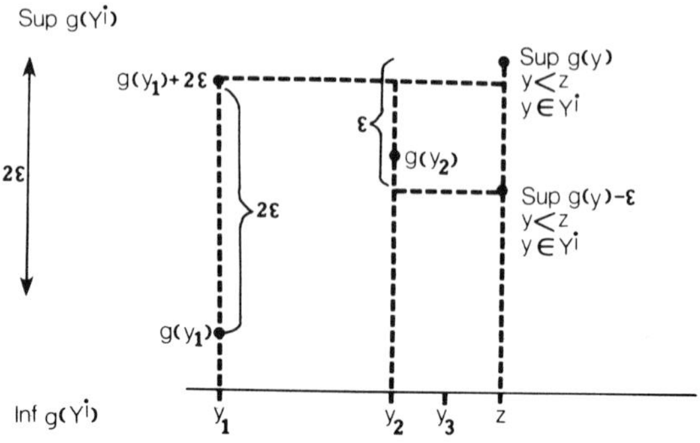

Fig. 1.

Given any ϵ such that $0 < 2\epsilon < \operatorname{Sup} g(Y^i) - \operatorname{Inf} g(Y^i)$, there are three points y_1, y_2, y_3 of Y^i such that

$$y_1 < y_2 < y_3, \tag{1}$$

$$g(y_1) < g(y_2) - \epsilon, \tag{2}$$

and

$$g(y_3) < g(y_2) + \epsilon. \tag{3}$$

To show this, select first y_1 in Y^i so that

$$g(y_1) < \operatorname{Sup} g(Y^i) - 2\epsilon.$$

Then choose z in Y^i so that

$$\operatorname*{Sup}_{\substack{y<z\\ y\in Y^i}} g(y) > g(y_1) + 2\epsilon.$$

Next select in Y^i a number $y_2 < z$ so that

$$g(y_2) > \operatorname*{Sup}_{\substack{y<z\\ y\in Y^i}} g(y) - \epsilon.$$

Therefore, $y_1 < y_2$, and (2) holds. Finally, select y_3 so that $y_2 < y_3 < z$. Then (3) holds.

Next, we prove:

(a) *If* $x_0 \in X^d$, *then* $f(x_0) = f(x_{0^-})$, where

$$f(x_{0^-}) = \lim_{\substack{x\to x_0\\ x<x_0}} f(x).$$

Clearly, $f(x_0) \le f(x_{0^-})$. We assume that $f(x_0) < f(x_{0^-})$ and show that this leads to

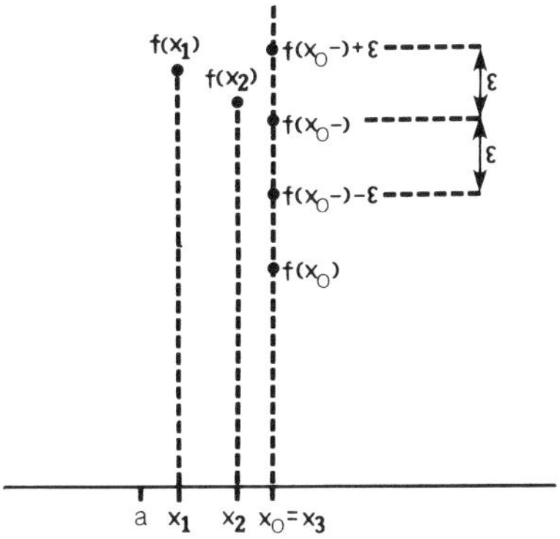

Fig. 2.

a contradiction. Select $\epsilon > 0$ such that

$$\epsilon < f(x_{0^-}) - f(x_0) \quad \text{and} \quad 2\epsilon < \operatorname{Sup} g(Y^i) - \operatorname{Inf} g(Y^i).$$

Thus, there are three points y_1, y_2, y_3 in Y^i satisfying (1), (2), (3). There is also a number a in X such that $a < x_0$ and

$$(*) \qquad a \leq x < x_0 \text{ implies } f(x_{0^-}) \leq f(x) < f(x_{0^-}) + \epsilon.$$

We can choose two real numbers $\alpha > 0$ and β such that $x_i = \alpha y_i + \beta$ $(i = 1, 2, 3)$ satisfy $a \leq x_1 < x_2 < x_3 = x_0$.

Then, by $(*)$, since $f(x_1) < f(x_{0^-}) + \epsilon$ and since also $f(x_{0^-}) \leq f(x_2)$, one has

$$f(x_1) < f(x_2) + \epsilon. \tag{4}$$

Since $f(x_3) < f(x_{0^-}) - \epsilon$ and $f(x_{0^-}) \leq f(x_2)$, one has

$$f(x_3) < f(x_2) - \epsilon. \tag{5}$$

Therefore, by (2) and (4),

$$F(x_1, y_1) < F(x_2, y_2),$$

while, by (3) and (5),

$$F(x_3, y_3) < F(x_2, y_2).$$

These two inequalities contradict the quasiconvexity of F on the straight line segment $[(x_1, y_1), (x_3, y_3)]$.

Having established (a), we now prove the continuity of f:

(b) *For every $x_0 \in X$, one has $f(x_{0^-}) = f(x_{0^+}) = f(x_0)$.*

Since locally f is weakly monotone on the left of x_0, as well as on the right of x_0, the two numbers $f(x_{0^-})$ and $f(x_{0^+})$ (one or both of which might be $-\infty$) are

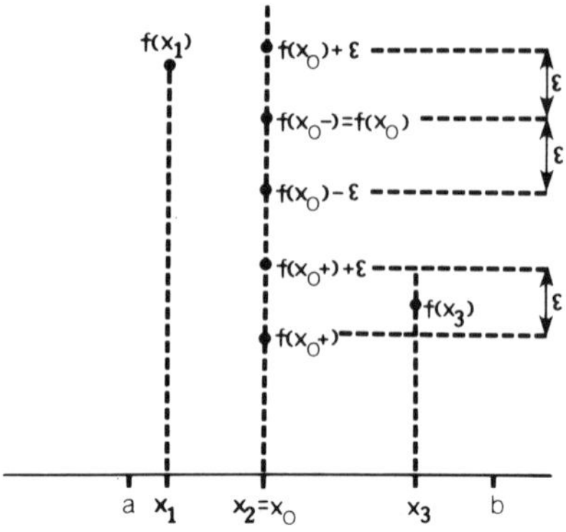

Fig. 3.

defined. Suppose that they are not equal. We can assume without loss of generality that $f(x_{0^-}) > f(x_{0^+})$, which implies that $x_0 \in X^d$, and, consequently by (a), $f(x_0) = f(x_{0^-})$. We select $\epsilon > 0$ such that

$$2\epsilon < f(x_0) - f(x_{0^+}) \quad \text{and} \quad 2\epsilon < \operatorname{Sup} g(Y^i) - \operatorname{Inf} g(Y^i).$$

Thus there are three points y_1, y_2, y_3 in Y^i satisfying (1), (2), and (3). As before, there is a number a in X such that $a < x_0$ and

$$a \leq x < x_0 \text{ implies } f(x) < f(x_0) + \epsilon.$$

There is also a number b in X such that $x_0 < b$ and

$$x_0 < x \leq b \text{ implies } f(x) < f(x_0) - \epsilon.$$

This last assertion is obvious if $f(x_{0^+}) = -\infty$. If $f(x_{0^+})$ is finite, then there is b in X such that $x_0 < b$ and $x_0 < x \leq b$ implies $f(x) < f(x_{0^+}) + \epsilon$, and consequently, $f(x) < f(x_0) - \epsilon$.

We can now choose two real numbers $\alpha > 0$ and β such that $x_i = \alpha y_i + \beta$ $(i = 1, 2, 3)$ satisfy $a \leq x_1 < x_2 = x_0 < x_3 \leq b$.

Since $f(x_1) < f(x_0) + \epsilon$, one has

$$f(x_1) < f(x_2) + \epsilon. \tag{4'}$$

Since $f(x_3) < f(x_0) - \epsilon$, one has

$$f(x_3) < f(x_2) - \epsilon. \tag{5'}$$

Therefore, by (2) and (4′),

$$F(x_1, y_1) < F(x_2, y_2),$$

while, by (3) and (5′),

$$F(x_3, y_3) < F(x_2, y_2).$$

We have again a contradiction of the quasiconvexity of F on the straight line segment $[(x_1, y_1), (x_3, y_3)]$.

Theorem 2. *Under* A.1, *if f is not convex, then g has the property*

(P) *If y_1, y_2 are two points of Y such that $g(y_1) \neq g(y_2)$, then for every t in* $(0, 1)$, *one has* $g[(1-t)y_1 + ty_2] < (1-t)g(y_1) + tg(y_2)$.

Proof. The proof rests on the same basic ideas as Yaari's (1977) proofs. We assume without loss of generality that f is not convex on X^i. Therefore, there are two points a_1, a_2 in X^i such that $a_1 < a_2$ and that there are points of the graph of f strictly above the chord $A = [(a_1, f(a_1)), (a_2, f(a_2))]$. Since f is weakly increasing on X^i, one cannot have $f(a_1) = f(a_2)$. Thus $f(a_1) < f(a_2)$. By continuity of f, there is a straight line L parallel to A and supporting from above the graph of f restricted to $[a_1, a_2]$. Since L is not horizontal, there is a highest point $(x^*, f(x^*))$ in the intersection of L with the graph of f restricted to $[a_1, a_2]$.

For every sufficiently small number $s > 0$,

(i) $\frac{1}{2}[f(y^* + s) + f(y^* - s)] \leq f(y^*)$.

Now consider the continuous function ϕ defined by

$$\phi(s) = f(x^* + s) - f(x^* - s).$$

One has $\phi(0) = 0$ and for every sufficiently small $s > 0$, $\phi(s) > 0$. Therefore, for every sufficiently small $\delta > 0$,

(ii) there is $s > 0$ such that $f(x^* + s) - f(x^* - s) = \delta$.

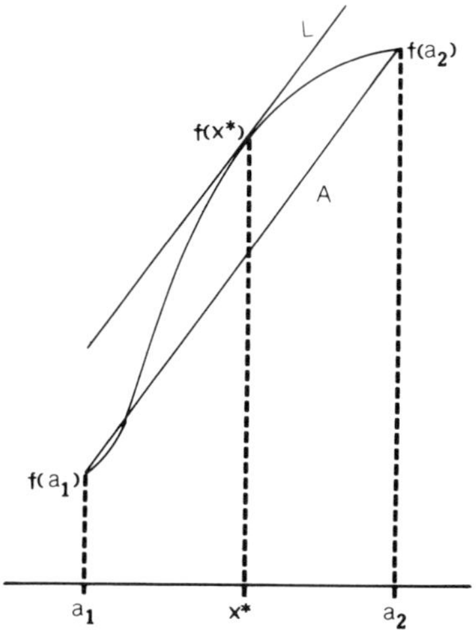

Fig. 4.

Let us then assume that there are two points b_1, b_2 in Y such that $b_1 < b_2$; $g(b_1) < g(b_2)$; and the graph of g is not strictly below the chord $B = [(b_1, g(b_1)), (b_2, g(b_2))]$. Reasoning as above, we observe that there is a straight line M parallel to B and supporting the graph of g restricted to $[b_1, b_2]$ from above. However, in the present case M may contain B. Next, we select a point $(y^*, g(y^*))$ in the intersection of M and the graph of g restricted to $[b_1, b_2]$, and different from the endpoints of B.

For every sufficiently small $t > 0$, we have this time that

(i′) $$\tfrac{1}{2}[g(y^* + t) + g(y^* - t)] \leq g(y^*).$$

As before, we define the continuous function ψ by

$$\psi(t) = g(y^* + t) - g(y^* - t).$$

One has $\psi(0) = 0$. Moreover, the inequality $g(b_1) < g(y^*)$ implies that y^* is in Y^i. Therefore, for every sufficiently small $t > 0$, $\psi(t) > 0$. Consequently, for every sufficiently small $\delta > 0$,

(ii′) there is $t > 0$ such that $g(y^* + t) - g(y^* - t) = \delta$.

We now choose $\delta > 0$ small enough so that both (ii) and (ii′) are satisfied. Thus, there are $s > 0$ and $t > 0$ such that

(iii) $$f(x^* + s) - f(x^* - s) = \delta = g(y^* + t) - g(y^* - t).$$

Defining $x_1 = x^* + s$, $x_2 = x^* - s$, $y_1 = y^* - t$, and $y_2 = y^* + t$, we obtain from (iii), (i), and (i′),

(iv) $$F(x_1, y_1) = F(x_2, y_2) = \tfrac{1}{2}[F(x_1, y_1) + F(x_2, y_2)] < F(x^*, y^*).$$

Since $\tfrac{1}{2}[(x_1, y_1) + (x_2, y_2)] = (x^*, y^*)$, (iv) contradicts the quasiconvexity of F.

(P) says that the graph of the function g is strictly below any chord $B = [(y_1, g(y_1)), (y_2, g(y_2))]$ that is not horizontal. In fact, if y_1, y_2 are two points of Y such that $y_1 < y_2$ and $g(y_1) = g(y_2) \neq \text{Inf}\, g(Y)$, then the graph of g is also strictly below the chord B. To see that this is implied by (P), select a point y_0 in Y such that $g(y_0) < g(y_1) = g(y_2)$. Since the graph of g is strictly below the chord with endpoints $(y_0, g(y_0))$ and $(y_1, g(y_1))$, and strictly below the chord with endpoints $(y_0, g(y_0))$ and $(y_2, g(y_2))$, it is strictly below B.

Moreover, $y_1 < y_2$ and $g(y_1) = g(y_2) = \text{Inf}\, g(Y)$ implies $g(y) = \text{Inf}\, g(Y)$ for every y in $[y_1, y_2]$ by quasiconvexity of g. Therefore, the function g is actually convex (and strictly convex on $Y^d \setminus Y^i$ and on $Y^i \setminus Y^d$.

Theorem 3. *Under* A.1, *at every point x of X, the function f has a finite left-derivative and a finite right-derivative satisfying $f'_-(x) \leq f'_+(x)$. Both derivatives are strictly positive in $X^i \setminus X^d$ and strictly negative in $X^d \setminus X^i$. The function f'_- is continuous on the left and the function f'_+ is continuous on the*

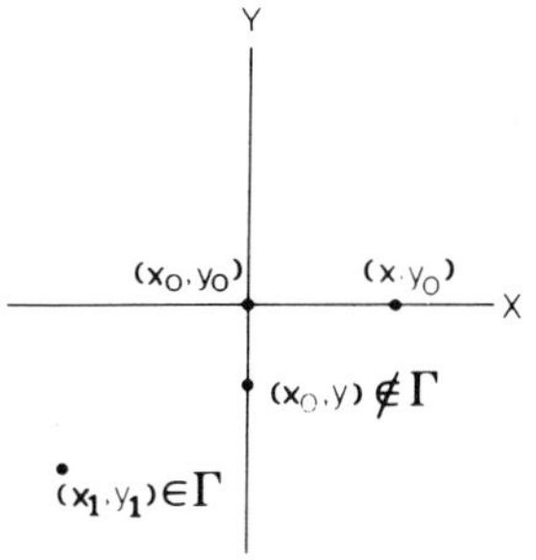

Fig. 5.

right. At every point x of X outside a countable set, $f'_-(x) = f'_+(x)$ and the functions f'_- and f'_+ are continuous. At every point x of X outside a set of Lebesgue measure zero, $f'_-(x) = f'_+(x)$ and the functions f'_- and f'_+ have the same finite derivative $f''(x)$.

Proof. If f is convex, it has all the properties listed above. Therefore, we study the case in which f is not convex.

First, we assume that the open interval $X^i \smallsetminus X^d$ is not empty and we prove that f is strictly increasing in that interval. Consider a point x_0 in $X^i \smallsetminus X^d$. There is a point x_1 in $X^i \smallsetminus X^d$ such that $x_1 < x_0$ and $f(x_1) < f(x_0)$, because otherwise x_0 would belong to X^d. We can without loss of generality assume that there is a point y_0 of Y such that the convex function g is strictly decreasing in a neighborhood of y_0.

We define the set

$$\Gamma = \{(x, y) \in X \times Y \mid f(x) + g(y) \leq f(x_0) + g(y_0)\},$$

which is convex and closed relative to $X \times Y$. By continuity of g, there is a point y_1 of Y such that $y_1 < y_0$ and $g(y_1) \leq g(y_0) + f(x_0) - f(x_1)$. Thus

(i) $\qquad x_1 < x_0,\ y_1 < y_0,\quad \text{and} \quad (x_1, y_1) \in \Gamma.$

Moreover, for every y in Y such that $y < y_0$, one has $g(y) > g(y_0)$. Consequently,

(ii) $\qquad y \in Y$ and $y < y_0$ imply $(x_0, y) \notin \Gamma$.

(i), (ii), and the convexity of Γ imply that for every x in X such that $x > x_0$, the point (x, y_0) is not in Γ (see Fig. 5). Therefore, x in X and $x > x_0$ imply $f(x) > f(x_0)$.

Having established that f is strictly increasing on $X^i \smallsetminus X^d$, we choose an open interval I around x_0 sufficiently small so that $I \subset X^i \smallsetminus X^d$ and that the open interval $f(x_0) + g(y_0) - f(I)$ is contained in $g(Y^d)$. Clearly, there is an open

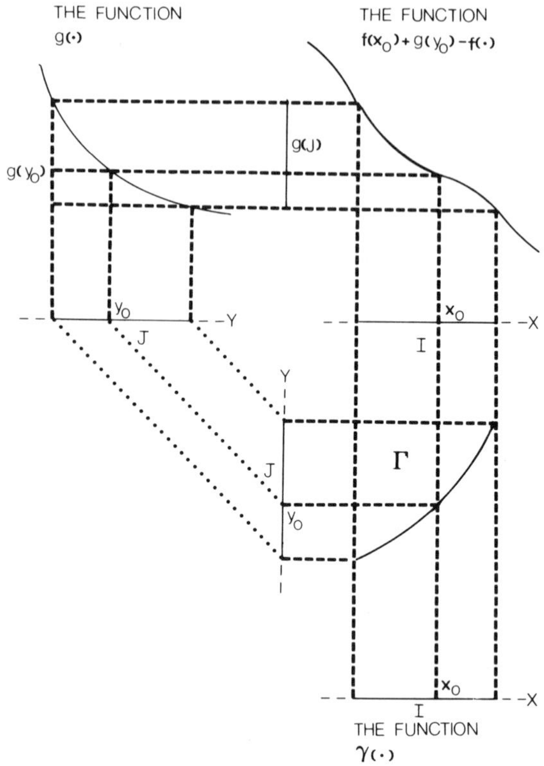

Fig. 6.

interval J around y_0 and contained in $Y^d \smallsetminus Y^i$ such that $g(J) = f(x_0) + g(y_0) - f(I)$.

For every x in I, there is a unique y in J such that $g(y) = f(x_0) + g(y_0) - f(x)$. Let γ be the function from I to J defined in this manner (see Fig. 6). γ is strictly increasing on I. Moreover, for every x in I, the point $(x, \gamma(x))$ is in the lower boundary of the convex set Γ. To see this, note that obviously $(x, \gamma(x))$ belongs to Γ, while, as in (ii), for every y in Y such that $y < \gamma(x)$, one has $(x, y) \not\in \Gamma$. Thus, the function γ is convex.

Let x tend to x_0 from the left. Then $\gamma(x)$ tends to $\gamma(x_0)$ from below. One also has

$$\frac{f(x) - f(x_0)}{x - x_0} = \frac{g[\gamma(x_0)] - g[\gamma(x)]}{\gamma(x) - \gamma(x_0)} \cdot \frac{\gamma(x) - \gamma(x_0)}{x - x_0}.$$

Since g is convex, the first factor of the right-hand side tends to $-g'_-[\gamma(x_0)]$. The second factor tends to $\gamma'_-(x_0)$. Therefore,

$$\frac{f(x)-f(x_0)}{x-x_0}$$

has a limit $f'_-(x_0) = -g'_-(y_0)\gamma'_-(x_0)$, where $g'_-(y_0) < 0$ and $\gamma'_-(x_0) > 0$. Consequently, $f'_-(x_0) > 0$. Similarly, $f'_+(x_0)$ exists and equals $-g'_+(y_0)\gamma'_+(x_0)$.

We have chosen for y_0 any point of Y where g is strictly decreasing. Since the convex function g has a finite derivative at every point of Y outside a countable set, we could have chosen y_0 in Y such that $g'_-(y_0) = g'_+(y_0) < 0$. But then $\gamma'_-(x_0) \leq \gamma'_+(x_0)$ implies $f'_-(x_0) \leq f'_+(x_0)$.

In the preceding reasoning we have associated with every point a in $X^i \smallsetminus X^d$, an open interval ${}_aI$ around a and contained in $X^i \smallsetminus X^d$, and a strictly increasing convex function ${}_a\gamma$ on ${}_aI$ such that for every point x in ${}_aI$ one has

$$f'_-(x) = -g'_-({}_a\gamma(x))\,{}_a\gamma'_-(x) \quad \text{and} \quad f'_+(x) = -g'_+({}_a\gamma(x))\,{}_a\gamma'_+(x).$$

Since the functions g'_- and ${}_a\gamma'_-$ are continuous on the left and the function ${}_a\gamma$ is increasing, the function f'_- is continuous on the left. Similarly f'_+ is continuous on the right.

At every point x of ${}_aI$ outside a countable set ${}_aD_1$, one has ${}_a\gamma'_-(x) = {}_a\gamma'_+(x)$ and the functions ${}_a\gamma'_-$ and ${}_a\gamma'_+$ are continuous. And at every point y of ${}_a\gamma({}_aI)$ outside a countable set ${}_aD_2$, one has $g'_-(y) = g'_+(y)$ and the functions g'_- and g'_+ are continuous. Therefore at every point x of ${}_aI$ outside the countable set ${}_aD = {}_aD_1 \cup {}_a\gamma^{-1}({}_aD_2)$, one has $f'_-(x) = f'_+(x)$ and the functions f'_- and f'_+ are continuous.

At every point x of ${}_aI$ outside a null (i.e. of Lebesgue measure zero) set ${}_aN_1$, one has ${}_a\gamma'_-(x) = {}_a\gamma'_+(x)$ and the functions ${}_a\gamma'_-$ and ${}_a\gamma'_+$ have the same finite derivative ${}_a\gamma''(x)$. And at every point y of ${}_a\gamma({}_aI)$ outside a null set ${}_aN_2$, one has $g'_-(y) = g'_+(y)$ and the functions g'_- and g'_+ have the same finite derivative $g''(y)$. We claim that ${}_a\gamma^{-1}({}_aN_2)$, the image of the null set ${}_aN_2$ by the concave function ${}_a\gamma^{-1}$, is null. Given any compact interval E contained in ${}_a\gamma({}_aI)$, the function ${}_a\gamma^{-1}$ is Lipschitzian on E and consequently the image of the null set $E \cap {}_aN_2$ by ${}_a\gamma^{-1}$ is null. However the open interval ${}_a\gamma({}_aI)$ can be covered by a countable union $\bigcup_i E_i$ of compact subintervals E_i. The equality

$${}_a\gamma^{-1}({}_aN_2) = \bigcup_i {}_a\gamma^{-1}(E_i \cap {}_aN_2)$$

proves our claim. Consider now a point x_0 of ${}_aI$ outside the null set ${}_aN = {}_aN_1 \cup {}_a\gamma^{-1}({}_aN_2)$. One has $f'_-(x_0) = f'_+(x_0)$. Moreover for any $x \neq x_0$ in ${}_aI$,

$$\begin{aligned}\frac{f'_-(x)-f'_-(x_0)}{x-x_0} &= \frac{-g'_-({}_a\gamma(x))\,{}_a\gamma'_-(x) + g'({}_a\gamma(x_0))\,{}_a\gamma'(x_0)}{x-x_0}\\ &= -g'_-({}_a\gamma(x)) \cdot \frac{{}_a\gamma'_-(x) - {}_a\gamma'(x_0)}{x-x_0}\\ &\quad - {}_a\gamma'(x_0) \cdot \frac{g'_-({}_a\gamma(x)) - g'({}_a\gamma(x_0))}{{}_a\gamma(x) - {}_a\gamma(x_0)} \cdot \frac{{}_a\gamma(x) - {}_a\gamma(x_0)}{x-x_0}.\end{aligned}$$

When x tends to x_0,

$$\frac{f'_-(x)-f'_-(x_0)}{x-x_0} \text{ tends to } -g'({}_a\gamma(x_0))\,{}_a\gamma''(x_0)-g''({}_a\gamma(x_0))[{}_a\gamma'(x_0)]^2.$$

Clearly

$$\frac{f'_+(x)-f'_+(x_0)}{x-x_0}$$

tends to the same finite limit when x tends to x_0.

In summary, with every point a of $X^i \smallsetminus X^d$ we have associated an open interval, ${}_aI$, around a and two exceptional subsets of ${}_aI$, one of them, ${}_aD$, countable, and the other, ${}_aN$, null. The intervals I_a cover $X^i \smallsetminus X^d$. Thus, by Lindelöf's theorem (Kelley, 1955, p. 49), we can cover $X^i \smallsetminus X^d$ with a countable collection of intervals ${}_aI$. The countable unions of the corresponding exceptional sets ${}_aD$ and ${}_aN$ form the two exceptional subsets D and N of $X^i \smallsetminus X^d$ respectively, the former being countable and latter being null.

The properties of the function f listed in Theorem 3 have been established in $X^i < X^d$. In a similar manner they hold in $X^d \smallsetminus X^i$. They also hold trivially in the interval (Inf X^i, Sup X^d). Only the cases in which $x = \text{Inf } X^i$ or $x = \text{Sup } X^d$ remain to be considered. A minor modification of the preceding proof, namely choosing an interval I having x as an endpoint, establishes that in the first case f has a finite left derivative $f'_-(x) \leq 0$ continuous on the left, and in the second case f has a finite right derivative $f'_+(x) \geq 0$ continuous on the right.

The function g obviously has in Y the properties that the function f has in X.

3. The convexity index of a quasiconvex function and a class of separating functions

We have shown that under A.1, the function f is continuous and the interval X is partitioned into three intervals $X^{sd} = X^d \smallsetminus X^i$, $X^c = X^d \cap X^i$, and $X^{si} = X^i \smallsetminus X^d$ (some of which may be empty) such that $X^{sd} < X^c < X^{si}$, f is strictly decreasing in X^{sd}, constant in X^c, and strictly increasing in X^{si}. To define the convexity index of f on X, we first define and study the convexity index of f on X^{si}. Then, letting $\hat{f}$ be the function with domain $\hat{X} = -X$ such that $\hat{f}(x) = f(-x)$, we define the convexity index of f on X^{sd} as the convexity index of $\hat{f}$ on $-X^{sd}$. Next we set the convexity index of f on X^c to be $+\infty$. Finally the convexity index of f on X is defined as the smallest of the convexity indices of f on X^{sd}, X^c, and X^{si} that are determined, i.e., for which the corresponding interval is not empty. Thus in Section 3 (with the exception of the last three paragraphs) we make the assumptions:

A.2. *X and Y are non-empty open real intervals. f and g are strictly increasing continuous real-valued functions on X and Y respectively. The function $F: X \times Y \to R$ is defined by $F(x, y) = f(x) + g(y)$.*

The inverse $\phi = f^{-1}$ of f is defined on the non-empty open real interval $U = f(X)$, and the inverse $\chi = g^{-1}$ of g is defined on the non-empty open real interval $V = g(Y)$.

Given a real number Δ such that $0 < \Delta < \frac{1}{2}(\text{Sup } U - \text{Inf } U)$, we let

$$\bar{\lambda}(\Delta) = \operatorname*{Inf}_u \log\left[\frac{\phi(u) - \phi(u - \Delta)}{\phi(u + \Delta) - \phi(u)}\right]^{1/\Delta}$$

In the last Infimum, u is restricted to be such that $u - \Delta$, u, and $u + \Delta$ belong to U.

The *convexity index* of the function f is defined as

$$\lambda = \limsup_{\Delta \to 0} \bar{\lambda}(\Delta).$$

Equivalently the convexity index can be defined in the following, perhaps more intuitively appealing, manner. Let

$$\beta(u, \Delta) = -\frac{\dfrac{1}{\Delta^2}[\phi(u + \Delta) - \phi(u)] - \dfrac{1}{\Delta^2}[\phi(u) - \phi(u - \Delta)]}{\dfrac{1}{\Delta}[\phi(u + \Delta) - \phi(u)]}.$$

We claim that

$$\lambda = \limsup_{\Delta \to 0} \operatorname*{Inf}_u \beta(u, \Delta) \tag{6}$$

Proof of (6). Let

$$\alpha(u, \Delta) = \frac{1}{\Delta} \log\left[\frac{\phi(u) - \phi(u - \Delta)}{\phi(u + \Delta) - \phi(u)}\right]$$

so that $\lambda = \limsup_{\Delta \to 0} \text{Inf}_u\, \alpha(u, \Delta)$. One has

$$\alpha(u, \Delta) = \frac{1}{\Delta} \log[1 + \Delta\beta(u, \Delta)].$$

For any $\Delta > 0$, the function $z \mapsto (1/\Delta) \log[1 + \Delta z]$ is strictly increasing; therefore

$$\operatorname*{Inf}_u \alpha(u, \Delta) = \frac{1}{\Delta} \log[1 + \Delta \operatorname*{Inf}_u \beta(u, \Delta)].$$

Let now

$$\gamma(\Delta) = \operatorname*{Inf}_u \beta(u, \Delta)$$

Since $(1/\Delta) \log[1 + \Delta\gamma(\Delta)] \le \gamma(\Delta)$, one has

(i) $$\limsup_{\Delta \to 0} \frac{1}{\Delta} \log[1 + \Delta\gamma(\Delta)] \le \limsup_{\Delta \to 0} \gamma(\Delta).$$

Next consider two real numbers k_0, k_1 such that $k_0 < k_1 < \limsup_{\Delta\to 0} \gamma(\Delta)$. There is an infinite sequence $\Delta_n > 0$ such that $\Delta_n \to 0$ and for every n, $\gamma(\Delta_n) \geq k_1$. Therefore

$$\frac{1}{\Delta_n}\log[1+\Delta_n\gamma(\Delta_n)] \geq \frac{1}{\Delta_n}\log[1+k_1\Delta_n].$$

The last expression tends to k_1. Hence for n large enough,

$$\frac{1}{\Delta_n}\log[1+k_1\Delta_n] \geq k_0.$$

Therefore

$$\limsup_{\Delta\to 0}\frac{1}{\Delta}\log[1+\Delta\gamma(\Delta)] \geq k_0,$$

and

(ii) $$\limsup_{\Delta\to 0}\frac{1}{\Delta}\log[1+\Delta\gamma(\Delta)] \geq \limsup_{\Delta\to 0}\gamma(\Delta).$$

We first show that under A.2, a convex function f is characterized by the fact that $\lambda \geq 0$. To this end we need two lemmata.

Lemma 1. *Under* A.2, *let u_1 and u_0 be two points of U such that $u_1 < u_0$; let Δ be a point in the domain of $\bar{\lambda}$ such that $\Delta \leq u_0 - u_1$; let k be a real number different from zero such that $k \leq \bar{\lambda}(\Delta)$; and let p be an integer such that $1 \leq p \leq (u_0 - u_1)/\Delta$. Then*

$$\phi(u_0) - \phi(u_1) \geq [\phi(u_0) - \phi(u_0 - \Delta)]\,\frac{e^{kp\Delta} - 1}{e^{k\Delta} - 1}.$$

Proof. One has $u_1 \leq u_0 - p\Delta$. Hence $\phi(u_1) \leq \phi(u_0 - p\Delta)$. Therefore

$$\begin{aligned}\phi(u_0) - \phi(u_1) &\geq [\phi(u_0) - \phi(u_0-\Delta)] + [\phi(u_0-\Delta) - \phi(u_0 - 2\Delta)] + \cdots \\ &\quad + [\phi(u_0 - (p-1)\Delta) - \phi(u_0 - p\Delta)] \\ &\geq [\phi(u_0) - \phi(u_0-\Delta)][1 + e^{k\Delta} + \cdots + e^{k(p-1)\Delta}] \\ &= [\phi(u_0) - \phi(u_0-\Delta)]\,\frac{e^{kp\Delta} - 1}{e^{k\Delta} - 1}.\end{aligned}$$

In a completely similar manner we establish

Lemma 2. *Under* A.2, *let u_0 and u_2 be two points of U such that $u_0 < u_2$; let Δ be a point in the domain of $\bar{\lambda}$; let k be a real number different from zero such that $k \leq \bar{\lambda}(\Delta)$; and let q be an integer such that $q \geq (u_2 - u_0)/\Delta$ and $u_0 + q\Delta \in U$. Then*

$$\phi(u_2) - \phi(u_0) \leq [\phi(u_0 + \Delta) - \phi(u_0)]\,\frac{e^{-kq\Delta} - 1}{e^{-k\Delta} - 1}.$$

Theorem 4. *Under* A.2, *the function* f *is convex if and only if* $\lambda \geq 0$.

Proof. Assume that f is convex. Then ϕ is concave and for every u and Δ, one has

$$\frac{\phi(u)-\phi(u-\Delta)}{\phi(u+\Delta)-\phi(u)} \geq 1.$$

Therefore for every Δ, one has $\bar{\lambda}(\Delta) \geq 0$. Hence $\lambda \geq 0$.

Conversely assume that $\lambda \geq 0$, and consider three points u_0, u_1, and u_2 of U such that $u_1 < u_0 < u_2$. Select a real number $k < 0$. There is an infinite sequence $\Delta_n > 0$ such that $\Delta_n \to 0$ and, for every n, $\bar{\lambda}(\Delta_n) \geq k$.

Denote by p_n the greatest integer $\leq (u_0 - u_1)/\Delta_n$, and by q_n the smallest integer $\geq (u_2 - u_0)/\Delta_n$. By Lemmata 1 and 2, for every n,

$$\phi(u_0) - \phi(u_1) \geq [\phi(u_0) - \phi(u_0 - \Delta_n)] \frac{e^{kp_n\Delta_n} - 1}{e^{k\Delta_n} - 1},$$

$$\phi(u_2) - \phi(u_1) \leq [\phi(u_0 + \Delta_n) - \phi(u_0)] \frac{e^{-kq_n\Delta_n} - 1}{e^{-k\Delta_n} - 1}.$$

Therefore

$$\frac{\phi(u_0)-\phi(u_1)}{\phi(u_2)-\phi(u_1)} \geq \frac{\phi(u_0)-\phi(u_0-\Delta_n)}{\phi(u_0+\Delta_n)-\phi(u_0)} \cdot \frac{1-e^{kp_n\Delta_n}}{e^{-kq_n\Delta_n}-1} \cdot \frac{e^{-k\Delta_n}-1}{1-e^{k\Delta_n}}$$

$$\geq e^{k\Delta_n} \cdot \frac{1-e^{kp_n\Delta_n}}{e^{-kq_n\Delta_n}-1} \cdot e^{-k\Delta_n} = \frac{1-e^{kp_n\Delta_n}}{e^{-kq_n\Delta_n}-1}.$$

As $n \to +\infty$, $p_n\Delta_n \to u_0 - u_1$ and $q_n\Delta_n \to u_2 - u_0$. Hence

$$\frac{\phi(u_0)-\phi(u_1)}{\phi(u_2)-\phi(u_1)} \geq \frac{1-e^{k(u_0-u_1)}}{e^{-k(u_2-u_0)}-1}.$$

Now let $k \to 0$. One obtains

$$\frac{\phi(u_0)-\phi(u_1)}{u_0-u_1} \geq \frac{\phi(u_2)-\phi(u_0)}{u_2-u_0},$$

which implies that ϕ is concave.

We note that if the function f is convex but *not* strictly convex, there is a non-empty open interval on which f is linear, hence a non-empty open interval U_0 on which ϕ is linear. Given any $u \in U_0$, for every Δ small enough, $u + \Delta$ and $u - \Delta$ belong to U_0, hence $\bar{\lambda}(\Delta) = 0$. Therefore $\lambda = 0$.

In the case of a C^2 function it is possible (Theorem 8) to give a simple expression of the convexity index. To prepare for that result we remark

Under A.2, *if* f *is* C^2 *and at a point* x_0 *of* X, $f'(x_0) \neq 0$, *then letting* $u_0 = f(x_0)$, *one has*

$$\lim_{\Delta \to 0} \log\left[\frac{\phi(u_0)-\phi(u_0-\Delta)}{\phi(u_0+\Delta)-\phi(u_0)}\right]^{1/\Delta} = \frac{f''(x_0)}{(f'(x_0))^2}. \tag{7}$$

Proof of (7). Since $f'(x_0) \neq 0$, the function ϕ is locally C^2 at u_0. An application of Taylor's theorem yields

$$\lim_{\Delta \to 0} \log\left[\frac{\phi(u_0) - \phi(u_0 - \Delta)}{\phi(u_0 + \Delta) - \phi(u_0)}\right]^{1/\Delta} = -\frac{\phi''(u_0)}{\phi'(u_0)}.$$

But $\phi = f^{-1}$ yields

$$-\frac{\phi''(u_0)}{\phi'(u_0)} = \frac{f''(x_0)}{(f'(x_0))^2}.$$

Of special interest is the class $\mathcal{H}$ of C^2 functions h, defined on the nonempty open real interval Z, such that for every z, $h'(z) > 0$, and, denoting h^{-1} by ψ,

$$\log\left[\frac{\psi(w) - \psi(w - \Delta)}{\psi(w + \Delta) - \psi(w)}\right]^{1/\Delta}$$

is independent of w and Δ, hence equal to a real number θ. In that case, according to (7), for every z, $h''(z)/(h'(z))^2 = \theta$. Now two functions f and f^* such that $\phi^* = a\phi + b$, where $a > 0$ and b are two real numbers, obviously have the same convexity index. Therefore there is no essential loss of generality in assuming that $0 \in Z$ and in normalizing h in such a way that $h(0) = 0$ and $h'(0) = 1$. By integration one obtains

if $\theta \neq 0$, $h_\theta(z) = -(\log(1 - \theta z))/\theta$ *defined in* $Z_\theta = \{z \in R \mid \theta z < 1\}$;

if $\theta = 0$, $h_0(z) = z$ *defined in* $Z_0 = R$.

Note that if $\theta_1 < \theta_2$ and $0 \neq z \in Z_{\theta_1} \cap Z_{\theta_2}$, one has $h_{\theta_1}(z) < h_{\theta_2}(z)$.

The inverse $\psi_\theta = h_\theta^{-1}$ is defined on R by

$$\psi_\theta(w) = \frac{1 - e^{-\theta w}}{\theta} \quad \text{if} \quad \theta \neq 0; \qquad \psi_0(w) = w.$$

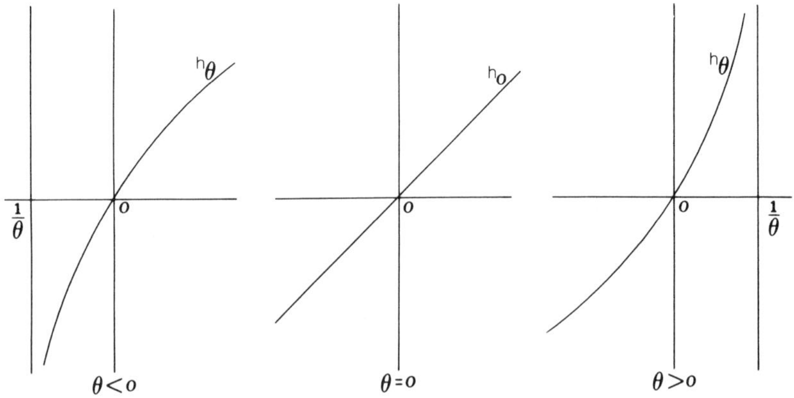

Fig. 7.

The convexity index of h_θ is easily seen to be θ since

$$\left[\frac{\psi_\theta(w)-\psi_\theta(w-\Delta)}{\psi_\theta(w+\Delta)-\psi_\theta(w)}\right]^{1/\Delta}=e^\theta.$$

Some properties of ψ_θ that we will use later on are also noted here. For any w, $\psi_\theta(w)$ is continuous in θ. For $w>0$, $\lim_{\theta\to+\infty}\psi_\theta(w)=0$. For $w<0$, $\lim_{\theta\to+\infty}\psi_\theta(w)=-\infty$. For $w\neq 0$, $\psi_\theta(w)$ is strictly decreasing in θ.

Theorem 5 gives conditions under which in any point x_0 of its domain, the function f is supported from below by a suitable linear transform of h_λ. Before stating and proving it we remark

Under A.2, *if* $\lambda>-\infty$ *and* $f'_-(x_0)$ *and* $f'_+(x_0)$ *exist at a point* x_0 *of* X, *then* $f'_-(x_0)\le f'_+(x_0)$. (8)

Proof of (8). Assume that $f'_-(x_0)>f'_+(x_0)$. Since f is increasing $f'_+(x_0)\ge 0$. Let $u_0=f(x_0)$. Then $0\le\phi'_-(u_0)<\phi'_+(u_0)$, where $\phi'_+(u_0)$ is defined to be $+\infty$ in case $f'_+(x_0)=0$. Moreover

$$0\le\lim_{\Delta\to 0}\frac{\phi(u_0)-\phi(u_0-\Delta)}{\phi(u_0+\Delta)-\phi(u_0)}=\frac{\phi'_-(u_0)}{\phi'_+(u_0)}<1.$$

Consider an arbitrary real number k. For every small enough Δ,

$$\log\left[\frac{\phi(u_0)-\phi(u_0-\Delta)}{\phi(u_0+\Delta)-\phi(u_0)}\right]^{1/\Delta}\le k,$$

hence $\bar{\lambda}(\Delta)\le k$. Therefore $\lambda\le k$. Consequently $\lambda=-\infty$, a contradiction.

Theorem 5. *Under* A.2, *the convexity index* λ *is strictly smaller than* $+\infty$.

If $\lambda>-\infty$ *and* $f'_-(x_0)$ *exists and is finite at a point* x_0 *of* X, *then* $f'_-(x_0)>0$ *and for every* $x\in X$ *such that* $x\le x_0$ *and*

$$\lambda(x-x_0)<\frac{1}{f'_-(x_0)},$$

one has

$$f(x)-f(x_0)\ge h_\lambda[f'_-(x_0)(x-x_0)].$$

If $\lambda>-\infty$ *and* $f'_+(x_0)$ *exists and is strictly positive at a point* x_0 *of* X, *then* $f'_+(x_0)$ *is finite and*

for every $x\in X$ *such that* $x\ge x_0$, *one has*

$$f(x)-f(x_0)\ge h_\lambda[f'_+(x_0)(x-x_0)].$$

Proof. Assume that $\lambda>-\infty$ and $f'_-(x_0)$ exists and is finite at x_0. Choose any $x\in X$ such that $x<x_0$ and let $u=f(x)$ and $u_0=f(x_0)$. Select a real number k such that $0\neq k<\lambda$. There is an infinite sequence $\Delta_n>0$ such that $\Delta_n\to 0$ and, for every n, $\bar{\lambda}(\Delta_n)\ge k$.

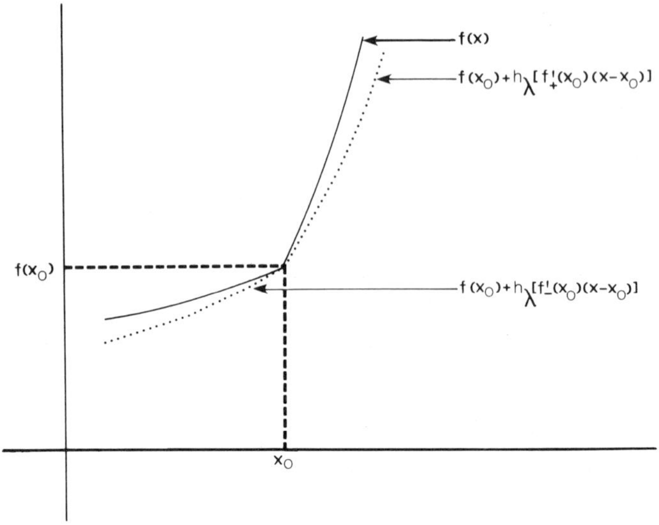

Fig. 8.

Denote by p_n the greatest integer smaller than or equal to $(u_0 - u)/\Delta_n$. By Lemma 1,

$$\phi(u) - \phi(u_0) \le \frac{\phi(u_0 - \Delta_n) - \phi(u_0)}{-\Delta_n} \cdot \frac{1 - e^{kp_n\Delta_n}}{\frac{1}{\Delta_n}(e^{k\Delta_n} - 1)}.$$

As $n \to +\infty$, one has $\Delta_n \to 0$;

$$\frac{\phi(u_0 - \Delta_n) - \phi(u_0)}{-\Delta_n} \to \phi'_-(u_0) = \frac{1}{f'_-(x_0)},$$

which may be $+\infty$; $p_n\Delta_n \to u_0 - u$;

$$\frac{1}{\Delta_n}(e^{k\Delta_n} - 1) \to k.$$

Therefore

$$\phi(u) - \phi(u_0) \le \phi'(u_0) \cdot \frac{1 - e^{k(u_0 - u)}}{k} = \phi'_-(u_0)\psi_k(u - u_0).$$

Since $\psi_k(u - u_0) < 0$, if $\phi'_-(u_0) = +\infty$, one obtains $\phi(u) = -\infty$, a contradiction of the fact that $\phi(u)$ is finite for every $u \in U$. Thus $0 < f'_-(x_0)$.

Next let $k \to \lambda$. If $\lambda = +\infty$, $\psi_k(u - u_0) \to -\infty$, and again $\phi(u) = -\infty$. Thus $\lambda < +\infty$, and, in the limit,

(i) for every $u \in U$ such that $u \le u_0$, $\phi(u) - \phi(u_0) \le \phi'_-(u_0)\psi_\lambda(u - u_0)$.

From (i), for every $x \in X$ such that $x \leq x_0$, one has

$$x - x_0 \leq \frac{1}{f'_-(x_0)} \psi_\lambda[f(x) - f(x_0)].$$

Hence

(i′) $$\psi_\lambda[f(x) - f(x_0)] \geq f'_-(x_0)(x - x_0).$$

Now $f'_-(x_0)(x - x_0)$ belongs to Z_λ if and only if $\lambda f'_-(x_0)(x - x_0) < 1$, i.e., if and only if

$$\lambda(x - x_0) < \frac{1}{f'_-(x_0)}.$$

Therefore from (i′), for every $x \in X$ such that $x \leq x_0$ and $\lambda(x - x_0) < 1/f'_-(x_0)$, one has

$$f(x) - f(x_0) \geq h_\lambda[f'_-(x_0)(x - x_0)].$$

We have shown that if $\lambda > -\infty$ and there is a point x_0 of X at which $f'_-(x_0)$ exists and is finite, then $\lambda < +\infty$. However, according to Lebesgue's theorem (Riesz and Sz.-Nagy 1955, pp. 5–9), the increasing function f has a finite derivative almost everywhere. Therefore $\lambda > -\infty$ implies $\lambda < +\infty$. So, obviously, does $\lambda = -\infty$.

Assume now that $\lambda > -\infty$ and $f'_+(x_0)$ exists and is strictly positive at x_0. In a completely similar manner one can show that for $u \in U$ such that $u > u_0$ and for $0 \neq k < \lambda$, one has

$$\phi(u) - \phi(u_0) \leq \phi'_+(u_0)\psi_k(u - u_0).$$

Since $\psi_k(u - u_0) > 0$, if $\phi'_+(u_0) = 0$, one obtains $\phi(u) \leq \phi(u_0)$, a contradiction of the fact that ϕ is strictly increasing on U. Thus $f'_+(x_0)$ is finite. Letting $k \to \lambda$, one obtains

(ii) for every $u \in U$ such that $u \geq u_0$, $\quad \phi(u) - \phi(u_0) \leq \phi'_+(u_0)\psi_\lambda(u - u_0)$.

From (ii), for every $x \in X$ such that $x \geq x_0$, one has

$$x - x_0 \leq \frac{1}{f'_+(x_0)} \psi_\lambda[f(x) - f(x_0)].$$

Hence

(ii′) $$\psi_\lambda[f(x) - f(x_0)] \geq f'_+(x_0)(x - x_0).$$

Now $f'_+(x_0)(x - x_0)$ belongs to Z_λ if and only if $\lambda f'_+(x_0)(x - x_0) < 1$. This inequality is obviously satisfied if $\lambda \leq 0$. It is also satisfied if $\lambda > 0$, for in this case (ii′) implies

$$\frac{1 - e^{-\lambda(u - u_0)}}{\lambda} \geq f'_+(x_0)(x - x_0),$$

hence

$$\lambda f'_+(x_0)(x - x_0) \leq 1 - e^{-\lambda(u-u_0)} < 1.$$

Therefore from (ii'), for every $x \in X$ such that $x \geq x_0$,

$$f(x) - f(x_0) \geq h_\lambda[f'_+(x_0)(x - x_0)].$$

We now establish two lemmata needed in the proofs of Theorems 6–8.

Lemma 3. *Assume that* A.2 *holds, and that f and g are C^2. The function F is quasiconvex if and only if*

(i) *for every $(x, y) \in X \times Y$, one has $f'(x) \neq 0$, $g'(y) \neq 0$,*

$$\frac{f''(x)}{(f'(x))^2} + \frac{g''(y)}{(g'(y))^2} \geq 0.$$

Proof. Consider $(x_0, y_0) \in X \times Y$ and let

$$\Gamma = \{(x, y) \in X \times Y \mid f(x) + g(y) \leq f(x_0) + g(y_0)\}.$$

One has, for the boundary $\partial\Gamma$ of Γ,

$$\partial\Gamma = \{(x, y) \in X \times Y \mid f(x) + g(y) = f(x_0) + g(y_0)\}.$$

Denote by proj_1 the projection from $X \times Y$ into X. Clearly $\text{proj}_1\, \partial\Gamma$ is a non-empty open real interval, and for every $x \in \text{proj}_1\, \partial\Gamma$, there is a unique point $\gamma(x)$ of Y such that $(x, \gamma(x)) \in \partial\Gamma$.

If $f'(x) \neq 0$ and $g'(y) \neq 0$ everywhere, the function γ is C^2 and one has for every $(x, y) \in \partial\Gamma$,

$$\frac{f''(x)}{(f'(x))^2} + \frac{g''(y)}{(g'(y))^2} = -\gamma''(x)\frac{g'(y)}{(f'(x))^2}.$$

Assume now that F is quasiconvex, then the set Γ is convex and the function γ is concave. By Theorem 3, $f'(x_0) > 0$ and $g'(y_0) > 0$. The concavity of γ implies $\gamma''(x_0) \leq 0$. Therefore (x_0, y_0) satisfies condition (i).

Conversely if (i) is satisfied, one has $\gamma''(x) \leq 0$ for every $x \in \text{proj}_1\, \partial\Gamma$. Therefore the function γ is concave, and the set Γ is convex. Consequently F is quasiconvex.

Lemma 4. *Assume that* A.2 *holds, and that for every $(x_0, y_0) \in X \times Y$, there are two open intervals I and J containing x_0 and y_0 respectively and two strictly increasing functions f^* and g^* defined on I and J respectively such that* (i) *$f^*(x_0) = f(x_0)$ and for every $x \in I$, $f^*(x) \leq f(x)$,* (ii) *$g^*(y_0) = g(y_0)$ and for every $y \in J$, $g^*(y) \leq g(y)$,* (iii) *the function from $I \times J$ to R defined by $(x, y) \mapsto f^*(x) + g^*(y)$ is quasiconvex. Then F is quasiconvex.*

Proof. Consider $(x_0, y_0) \in X \times Y$ and the sets

$$\Gamma_1 = \{(x, y) \in I \times J \mid F(x, y) \leq F(x_0, y_0)\}$$

and

$$\Gamma_2 = \{(x, y) \in I \times J \mid f^*(x) + g^*(y) \leq F(x_0, y_0)\}.$$

Since

$$f^*(x) + g^*(y) \leq f(x) + g(y),$$

one has $\Gamma_1 \subset \Gamma_2$. Since f, g, f^*, g^* are strictly increasing, $(x_0, y_0) \in \partial\Gamma_1 \cap \partial\Gamma_2$. Moreover Γ_2 is convex. Consequently there is through (x_0, y_0) a straight-line supporting Γ_2, hence Γ_1, from above. This implies that the set

$$\Gamma = \{(x, y) \in X \times Y \mid F(x, y) \leq F(x_0, y_0)\}$$

is convex. Hence F is quasiconvex.

In Theorem 6 and in its proof, the function $\bar{\mu}$ and the convexity index μ are associated with g as $\bar{\lambda}$ and λ are associated with f.

Theorem 6. *Under* A.2, *the function F is quasiconvex if and only if $\lambda + \mu \geq 0$ and at every $(x, y) \in X \times Y$, $f'_-(x)$, $f'_+(x)$, $g'_-(y)$, and $g'_+(y)$ exist and are finite.*

There is clearly some redundancy in the assumptions following "if and only if" since $\lambda + \mu \geq 0$ implies that at least one of the two convexity indices is ≥ 0. However, by Theorem 4, under A.2, a function whose convexity index is ≥ 0 is convex, and therefore has finite left and right-derivatives everywhere.

Proof of Theorem 6. Assume first that F is quasiconvex. Consider x, x', x'' in X and y, y', y'' in Y such that $x' < x < x''$, $y'' < y < y'$ and $F(x', y') = F(x, y) = F(x'', y'')$. Since f and g are strictly increasing, the point (x, y) is not strictly below the diagonal of the rectangle in Fig. 9.

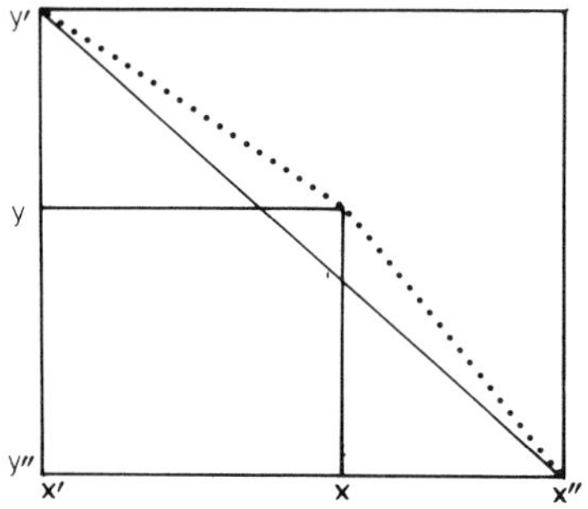

Fig. 9.

Therefore the absolute values of the slopes of the dashed segments satisfy

$$\frac{y'-y}{x-x'} \leq \frac{y-y''}{x''-x}.$$

Hence

$$\frac{x-x'}{x''-x} \cdot \frac{y-y''}{y'-y} \geq 1.$$

Let now u, v and $\Delta > 0$ be such that $u-\Delta$, u, and $u+\Delta$ are in U; $v-\Delta$, v, and $v+\Delta$ are in V. One has

$$\frac{\phi(u)-\phi(u-\Delta)}{\phi(u+\Delta)-\phi(u)} \cdot \frac{\chi(v)-\chi(v-\Delta)}{\chi(v+\Delta)-\chi(v)} \geq 1.$$

Therefore

$$\text{for every } \Delta \in (\text{domain } \bar{\lambda}) \cap (\text{domain } \bar{\mu}), \text{ one has } \bar{\lambda}(\Delta)+\bar{\mu}(\Delta) \geq 0. \quad (9)$$

Since, by Theorem 5, $\lambda < +\infty$ and $\mu < +\infty$, the sum $\lambda+\mu$ is well defined. If one had $\lambda+\mu<0$, there would be λ' and μ' such that $\lambda<\lambda'$, $\mu<\mu'$ and $\lambda'+\mu'<0$. For every Δ small enough, $\bar{\lambda}(\Delta)<\lambda'$ and $\bar{\mu}(\Delta)<\mu'$. Hence $\bar{\lambda}(\Delta)+\bar{\mu}(\Delta)<0$, a contradiction of (8). Therefore $\lambda+\mu \geq 0$. The existence of the finite left and right derivatives of f and g is asserted by Theorem 3.

Assume now that f and g have finite left and right derivatives everywhere and $\lambda+\mu \geq 0$. Since $\lambda < +\infty$ and $\mu < +\infty$, one has $\lambda > -\infty$ and $\mu > -\infty$. Consider $(x_0, y_0) \in X \times Y$.

According to Theorem 5 and (8), $0 < f'_-(x_0) \leq f'_+(x_0)$ and $0 < g'_-(y_0) \leq g'_+(y_0)$. Select two numbers α, β such that

$$f'_-(x_0) \leq \alpha \leq f'_+(x_0) \quad \text{and} \quad g'_-(y_0) \leq \beta \leq g'_+(y_0).$$

By Theorem 5, since h_λ is a strictly increasing function, for every $x \in X$ such that $x \geq x_0$, or such that $x \leq x_0$ and $\lambda(x-x_0)<1/\alpha$, one has $f(x)-f(x_0) \geq h_\lambda[\alpha(x-x_0)]$.

This leads us to define the function $\bar{f}$ and its domain $\bar{X}$ as follows.

If $\lambda \geq 0$, then $\bar{X} = X$. If $\lambda < 0$, then $\bar{X} = (\text{Max}\{x_0 + 1/\alpha\lambda, \text{Inf } X\}, \text{Sup } X)$. In either case, for every $x \in \bar{X}$, $\bar{f}(x) = h_\lambda[\alpha(x-x_0)]$. (10)

Therefore

$$\text{for every } x \in \bar{X}, \quad f(x) \geq f(x_0) + \bar{f}(x).$$

Note that $\bar{f}(x_0) = 0$, and for every $x \in \bar{X}$, $\bar{f}'(x) > 0$ and $\bar{f}''(x)/(\bar{f}'(x))^2 = \lambda$.

Similarly define the function $\bar{g}$ and its domain $\bar{Y}$ as follows.

If $\mu \geq 0$, then $\bar{Y} = Y$. If $\mu < 0$, then $\bar{Y} = (\text{Max}\{y_0 + 1/\beta\mu, \text{Inf } Y\}, \text{Sup } Y)$. In either case, for every $y \in \bar{Y}$, $\bar{g}(y) = h_\mu[\beta(y-y_0)]$. (11)

Therefore

$$\text{for every } y \in \bar{Y},\quad g(y) \geq g(y_0) + \bar{g}(y).$$

As before, $\bar{g}(y_0) = 0$, and for every $y \in \bar{Y}$, $\bar{g}'(y) > 0$ and $\bar{g}''(y)/(\bar{g}'(y))^2 = \mu$.

According to Lemma 3, the function from $\bar{X} \times \bar{Y}$ to R defined by $(x, y) \mapsto f(x_0) + g(y_0) + \bar{f}(x) + \bar{g}(y)$ is quasiconvex. According to Lemma 4, the function F is quasiconvex.

Note that if F is quasiconvex and f is not convex, then $\lambda < 0$ and, by Theorem 6, $\lambda + \mu \geq 0$. Hence $\mu > 0$. Consequently, according to the remark we made after proving Theorem 4, g is strictly convex, a restatement of Theorem 2.

As a consequence of the preceding results, the function F is quasiconvex if and only if the two functions f and g can be separated by a function of the class h_θ in the following sense.

Theorem 7. *Under* A.2, *the function F is quasiconvex if and only if for every $(x_0, y_0) \in X \times Y$, there are three real numbers $\alpha > 0$, $\beta > 0$, and θ and an open interval I containing x_0 such that*

$$\textit{for every } x \in I,\quad g(y_0) - g\left[y_0 - \frac{\alpha}{\beta}(x - x_0)\right] \leq h_\theta[\alpha(x - x_0)] \leq f(x) - f(x_0).$$

The greatest interval I in which both inequalities hold is given by (12).

Proof. Assume first that F is quasiconvex, and consider $(x_0, y_0) \in X \times Y$. By Theorem 3, $0 < f'_-(x_0) \leq f'_+(x_0)$ and $0 < g'_-(y_0) \leq g'_+(y_0)$. By Theorems 5 and 6, $\lambda + \mu \geq 0$, $\lambda > -\infty$, $\mu > -\infty$.

Select two numbers α and β such that

$$f'_-(x_0) \leq \alpha \leq f'_+(x_0) \quad \text{and} \quad g'_-(y_0) \leq \beta \leq g'_+(y_0).$$

For every x such that $y_0 - (\alpha/\beta)(x - x_0) \in Y$, i.e., $x \in x_0 - (\beta/\alpha)(Y - y_0)$, we define

$$\tilde{g}(x) = g(y_0) - g\left[y_0 - \frac{\alpha}{\beta}(x - x_0)\right].$$

Note that $\tilde{g}(x_0) = 0$; $\tilde{g}'_-(x_0) = (\alpha/\beta)g'_+(y_0) \geq \alpha \geq f'_-(x_0)$; $\tilde{g}'_+(x_0) = (\alpha/\beta)g'_-(y_0) \leq \alpha \leq f'_+(x_0)$.

The sets $\bar{X}$, $\bar{Y}$ and the functions $\bar{f}$, $\bar{g}$ are defined as in (10) and (11). For every $y_0 - (\alpha/\beta)(x - x_0) \in \bar{Y}$, one has

$$g\left[y_0 - \frac{\alpha}{\beta}(x - x_0)\right] - g(y_0) \geq \bar{g}\left[y_0 - \frac{\alpha}{\beta}(x - x_0)\right] = h_\mu[-\alpha(x - x_0)].$$

However, $z \in Z_\mu$ implies $-z \in Z_{-\mu}$ and $h_{-\mu}(-z) = -h_\mu(z)$. Consequently for every $x \in x_0 - (\beta/\alpha)(\bar{Y} - y_0)$,

(i) $\qquad \tilde{g}(x) \leq h_{-\mu}[\alpha(x - x_0)].$

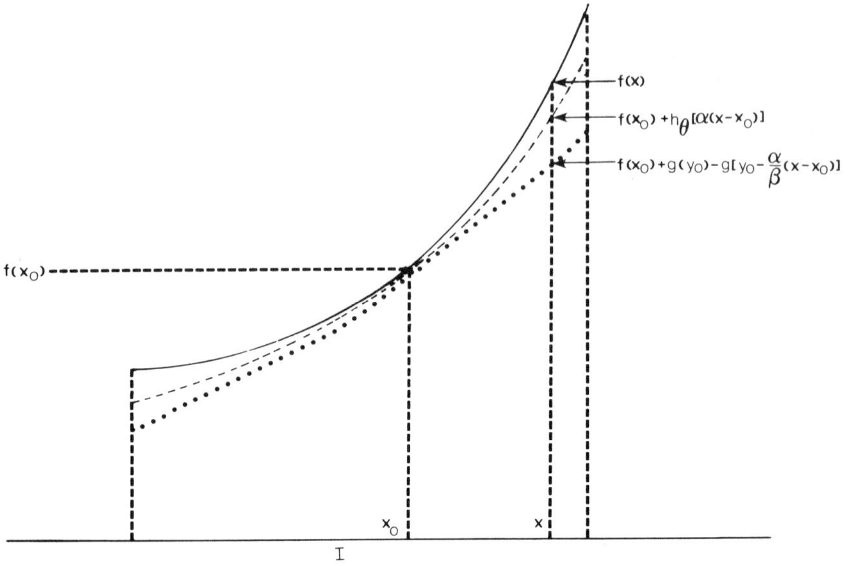

Fig. 10.

Moreover $-\mu \leq \lambda$ and $h_\theta(z)$ is increasing in θ. Therefore if $\alpha(x-x_0) \in Z_\lambda$, i.e., $x \in x_0 + (1/\alpha)Z_\lambda$, and $-\mu \leq \theta \leq \lambda$, one has

(ii) $$h_{-\mu}[\alpha(x-x_0)] \leq h_\theta[\alpha(x-x_0)] \leq h_\lambda[\alpha(x-x_0)].$$

Finally for every $x \in \bar{X}$,

(iii) $$h_\lambda[\alpha(x-x_0)] \leq f(x) - f(x_0).$$

Let

$$I = \left[x_0 - \frac{\beta}{\alpha}(\bar{Y} - y_0)\right] \cap \left[x_0 + \frac{1}{\alpha} Z_\lambda\right] \cap \bar{X}, \tag{12}$$

and note that I is an open interval containing x_0. Summing up (i), (ii) and (iii), one has for every $\theta \in [-\mu, \lambda]$, for every $x \in I$,

$$\tilde{g}(x) \leq h_\theta[\alpha(x-x_0)] \leq f(x) - f(x_0).$$

Conversely assume that for every $(x_0, y_0) \in X \times Y$, there are three real numbers $\alpha > 0$, $\beta > 0$, and θ, and an open interval I containing x_0 such that for every $x \in I$,

$$g(y_0) - g\left[y_0 - \frac{\alpha}{\beta}(x-x_0)\right] \leq h_\theta[\alpha(x-x_0)] \leq f(x) - f(x_0).$$

Let $J = y_0 - (\alpha/\beta)(I - x_0)$. For every $y \in J$, one has

$$g(y_0) - g(y) \leq h_\theta[-\beta(y - y_0)] = -h_{-\theta}[\beta(y - y_0)].$$

Hence

$$\text{for every } y \in J, \quad g(y) - g(y_0) \geq h_{-\theta}[\beta(y - y_0)].$$

Moreover,

$$\text{for every } x \in I, \quad f(x) - f(x_0) \geq h_\theta[\alpha(x - x_0)].$$

Now let $f^*(x) = h_\theta[\alpha(x - x_0)]$ and $g^*(y) = h_{-\theta}[\beta(y - y_0)]$. By Lemma 3, the function from $I \times J$ to R defined by $(x, y) \mapsto f^*(x) + g^*(y)$ is quasiconvex. By Lemma 4, the function F is quasiconvex.

Theorem 8 gives an explicit expression of the convexity index of a C^2 function.

Theorem 8. *Under* A.2, *if the function f is C^2 and for every $x \in X$, $f'(x) \neq 0$, then*

$$\lambda = \operatorname*{Inf}_x \frac{f''(x)}{(f'(x))^2}.$$

Proof. Assume that $\lambda > -\infty$ and select a real number $k < \lambda$. There is an infinite sequence $\Delta_n > 0$ such that

$$\Delta_n \to 0 \quad \text{and} \quad \text{for every } n, \quad \bar{\lambda}(\Delta_n) \geq k.$$

Therefore for every n, for every $u \in U$ such that $u - \Delta_n$ and $u + \Delta_n$ are in U,

$$\log\left[\frac{\phi(u) - \phi(u - \Delta_n)}{\phi(u + \Delta_n) - \phi(u)}\right]^{1/\Delta_n} \geq k.$$

Hence, by (7), for every $x \in X$, $f''(x)/(f'(x))^2 \geq k$. Consequently

$$\operatorname*{Inf}_x \frac{f''(x)}{(f'(x))^2} > \lambda.$$

This inequality also obviously holds if $\lambda = -\infty$.

Conversely assume that

$$\operatorname*{Inf}_x \frac{f''(x)}{(f'(x))^2} > -\infty$$

and let

$$k = \operatorname*{Inf}_x \frac{f''(x)}{(f'(x))^2}.$$

We have defined earlier the function h_{-k} from $Z_{-k} = \{y \in R \mid -ky < 1\}$ to R and noted that its convexity index is $-k$. Moreover for every $y \in Z_{-k}$, $h'_{-k}(y) > 0$ and

$h''_{-k}(y)/(h'_{-k}(y))^2 = -k$. Therefore for every $(x, y) \in X \times Z_{-k}$,

$$\frac{f''(x)}{(f'(x))^2} + \frac{h''_{-k}(y)}{(h'_{-k}(y))^2} \geq 0.$$

According to Lemma 3, the function defined on $X \times Z_{-k}$ by $(x, y) \mapsto f(x) + h_{-k}(y)$ is quasiconvex. Therefore by Theorem 6, $\lambda - k \geq 0$. Hence

$$\lambda \geq \operatorname*{Inf}_x \frac{f''(x)}{(f'(x))^2}.$$

This inequality also obviously holds if

$$\operatorname*{Inf}_x \frac{f''(x)}{(f'(x))^2} = -\infty.$$

The assumption that the intervals X and Y are open was made only to simplify the exposition. All the definitions and results of this section can be extended to the case in which X and Y are non-degenerate, i.e., contain at least two distinct points. It suffices to observe that (1) the convexity index of f on X is equal to the convexity index of the restriction of f to $\operatorname{int} X$, (2) if the restriction of F to $\operatorname{int} X \times \operatorname{int} Y$ is quasiconvex, then F is quasiconvex (Ferland, 1971, Proposition 11). To prove the last assertion we show that if K is a convex set with a non-empty interior, G is a continuous real-valued function on K such that the restriction of G to $\operatorname{int} K$ is quasiconvex, then G is quasiconvex. Let x, y be two points of K, and z be a point of the straight line segment $[x, y]$. Subjecting K to a translation if need be, we assume without loss of generality that the origin of the space belongs to $\operatorname{int} K$. Define

$$x_n = \left(1 - \frac{1}{n}\right)x, \qquad y_n = \left(1 - \frac{1}{n}\right)y, \qquad z_n = \left(1 - \frac{1}{n}\right)z,$$

where n is a positive integer. x_n, y_n and z_n are in $\operatorname{int} K$. The point z_n belongs to $[x_n, y_n]$. By quasiconvexity of G on $\operatorname{int} K$, one has $G(z_n) \leq \operatorname{Max}\{G(x_n), G(y_n)\}$. As $n \to +\infty$, $G(z) \leq \operatorname{Max}\{G(x), G(y)\}$.

The convexity index can readily be defined for a broader class of functions than those we have considered so far in this section. If f is a strictly *decreasing* continuous real-valued function on a non-degenerate real interval X, let $\hat{f}$ be the function defined on $\hat{X} = -X$ by $\hat{f}(x) = f(-x)$. The convexity index $c(f)$ of f is defined as $c(\hat{f})$, the convexity index of $\hat{f}$. If f is a *constant* real-valued function on a non-empty real interval X, the convexity index of f is defined to be $+\infty$.

Consider now the *class* $\mathscr{C}$ of continuous real-valued functions f such that (i) the domain of f is a non-empty real interval partitioned into three intervals $X^{sd} < X^{c} < X^{si}$ (some of which may be empty), and (ii) f is strictly decreasing on X^{sd}, constant on X^{c}, and strictly increasing on X^{si}. According to the results of Section 1, if f and g are non-constant real-valued functions defined on the non-empty open real intervals X and Y respectively, and the function from

$X \times Y$ to R defined by $(x, y) \mapsto f(x) + g(y)$ is quasiconvex, then f and g belong to $\mathscr{C}$. Let f be a function in $\mathscr{C}$ and denote by f^{sd}, f^{c} and f^{si} the restrictions of f to X^{sd}, X^{c} and X^{si} respectively. The convexity indices $c(f^{sd})$, $c(f^{c})$, and $c(f^{si})$ are determined if and only if the corresponding intervals X^{sd}, X^{c}, and X^{si} are non-empty. The convexity index $c(f)$ is defined as the smallest of the convexity indices $c(f^{sd})$, $c(f^{c})$, and $c(f^{si})$ that are determined. With this definition, the extension of the results of this section to the class $\mathscr{C}$ is straightforward.

4. Extensions to higher dimensions and to more than two factors

In this section we make the assumptions:

A.3. *S and T are finite-dimensional real vector spaces; X and Y are open convex subsets of S and T, respectively; f and g are non-constant real-valued functions on X and Y, respectively; the function $F: X \times Y \to R$ defined by $F(x, y) = f(x) + g(y)$ is quasiconvex.*

We first note

Theorem 9. *Under* A.3, *the functions f and g are continuous.*

Proof. Since g is non-constant on Y, there are two points y_1, y_2 of Y such that $g(y_1) \neq g(y_2)$. Let M be the straight line through y_1 and y_2 and let g_M be the restriction of g to $Y \cap M$, which is a convex subset of M open relative to M.

Consider now an arbitrary straight line L in S and let f_L be the restriction of f to $X \cap L$, which is a convex subset of L open relative to L. The function from $(X \cap L) \times (Y \cap M)$ to R defined by $(x, y) \mapsto f_L(x) + g_M(y)$ is quasiconvex. Therefore, by Theorem 1, if f_L is non-constant, it is continuous, while if f_L is constant, it is trivially continuous. Thus for every L, the function f_L is continuous. We shall show that, according to Proposition 4 of Crouzeix (1977) (see also Crouzeix, 1981, Proposition 6), this implies that the quasiconvex function f is continuous. Following Crouzeix,

(i) *f is lower semi-continuous.*

For this one has to show that for every real number k, the set

$$V_k = \{x \in X \mid f(x) \leq k\}$$

is closed relative to X. By quasiconvexity of f, the set V_k is convex. Moreover, for every straight line L in S, the set $V_k \cap L$ is closed relative to X by continuity of f_L. These two properties together imply that V_k is closed relative to X. To see this, consider a point x_0 of X adherent to V_k. Select a point x_1 in the relative interior of V_k. If $x_1 = x_0$, then x_0 is in V_k. If $x_1 \neq x_0$, then every point of the straight line segment $[x_1, x_0)$ is in V_k (Eggleston, 1969, pp. 9–11). Since the intersection of the straight line through x_1 and x_0 with V_k is closed relative to X, the point x_0 is in V_k.

(ii) *f is upper semi-continuous.*

For this one has to show that for every real number k, the set

$$U_k = \{x \in X \mid f(x) < k\}$$

is open. By quasiconvexity of f, the set U_k is convex. Moreover, for every straight line L in S, the set $U_k \cap L$ is open relative to L by continuity of f_L. These two properties together imply that U_k is open. To see this, assume that U_k is not empty and consider a point x_0 of U_k. Let $\{e_1, \ldots, e_m\}$ be a basis of S. For every $i = 1, \ldots, m$, there is $t_i > 0$ such that $x_0 - t_i e_i$ and $x_0 + t_i e_i$ belong to U_k. The convex hull of the $2m$ points obtained in this manner is a neighborhood of x_0, and is contained in the convex set U_k. Hence f is continuous.

We also note

Theorem 10. *Under* A.3, *if f is not convex, then g has property* (P) *of Theorem* 2.

Proof. If f is not convex, there is a straight line L in S such that the restriction f_L of f to $X \cap L$ is not convex. Let then y_1, y_2 be two points of Y such that $g(y_1) \neq g(y_2)$, and denote by M the straight line through y_1 and y_2, and by g_M the restriction of g to $Y \cap M$. By Theorem 2, the function g_M has property (P).

For every $i = 1, \ldots, m \geq 2$, let now S_i be a finite-dimensional real vector space, X_i be an open convex subset of S_i, f_i be a non-constant real-valued frunction on X_i, and assume that the function $f: \times_{i=1}^{m} X_i \to R$ defined by $x \mapsto f(x) = \sum_{i=1}^{m} f_i(x_i)$ is quasiconvex. By Theorem 9, every function f_i is continuous, and by Theorem 10, if a certain function f_j is not convex, then for every $i \neq j$, the function f_i has property (P) of Theorem 2.

Our next purpose is to extend the definition of the convexity index given in Section 3. Let K be a non-empty convex subset of a finite-dimensional real vector space, and G be a real-valued function on K such that for every straight line D intersecting K, the restriction G_D of G to $D \cap K$ belongs to the class $\mathscr{C}$ defined at the end of Section 3. By definition, the convexity index $c(G)$ of G is

$$c(G) = \operatorname*{Inf}_{D} c(G_D),$$

where the Inf is defined over the set of straight lines intersecting K.

We note that f and g satisfy all the conditions imposed on G.

Let L be a straight line in S intersecting X and such that f_L is not constant. Let M be a straight line in T intersecting Y and such that g_M is not constant. According to Theorem 6, $c(f_L) + c(g_M) \geq 0$. Therefore $c(f)$ and $c(g)$ are both finite and satisfy

$$c(f)+c(g)\geq 0.$$

Theorem 11. *Assume that* A.3 *holds, and that f and g are* C^2. *If* $c(f)+c(g)>0$, *then*

$$\frac{1}{c(F)}=\frac{1}{c(f)}+\frac{1}{c(g)}.$$

If $c(f)+c(g)=0$ *and* $c(f)\cdot c(g)\neq 0$, *then* $c(F)=-\infty$. *If* $c(f)=0=c(g)$, *then* $c(F)=0$.

In the case covered by the second sentence, if one of the two convexity indices, say $c(f)$, vanishes, the other is strictly positive. Thus $1/c(f)$ is infinite while $1/c(g)$ is finite. Therefore $1/c(F)$ is infinite and $c(F)=0$.

Proof of Theorem 11. We assume at first that X and Y are open real intervals and f and g are strictly increasing. Consider an arbitrary point $(x_0, y_0)\in X\times Y$ and an arbitrary straight line D through (x_0, y_0) with slope σ. If σ is finite, the restriction F_D of F to D satisfies $F_D(x, y)=f(x)+g[y_0+\sigma(x-x_0)]$ which we denote by $t(x; x_0, y_0, \sigma)$. If σ is infinite, the restriction F_D of F to D satisfies $F_D(x, y)=f(x_0)+g(y)$. Since t is C^2, by Theorem 8 we have if σ is finite and (x_0, y_0, σ) are such that $t'(x_0; x_0, y_0, \sigma)\neq 0$,

$$c(F)=\operatorname*{Inf}_{x_0,y_0,\sigma}\frac{t''(x_0; x_0, y_0, \sigma)}{(t'(x_0; x_0, y_0, \sigma))^2}.$$

To cover the case in which σ is infinite, it is sufficient to check that

$$\operatorname*{Inf}_{\sigma\text{ finite}}\frac{t''(x_0; x_0, y_0, \sigma)}{(t'(x_0; x_0, y_0, \sigma))^2}\leq\frac{g''(y_0)}{(g'(y_0))^2}$$

which we will do below in every case.

Now

$$t'(x_0; x_0, y_0, \sigma)=f'(x_0)+\sigma g'(y_0)$$

and

$$t''(x_0; x_0, y_0, \sigma)=f''(x_0)+\sigma^2 g''(y_0).$$

To lighten notation we let

$$\gamma(x_0, y_0, \sigma)=\frac{t''(x_0; x_0, y_0, \sigma)}{(t'(x_0; x_0, y_0, \sigma))^2},$$

$a'=f'(x_0)$, $a''=f''(x_0)$, $b'=g'(y_0)$, $b''=g''(y_0)$. Thus

$$\text{if } b'\sigma+a'\neq 0,\quad \gamma(x_0, y_0, \sigma)=\frac{b''\sigma^2+a''}{(b'\sigma+a')^2}. \tag{13}$$

For a given point (x_0, y_0), we seek the infimum of this ratio as σ varies, recalling that by Theorem 3, $a' > 0$ and $b' > 0$, and by Lemma 3,

$$\frac{a''}{(a')^2} + \frac{b''}{(b')^2} \geq 0.$$

The case in which

$$\frac{a''}{(a')^2} + \frac{b''}{(b')^2} > 0.$$

A routine study of the function

$$\sigma \mapsto \frac{b''\sigma^2 + a''}{(b'\sigma + a')^2}$$

shows that its minimum is

$$\frac{\dfrac{a''}{(a')^2} \cdot \dfrac{b''}{(b')^2}}{\dfrac{a''}{(a')^2} + \dfrac{b''}{(b')^2}}.$$

Moreover this number is indeed $\leq b''/(b')^2$.

The case in which

$$\frac{a''}{(a')^2} + \frac{b''}{(b')^2} = 0.$$

If $a'' \neq 0 \neq b''$, then

$$\frac{b''\sigma^2 + a''}{(b'\sigma + a')^2} = \frac{b''}{(b')^2} \cdot \frac{b'\sigma - a'}{b'\sigma + a'}.$$

Letting σ tend to $-a'/b'$ on the right if $b'' > 0$, on the left if $b'' < 0$, one obtains

$$\operatorname*{Inf}_{\sigma} \frac{b''\sigma^2 + a''}{(b'\sigma + a')^2} = -\infty.$$

If $a'' = 0 = b''$, then for every σ,

$$\frac{b''\sigma^2 + a''}{(b'\sigma + a')^2} = 0.$$

Therefore

$$\operatorname*{Min}_{\sigma} \frac{b''\sigma^2 + a''}{(b'\sigma + a')^2} = 0,$$

which is indeed $\leq b''/(b')^2 = 0$.

In the following we appeal to the properties of the function

$$(u, v) \mapsto e(u, v) = \frac{uv}{u + v}$$

defined on $H = \{(u, v) \in R^2 \mid u + v > 0\}$.

The function e is continuous and strictly increasing in u and in v. Moreover let $(u_0, v_0) \in \partial H$. If $u_0 \neq 0 \neq v_0$, then as (u, v) in H tends to (u_0, v_0), $e(u, v) \to -\infty$. If $u_0 = 0 = v_0$, then as u tends to 0 on the right and v tends to 0 on the right in such a way that $(u, v) \in H$, one has $e(u, v) \to 0$ because $e(u, v) < u + v$.

We now distinguish two cases.

Case 1: $c(f) + c(g) > 0$.

For any $(x, y) \in X \times Y$, one has

$$\frac{f''(x)}{(f'(x))^2} \geq c(f)$$

and

$$\frac{g''(y)}{(g'(y))^2} \geq c(g),$$

hence

$$\frac{f''(x)}{(f'(x))^2} + \frac{g''(y)}{(g'(y))^2} > 0.$$

According to the above

$$\operatorname*{Inf}_{\sigma} \gamma(x, y, \sigma) = \frac{\dfrac{f''(x)}{(f'(x))^2} \cdot \dfrac{g''(y)}{(g'(y))^2}}{\dfrac{f''(x)}{(f'(x))^2} + \dfrac{g''(y)}{(g'(y))^2}}.$$

By continuity and monotony of the function e,

$$c(F) = \operatorname*{Inf}_{x,y} \operatorname*{Inf}_{\sigma} \gamma(x, y, \sigma) = \frac{\operatorname*{Inf}_{x} \dfrac{f''(x)}{(f'(x))^2} \cdot \operatorname*{Inf}_{y} \dfrac{g''(y)}{(g'(y))^2}}{\operatorname*{Inf}_{x} \dfrac{f''(x)}{(f'(x))^2} + \operatorname*{Inf}_{y} \dfrac{g''(y)}{(g'(y))^2}} = \frac{c(f) \cdot c(g)}{c(f) + c(g)}.$$

Case 2: $c(f) + c(g) = 0$.

Two subcases have to be considered.

(i) $c(f) \neq 0 \neq c(g)$. There is a sequence $(x_n, y_n) \in X \times Y$ such that $f''(x_n)/(f'(x_n))^2$ tends to $c(f)$, and $g''(y_n)/(g'(y_n))^2$ tends to $c(g)$. If for some n,

$$\frac{f''(x_n)}{(f'(x_n))^2} + \frac{g''(y_n)}{(g'(y_n))^2} = 0,$$

then

$$\frac{f''(x_n)}{(f'(x_n))^2} = c(f) \quad \text{and} \quad \frac{g''(y_n)}{(g'(y_n))^2} = c(g).$$

According to the above, $\operatorname{Inf}_\sigma \gamma(x_n, y_n, \sigma) = -\infty$. Hence $c(F) = -\infty$. If for every n,

$$\frac{f''(x_n)}{(f'(x_n))^2} + \frac{g''(y_n)}{(g'(y_n))^2} > 0,$$

then according to the above,

$$\operatorname*{Inf}_{\sigma} \gamma(x_n, y_n, \sigma) = \frac{\dfrac{f''(x_n)}{(f'(x_n))^2} \cdot \dfrac{g''(y_n)}{(g'(y_n))^2}}{\dfrac{f''(x_n)}{(f'(x_n))^2} + \dfrac{g''(y_n)}{(g'(y_n))^2}}.$$

Moreover as $n \to +\infty$, the last ratio tends to $-\infty$. Hence again $c(F) = -\infty$. In summary, in subcase (i), $c(F) = -\infty$.

(ii) $c(f) = 0 = c(g)$. Consider an arbitrary $(x, y) \in X \times Y$. One has $f''(x) \geq 0$ and $g''(y) \geq 0$. According to (13), for every σ, one has $\gamma(x, y, \sigma) \geq 0$. Therefore $c(F) \geq 0$. Moreover there is a sequence $(x_n, y_n) \in X \times Y$ such that $f''(x_n)/(f'(x_n))^2$ tends to 0, and $g''(y_n)/(g'(y_n))^2$ tends to 0. If for some n,

$$\frac{f''(x_n)}{(f'(x_n))^2} + \frac{g''(y_n)}{(g'(y_n))^2} = 0,$$

then $f''(x_n) = 0 = g''(y_n)$, and by (9), $\gamma(x_n, y_n, \sigma) = 0$ for every σ. Hence $c(F) = 0$. If for every n,

$$\frac{f''(x_n)}{(f'(x_n))^2} + \frac{g''(y_n)}{(g'(y_n))^2} > 0,$$

then

$$\operatorname*{Inf}_{\sigma} \gamma(x_n, y_n, \sigma) = \frac{\dfrac{f''(x_n)}{(f'(x_n))^2} \cdot \dfrac{g''(y_n)}{(g'(y_n))^2}}{\dfrac{f''(x_n)}{(f'(x_n))^2} + \dfrac{g''(y_n)}{(g'(y_n))^2}}.$$

When $n \to +\infty$, the last ratio tends to 0. Hence again $c(F) = 0$. In summary, in subcase (ii), $c(F) = 0$.

This concludes the proof in the case in which X and Y are open real intervals and f and g are strictly increasing. The preceding results hold as well if f and g are no longer restricted to be strictly increasing. In that case f and g belong to the class $\mathscr{C}$ defined at the end of Section 3 and the definition of the convexity indices $c(f)$ and $c(g)$ makes the extension immediate.

Finally we consider the case in which X and Y are open convex subsets of finite-dimensional real vector spaces. In the remainder of this proof, L denotes a straight line in S intersecting X; M denotes a straight line in T intersecting Y; K denotes the product $L \times M$; F_K denotes the restriction of F to K; L_n denotes a sequence such that $c(f_{L_n})$ tends to $c(f)$; M_n denotes a sequence such that $c(g_{M_n})$ tends to $c(g)$.

As we noted before stating Theorem 11, one has $c(f) + c(g) \geq 0$.

The case in which $c(f) + c(g) > 0$.

Consider a straight line D in $S \times T$ intersecting $X \times Y$. There are L and M such that $D \subset K$. One has $c(f_L) + c(g_M) > 0$, hence

$$c(F_D) \geq c(F_K) = \frac{c(f_L) \cdot c(g_M)}{c(f_L) + c(g_M)} \geq \frac{c(f) \cdot c(g)}{c(f) + c(g)}.$$

Consequently

$$c(F) \geq \frac{c(f) \cdot c(g)}{c(f) + c(g)}.$$

Consider now the sequences L_n, M_n, and K_n. One has

$$c(F_{K_n}) = \frac{c(f_{L_n}) \cdot c(g_{M_n})}{c(f_{L_n}) + c(g_{M_n})}.$$

As $n \to +\infty$, $c(F_{K_n})$ tends to

$$\frac{c(f) \cdot c(g)}{c(f) + c(g)}.$$

However $c(F) \leq c(F_{K_n})$. Hence

$$c(F) = \frac{c(f) \cdot c(g)}{c(f) + c(g)}.$$

The case in which $c(f) + c(g) = 0$.

Two subcases have to be considered.

(i) $c(f) \neq 0 \neq c(g)$. Let L_n, M_n, K_n be as above. If for some n, $c(f_{L_n}) + c(g_{M_n}) = 0$, then $c(f_{L_n}) = c(f)$ and $c(g_{M_n}) = c(g)$. Consequently $c(F_{K_n}) = -\infty$. Hence $c(F) = -\infty$. If for every n, $c(f_{L_n}) + c(g_{M_n}) > 0$, then

$$c(F_{K_n}) = \frac{c(f_{L_n}) \cdot c(g_{M_n})}{c(f_{L_n}) + c(g_{M_n})}.$$

As $n \to +\infty$, $c(F_{K_n})$ tends to $-\infty$. Hence again $c(F) = -\infty$.

(ii) $c(f) = 0 = c(g)$. Let D be a straight line in $S \times T$ intersecting $X \times Y$. There are L and M such that $D \subset K$. If $c(f_L) + c(g_M) > 0$, then

$$c(F_K) = \frac{c(f_L) \cdot c(g_M)}{c(f_L) + c(g_M)} \geq 0.$$

If $c(f_L) + c(g_M) = 0$, then $c(f_L) = 0 = c(g_M)$ and $c(F_K) = 0$. In either case, $c(F_D) \geq c(F_K) \geq 0$. Consequently $c(F) \geq 0$.

Let now L_n, M_n, K_n be as above. If for some n, $c(f_{L_n}) + c(g_{M_n}) = 0$, then $c(f_{L_n}) = 0 = c(g_{M_n})$. Consequently $c(F_{K_n}) = 0$. Hence $c(F) = 0$. If for every n, $c(f_{L_n}) + c(g_{M_n}) > 0$, then

$$c(F_{K_n}) = \frac{c(f_{L_n}) \cdot c(g_{M_n})}{c(f_{L_n}) + c(g_{M_n})}.$$

As $n \to +\infty$, $c(F_{K_n})$ tends to 0. Hence again $c(F) = 0$.

For every $i = 1, \ldots, m \geq 2$, let S_i be a finite-dimensional real vector space, X_i be an open convex subset of S_i, f_i be a C^2 non-constant, real-valued function on X_i such that the restriction of f_i to every straight line intersecting X_i belongs to the class $\mathscr{C}$. Define the function $f: \times_{i=1}^{m} X_i \to R$ by $x \mapsto f(x) = \sum_{i=1}^{m} f_i(x_i)$.

Theorem 11 permits a complete characterization of the functions f that are quasiconvex.

Consider first the case of two factors S_1 and S_2. As we noted before stating Theorem 11, if the function f is quasiconvex, one has $c(f_1)+c(f_2)\geq 0$. Conversely assume that $c(f_1)+c(f_2)\geq 0$. For $i=1,2$, let L_i be a straight line in S_i intersecting X_i. Denote by $f_{i \cdot L_i}$ the restriction of f_i to L_i. One has $c(f_{1 \cdot L_1})+c(f_{2 \cdot L_2})\geq 0$, and by Theorem 6, the restriction of f to $L_1 \times L_2$ is quasiconvex. Let D be a straight line in $S_1 \times S_2$ intersecting $X_1 \times X_2$. Choose L_1 and L_2 such that $D \subset L_1 \times L_2$. The restriction of f to D is quasiconvex. Therefore f is quasiconvex. Summing up, f is quasiconvex if and only if $c(f_1)+c(f_2)\geq 0$.

Consider now an arbitrary number $m \geq 2$ of factors. Two cases must be distinguished.

(a) If f is convex (equivalently if $c(f)\geq 0$), then for every i, f_i is convex, and $c(f_i)\geq 0$. Conversely if for every i, $c(f_i)\geq 0$, then every f_i is convex, and f is convex.

(b) If f is quasiconvex but not convex (hence $c(f)<0$), then there is j for which f_j is not convex, hence $c(f_j)<0$. For every $i \neq j$, f_i is convex, hence $c(f_i)\geq 0$. Let $I=\{1,\dots,m\}\smallsetminus\{j\}$, and f_I be the function $\times_{i\in I} X_i \to R$ defined by $x \mapsto f_I(x)=\sum_{i\in I} f_i(x_i)$. According to the preceding paragraph $c(f_j)+c(f_I)\geq 0$. Therefore $c(f_I)>0$. Consequently by Theorem 11, $c(f_i)>0$ for every $i \in I$, and

$$\frac{1}{c(f_I)}=\sum_{i\in I}\frac{1}{c(f_i)}.$$

However, $c(f_I)\geq -c(f_j)$ implies

$$\frac{1}{c(f_I)}\leq -\frac{1}{c(f_j)}.$$

Hence

$$\frac{1}{c(f)}=\sum_{i=1}^{m}\frac{1}{c(f_i)}\leq 0.$$

Conversely assume that for some j, $c(f_j)<0$; for every $i\neq j$, $c(f_i)>0$; and

$$\sum_{i=1}^{m}\frac{1}{c(f_i)}\leq 0.$$

Then

$$\frac{1}{c(f_I)}=\sum_{i\in I}\frac{1}{c(f_i)},$$

and

$$\frac{1}{c(f_I)}+\frac{1}{c(f_j)}\leq 0.$$

Hence $c(f_I)+c(f_j)\geq 0$, and f is quasiconvex.

Summing up, f is quasiconvex if and only if either (1) for every i, $c(f_i) \geq 0$, or (2) for some j, $c(f_j) < 0$; for every $i \neq j$, $c(f_i) > 0$; and

$$\sum_{i=1}^{m} \frac{1}{c(f_i)} \leq 0.$$

Acknowledgment

The work of G. Debreu was done partly at the Cowles Foundation for Research in Economics at Yale University in 1976, and thereafter partly at the University of Bonn under the auspices of the Alexander von Humboldt Foundation, and partly at the University of California, Berkeley, under grants of the National Science Foundation. The work of T.C. Koopmans was done at the Cowles Foundation under successive grants of the National Science Foundation, and was presented in an early form to a Symposium on Mathematical Methods of Economics at the Institute of Mathematics of the Polish Academy of Sciences (IMPAN), in Warsaw in the summer of 1972. The support or hospitality of all these institutions is gratefully acknowledged. We also wish to thank V.P. Crawford, W.E. Diewert, G. Heal, R.E. Kihlstrom, A. Mas-Colell, and R.S. Russell for several items in our bibliography, and D. Brown, J.P. Crouzeix, R. Howe, K. Vind, and an anonymous referee for valuable observations.

In particular, Karl Vind has pointed out to us that Thorlund-Petersen (1980) has independently obtained the result that appears in our paper as Theorem 2, and, from slightly stronger assumptions, the result that appears as the first sentence of Theorem 3.

In addition we have received four papers by Lindberg (1980a, b, c, 1981), all written independently of ours, and dealing with some of the problems that we treat here by means of r-convex functions (Avriel, 1972).

References

M. Aoki, "An investment planning process for an economy with increasing returns", *Review of Economic Studies* 38 (1971) 273–280.

K.J. Arrow, "Le rôle des valeurs boursières pour la répartition la meilleure des risques", *Econométrie*, Paris, Centre National de la Recherche Scientifique (1953) 41–48. Translated as "The role of securities in the optimal allocation of risk-bearing", *Review of Economic Studies* 31 (1964) 91–96.

K.J. Arrow and A.C. Enthoven, "Quasi-concave programming", *Econometrica* 29 (1961) 779–800.

M. Avriel, "r-convex functions", *Mathematical Programming* 2 (1972) 309–323.

C. Blackorby, R. Davidson and D. Donaldson, "A homiletic exposition of the expected utility hypothesis", *Economica* 44 (1977) 351–358.

J.C. Cox, "A theorem on additively-separable quasi-concave functions", *Journal of Economic Theory* 6 (1973) 210–212.

J.P. Crouzeix, "Conjugacy in quasi-convex analysis", in: A. Auslander, ed., *Convex analysis and its applications* (Springer-Verlag, Berlin, 1977) pp. 66–99.

J.P. Crouzeix, "Continuity and differentiability properties of quasiconvex functions on R^n", in: S. Schaible and W.T. Ziemba, eds., *Generalized concavity in optimization and economics* (Academic Press, New York, 1981).
G. Debreu, "Topological methods in cardinal utility theory", in: K.J. Arrow, S. Karlin and P. Suppes, eds., *Mathematical methods in the social sciences*, 1959 (Stanford University Press, Stanford, CA, 1960) pp. 16–26.
E. Dierker, C. Fourgeaud and W. Neuefeind, "Increasing returns to scale and productive systems", *Journal of Economic Theory* 13 (1976) 428–438.
H.G. Eggleston, *Convexity* (Cambridge University Press, London, 1969).
W. Fenchel, "Convex cones, sets, and functions", Lecture notes, Department of Mathematics, Princeton University (Princeton, NJ, 1953).
J.A. Ferland, "Quasiconvex and pseudoconvex functions on solid convex sets", Dissertation, Stanford University (Stanford, CA, 1971).
C. Fourgeaud, B. Lenclud and P. Sentis, "Equilibre, optimum et décentralisation dans un cas de rendement croissant", *Cahiers du Séminaire d'Econométrie*, Centre National de la Recherche Scientifique, Paris, 15 (1974) 29–46.
W.M. Gorman, "The concavity of additive utility functions", Research Memorandum, The University of North Carolina (1970).
J. Green, "Direct additivity and consumers' behaviour", *Oxford Economic Papers* 13 (1961) 132–136.
H.J. Greenberg and W.P. Pierskalla, "A review of quasi-convex functions", *Operations Research* 19 (1971) 1553–1570.
B. Grodal, "Some further results on integral representation of utility functions", unpublished manuscript, Institute of Economics, University of Copenhagen (Copenhagen, 1978).
R. Guesnerie, "Pareto optimality in non-convex economies", *Econometrica* 43 (1975) 1–29.
J. Hirshleifer, "Investment decision under uncertainty: Choice-theoretic approaches", *Quarterly Journal of Economics* 79 (1965) 509–536.
J.L. Kelley, *General topology* (Van Nostrand Reinhold, New York, 1955).
T.C. Koopmans, "If $f(x)+g(y)$ is quasi-convex, at least one of $f(x)$, $g(y)$ is convex", Mimeographed, Yale University (New Haven, CT, 1971).
J.J. Laffont, "Une note sur la compatibilité entre rendements croissants et concurrence parfaite", *Revue d'Economie Politique* 82 (1972) 1188–1193.
P.O. Lindberg, "On classes of quasiconvex functions on R, closed under addition and translation", unpublished manuscript, Department of Mathematics, Royal Institute of Technology (Stockholm, 1980a).
P.O. Lindberg, "On r-convex functions", unpublished manuscript, Department of Mathematics, Royal Institute of Technology (Stockholm, 1980b).
P.O. Lindberg, "On separable quasiconcave functions", unpublished manuscript, Department of Mathematics, Royal Institute of Technology (Stockholm, 1980c).
P.O. Lindberg, "A class of convexifiable functions", in: S. Schaible and W.T. Ziemba, eds., *Generalized concavity in optimization and economics* (Academic Press, New York, 1981).
T. Rader, *Theory of microeconomics* (Academic Press, New York, 1972).
F. Riesz and B. Sz.-Nagy, *Functional analysis* (Ungar, New York, 1955).
A.W. Roberts and D.E. Varberg, *Convex functions* (Academic Press, New York, 1973).
R.W. Shephard, *Cost and production functions* (Princeton University Press, Princeton, NJ, 1953).
E.E. Slutsky, "Sulla teoria del bilancio del consumatore", *Giornale degli economisti* 51 (1915) 1–26. Translated as "On the theory of the budget of the consumer", in: *Readings in price theory*, American Economic Association (Richard Irwin, 1952) pp. 27–56.
J. Stoer and C. Witzgall, *Convexity and optimization in finite dimensions I* (Springer-Verlag, Berlin, 1970).
L. Thorlund-Petersen, "Concave, additive utility representations and fair division of a random income", unpublished manuscript, Institute of Economics, University of Copenhagen (Copenhagen, 1980).
M.E. Yaari, "A note on separability and quasi-concavity", *Econometrica* 45 (1977) 1183–1186.
M.E. Yaari, "Separably concave utilities or the principle of diminishing eagerness to trade", *Journal of Economic Theory* 18 (1978) 102–118.

Publications of Tjalling C. Koopmans, 1969–1985

Asterisk indicates inclusion in present volume.

* Note on a Social System Composed of Hierarchies with Overlapping Personnel. *Orbis Economicus* 13 no. 3/4 (1969) (special issue in honor of P. de Wolff), pp. 61–72.

* Maximizing Stationary Utility in a Constant Technology (with Richard Beals). *SIAM Journal of Applied Mathematics* 17, no. 5 (1969), pp. 1001–1015.

* On the Description and Comparison of Economic Systems (with John Michael Montias). In *Comparison of Economic Systems: Theoretical and Methodological Approaches*, ed. Alexander Eckstein. Berkeley: University of California Press, 1971.

A Model of a Continuing State with Scarce Capital. *Zeitschrift für Nationalökonomie* suppl. 1, 1971, pp. 11–22.

* Representation of Preference Orderings with Independent Components of Consumption. In *Decision and Organization: A Volume in Honor of Jacob Marschak*, ed. C. B. McGuire and Roy Radner. Amsterdam: North-Holland, 1972.

* Representation of Preference Orderings Over Time. In *Decision and Organization: A Volume in Honor of Jacob Marschak*, ed. C. B. McGuire and Roy Radner. Amsterdam: North-Holland, 1972.

* On the Definition and Computation of a Capital Stock Invariant Under Optimization (with Terje Hansen). *Journal of Economic Theory* 5, no. 3 (1972), pp. 487–523.

* Some Observations on 'Optimal' Economic Growth and Exhaustible Resources. In *Economic Structure and Development: Essays in Honour of Jan Tinbergen*, ed. H. C. Bos, H. Linneman, and P. de Wolff. Amsterdam: North-Holland, 1973.

Ways of Looking at Future Economic Growth, Resource and Energy Use. In *Energy: Demand, Conservation, and Institutional Problems*, ed. M. S. Macrakis. Cambridge, Mass.: MIT Press, 1974.

* Is the Theory of Competitive Equilibrium With It? *American Economic Review* 64, no. 2 (1974), pp. 325–329.

* Proof for a Case where Discounting Advances the Doomsday. *Review of Economic Studies,* Symposium on the Economics of Exhaustible Resources, 1974, pp. 117–120.

* Concepts of Optimality and Their Uses. Nobel Lecture, December 11, 1975, Stockholm. In *Les Prix Nobel en 1975* (Stockholm: Nobel Foundation, 1976). Reprinted in *American Economic Review* 67, no. 3 (1977), pp. 261–274; *Mathematical Programming* 11, no. 3 (1976), pp. 212–228; *Scandinavian Journal of Economics* 78, no. 4 (1976), pp. 542–560.

Analytical Aspects of Policy Studies. In Proceedings of 1976 IIASA Conference, vol. 1, pp. 213–231.

* Examples of Production Relations Based on Microdata. In *The Microeconomic Foundations of Macroeconomics,* ed. G. C. Harcourt. London: Macmillan, 1977.

Energy Modeling for an Uncertain Future (with Robert Litan, John Weyant, and many others). Report of Modeling Resource Group, Synthesis Panel, Committee on Nuclear and Alternative Energy Systems (CONAES), National Research Council. Washington, D.C.: National Academy of Sciences, 1978.

* Economics Among the Sciences. Presidential address, American Economic Association. *American Economic Review* 69, no. 1 (1979), pp. 1–13.

* Alternative Futures With or Without Constraints on the Energy Technology Mix. In *Directions in Energy Policy: A Comprehensive Approach to Energy Resource Decision-Making,* ed. B. Kurşunoğlu and A. Perlmutter. Cambridge, Mass.: Ballinger, 1978.

* The Transition from Exhaustible to Renewable or Inexhaustible Resources. In *Economic Growth and Resources, volume 3: Natural Resources,* ed. C. Bliss and M. Boserup. London: Macmillan, 1980.

Projecting Economic Aspects of Alternative Futures. In *Global Resources: Perspectives and Alternatives,* ed. Clair N. McRostie. Baltimore: University Park Press, 1980.

* Additively Decomposed Quasiconvex Functions (with Gerard Debreu). *Mathematical Programming* 24, no. 1 (1982), pp. 1–38.

Constancy and Constant Differences of Price Elasticities of Demand (with Hirofumi Uzawa). In [*title to be inserted later*], *Essays in Honor of Leonid Hurwicz,* ed. John S. Chipman, Daniel McFadden, and Marcel K. Richter. Minneapolis: University of Minnesota Press, 1985.

Index

Acid rain, 254
Actions, 31–32, 35
 informational and effective, 59–63
 system-bound, 56–57
"Acts of God," 62
Additive decomposition, of a function, 273–310
Adelman, I., 205
Adjustment processes, 183–184
Aggregator function, 117
Air quality, 77, 247
Anderson, K., 173n.
Aoki, M., 276, 309
Apter, D., 56n.
Arrow, K. J., 83n., 96n., 122, 182–183, 202, 275–276, 309
Assignment, 69, 71–72, 74
Associations, 41–42
Aumann, R. J., 83n., 122, 183
Autarky, organizational, 75–76
Automobile emission controls, 238, 247
Avriel, M., 309

Barnett, H. J., 173, 270
Barone, E., 194
Base case, 253
Bausch, A., 39n., 193n.
Beals, R., 197n.
Bienstock, G., 73n.
Blaschke, W., 90, 95, 122
Blackorby, C., 276, 309
Blitzer, C. R., 205
Bol, G., 90, 95, 122
Block, W. A., 177
Brumberg, R., 45n.

Capital
 aggregation of, 209–211
 depreciation of, 14–15
 marginal productivity of, 199, 200
Capital cost levels, 241
Capital index, 209–211
Capital model, 199–201
 discounting in, 166, 175–177
 example of, 164–166
 and exhaustible resources, 171–178
Capital paths
 feasible, 14, 22, 24, 139
 optimal, 17–25, 176–177, 215–216
Capital program, 13
Capital saturation, 165–166, 198
Capital stock
 and discount rate, 210–211, 226–236
 initial, 197, 265
 invariant, 125–161, 184, 210, 215, 224–226, 233–236
 and one-period problem, 130–133
 prolific, 139
 reproducible, 128, 132, 140
 stability of, 233–236
 uniqueness of, 215, 227–228
Carlsen, S., 192
Cartwright, D., 3n.
Cass, D., 27, 177, 198
Cassel, G., 192
Casual empiricism, 242
Centralization, 38, 49
Chains
 directed, 68
 in hierarchies, 68, 73–75
Chakravarty, S., 204

Chenery, H., 204–205
Choice space, 105
Clark, P. C., 205
Coal and oil
 ceilings on, 254, 256, 257
 depletion of, 270
Colonialism, 79
Commodity space, 275
Comparative statics, 182
Commercialism, 49, 51
Communist Party, 58n., 72–73
Computation, 127, 140, 196
Committee on Nuclear and Alternative Energy Systems (CONAES), 240, 252, 268
Conservation tax, 241–242, 257, 260, 269
Constant programs, 111–113, 119
Consumer satisfaction, maximization of, 242, 246
Consumption, 44–45
Consumption path, 14, 18, 20
 optimal, 16, 198
Consumption program, 13
Convexity index, 273–274, 286–301, 306
Core of an economy, 183
Core-type bargaining, 183
Costs
 minimization of, 246
 and mutuality, 62
Cox, J. C., 276, 309
Crouzeix, J. P., 301, 309–310
Custody
 and efficiency, 66
 and ownership, 65
 transfers of, 54–56
Czechoslovakia, organizational change in, 70n.

Dantzig, G., 193–195
Dasgupta, P., 202, 264
Decision, 35
Decision making, 48, 64
Decision rule, 33
Decision theory, under uncertainty, 263
Decomposition principle, 195
Demsetz, H., 62n.
Depletion, 263–266
 of coal and oil, 270
 optimal, 264
 of phosphate, 270
Desiderata, 43–44
 common, 44–48
 in "East," 47–48
 and norms, 48–50
 in "South," 47–48
 in "West," 47
DESOM energy-supply model, 255, 267
Development programming, 196, 204
 over several generations, 196
Diamond, P. A., 105, 108, 117, 120–122, 197n.
Dierker, E., 276, 310
Digraph, 3, 68
 directed arcs of, 5
 as directed tree, 5
 nodes of, 5, 7
Directed forest, 7
Discount factor, 13, 115–116, 118–120, 125, 131–132, 210, 215, 226–233, 276
Discounting, 184, 199, 201, 240, 243, 244
 of future utility levels, 187–188
 and survival time, 169, 171
Distance function
 in infinite-dimensional space, 105, 108n., 111, 121
 in prospect space, 84

"East"
 as classification, 30
 economic desiderata in, 47–48
 neocolonialism in, 79
 organizational change in, 70
Eastern Europe, range of activities of enterprises in, 75
Eaves, B. C., 127, 160
Eckstein, A., 28n.
Economic system, definition of, 34
Economics, definition of, 191
Economies of scale, 205

Economist, role of, 205
Edinoachalie, 72, 73
Efficiency
and custody, 65–66
as desideratum, 45–46, 51
intertemporal, 46–47, 49, 214, 243–244
single-period, 46–47
static, 46n.
Eggleston, H. G., 302, 310
Eilenberg, S., 85n., 122
Elasticity of demand, 249, 255, 261, 267–269
constant, 266
for energy, 253, 286
Elasticity of substitution, 173
Electricité de France, 251
Empirical validation of premises, 248
Employment, stability of, 47
Energy demand, 246, 267–270
Energy modeling, 251–262, 266–271
Energy policy, and growth rate, 257, 268
Energy supply, 237, 240, 253
Energy use
and GNP, 241, 243, 258–260
growth of, 242, 257, 261, 268
Engagements, 2, 5, 8, 10
Enthoven, A. C., 275–276, 309
Entities, 41
custodial, 54–55
Entropy, 249
Environment
and economic systems, 37–38, 40
of an individual, 35
in models, 31
Environmental problems, 237, 240, 254
Environmental protection, 173
Equilibrium, 246
competitive, 181–184
intertemporal, 242–244
of prices and quantities, 242
and time, 182
Equity, in distribution, 47
ETA energy model, 255, 267
Exchange price, 62
Experiments, in economics, 242, 247
External factors, 31–32
Externalities, 62n., 77n., 249

Fabian, T., 54n.
Feasible basis, 142–154
Fenchel, W., 310
Ferland, J. A., 310
Fisher, I., 118, 122, 163
Fixed-point algorithm, 127, 141
Fixed-point methods, 183, 184
Fixed-point theorem, 126, 193n.
Fossil, fuel, supply of, 270
Fourgeaud, C., 276, 310
France, planning in, 60
Freedman, D., 182
Frisch, R., 192

Galbraith, J. K., 52, 181
Gale, D., 82, 116, 122, 160, 166–167, 194
Game theory, 194
Gavurin, M. K., 193
Geometry of webs, 90
Gerstenhaber, M., 159, 160
Gibrat R., 194n.
Gloerfelt Tarp, B., 192
Goal displacement, 51
Goal function, 33
Goeller, H. E., 174, 270
"Golden rule stock," 84, 215
Goldman, S. M., 123
Gordon, R., 172
Gordon, R. A., 248
Gorman, W. M., 88, 90n., 100, 106n., 123, 275, 310
GNP, 240
and energy use, 241, 243, 253, 258–260, 267
Goreux, L. M., 204
Government, as an aggregate of organizations, 58
Graphs
directed, 68
organizational, 66–69, 71
Great Britain, competition among nationalized enterprises in, 70
Green, J., 275, 310

Greenberg, H. J., 310
Grodal, B., 275, 310
Grossman, G., 31
Growth capability condition, 143–154
Growth, as desideratum, 44–45, 57
Guesnerie, R., 276, 310

Häfele, W., 263
Hahn, F. H., 182–183
Hansen, T., 125, 127, 146, 153, 160, 166, 183–184, 216
Harary, F., 3n.
Hayek, F. A., 194
Heal, G., 202, 264
Helium, 174–175, 238–241, 244
Helium Study Committee, 238–239
Hierarchies, 3
 complete, 5, 8, 10–11
 conflict of interest between, 76–77
 and information, 73–76
 in market economy, 72
 personnel of, 8
 and quasi-hierarchies, 41–42, 70–73
 for set of activities, 7
 for single activity, 3–7
Hildenbrand, W., 183
Hirschman, A. O., 38n.
Hirshleifer, J., 276, 310
Hitchcock, F. L., 193
Hoffman, K., 252, 255, 267
Hogan, W., 252
Hotelling, H., 166, 264
Houthakker, H. S., 211, 236
Hudson, E., 243
Hungary, 49, 182, 195, 204
Hurwicz, L., 77n.
Hypotheses, testing and verification of, 242

Ideology, 35
"If . . . then" statements, 247, 252
Impatience, 117–122
Imports, ceilings on, 254
Independence postulate, 106, 109–111, 117–120
India, 205
Indicators, statistical, 44
Information handling, requirements for, 183
Information hierarchies, 73–76
Information set, 35
Input-output analysis, 193, 204, 266
Input-output coefficients, 216
Interactions, 40
 actions and, 59–63
 incomplete, 33
 interdisciplinary, 237, 242, 248–249, 251, 263–264, 266
 patterns of, 66–67
Interactivities, 56
Interdisciplinary studies, 237, 242
Interest, 163–164
International Institute for Applied Systems Analysis (IIASA), 251, 269
Intertemporal preference structure, 163, 246
Investment, 95, 105
Italy, 204
Iwai, K., 235–236

Johansen, L., 211–213, 236
Jorgensen, D., 243

Kakutani's fixed-point theorem, 126
Kaldor, N., 181–182
Kantorovich, L. V., 46n., 192–195
Kelley, J. L., 27, 286, 310
Kemeny, J. G., 160
Kirschen, E., 43n.
Koopmans, T. C., 15, 23, 27, 33n., 39n., 49n., 66n., 72n., 81n., 103n., 105, 108, 116–118, 123, 125, 129n., 160, 166, 177, 184, 193, 194, 197n., 198, 200, 202
Kornai, J., 181–183, 195, 204
Kretschmer, K., 204
Kuhn, H. W., 127, 160–161, 194
Kuhn-Tucker conditions, 150
Kuhn-Tucker theorem, 131, 135–136
Kurz, M., 202

Labor force, growth of, 14–15
Laffont, J.-J., 276, 310
Lake Baikal dispute, 77n.

Lancaster, K. J., 82, 123
Lange, O., 194
Laws
 and the economy, 42
 and systems, 58–59
Lebesgue measure, 283, 285
Lebesgue's theorem, 293
Leontief, W., 87, 123, 192, 204, 248, 266
Lerner, A., 194
Levhari, D., 211, 236
Life, calculation and valuation of, 244–246
Lindberg, P. O., 310
Linear graphs, theory of, 66
Linear programming, 193, 194
Linear transforms, 274, 291
Lipták T., 194
Litan, R., 252
Lower semi-continuity, 301

Mafia, 58n.
Malinvaud, E., 27, 166, 195, 198, 209
Managers, motivation of, 64–65
Manganese, 270
Manne, A., 54n., 204–205, 252, 255, 267
March, J. G., 51
Marcuse, W., 255, 267
Markowitz, H., 54n., 205
Marschak, J., 33n., 39n., 81, 103, 237, 242
Massé, P., 194n.
Mathematical programming, 141–154, 266
McGuire, C. B., 81, 103
Meade, J., 202
Merton, R., 51
Messages, 59–60
Modigliani, F., 45n.
Monotonicity postulate, 108, 116, 120
Moratoria, 241, 254, 256–257
Morgenstern, O., 160, 194
Morrissens, L., 43n.
Morse, C., 173, 270
Motivation, 42–43, 63–66
Motzkin, T., 194
MRG (Modelling Resource Group of CONAES), 240–244, 246, 247, 252, 268
Multinational organizations and enterprises, 77–80
Mutuality, in interactions, 59–62

Nation, strength of, 48, 77–80
National Research Council, 238, 252
Negative income tax, 247
Neoclassical economics, 242
Neocolonialism, 79
Nondegeneracy assumption, 141–154
Nonlinear programming, 194
Nonlinearity, 195
Nonslack vectors, 141–154
Nordhaus, W. D., 170n., 173, 177, 255
 energy model of, 255, 267
Normal goods, 228–229
Norman, R. Z., 3n.
Norms, 33, 36–39, 50
 explicit, 36
 prevailing, 36–37, 50
 and system comparisons, 31, 40, 43–52
 unavailing, 37
 and variables, 38–39
Novozhilov, V. V., 195
Nuclear technology, 245

Objective function
 for generations, 197
 in "optimal growth" theory, 129, 196
 with variable discount rate, 197n.
Oil
 depletion of, 270
 import ceilings on, 241
One-person leadership, 72–73
OPEC, 268
"Optimal growth" theory, 184, 196
Optimal path, 17–25, 165
Optimal program, 13
Optimality, conditions for, 13, 20–21, 24

Optimization, 192, 217–224, 241, 254–255
Optimizing cake eater, 166–167
Orders, 40, 42
Organizations, 40–41, 57–58
and change, 69–70
graphs for, 66–69
and interaction between systems, 77–80
multinational, 77–80
ruling, 42, 57–68
structures of, 40–43
Overtaking criterion, 116
Ownership, 43, 55, 65. *See also* Custody

Pareto optimality
and efficiency, 45
and interactions, 60–61
Perfect markets, 209
Phosphates, depletion of, 270
Phosphorus, 174, 270
Pierskalla, W. P., 310
Pigou, A. C., 191
Pitchford, J. D., 203–204
Planning
in France, 195
of investment, 195
two-level, 195
in USSR, 195
Policies, 35
and economic systems, 38–40
Policy variables, 253–254, 256
Political systems, 34n.
Pollution, 77
Population, 197, 202–204
Preference ordering, 32–33, 81–122, 133
assumptions on, 82–83
with independent components of consumption, 87–102
partial, 83
on prospect space, 82
representation of, 81–102
unique representation of, 90, 100–102, 112
Preference over time, 103–124, 214
interpretation of, 103–104, 214, 227
postulates on, 104–108
Preferences, initial, 31–32
Pre-institutional terms, 30–31, 196
Prices
notion of, 43
role or use of, 194
shadow, 131, 134, 154–155, 177, 193, 195, 198–199, 224, 226, 245
Primal variables, 193–194
Primitive set, 141–154
Process model, 252, 266
Process vector, 211–212
Production function, 15, 126, 210, 266–267, 275
CES, 266
Cobb-Douglas, 265
short-run, 211
Production, model of, 192–193
Production possibility, 191–192, 211, 266
Production processes, 128, 209–215
linear, 210
von Neumann type, 127, 132
Production programs, 191
Production theory, 276
Profit, 64
maximization of, 242
Program space, 104
Programs, bounded in utility, 113–115, 166
Projections, 252
Propaganda, 35
Prospect space, 82, 84, 99, 103
Public goods, 47

Quantitative economic knowledge, empirical basis of, 246–247
Quasi-concave function, 18–19, 22, 24–26, 275–276
Quasi-convex function, 273–310
Quasi-hierarchies, 41–42, 70–73

Rader, T., 85n., 123, 275, 310
Radner, R., 24–25, 81, 103, 166, 183
Railroads, cooperation among, 75n.
Ramsey, R. P., 27, 164, 166–167, 175, 196, 198, 200–201, 215, 264
Random events, 31–32
Realization variables, 252–253
Reiter, S., 193

Resolving multipliers, 193
Resources
allocation of, 193–196
availability of, 163–165
best use of, 191–192
in an economic system, 31–32
exhaustible, 164, 166–178, 200–202
extractability of, 270
generally accessible, 54
growth of, 126–127, 215
scarce, 191
supply of, without substitutes, 174
Returns to scale
constant, 265
increasing, 181–182, 195–196
Revolutionary change, 51
Riesz, F., 293, 310
Roberts, A. W., 310
Rules, 40, 42
Ruling units, 58n.

Samuelson, P. A., 87, 123, 194
Sato, K., 211, 236
Savage, L. J., 33n.
Scarf, H. E., 127, 141, 146, 153, 161, 183
Scarcity rent, 172
Schmidt, E., 192
Schneider, E., 192
Separating functions, 286–301
Separation theorem, 193
Shephard, R. W., 276, 310
Shoven, J. B., 183
Shubik, M., 181–83
Simon, H., 33n., 39n., 51, 64, 71n.
Simplex method, 194
Slack vectors, 141–154
Slutsky, E. E., 275, 310
Smith, A., 194
Social preference function, 32–33, 214
Social sciences, and other disciplines, 237
Social services, 47
Social-welfare functional, 163
"South," 30
economic aspects of, 49, 79
economic desiderata in, 47–48
Soviet Union. *See* USSR
Specialization, economic, 38, 53
Stability, of employment and incomes, 47
Stackelberg, H. von, 192
Stationarity postulate, 107–108, 120–122
Stationarity requirement, 130
Stigler, G. J., 38n., 53n.
Stoer, J., 276, 310
Strotz, H., 88, 108n., 123–124
Subsistence level, 167–168
Substitutability, 270–271
Substitute technology, 265
Substitution
elasticity of, 173
of electric and nonelectric energy, 246
rates of, 193, 202
for a resource, 263, 265
Superior, 2
lowest common, 3
Superiority relation, 3, 7
Superordination, 41
Supervision, 1–2, 5, 7, 41, 71–72
Supervisors, 5
Survival period, 187, 201, 203n.
Survival time, 168–169
and discounting, 169, 171
Sutherland, W. R. S., 126, 132, 161, 184
System-free terms, 30–31. *See also* Pre-institutional terms
Systems, 33–34
changes in 48, 50–51, 69–70
conceptual framework of, 31
description of, 40–43
interaction between, 50–52, 77–80
participants in, 40–41
perception of, 34–35
Sz.-Nagy, B., 293, 310

Taxation, 183
Taylor, L., 205
Technological change, 163, 173, 263–267
Technology
activities involving, 52–53
availability of, 254

Technology (cont.)
initial, 31–32
and systems, 55
Technology mix
and benefits and costs, 256
of future energy supply, 238
shifting of, 269
Thompson, G. L., 160
Thorbecke, E., 205
Thorland-Petersen, L., 310
Time consistency, of orderings, 108
Tobin, J., 45n., 173
Transfer price, 62
Transfer states, of custody, 54
Transportation problem, 193
Trees
directed, 5
in graph theory, 71
Tucker, A. W., 161, 194

Uncertainty, 274
and discounting, 244
and risk, 202
Unemployment, 231
United Nations, 79
United States
energy sector of, 241, 267–270
ruling units of, 58n.
trade restrictions imposed by, 79
Upper semi-continuity, 302
USSR
planning in, 60
range of activities of enterprises in, 75–76
reorganization of industry in, 69
ruling units of, 58n.
Utility, 45–46, 51
discounted sum of, 125, 215
expected, 42
maximization of, 178–190
unique optimal level of, 220
Utility flows, 210, 215
Utility function, 32–33, 83, 85, 103, 121, 275–276
ordinal and cardinal, 85, 88, 90, 115–117, 119
over time, 109–113
quasi-cardinal, 119
recursive relation on, 14, 117
separable, 89–99, 101–102
single-period, 13, 120, 125–126, 133
stationary, 13
Utility-function assumptions, 14–17, 25–26
Utility theory, 274
Utility tree, 88
Utilization factor, 212
Uzawa, H., 123, 204, 269

Varberg, D. E., 310
Variables
blend, 254
driving, 253
dual, 193–194
exogenous ("realization"), 241
policy, 241
Vector space, 263, 276, 301–302, 306–307
vernon, R., 79n.
Viability condition, 128, 139
Vind, K., 183
von Neumann, J., 128, 161, 192
models of, 144, 157, 193–194
von Weizsäcker, C. C., 116, 124
Vousden, N., 178

Wallich, R. C., 38n.
Walras, L., 192
Weinberg, A. M., 270–271
Weitzman, M. L., 181
Wells, F., 174
"West," 30
commercialism in, 49, 51
dispersion of economic decisions in, 48
economic desiderata in, 47
and international business organizations, 78–80
organizational change in, 70
Whalley, J., 183
Williamson, R. E., 105, 117, 197n.
Wittfogel, K. A., 38
Witzgall, C., 276, 310
Wold, H., 84n. 124
Wolfe, P., 195

Yaari, M. E., 104, 124, 275, 281, 310
Yugoslavia, 30, 70
  decentralization of economic decisions in, 49
  and international business activities, 78–79

Zeuthen, F., 192